# Scott Nearing    The Making of a Homesteader

The Good Life Series

IN 1932, at the height of the great Depression, Helen and Scott Nearing moved from their small apartment in New York City to a dilapidated farmhouse in Vermont. For over twenty years, they created fertile, organic gardens, handcrafted stone buildings, and a practice of living sustainably on the land. In 1952, they moved to the Maine coast, where they continued to give practical meaning to the values that are the basis for America's Back to the Land and Simple Living movements.

To continue this vision of "the good life" beyond their own lives, after Scott's death in 1983 and before her own in 1995, Helen arranged for the creation of The Good Life Center, a nonprofit organization based at their homestead Forest Farm, in Harborside, Maine. The Good Life Center was founded between 1995 and 1998 by the Trust for Public Land, a national organization dedicated to conserving land for public benefit and protecting natural and historic resources for future generations. The mission of The Good Life Center is to perpetuate the philosophies and way of life exemplified by two of America's most inspirational practitioners of simple, frugal, and purposeful living.

Building on the Nearing legacy, The Good Life Center supports individual and collective efforts to live sustainably into the future. Guided by the principles of kindness, respect, and compassion in relationships with natural and human communities, The Good Life Center promotes active participation in the advancement of social justice; creative integration of the mind, body, and spirit; and deliberate choice in efforts to live responsibly and harmoniously in an increasingly complicated world.

Volunteers are the foundation of The Good Life Center. Please contact us if you are interested in visiting, or in lending helping hands to various garden, maintenance, and office projects. Financial contributions help keep Forest Farm open, Nearing publications in print, and educational programs reaching outward.

The Good Life Center
Box 11
Harborside, Maine 04642
(207) 326-8211

# Scott
# Nearing

**The Making of a Homesteader**

# John A. Saltmarsh

Chelsea Green Publishing Company
White River Junction, Vermont

First published in 1991 in a clothbound edition under the title, *Scott Nearing: An Intellectual Biography*. First Chelsea Green paperback edition published in October, 1998.

Printed in the United States of America.

02 01 00 99 98  1 2 3 4 5

Library of Congress Cataloging-in-Publication Data

Saltmarsh, John A., 1957–
    Scott Nearing : an intellectual biography
    Includes bibliographical references and index.
    ISBN 0-8722-844-2 (cl.) ISBN 1-890132-21-7 (pbk.)
    1. Nearing, Scott, 1883–1983.  2. Socialists—United States—
Biography.  3. Radicals—United States—Biography.
4. Intellectuals—United States—Biography.  I. Title.
HX84.N4S25  1991  335'.0092—dc20
[B]                                               90-28914

Chelsea Green books may be purchased for educational, business, or sales promotional use. For information, please contact Special Markets Department at the address below.

Chelsea Green Publishing Company
P.O. Box 428
White River Junction, Vermont 05001
telephone (800) 639-4099
www.chelseagreen.com

Scott Nearing! You have heard of Scott Nearing. He is the greatest teacher in the United States.

— Eugene V. Debs,
Canton Speech, 1918

Dr. Nearing is not to be dismissed as a mere vapid dreamer . . . under any genuine civilization he would be better appreciated than he is in the United States. When one hears of him it is commonly to the effect that some ass of a college president has forbidden him from the campus, or some gorilla of a policeman has jailed him for sedition. What our third-rate snivilization fails to estimate at its real worth is the resolute courage and indomitable devotion of such a man. His virtues are completely civilized ones; he is brave, independent, unselfish, urbane and enlightened. If I had a son growing up, I'd want him to meet Nearing, though the whole body of doctrine Nearing preaches seems to me to be false. There is something even more valuable to civilization than wisdom, and that is character. Nearing has it.

— H.L. Mencken,
*American Mercury*, 1929

There have always been native sons in each generation to voice the old revolt against privilege and power. Scott Nearing is not merely one of them, he is doubtless the best known of them, both at home and abroad.

— Roger Baldwin,
*World Tomorrow,* 1930

Scott Nearing was a grand old man and a real mensch.

— Allen Ginsberg,
"America," 1956

# Contents

# Illustrations

# Preface to the Second Edition: *Creating Lives of Integrity*

WHEN I WENT to Forest Farm early in the summer of 1995, it had been more than a dozen years since I had first made my way to Maine to interview Scott Nearing, late in his 99th year. At that time, his wife Helen was guiding him steadily toward a conscious and deliberate death, and I, as a young graduate student, was asking questions—in hindsight, often naive and uninformed—that would lead to this biography. I returned years later, drawn back by persistent questions to the presence of Helen, now 91 years old and blossoming.

My reconnection with Helen that summer of 1995 dissolved in sorrow at her death in an automobile accident late in September, just as she was preparing for a tour to promote what would be her last book. That Helen was ready to go, even looking forward to her "next adventure," hardly compensated for the deep sense of loss. Yet my time with Helen that summer, along with the emotional turmoil following her death, allowed me to reflect upon the meaning of the Nearings' lives, to ask again what it is about these two people that influences and inspires so many.

Perhaps the defining feature of their lives was the fundamental consistency of living according to their values, living in a way that combined the personal and the political, integrating simple living with social justice, creating lives of integrity. Homesteading as practiced by the Nearings — building, gardening, energy self-reliance, using local indigenous resources — embodies our highest aspirations for principled, sustainable living.

The Nearings' legacy demonstrates that living a life of integrity, reconciling a personal and a social identity, can provoke meaningful social change. The connecting thread between Scott's early life as an economist at the University of Pennsylvania and his later life as a conscientious homesteader is the principle of non-exploitation, which defined his notion of social justice from his earliest days as an academic. The exploitation of children as workers addressed in *The Solution of the Child Labor Problem,* a book Nearing wrote in 1911, finds broader expression, decades later, in a life of austere simplicity and homesteading based upon non-exploitation of humans, animals, the land, and all of nature. Living the practice of non-exploitation meant including both humans and non-humans as members of the community, and also meant pursuing the political logic of non-exploitation through pacifism, vegetarianism, and environmentalism. "We desired to liberate ourselves," the Nearings wrote in 1954 in their most famous book, *Living the Good Life,* "from the cruder forms of exploitation: the plunder of the planet, the slavery of man and beast, the slaughter of men in war, and animals for food." What the Nearings called "the good life," expressed a politics of praxis: "one's personal conduct may either follow the belief pattern or diverge from it . . . The most harmonious life is one in which theory and practice are unified."

Although he wasn't writing about the Nearings or homesteading, Wendell Berry could have been addressing their situation when he discussed the possibility of individuals living in protest, rather than simply engaging in acts of protest. It is "in the long run richer in promise, to remove oneself as far as possible from complicity in the evils one is protesting, and to discover alternative possibilities." How could one be true to one's beliefs and conscience in one's daily life? Berry continues:

> To make public protests against an evil, and yet live dependent on and in support of the way of life that is the source of the evil, is an obvious contradiction and a dangerous one. If one disagrees with the nomadism and violence of our society, then one is under an obligation to take up some permanent dwelling place and cultivate the possibility of peace and harmlessness in it. If one deplores the destructiveness and wastefulness of the economy, then one is under obligation to live as far out on the margin of the economy as one is able: to be as economically independent of exploitive industries, to learn to need less, to waste less, to make things last . . . If one feels endangered by meaninglessness, then one is under an obligation to refuse meaningless pleasures and to resist meaningless work, and to give up the moral comfort and the excuses of the mentality of specialization. (*The Long-Legged House,* 1969, pp. 76–92.)

One way to do this, Berry suggests, is "to reject the dependencies and the artificial needs of urban life, and to go into the countryside and make a home there in the fullest and most permanent sense." This was the choice made by the Nearings in 1932 in an attempt to create a "subsistence homestead economy."

Prior to their homesteading experiment, Scott had already spent decades both developing a clearly defined ideology and engaging in active political dissent and protest. He wrote pamphlets and made speeches, engaged in civil disobedience and ran for public office, and he endured arrests, legal persecution (under the Espionage Act in 1918), firings (from two universities), and expulsion (from the

Communist Party in 1930). All his early political struggles were defined by the negative; they were against certain values and practices associated with social and economic exploitation. That political stance shifts dramatically when Helen and Scott commence to live the good life, when they live their political beliefs, when they live in protest. At that point the politics of simple living is no longer a negative reaction but a positive commitment. As they wrote in *Living the Good Life,* "we were seeking an affirmation, a way of conducting ourselves, of looking at the world and taking part in its activities that would provide at least a minimum of those values we considered essential to the good life."

It is that affirmation that lives on in the Nearings' writings and at Forest Farm itself, with the creation of the Good Life Center, in keeping with Helen's wishes. For thousands of readers freshly intrigued by the prospect of fashioning a conscientious, meaningful way of life, the Nearings will continue to raise the example, and the exacting standard, of life lived closely to deeply held social and personal values. Their example will make complacency with our compromises ever so uncomfortable, and it will inspire principled action beyond our own homes.

I still make an occasional trip to Forest Farm, seeking grounding and inspiration on my own life's journey. It provides a sense of wholeness. It is a place that nurtures both the example and the possibility of a life of integrity. I can see now that my first visit to Forest Farm years ago was indeed a pilgrimage in the best sense, leading to discovery and transformation, defined by both venturing and returning. No pilgrimage is complete until the pilgrim returns home to tell his story as a way of recomposing both the self and the world. This biography is the story I've tried to tell, begun on that first pilgrimage.

*— September, 1998*

# Acknowledgments

NEARING would appreciate the fact that any work of this type is throughout a cooperative venture; thus, I would like to thank those who offered assistance along the way and helped shape this biography.

Among the teachers whose influence on the historian and the history is prevalent throughout, the most significant is Milton Cantor, who cultivated the nascent historical imagination of a young graduate student and impressed upon him the standards of rigorous scholarship and the need to be sure that history does not lose sight of its essential humanity. Special gratitude also goes to Henry Commager, who suggested Nearing as a figure worthy of study in the first place.

To those who read the manuscript in full or in part and offered critical and oft-heeded suggestions, I am especially grateful: David D. Hall, Arnold Offner, William Keylor, Joseph Boskin, Saul Englebourg, Stephen Whitfield, Mark Naison, Norman Markowitz, Richard Wightman Fox, and Fouad Ajami. A special thanks is owed to Alan Lawson, who acted as a model advisor, teacher, and historian. I would also like to acknowledge the assistance of Greg Kaster, Vivien Dreves, and all the graduate students at Boston University. Norman Schneider and Michelle Ajami provided valuable research assistance.

A dissertation scholarship provided by the Graduate School of Boston University provided an uninterrupted semester to complete the manuscript. Important support and encouragement came at critical times from William Carroll and Linda Lear.

Special thanks go to Helen Nearing for providing important papers and encouraging the project and to Robert Nearing for taking the time to relive the past with me and opening the door to largely hidden dimensions of his father's life.

I deeply appreciate the archival assistance provided by Howard Gottlieb, who took an interest in preserving Nearing's past for future scholars, and the research assistance provided by the staff of Special Collections at Boston University.

My son Joshua arrived toward the end of this project and offered assistance in the form of welcome distractions. He represents the spirit behind these pages, embodying the potential, promise, and hope for the future.

Much thanks goes to Janet Francendese and Mary Capouya at Temple University Press. Janet took an early interest in the biography and never wavered in her enthusiasm for the project. Mary carefully and ably shepherded the manuscript through the production process.

Finally, and most important, I would like to offer inadequate but much deserved thanks to my wife, Gisele Grenon, who saw this undertaking through from the beginning. She read more drafts than I'm sure she'd like to recall and never hesitated to push me to clarify my thinking and writing. In the process of coming to an understanding of Scott Nearing's life, she reminded me of the need to recognize the enormous complexity of the human experience and to remain humbled by the hidden dimensions of the past. I am grateful to her for pointing out the following passage from Margaret Atwood's *The Handmaid's Tale:* "As all historians know, the past is a great darkness, and filled with echoes. Voices may reach us from it; but what they say is imbued with the obscurity of the matrix out of which they come; and, try as we may, we cannot always decipher them precisely in the clearer light of our own day." Gisele lived through this book with me. It is for her.

**Scott Nearing**  The Making of a Homesteader

# The Terrible Freedom

## An Introduction

*The Terrible Freedom—. . . It is awful to look into the mind of a man and see how free we are, to what frightful excesses our vices may run under the whited wall of a respectable reputation. Outside, among your fellows, among strangers, you must preserve appearances, a hundred things you cannot do; but inside, the terrible freedom!*
*Ralph Waldo Emerson,* Journals, *October 2, 1832*

ON RARE occasions the intellectual life of an individual—his or her thoughts, ideas, writings, and experience—can serve to illuminate the cultural developments of an era. It is this dynamic that makes biography the historian's prism through which the purified light of the past refracts through a single crystal and emerges in its wholly transformed and clarified components. Scott Nearing's life (1883–1983) is in this sense emblematic; it illuminates twentieth-century America itself.

This is a biography of Scott Nearing's intellectual life. It focuses on his ideas and the manifestations of those ideas in his life. Nearing's thought was enormously complex, an eclectic amalgam of the social gospel, transcendentalism, pragmatism, naturalism, utopianism, nineteenth-century socialism, and twentieth-century communism. This broad eclecticism created intellectual paradoxes that became in the end an obstacle to understanding him and a convenient means for his critics to dismiss him.[1]

Yet it is too easy to characterize Nearing, as Sidney Hook did, as simple-minded.[2] It is also somewhat facile merely to point out certain obvious contradictions. More important in understanding Nearing is to recognize the central incongruity between the public intellectual and the private thinker without negating the value of his ideas. Joseph Freeman, a close friend of Nearing's, explained that for those who were in personal contact with him, "it was typical of his sincerity, a sincerity so profound that it moved people even when they least agreed with him, that he never attempted to deceive either himself or anyone else about his political contradictions." According to Freeman, Nearing was well aware of these inconsistencies and "struggled to overcome them, but until he did overcome them, he neither ignored or concealed them." In his personal life, the chief impression Nearing created "was not one of assurance but of search."[3]

In his public life, the image he projected was just the opposite. His manner of his speaking, his authoritative presence, his honesty and conviction, all gave the impression of absolute certainty. This tendency to conceal personal uncertainty and struggle with a public air of resolute confidence was perhaps the central flaw of his being. To understand Nearing, one must assess both the public and private intellectual, which this biography attempts to do.

Nearing was raised in a prominent family that controlled the coal town of Morris Run, Pennsylvania. In his youth he was educated in Philadelphia and was graduated from the University of Pennsylvania's Wharton School in 1905. He went on to teach there as an economist and engaged himself in the political and social causes of progressivism, preaching the social gospel and denouncing child labor. He gained national attention when he was fired from the Wharton School in 1915 for his religious and economic views in what became a major academic-freedom case. Two years later, he was dismissed from the University of Toledo for his antiwar activities. While he had been sympathetic to the socialist movement prior to 1917, after he severed his ties with academia he joined the Socialist party and ran for a congressional seat from New York as a Socialist candidate. His antiwar stance also led to an indictment under the Espionage and Sedition Acts and his eventual acquittal.

When the Left split in 1919, Nearing's sympathies went with the Communists, but he remained with the Socialist party until 1922. He was a prominent figure in the Left throughout the 1920s, visited China and Russia, and joined the Communist party in 1927. He was expelled from the party in 1930 over issues of doctrine and intellectual independence. In the early 1930s, Nearing cut his ties with the organized Left and began what became a fifty-year experiment in subsistence living, homesteading in Vermont and then Maine, adhering to a philosophy of simple living and self-sufficiency. In the 1970s, he gained the attention of the countercultural Left, which sought a retreat back to the land as a solution to political and cultural alienation, and he was considered one who implicitly contributed to an environmentalism stressing one's ethical duty toward nature and animal welfare as an affirmation of values that would serve the common good.

Nearing's intellectual development followed a path of increasing awareness of the intransigence of the dominant classes of capitalist culture to adopt reforms that would spread the enlightenment and opportunities of the leisure classes to society as a whole. From the time of his firing from the University of Pennsylvania in 1915 through the aftermath of World War I, he experienced the limits of permissible questioning of conventional wisdom. His long, difficult journey from an orthodox reformer of the ruling class from within to a complete secessionist from capitalist cultural hegemony led him by 1932 to choose homesteading—an experiment Nearing called "living the good life."

In that spirit, Nearing moved through a series of secessions—from Christianity, from politics, and finally from American society itself. He voyaged to the wilderness as if on a pilgrimage to a sacred place. His experience, along with a deeper understanding of American culture, led to the inescapable consciousness that capitalist cultural dominance was too strong to eliminate and therefore too powerful to control or mold to liberal purposes. The secessions in his life were progressive repudiations of American canons of moral conduct as well as indications of Nearing's perception of the fragmented, segmented, discontinuous nature of American society. Only in the isolated private sphere provided by homesteading could a radical resistance and constructive challenge to capitalist culture be nurtured.

In his devotion to conscientious self-reliance, Nearing emerged as a twentieth-century colleague of Emerson and Thoreau. He was perhaps closer to Thoreau, whose writings touched more directly on the problem of the self in relation to society, the public and political in relation to the individual, whose reclusiveness and institutional withdrawal presented no contradiction to social transformation. Yet it is Emerson who, when musing in his journal about "the terrible freedom," captures a number of critically important themes essential to understanding Nearing's thought.

Drawing on Emerson, on one level, directs attention to the nineteenth century and provides a crucial starting point for discerning the contours of Nearing's intellectual nature. However much Nearing is portrayed as a twentieth-century figure, he was also a product of the late nineteenth century, and his thought is rooted in the vital uncertainty that distinguished turn-of-the-century intellectual life. His was a deeply naturalistic mind that confronted pragmatism and shed the excesses of determinism while shying away from experience unguided by ethics. Similarly, Nearing's economic thought turned to the social facts discovered through modern science, but he acquired his moral sensibilities in the nineteenth century, never doubting that economics merged science and ethics. The roots of Nearing's mind—his philosophy, religion, character, vocation—allowed him to consider without contradiction both the external reality of collective experience and the idealism of voluntary action. He sought empirical evidence to reinforce the significance of individual moral choice.

That freedom could lead to what Emerson called "frightful excesses" is easily embraced as a dominant motif encompassing the tragic qualities of twentieth-century history. Nearing's writings throughout his life never strayed far from the central problem of realizing social transformation while retaining personal freedom. Obligations and duties had to be self-imposed, for authentic personal freedom meant that the individual would exercise freedom responsibly. True freedom was attained not simply by granting positive rights or imposing social restraints but more nearly by means of Emersonian "self-reliance."

What Emerson saw as the need to "preserve appearances" among one's peers, Nearing would lament as the deadening, artificial conformity attendant upon the mass culture of a consumer society. Anticapitalist assumptions formed the basis for Nearing's socialism, which provided a conceptual framework for criticizing industrial capitalism and envisioning the construction of a society that would pierce societal restraints and release individual potential. Society would have to be changed, but more important, the individual would have to be transformed.

Furthermore, like the transcendentalists, Nearing's conception of individual transformation was expressed in the religious overtones of a conversion experience. Nearing saw his role not only as a social scientist investigating modern society but as a teacher working "for the liberation of the individual soul." Just as the transcendentalist faith rested upon the belief that the "facts" of nature would flower into a transcending spiritual truth, Nearing's faith relied on the social facts as the primary source of moral inspiration. Like Emerson, Nearing could find a home in none of the existing religious bodies but was attracted to the religious teachings of several traditions. The inner liberation of the individual was to be founded upon the principles inhering in the remnants of nineteenth-century liberal religion, a religion of love, fellowship, brotherhood, and social service. Inner emancipation came about through the recognition that social religion encompassed both an individual and a social morality, and that the salvation of each was dependent upon the redemption of all. Nearing's profound religious sensibility informed all his thinking, even his most "dismal" economic writings. He was haunted by the terrifying results in the twentieth century of freedom exercised without conscience.

Underscoring the somber aspects of freedom is not meant to suggest that Nearing ever became resigned to the view that freedom is not a worthwhile attainment. His radical individualism did not age into nihilism. Just as Emerson would remain eternally optimistic while understanding the terrifying qualities of freedom, so would Nearing devote his life to a quest for true individual freedom as a social goal while expressing an acute dread of the dangers of superficial freedoms. Although freedom had its fearful side, Nearing's efforts to bring attention to both its promise and its peril should be seen not as despair but in the way Sacvan Berkovitch explains the Puritan's "political sermon": "Cries of declension and doom were part of the strategy designed to revitalize the errand." His purpose, like Thoreau's, was not to compose an "ode to dejection, but to brag as lustily as a chanticleer in the morning, standing on his roost, if only to wake my neighbors up."

Nearing's century-long search for the "good life" explored the possibilities of freedom in the twentieth century. "Of course, we are a democracy," he told an audience in 1916, "on the Fourth of July and other public occasions."[4] But, he continued, "in the privacy of our own intellects, in the privacy of our own consciousness we know certain things." In the mountains of Vermont and on the shoreline of Maine he found solace and experimented with a life of principle and personal liberation, joining social criticism to spiritual renewal, and private to public identity—all the while his conscience haunted, like Emerson's, for "inside, the terrible freedom!"

# American Promise

## Part One

# Life among the Oligarchs

## Chapter 1

FOR a boy growing up among one of the leading families of a coal-mining community in the rugged mountains of Pennsylvania, late-nineteenth-century America offered the promise of greatness, both for the individual and for the highest ideals of civilization. This sense of advancement and of America's wonder was easily absorbed by the young Scott Nearing, born on August 6, 1883, a member of the third generation of Nearings established in the township of Morris Run. Born to the dominant class of his community, he readily believed in America's "principles, was hopeful of its possibilities, and convinced of its improvability."[1] In his youth "there were still patches of light in the sky," he recalled many years later; "for years I enjoyed those last glimmerings of twilight and believed that they were the first streaks of a new dawn."[2]

Scott was named for his grandfather Winfield Scott Nearing, whose namesake was the hero–general of the Mexican war. Winfield Scott Nearing, or as he was known about Morris Run, W.S.N., brought his family to the coal-mining region of Tioga County in 1864 at the age of thirty-five when he accepted a job as a civil and mining engineer. Before the end of the year he had assumed full control of the mining operations as superintendent of the Morris Run Coal Mining Company, a position he held for the next forty-three years.[3] From that post, W.S.N. earned the appellation "Tzar Nearing," because, it was recalled, he ruled the company town "almost as a benevolent despot."[4] Yet this was not rule for the purposes of outright selfish aggrandizement but rather in the traditions of republican civic responsibility, a belief that the betterment of the community was fostered by the leadership of the well-to-do. This civic consciousness advanced mining reforms whereby he adopted "every improvement or appliance tending to facilitate the working of the mines or promote the health and safety of the miners"; "the mines under his charge are reputed to be among the best ventilated and best managed in the State."[5] It also led to civic improvements. "Mr. Nearing," one local observer wrote in 1883, "has done much to assist . . . in organizing churches, lodges and associations, and stimulating them in maintenance of good order and morality."[6] W.S.N. exercised his elevating and refining influence in organizing the first school in the town and serving at different times as treasurer of the School Board, president of the State Hospital in nearby Blossburg, justice of the peace, and treasurer of the town. Civic improvement meant partnerships incorporating the Tioga and Morris Run Telegraph Company in 1879 and serving as a trustee for the Welsh Baptist Church.[7] It was only natural that Scott recognized that he began his "life among the United States oligarchs— minor oligarchs to be sure, but oligarchs none the less." Morris Run was, he recalled, "the oligarchy in miniature—rule by the selected few."[8]

Little is known about Scott's father, Louis Nearing. He was born in 1860 in upstate New York, and when he married Minnie Zabriskie in 1882, he worked as an engineer in Morris Run. Louis appears to have been the typical Victorian gentleman, cultivated and unassuming, a model of exemplary behavior for his family and community.[9] In keeping with his Victorian sensibility, his was not the primary influence in the home; the domestic sphere belonged clearly to his wife. Hence, it was Minnie Nearing who would be the dominant influence on her three sons and three daughters. Louis remained on the periphery of the home and family, referring to his wife and children as "the Nearing debating society," a club of which he was not fully a member. Quiet, reserved, and upstanding, he reprimanded his oldest son for his outspokenness. Scott counted his mother as one of the key formative influences of his youth. Emblematic of the cult of domesticity, she lived, according to Scott, "chiefly for her family."[10]

Nearing described his mother as "young and vigorous, energetic, impetuous, idealistic" and credited her with providing an appreciation for the higher things in life. Indebted to her "for the beginnings of a cosmopolitan education," he claimed that it was his "mother who introduced me to nature, books, and the arts," and he identified strongly with her cultured world, while he recalled a veiled indifference toward his father. He was closer to her domestic "feminine" cultured world than to that of his father, who became a small businessman and stockbroker. His father was all practicality and engagement, removed from the contemplation of life. Not only in the community but in his family young Scott experienced ambivalence founded upon the basic distinction of Victorian morality between "masculine" business engagement and the values associated with the idealism, culture, and morality of "feminine" withdrawal to the domestic realm.[11]

Perhaps a more lasting impact was made by W.S.N., one who bridged the cultural divisions in society. Scott described him as a "skilled" worker and "self-educated," working with both hands and head. The young Nearing had great admiration for the man who introduced him to "science, technology, and some of the simpler practices of civil engineering." He recalled fondly having the run of his grandfather's "huge library, filled with books on travel, natural science, economics, history, biography, eastern religions, and metaphysics [and] complete sets . . . of Dickens, Thackery, Walter Scott, Dumas, Balzac, Victor Hugo, Shakespeare, and the leading English and American poets."[12] He also followed his grandfather into the field and under his supervision took odd jobs around the town. The grandson clerked in the company store, "worked in the town butcher shop and with the town blacksmith, did road building and railroad construction, drove team, chopped in the woods, and was an assistant on surveying crews" as well as occasionally entering the mines.[13]

"Our Grandfathers," Nearing wrote some years later, "were men of affairs" who "belonged to the group in which they lived; they helped to perform its labor; and they shared in its rewards."[14] W.S.N., it seems, was the embodiment of Thorstein Veblen's enlightened engineer, embracing values that Nearing himself would come to cherish, what Veblen referred to as "the propensity for achievement—the instinct of workmanship." Nearing could easily have likened W.S.N. to the ideal type of character needed for social advancement that Veblen described: "By force of his being such an agent he is possessed of a taste for effective work, and a distaste for futile effort. He has a sense of serviceability or efficiency and the demerit of futility, waste, or incapacity. This aptitude or propensity may be called the instinct of workmanship."[15]

Veblen had in mind workmanship, not power, as the social standard, yet W.S.N. was a powerful man whose Whiggish civic sensibility could not bear the weight of a crushing industrial economy. A dark side to this pro-totechnocrat emerged that posed an ugly paradox. While he represented "planning, building, and directing," he was also the dictatorial superintendent of a company town who resorted to harsh means to maintain dominance. It was this learned technician who ran a company that profited from breaking unions and promoting ethnic divisions in the community.[16] His reputation suffered with the years. First came the 1873 incident when he ordered the wholesale eviction of tenants who had attempted to unionize the company town. His indifference took no account of the hardships of midwinter weather. He confronted organized labor again when John Mitchell and the Mine Workers Union organized a strike in 1904 instead of submitting to a 14 percent reduction in wages. W.S.N., the republican steward, aged into an industrial autocrat.[17] "My grandfather," Nearing recalled in a draft of his autobiography, "in carrying out company policy, cut wages and faced a spontaneous strike by the miners." The strike committee "represented the people of the town . . . a democratically selected body." Yet "the representatives of the people of Morris Run were brushed aside summarily . . . that was the way the American oligarchy operated in a Pennsylvania company town, and I grew up as a trouble shooter for the local oligarch."[18]

▬ Nearing had been "born into a family that had all the economic necessities, most of the comforts, and for that day, many of the luxuries" available to the dominant classes. The distinction of his social status was enforced from early on. He recalled that "our yard, behind the house, was bordered by a high wooden fence. . . . In early years I was forbidden to pass that fence, under heavy penalties. Neighbors' children played 'kick the wicket' out there in the pasture. How I longed to get through the fence."[19] When he was age thirteen, his family took up a winter residence in Philadelphia to provide an "advanced education" for the Nearing children. In the "teeming life of Philadelphia" he encountered social circumstances that effected a "crucial period of transition" in his life—he discovered life on the other side of the fence.[20]

His encounter with formal schooling consisted of enrollment in the Central Manual High School, a public institution founded by the city of Philadelphia in 1885 under the increasingly acceptable notion that education had to be transformed to meet the need of an industrialized society. The manual-training idea was rooted in the belief that the public school system was too narrowly committed to mental training removed from the activities of real life. Furthermore, manual-training reforms were fueled by the conviction that industrialization had developed such stark divisions of labor and specialization that the apprenticeship system could no longer effectively function as an educative force in the new factory setting. Because the work process in an industrialized society had become exploitative rather than educative, popular education could not remain isolated from practical affairs. With the new manual-training school, public education would wed the mental and the manual to provide practical preparation for life in the industrial age.[21]

In 1901, Nearing continued his education at the University of Pennsylvania where after a year in the law school, he transferred to the Wharton School of Finance and Economy, recalling later that he had "been repelled by the big business domination of the law and lawyers."[22] His ambivalence reflected a real crisis surrounding the question of vocation. What civic role was there for one who believed that "America to-day presents rare opportunities . . . of man's possibilities"?[23] And what vocational choice could harmonize worthy achievement with his childhood republican and Christian ideals— could reconcile public duty with private beliefs?

In 1903, another vocational direction was military service. His parents had encouraged him to attend West Point, and he was attracted by military virtues and the "glamor of military life," especially following the patriotic fervor of the Spanish-American War. A military career could fulfill the needs of practical service and a vital existence, much in the same way that Edward

Bellamy's notion of the industrial army harmonized national and individual existence into virile and purposeful action in the name of the higher values of duty, cooperation, service, and sacrifice. One cannot escape the irony that the "military yearnings" of this future pacifist were brought to an end by an eye injury. But the need to bring his values into a practical social endeavor remained.[24]

Another possibility was the ministry. Nearing had been a Sunday school teacher and leader of the Christian Endeavor in the Philadelphia Baptist Church during the early years of the century. He began attending Sunday school classes as soon as his family arrived in Philadelphia and in due course joined the church. In considering why Nearing identified with the Grace Baptist Church, a number of possibilities present themselves. First, at least back to W.S.N. there was some family association with the Baptist church. Second, he might have found the denomination congenial because, in deemphasizing formal creeds or dogma it offered a degree of theological autonomy. As Walter Rauschenbusch explained in his essay "Why I Am a Baptist," it was because "experience," not "a creed or catechism . . . is our sole requisite." Additionally he noted that the Baptist religion "demands social expression, and will come to its full strength and riches only when it is shared with others."[25]

The Grace Baptist Temple seemed to fulfill this evangelical fervor, looking toward a kingdom of God in the Philadelphia community. Under the ministry of Dr. Russell Conwell, the Temple had become "the greatest of institutional churches."[26] Conwell worked to extend the values of teaching and healing into the community, establishing Temple College and the Samaritan Hospital to those ends. For Nearing, Conwell was a man who put ideals into action; he was attracted to Conwell's message that "Jesus preached, taught, and healed. We should be doing the same things today."[27] Nearing may also have identified with Conwell's attitude toward work and wealth. "There is no class of people to be pitied so much as . . . the sons and daughters of the rich of our generation," he admonished. "I pity the rich man's son. He can never know the best things in life [because he has not] earned his own living."[28]

Yet Nearing's youthful zeal was apparently initially blind to the worldly interests inherent in Conwell instructions to "apply" oneself. In his famous "Acres of Diamonds" sermon, Conwell not only revealed a belief in the depravity of the poor but linked success to morality, telling his audience that "you ought to get rich, and it is your duty to get rich."[29] Any ambiguities in Conwell's morality were shattered with his political endorsement of what Nearing considered to be a case of blatant political corruption. This incident precipitated a crisis of faith and led, Nearing explained, to his "withdrawal . . . from all connection with [organized] Christianity." Conwell's "Acres of Diamonds" was revealed as a moral wasteland, its gospel of wealth a poisonous sermon of corrupted Christianity. "After my disillusioning adven-

A family group c. 1887. From left, Louis Nearing, Mrs. Winfield Scott Nearing, Scott Nearing, Mary Nearing (in carriage), and Minnie Nearing. Courtesy of Robert Nearing

The Nearing family at Morris Run, Pa., c. 1892. Winfield Scott Nearing with grand-children, from left to right, Mary, Guy, Dorothy, and Scott. Courtesy of Robert Nearing

Scott Nearing at Morris Run, 1902. Courtesy of Robert Nearing

he Nearing children, 1906: Scott, Mary, Dorothy, Guy, Beatrice, and Max. Courtesy
f Robert Nearing

ture into that labyrinth that linked politics with Christian beliefs and tied professing Christians to the coattails of monopolistic capitalism," Nearing recalled, "I did not want to commit myself to any set of authoritarian beliefs." He had become convinced that "the Christian church had become an instrument of reaction and corruption."[30]

Nearing's response was typical of social reformers who turned away from the corrupted dogma taught by the established churches as a historical distortion of the true teachings of Christ. These reformers yearned for the simple pure faith of the primitive church and focused their Christianity on the New Testament for the true spirit of their religion and a model of applied Christianity.[31] This crisis of faith and associated vocational consequences marked a turning point in his life; it "eliminated the ministry as a self-respecting career." Although adrift, he also recognized that he was living in an "age of unparalleled activity." "The present," he wrote, "is an age of dynamic achievement, leading on into the future of human development."[32] But what field of service did America offer for one born to advantages yet recognizing the civic responsibility of the well-to-do, one who sought to harmonize ideals with practice, one who wanted to experience a vitalized existence and contribute to the promise of American progress?

During his undergraduate years, Nearing's interests coalesced around teaching and the study of economics. By the time he taught Sunday school classes at the Grace Baptist Temple, he had already "taught groups of boys in a Philadelphia Settlement House." In 1903, he taught classes in sociology for theology students at Temple College,[33] an institutional affiliate of Conwell's church. And to enhance his abilities as an effective instructor, he enrolled in a four-year course of study in the School of Oral Expression, receiving a Bachelor of Oratory degree at the same time that he earned his Bachelor of Science degree in economics from the Wharton School. His teaching found direction when, in the fall semester of 1903, he encountered the economist Simon Nelson Patten, a man who Nearing claimed "had a profound effect in determining the course of my life."[34]

▬ Nearing arrived at the Wharton School eight years after Patten had assumed its chairmanship and began to shape it to his purposes. Patten's goals were largely an expression of the ideals and training that had led the economist Edmund J. James to recruit him in 1887. He brought with him to Philadelphia just what his former classmate from Halle could appreciate—solid German credentials for the advancement of social science and the reform of the university. Raised in the Midwest, Patten studied for two years in Germany where he absorbed the German university ideal, which was currently enjoying a warm reception in America for its scientific discovery and practicality. The German school's "historical" method centered on the research laboratory and seminar, drawing heavily upon original documents and empirical evidence as the basis for studying the development of social institutions. Patten experienced, as did a generation of American scholars who migrated to Germany in the late nineteenth century, the intellectual liberation of a method that directly challenged the foundations of traditional moral philosophy and classical economics and focused on society instead of the self, offered organic and statist premises as an alternative to the individualistic bias of laissez-faire. The emphasis in German scholarship fell heavily on the use of research in the training of leaders and the formulation of public policy; the university had a social function, and the active state had a positive role to play in social change.[35]

This background seemed to complement the original purposes of the founder of the Wharton School. Joseph Wharton, a Philadelphia captain of industry, endowed a "School of Economy and Finance" at the University of Pennsylvania in 1881 to train the young men of "inherited intellect, means, and refinement," believing that "adequate education in the principles underlying successful business management and civil government would greatly aid in producing a class of men likely to become pillars of the state."[36] He envisioned a vocationally oriented professional college that would educate society's business and political elite and turn the nation's genteel youth into a class of responsible leaders. When Patten joined the Wharton faculty, Joseph Wharton still exercised considerable influence over his "project," particularly in overseeing what was taught on the issue of tariffs. Wharton, like most Pennsylvania industrialists, was a strong defender of protectionism; his belief in national assistance in economic development fostered a deep aversion to the free-trade doctrines of the classical economists. He had little trouble accepting the arrival of Patten with whom he shared a distrust of classical economics, advocacy of protectionism, and belief in a role for the state in economic development—even if it emanated from different roots and reasoning.[37]

By the time Nearing arrived at Wharton, Patten had moved well beyond the issue of protectionism and had become a leading American economist as well as a major force at the school. Variously focusing on the issues of protectionism, consumption, and distribution, he drew on the fields of economics, history, psychology, sociology, philosophy, and religion for his analysis.[38] Perhaps his most lasting contribution to economic thought, the basis of all his economic interpretations, was his belief in a dynamic expanding economy, producing a social surplus and creating a society of abundance. And while Patten's tremendously optimistic vision of economics repudiated the classical doctrine of the economic law of decreasing returns in a deficit society, "there was nothing revolutionary in Patten's teaching," explained Nearing after Patten's death in 1922, "if by that word is meant a demand for sudden change in any of the existing forms of society."

> He desired changes and fundamental ones, but he believed that they should be made within the bounds of the established order. . . . He was essentially an inside worker—going to church, voting the Republican ticket, helping to build an efficient business system, but doing all of these things with one central thought—the possibility of bettering the conditions under which the human race lived.[39]

Nearing's youthful zeal found direction and flourished under Patten's tutelage. He was a "Wharton man" protégé in the Progressive Era, one who would be trained in practical economics for his place as a responsible leader of the community. Patten showed how social science could lead to a progressive future by destroying deterministic dogma while retaining moral certainty. The science he impressed upon his student was primarily associated with the power of creative intelligence to master new situations and overturn traditional theory. Although economics was then in the process of establishing itself as a clearly delineated discipline, Patten would not ignore "our origin in the undifferentiated field from which also came the moralist, the political scientist, and the historian."[40] The economics he embraced encompassed virtually the whole expanding field of social science and philosophy, and was passionately committed to ethical values and their practical application. The economist belonged, he declared, "on the firing line of civilization,"[41] which was both an activist and a moral prescription.

Patten's dynamic economics offered Nearing a way of reconciling progressive social science with the ideals retained from the moral universe of his youth. It was Patten, wrote Nearing, "who turned me from preaching to teaching."[42] The vocation of teaching economics provided Nearing with a rostrum to preach from instead of a pulpit, and a classroom instead of a congregation. Patten's larger contribution to Nearing's thought was first the notion, as another of Patten's students explained, of "the power of creative intelligence to master situations irrespective of received dogma—in other words, to make a new start and to think itself clean out of difficulties as they arise,"[43] and second a concern with ethical and humanitarian ideals as a necessity in the moral emphasis of economic study. Because of the importance of Patten's intellectual contribution to the development of Nearing's thought, we must briefly consider Patten's mind.

■■■ Under Patten's influence, Nearing was the intellectual heir to the attempt of the "historical school" to revitalize economics through criticism of traditional economic theory and its presumptions concerning human nature.[44] This school, notes one historian, "was attempting primarily to get behind the basic assumption of British classicism and study economics as an aspect of the entire cultural tradition. Such assumptions as self-interest and private property were examined in terms of their development rather than as immutable laws."[45] Patten taught that "many economic laws are expressions of human nature." These laws were "not only capable of modification, but are continually being altered . . . features we regard as human are subject to evolutionary modification."[46] He posited a dynamic economics that was not determined strictly by the objective environment but was shaped instead by "a series of progressive movements in society through the reactions between the subjective and objective worlds . . . a new standard of life is formed through which the feelings and mental characteristics of men are changed."[47] "The errors of the day," he explained, "are merely old truths that have outlived their usefulness. The economist therefore seems in revolt because of the importance he attaches to present facts."[48] This attempt to revise economic theory through discovery of the current economic and social facts and to overthrow narrow economic determinism reflected the Progressive's faith in the transformation and control of society. Patten forcefully advocated a "new economics," believing that "the traditional laws of economics were not natural but social laws, developed by non-progressive people."[49]

Patten impressed upon Nearing the need for "a new social science, a new philosophy, and a new mental discipline which will face the facts of today without the presuppositions the old thought imposed."[50] It followed that this broad perspective of economics was closely linked to and drew heavily on pragmatism in philosophy.[51] Drawing upon the writings of William James and John Dewey, the "new" economists found that "pragmatism seemed to offer a better explanation of individual and group behavior than did the hedonistic psychology and philosophy of classical British rationalism."[52] Patten admitted being influenced by James's "view of pragmatism, not that it seemed new, but that it was a better expression of a view toward which economists like myself were struggling, but into which they had never clearly come."[53] Reconstructed economic theory rejected "dogmatic rationalism," he declared; "the new epoch in American thought begins with the contrast of rationalism with pragmatism." Pragmatism applied to economic thought meant testing "historical epochs by the results that flowed from them. . . . It is not what Mill, Carlyle, Spencer or Marx thought would take place but what has actually happened that should interest us."[54] Pragmatists and economists shared a particular logic, method, and mode of verification. They both "must accept consequences as the ultimate test of truth," he explained, "and these consequences are measured in the same broad field of social endeavor. To this end, the intellectual reliance on premises must be broken."[55]

If this process of breaking free of received dogma would open the way for an economics appropriate to dealing with current social problems, then could not the same intellectual attitude be applied to religious thought to adapt Christianity to meet modern ethical demands? Could morality and social science, restraint and economic growth, be reconciled for a shared social purpose?[56] "Religion," Patten wrote, "has for its problem social reconstruction."[57] Applying a historical interpretation to Christianity, Patten saw that at one time the emphasis on personal rather than social redemption had a certain social validity. But now this ethic operated to the disadvantage of society as a whole, failed the test of experience, and hence was false. As with any other system of thought, religious notions changed with changing social circumstances. Religion's new task, according to Patten, was to convert the "economically prosperous individualist to work for society instead of his own aggrandizement."[58] A new era of industrialism and economic surplus called for a corresponding change in values. A social Christianity compatible with the new economics was found in a religion that returned to the pure, uncorrupted teachings of Christ.

Patten's most extensive commentary on the social influence of religion appeared in his study *The Social Basis of Religion* (1914) where he proclaimed that "a new missionary movement is demanded in our age" that "must have the vigor and clearness of thought that Paul gave to the first extensions of Christ's influence." "The impress of past centuries," he wrote, "has put modern religion in as helpless a condition to meet present emergencies."

> The work that Christ began could not be fully developed in the early centuries because of adverse economic conditions. It can, however, be successfully completed now because favorable environing [*sic*] conditions have replaced race antagonisms with a spirit of social cooperation. This has opened the road to social regeneration as contrasted with social elimination. To meet this new challenge is the religious need of the day.[59]

Religious truth, like economic truth, was relative. And concern with ethical and humanitarian ideals emphasized the moral element in economic study.

Patten's ethical economics persuaded Nearing to regard scientific economic questions in relation to Christian principles and practical religion. This was precisely what Patten had in mind when he suggested that religion should be "given a scientific foundation and its doctrines . . . transferred from the traditional basis to the realm of social science."[60] In reference to the economists of this period who easily merged religious solutions with economic analysis, one historian has noted that "what was needed, it seemed, was a new kind of specialist: one who could analyze and guide social policy from the comprehensive, disinterested, ethical perspective which the ministry had once maintained and speak with the authority which ministers had once commanded, but with a modern, scientific voice."[61]

It was, Patten found, only natural for the economist to be a theologian of religion in social science. "It should be remembered," he reminded his students, "that the early economists were theologians, and that the basis of their thought was known as natural theology."[62] Hence, there were not "two programmes of reform, the one economic and the other religious; the group interests that excite religious and economic activity are the same, . . . the religious and economic motives and ideals are felt by the same men, and the forces that make society economic also make it religious."[63] It was "no wonder," he claimed, "that these two essentially different types of thinking should use different terms to express similar ideas . . . the moral education should begin with lessons from the economic world because the mechanism of morality is the same as that of the standard of life."[64]

For Patten, and for others, it was undeniable that the consequences of this practical religion, the social expression of ethical economics, seemed to resemble a socialist program. As such, his economic teachings could be construed as radical and partisan and could thus throw into doubt the professional legitimacy of this new economics, which proclaimed an objective adherence to the scientific study of economic facts.[65] Yet Patten was not interested in overthrowing existing society, only in assaulting formal ways of thinking. The social transformation he envisioned was focused on the changed social conscience of the dominant classes in society because he believed that "social thought . . . is impressed by the action of the dominant class."[66] Patten envisioned social reform not only as a process initiated by the well-to-do but one that would also reinvigorate the upper class. The degradation of the dominant classes was simply the concurrent result of an economic order that led to the existence of widespread poverty, producing similar effects among the producing classes. "Wealth and want," he explained, "oppose each other in their influence on human nature." "Riches sate desire and stifle impulses with lethargic fullness," he wrote; "chronic want, starved desires, and dwarfed impulses render many of man's faculties inert. . . . While the weakening of stimuli is clogging the primary instincts of the leisure rich, the poor degenerate under the throttling of want."[67]

For the wealthy, the key to social change was to be found in leisure activity. A life "without purposeful and occupied leisure is unfulfilled purpose," Patten declared: "At this moment of social evolution one might indeed say that while the economic virtues are the product of work, the whole character is formed in leisure—its other half—because the motives of the ideal society are there."[68] The rich could be rescued from a nonproductive life through the pursuit of strenuous, revitalized, constructive leisure.

For the poor, those who engaged in productive labor, the problem was not the squandering of leisure—the producing classes were deprived of adequate free time—but deadening work. "It has come up in America," Patten observed in 1909, "a neglected commercialized growth, which does not satisfy men's desire for the surprises, varieties and stimulants" of life. Quite simply, "there is product without climax in the industrial age." He feared that "the dead monotony of product . . . has removed the goals toward which men strive in moments of inspiration." He prescribed "intense action," "climax, vivid attention, strenuous bodily coordination," "enthusiastic work" as the "intenser motives for men subjected to depression and degeneration."[69]

Patten's program for radical social reform under the auspices of the dominant classes did not mean a threat to fundamental American ideals because, he explained, "there is no difference at present between socialism and democracy."[70] It was based upon the distinction that

> the desire of upper class men to improve the conditions of the lower classes is a radically different phenomenon from the pressure exerted by the lower classes for their own betterment. The lower class movement stands for the control of the state by themselves in their own interests. The upper class movement directs itself against the bad environmental conditions preventing the expression of character.[71]

This upper-class socialism was emerging most forcefully at the same time that Nearing was finding his intellectual bearings in a form Patten labeled "collegiate socialism, because universities and colleges are the centers of its propagation." The "moral program" of this reform, wrote Patten, "can be summarized as the regeneration of character and its economic program is the abolition of poverty."[72]

This conception of socialism was not antagonistic to Patten's professional role, nor was it a direct affront to the elite student body he taught or the wealthy supporters of the university. Yet it was a socialism that departed sharply from Marxism, largely because of the strength of Patten's antideterminist, evolutionist, and idealistic premises. Patten was familiar with Marx's work and his concern with the question of institutional change in his economics. He repudiated Marxism on largely the same grounds that he rejected the deterministic natural laws of the classical economists. He could not accept Marx's notion that man "is in the crushing grip of an economic law which operates wherever land or tools are rented as inevitably as gravitation acts where matter is." Man, declared Patten, "is not to be singly accounted for by a single all-prevailing law."[73] The new movement in economics would both reject Marx and rescue socialism: "It will not accept socialism; and to free itself from the snares into which it has fallen through the careless statements of its creators, it must isolate itself more fully from history, sociology, and other disciplines that give undue weight to past experience."[74] Furthermore, the reform associated with the new economics was not tied to rapid change. "The difference between Marx and the American radical," explained Patten, "does not lie in the positions taken but in the remedies to be applied. . . . As it is, every doctrine claiming that progress comes by slow evolution has been gaining ground."[75]

Finally, Marxism, and other economic schemes, placed too much emphasis upon material cures for what was more properly a spiritual dilemma. The solution to the problem of industrial America was to be found in the rebirth of religion in social terms.[76] Marx had, according to Patten, transformed "socialism from a sentimental to a scientific basis." "But," he continued, "the sentimental socialists remained in America as they were."

> The keynote to their sentimental attitude is a repugnance toward anything materialistic. Consequently, so long as socialism was put in purely materialistic terms, they would not accept it. . . . American socialists are not scientific socialists of the type Marx sought to create. Every leading socialist writer is clearly idealistic in his attitude, and would repudiate socialism if it were put in a materialistic shape.

"Marx," Patten was convinced, "may continue as a myth and a terror to the uninformed, but the type of thinking he introduced belongs to the past rather than to the present."[77]

Patten's economics created enthusiasm among his students, largely because of its activist implications; like the German university ideal of his training, his economic thought and teaching stressed a practical contribution to social reform. He emphasized first that economic study was purposeless unless it was taken out of the classroom and into society, and second that it would not be possible to see the progressive achievements of the new economic thought if the public was not educated—the boundaries of legitimate discussion could be broadened only if public opinion were cultivated.

Patten's views here were shaped not only by the implications of the German method but by another key element of the German university that had great appeal for American scholars—the concept of academic freedom. The German conception of academic freedom had largely pedagogical implications and carefully distinguished between freedom within the university and freedom outside it. But in the American setting scholars trained in Germany attempted to extend the notion democratically and define academic freedom institutionally, claiming no separation between inquiry and reform.[78] In the American experience, the notion that academic freedom functioned in the realm of social and political reform was reinforced by the pragmatic dictum of applying a trained intelligence to social problems. Patten's call to action incorporated the presumption that the scholar had not only a university role but a larger responsibility to the community.

According to this logic, Patten wanted his students to bring their work to the attention of the public as the basis for constructive social action. In his presidential address to the American Economics Association of 1908, the year that Nearing took his Ph.D., Patten lamented the failure of economists to find a popular audience and institute a new vision of society as well as an activism to bring it about. "There is . . . no great American problem that has been solved. With every vital question we stand on half-way ground, halting between the old and the new. We must lay the foundation of a new civilization and show how economic forces will remedy evils that soon may be unbearable."[79] Predating Walter Lippmann's clarion call, Patten perceived a critical juncture in America's development and asked his audience whether "we are mastering it or merely drifting with the tide." Young economists had "pushed forward neither the science nor the nation."[80]

The place for economists to begin as "actors in the momentous struggles of the present" was in reaching "the public consciousness." Patten observed that there was "a real public at hand craving for information and inspiration." The economist needed to direct his attention to "the control of public opinion" by "giving clearer ideals and better programs to those who direct public affairs."

> His home should be not in the library but in the classroom, and when sufficiently proficient to investigate, he should be loaned by the university to the government, to local committees or institutions capable of handling social problems on a scale that commands success. . . . His vehicle should be the newspaper and the magazine, not the scientific journal.

"There can be no economic literature," Patten declared, "apart from the general literature." The economist had a public role to play in the organic community where "thought is no longer in isolated compartments affecting only particular persons or classes." With public opinion as an effective counterforce, economists could actively work to construct a new vision of society. Economists "should work in the open and get their inspiration from the struggle and evolution which passing events reveal; for where change is there should also the economist be."[81]

━━ Nearing absorbed not only his mentors' economic teachings but the ideal of academic freedom as a necessary principle of Patten's activist prescription and "saw no real distinction between on-campus and off-campus" activities. In an organic, interdependent society, Nearing believed, "the campus, its affairs, and the outside world were all parts of the same historical process."[82] According to his view of academic freedom,

> a teacher, to be effective, must communicate efficiently and honestly . . . when questions are raised, in class or outside the classroom, by concerned students or members of the public, the teacher must answer the questions factually, thoroughly, honestly. The possibility of doing so is called "academic freedom." The duty to do it is part of the responsibility assumed by every conscientious practitioner of the teaching profession.[83]

Nearing and others at the Wharton School concluded that Patten's vision of social change boiled down to a simple formula: "to learn the truth, to teach the truth, and to help build the truth into the life of the community."[84]

One way that Nearing adhered to these principles and crossed that permeable boundary between the campus and the world was by disseminating his scholarly work through the popular press. So in addition to writing for professional and scientific journals, such as the *Annals of the American Academy of Political and Social Science* (a Wharton School creation under Patten's counsel), the *Journal of Politics and Economics*, the *Journal of Education*, the *American Journal of Sociology*, and the *Quarterly Publication of the American Statistical Association*, he published much more frequently in such popular magazines as *Everybody's*, *Popular Science Monthly*, the *Nation*, *Ladies Home Journal*, *American Magazine*, the *Woman's Magazine*, the *Survey* ("a Journal of Constructive Philanthropy"), and the *Public* ("a National Journal of Fundamental Democracy, and a Weekly Narrative of History in the Making").[85]

Another way to build truth into the life of the community was actively to seek practical application of his economic views. "Very early in the game," Nearing "took on off-campus work to help . . . carry out my program."[86] While still an undergraduate, he ventured into Philadelphia politics as part of a course in political science. A professor outraged at political corruption sent Nearing into Philadelphia's notorious Fifth Ward where he discovered a textbook example of machine politics. This assignment allowed him to see "Philadelphia politics in the raw" and sparked his "interest in political reform."[87]

While in graduate school and assigned as an assistant instructor, Nearing's off-campus activities included a position as assistant to the secretary of the Philadelphia Child Labor Committee, a post he later assumed himself. In his work for the committee, he "saw many aspects of child labor and tenement life" and "came into intimate contact with working children, their parents, and their employers."[88]

Nearing was not alone in his activism. He noted that Patten's "students left the classroom to investigate the doings of the United Gas Improvement Company, the Philadelphia Electric Company, the Hard Coal Combine, and other aggregations of capital that held the city and state in the hollow of their hands."[89] Patten's enthusiasm rubbed off on at least eight members of the Wharton faculty—some who had been students of Patten—who "met occasionally to discuss matters of common interest." The "Wharton Eight" assembled out of the conviction that they "should make a contribution not only to our students and the university but also to the society at large."[90] "Patten's men," as Nearing referred to them, "attacked the problems that lay all around them in the economic and social world,"[91] at the same time fighting to "guarantee the right of off-campus activities to the members of the teaching staff."[92]

It was under Patten that Nearing discovered an intellectual and moral universe in which the professional social scientist had a vital role to play. He wrote that "as a freshman I had learned to regard economics as a rather stodgy subject," and he had no greater expectations when he enrolled in Patten's "sophomore course in John Stuart Mill's *Principles*." While he "sat listening to a talk on Adam Smith and his reasoning concerning capital" given by Patten, he was astonished.[93] Here was a teacher who "suggested to us that the established order was not all that it might be."[94] Nearing concluded that compared with the law, the military, or the ministry, "economics offered a more practical field." He "decided in favor of teaching economics because of the role which economic forces played in public affairs."[95] He believed that in capitalist society the means to enhance the general welfare were largely economic and that economic conditions critically influenced political affairs. Patten, Nearing noted, had "pointed out the road to me."[96]

Despite the vitality of Patten's thinking, the Wharton School was a rather conventional place. Nearing recorded in notes for his autobiography that "I must confess that I spent a dozen years in undergraduate and graduate social science classes without ever hearing the doctrine of Marx . . . explained in the classroom." It was the study of Mill and "other social scientists" like Saint-Simon, Fourier, and Comte that "absorbed our time and attention."[97] He recalled that his "Wharton School training was severely limited by the economic and social interests of those who founded and financed the institution and those who were responsible for its day-to-day administration," those who "supported the establishment quite frankly and openly, and believed firmly in the American way."

As a Wharton School protégé, he counted himself "a loyal devoted citizen" who was "among those to whom these strictures applied." By inheritance, education, and training, he "was part and parcel of the United States Establishment in the early years of the present century."[98] Imbued with the advantages and privileges of his class, he had acquired a strong sense of civic duty and social responsibility, which he associated with a deep optimism concerning American progress. If there were tensions between his social position and the kind of America he envisioned, they were not serious enough to create skepticism. This paradox of progressivism would thrive undisturbed for the time being.

# The New Economics

## Chapter 2

BY THE time Nearing discovered his calling, his experience and training had established the fact that he was living in an "age when a small leisured money class are impressing their standards on the masses."[1] As a member of the dominant class, this was his age, his historical and cultural moment, a chance to shape society under the unshakable assumption of social advancement. "The new view" of society, he claimed, was "full of hope and promise" that "progress is always attainable." He explained that "man himself is thought to be thoroughly capable of improvement . . . this concept of the natural capacity of man dominates the thought of a progressive society."[2] Nearing noted that this faith in America's progress "played a larger and larger part of my thinking, my teaching, lecturing and writing during nine years in the Wharton School, concentrating my attention on the economics of distribution which I saw as the economic key that was to open the door to the glorious possibilities of 20th century civilization."[3] It was a faith in progress and social perfection that, if clung to too fiercely, could become little more than a set of cherished illusions.

▬ Between 1908 and 1915, Nearing devoted himself to educating his students at the Wharton School and educating the American public—in both cases his audience was the dominant classes in society whose members were in social positions to promote a progressive future. In his *Economics* (1908), *Social Adjustment* (1910), *Elements of Economics* (1912), *Financing the Wage*

*Earners' Family* (1913), *Social Sanity* (1913), *Wages in the United States* (1914), *Income* (1915), and *Anthracite: An Instance of a Natural Resources Monopoly* (1915) as well as numerous scholarly and popular articles, Nearing turned to teaching the new economics. He believed that institutional reform alone would not be sufficient; changes in values had to accompany political, economic, and social reforms. He hoped to effect the reorientation of the conscience of the well-to-do toward social responsibility, to foster a transformation of values. There was no need to doubt this expectation in light of America's abundance. "Where there is a great mass of social wealth in the community," he believed, "society may offer opportunities for individual improvement."[4] "The community abounds in latent ability which awaits the opportunity for development,"[5] he explained, and "the loss and pain are due to social conditions which are remedial through education and legislation."[6] He was "living in a land of plenty; a land of prosperity as contrasted with misery; a land in which there is a surplus of economic goods rather than a deficit."[7]

An evolutionary premise made it apparent that economic thought, like all other aspects of life, was in a process of change. The "old philosophy was hopeless" and "static," and based upon "despondent resignation to the divine will," it produced individuals who were "fatalists." In contrast, the new thought, "full of inspiration and promise," was "dynamic," fostering "vigorous, well-directed efforts" by "enthusiastic workers."[8] The older view of economics and society was highly deterministic, relegating the individual to impotence as an agent for social change.[9] The beginnings of a new economics was

> an insistence that the economists part company with the ominous pictures of an overpopulated, starving world, prostrate before the throne of "competition," "psychic value," "individual initiative," "private property," or some other pseudo-god, and tell men in simple, straightforward language how they may combine, re-shape, or overcome the laws and utilize them as a blessing instead of enduring them as a burden and a curse. The day has dawned when economists must explain that welfare must be put before wealth; that the iron law of wages may be shattered by a minimum wage law; that universal overpopulation is being prevented by universal restriction in the birth rate; that overwork, untimely death, and a host of other economic maladjustments will disappear before an educated, legislating public opinion; and that combination and cooperation may be employed to silence forever the savage demands of unrestricted competition.[10]

Under the new economics, which attributed social problems "not to personal depravity, but to economic causes, the world is filled with opportunities for improvement."[11]

Yet this new view meant voluntarism and environmentalism within limits. One could not escape the evidence from naturalism that fostered the notion "that there are many social forces operating in the economic world which are beyond the power of immediate control." Over some social forces, such as "population increase, changing gold supply, discovery and invention of improved methods and process . . . men may exercise but meager sway."[12] One had to turn attention to both the individual and the environment, Nearing explained, because "while recognizing the desirability of purity in thought and action, modern society demands that the environment be changed also in order to afford universal opportunity for the purifying of thought and action. . . . Men need regeneration, but so does the environment." In the end, "the only effective way of securing the regeneration of humanity is to provide a wholesome environment."[13]

Nearing recognized that the individual's free will was to be fully realized in direct proportion to his understanding of the limitations imposed by social forces. He explained that "clever plotting or planning will bend [social forces] in the service of mankind," while "for the time being they must be counteracted or offset, since they will continue to operate."[14] This also meant that there was a close association between freedom and intelligence, knowledge, and education. This way of thinking led Nearing to claim that a transformation had occurred that "bent immutable nature to the service of man through applied science." Thus, "the twentieth century voice demands that economics undergo the same process of transformation from a science that serves laws to a science that serves society." With the "conversion to social science," all "so-called laws may be employed to serve man, or else, if their influence is harmful, counteracted and offset." "Men have triumphed everywhere," he explained, "through the mastery of human thought."[15]

Nearing's single most important writing on the thinking behind the new economics, "Welfare and the New Economics," appeared in the May 1913 issue of *Popular Science Monthly*. In response to the question of "what relief may economics—'the dismal science'—afford?" he explained that "economic thought is undergoing a profound and rapid transformation" against which the older voices were fading. "Vainly do the classicists protest. Futility grips the throats of the doctrinaires." He likened the new economics to the "questioning of the infallibility of a corrupt and dissolute church . . . the infallibility of the scripture."[16] "So long as men regard the laws of political economy as immutable," he declared,

> so long they will be in the grip of the powers which these laws express. It is in vain that Karl Marx argues regarding economic determinism; it is futile for Henry George to "seek the law which associates poverty with progress"; the future is hopeless so long as men believe that political economy is "as exact a science as geometry." Under the domination of economic law, the exploiter will continue to exploit, and the exploited to suffer. Not until men realize that they are creators and arbiters of economic laws will economic laws subserve human welfare. The dawning lies beyond the fetish of economic determinism; the hope for the future rests upon man's ability to make of political economy an eclectic philosophy.[17]

The new economist thus recognized that "the whole subject matter of economics is man-made—the product of human activity." It was man who was the "economic law giver—man, who can unmake or re-make that which he has made."[18] "Political economy," Nearing concluded, was "not a science founded on eternal principles, but a philosophy of livelihood."[19] The economist, then, was not simply a scientist, but with economics so broadly conceived, became a philosopher as well, who in the modern era would have a vital role to play in society. Nearing's social role was implicit in his claim that "the day has dawned when economists must explain that welfare must be put before wealth; that the iron law of wages may be shattered by a minimum wage law. . . . In short, the economists, if they are to justify their existence, must provide a theory which will enable the average man, by cooperating with his fellows, to bear more easily the burden and heat of the day."[20]

The significance of this view was, first, that the definition of economics gave the meaning of wealth an enlarged scope and a human element. Drawing on the teachings of the English ethical and art critic John Ruskin, Nearing declared that "there is no wealth but life";[21] it followed that because life is wealth, all that which contributed to life was subsumed under the field of economics. "Wealth," he found, "may be either material or immaterial," and when "immaterial wealth becomes productive of material wealth, economics becomes indirectly interested in some of its problems."[22] Second, because it was "linked, as it must be, with the problems of government," this philosophy of the new economics had "been drawn into the maelstrom of progressivism which has gripped the Western world,"[23] because "great as has been our material prosperity, one cannot fail to realize that we have far from attained an ideal civilization or anything as good as we have a right to expect."[24]

■■ The evidence of social conditions and the logic of reform seemed to point toward the issue of redistribution of wealth in America. Drawing on Patten's discovery of an economics of abundance, Nearing believed that there was "enough income to go around"; "if all those who participated in the production of wealth received an equal share of the wealth produced, the whole of American society would be able to live on a standard of splendid comfort."[25] The economic–historical fact that American society was a society of abundance was for Patten as much something to fear as to celebrate; the promise of abundance raised the problem of restraints. What would happen to character and morality in the midst of a materialist orgy?[26]

These problems, and the more practical ones of teaching economics at a private university under the wary eyes of trustees who had a financial stake in economic controversies, led Patten to focus on the issue of consumption, not distribution. The problems associated with abundance would be avoided through properly trained consumption. Since the subject of distribution was professionally dangerous, Patten would try to dissuade his students from its study. Nearing recalled that after he began teaching freshman economics at

Wharton School in 1906, Patten called him into his office: " 'Stress anything you care to in the field,' he advised, 'though it might be wise to go light on the distribution of income. It is a delicate subject here.' "[27] Patten's biographer has written that "Nearing became a champion of principles based upon the implications of Patten's logic—implications which Patten himself hesitated to draw."[28]

Driven by the social evidence rather than by the advice of his mentor, Nearing "decided to find out the facts of distribution and perhaps to make a contribution toward the solution of the problem." The problem modern society faces, he claimed, "involves an equitable distribution of the abundant wealth produced by cooperative industry."[29] "Modern industry has created sufficient economic goods," Nearing believed, which led him to declare that it was "merely the archaic system of distribution which has nullified our productive triumphs."[30]

His analysis and conclusions then made their way into his courses, which "became a real forum where opinions were tested and ideas were formulated, presented, controverted, and expanded." One of Nearing's students, Rexford Tugwell, who would later become one of the more radical-minded braintrusters of the New Deal, recalled one of Nearing's courses:

> Since it had a hard core of satisfyingly difficult theory, much of the students' efforts had to go into learning the elements of production, consumption, exchange, and distribution. Production did not detain us long; neither did consumption . . . much of the attention necessarily went to the elaboration of value theory and its effects on the exchange of goods and services. But there was, at the latter end, long consideration of the distributive shares and their adequacy. This is where the quarrels of those days centered. No one suggested more than modifications of the orthodox theory. Even the more radical accepted that system; their radicalism consisted of showing that businessmen were violating the canons of the theory they accepted. . . . Most students took Nearing's criticism of the economic system as something a good deal less than a questioning of its values.[31]

"Distribution," Nearing discovered, was the "most difficult as well as the most interesting part of our science."[32] American society had reached the stage where "people have learned how to produce wealth, but as yet they have never learned to distribute it so as to satisfy all the interested parties." All "the reform movements and agitations" of the day were "largely due to dissatisfaction with the present method of distributing wealth"; "whether it be the strike of a union laborer to secure higher wages, the demands of the Single Taxer that the land alone should be taxed, or the contention of the socialist for a more equitable distribution of the social surplus, at its root is the great question of distribution."[33] Nearing concluded that the case he was building showed that "private enterprize capitalism had created a distribution apparatus that was unethical and anti-social."[34]

While the logical implications of Nearing's work on distribution appeared to make him a spokesman for the interests of the working class, he was more correctly addressing the needs of the leisure class from within it, for he understood its cultural dominance and hence the fact that social change rested in its hands. His economic analysis revealed that modern society was fragmenting and degenerating because of the failure of the dominant class to meet its social duty. The results were especially ominous for the wealthy, who no longer worked for their living, weakening their moral fiber and creating a situation of dependence upon those who did the productive work of society, but were debased in the process. The responsibility for this social and class degradation rested clearly at the feet of the wealthy. According to Nearing's economics, "If I am rich and you are poor, both of us are corrupted by inequality."[35]

His economic analysis led him to a social classification based upon the distinction between "earned" and "unearned" income or "service" and "property" income. "The discussion of economic questions bearing upon the distribution of income," he found, "would be greatly facilitated if a classification could be established of the receipts of income that would conform in some measure to the facts of distribution." Such a classification was offered by "the distinction between income as a return for services, and income as a return for property ownership."[36] Citing the "failure of the classical economists to make good their distinction between productive and unproductive labor,"[37] he then drew upon this distinction claiming that "the time has come when a new classification of the reasons for paying income must be formulated."

> This classification will be based on function rather than tradition. It will be made personal and concrete, rather than impersonal and abstract. . . . [It] exists in fact in the contrast between property income (the income from property ownership) and service income (the income from human effort). The distinction . . . measures the relation of the income-earner as an individual to the productive process.[38]

It was not unusual for economists and social critics at this time to perceive a social division forming, based upon, as Veblen put it, "the distinction between the leisure and the laboring class." "The relation of the leisure (that is, propertied non industrial) class to the economic process," he observed, "is a pecuniary relation—a relation of acquisition, not of production; of exploitation, not of serviceability."[39] But it was Nearing, remarked Tugwell, who "was the first to make 'earned' and 'unearned' major categories of national income studies. . . . He was one of the first, in fact, to study the yield and source of our wealth as a whole." "But otherwise," he continued, Nearing "was one of those dissenters from business practice who leaned hard on economic orthodoxy to sustain his criticisms. . . . Scott had wanted business to perform in the enlightened way classical theory said they were supposed to."[40]

One commentator noted that the categories of "earned" and "unearned" income employed by Nearing were "bound, sooner or later, to be put into practical use in our own financial policy." "As an ethical view, it is not so discordant with the spirit of the times as at first appears," he continued: "To challenge the institutions of property income . . . is a valuable service to social science."[41] Another observer of Nearing's economics noted at the time that "Professor Nearing undoubtedly takes advanced ground, and some of his remedies are socialistic in their tendencies." Yet Nearing's views were in "substantial agreement" with the "great body of economists, in their advocacy of largely increased social control over economic affairs." Nearing's position was that "the present distribution of wealth is largely the result of legalized special privilege, increasing the returns to capital, in its various forms, at the expense of wage labor; that a large proportion of wealth privately held today has been acquired by the owners as a result of predation, and not production on their part." He "advocates, in short, a greatly increased social control over production and distribution, so as to eliminate unearned income, and make impossible future predation, in order to bring about a more equitable and wholesome condition in society, and permit of true progress; and he has been open and fearless in the advocacy of those things."[42]

Pressing his case for formulating a systematic analysis of distribution of income based upon the distinction between earned and unearned income, Nearing's "The 'Why' of Income" appeared in the *American Journal of Sociology* in May 1915. There he stated boldly that "the modern economic world presents this significant picture: many people striving to create wealth and enjoying a part of the wealth they create; other people, who have never participated in the activities of production, receive income." Economic analysis of production "leads at once to the conclusion that the participants in production and the sharers in distribution are not identical groups." The new economics revealed that there could "be no simple contrast between activity in production and participation in distribution. . . . The old explanation was naive and simple."

Opposition to the classical economists had come from "the rhetoric of Ruskin, the front attack of Karl Marx, the vigorous assaults of Henry George" with the effect of "turning the main stream of economic thought from wealth and production to welfare and consumption." There remained but "one major task for the champions of economics as a science." The "theories of distribution," Nearing concluded, "must be revised to correspond with distribution facts. . . . The time has come when a new classification of the reasons for paying income must be formulated."[43]

If there was an ominous shadow darkening the light of progressive reform, it was cast by the fear of the development of rigid class distinctions in American society. With trepidation Nearing observed that "economic issues are rapidly shaping themselves in a manner calculated to draw a sharp line between the recipients of service and of property income."[44] Yet "the importance of the contrast between service and property income," he explained, "is represented not by the fact that it will separate the working class from the leisure class, but that it will lay the basis for the elimination of exploitation, on the one hand, and of economic parasitism, on the other hand." "Economic salvation," he continued, "does not lie through class conflict, but through distinctions which will pay the worker the full value of his work, and drive the idler out of society."[45]

Much of Nearing's professional writing pointed out to the dominant class the dangers of their exploitation of wage earners. By the time he wrote *Income: An Examination of the Returns for Services Rendered and from Property Owned in the United States* (1915), he noted a "cleavage that is becoming more manifest" corresponding to the "contrast between property income and service income." This would eventually cause the "unpropertied masses . . . to question, to protest, to revolt. . . . The workers and the owners are contending on opposite sides and with unabated vigor for a larger share of the wealth which the industrial activities of the community produce."[46]

The ideal of an "economic life" was centered on the belief that "a man's energy must be *efficiently* used in making *only* those goods which *give him back* his energy when he consumes them." "The economic life is a complete, full life containing its share of recreation as well as of work"; but this had become disjointed, for the wealthy had all the leisure without the vivifying virtues of productive labor, and the workers had become exploited to such a degree that they were denied the leisure time necessary for individual improvement and moral enlightenment. "Neither a human machine [the worker] nor a social parasite [the idle rich]," he claimed, was "leading an economic life."[47] His fear was that "the rigidity of the present economic system makes a material increase in service income unlikely, for either a man or his descendants. Arbitrary to the point of fatalism, the economic system ties the worker hand and foot to a standard of service income over which he has the most meager control."[48] His hope and solution of reform was for "an effective system of income distribution [that would] recognize service as the greatest economic asset; will reward service with the values that service creates."[49] "The world must learn that no one who is able to serve should idle," he concluded. "That any one should receive a return for services above the value of those services to the world seems inethical to the last degree."[50]

Nearing wrote that it was "during my student days that I became aware of the menace of riches, which corrupt [the rich] . . . and are financed by exploiting the poor and helpless."[51] Exploitation persisted, and reform was inhibited simply because the rich were "economically parasitic."[52] This condition seemed endemic since "the belief in riches is so general in the United States that it resolves itself into a kind of creed or confession of faith . . . confronted by the choice between the service of God and of Mammon, Americans, for the most part, have frankly chosen Mammon."[53] He concluded that the burden of the economic system was not felt most critically by the workers but that the most immediate result of riches is their disastrous effect on the rich. . . . The rich, particularly in the second generation, are not called upon to achieve anything. They are relieved from the necessity of existence. Their power and initiative atrophies. . . . This denial of achievement undermines the self-respect of the rich and is one of the surest explanations of that profound dissatisfaction, world-weariness, and ennui that is the spiritual scourge of the well-to-do.[54]

He had nothing but disdain for those devitalized members of his class who had failed in their mission to enhance civilization and had landed in a state of "dependency—inability for self-support."[55] His indignation emerged forcefully in his book *Social Sanity* (1913):

There is, of course, a handful of people to whom labor is but a word. Living lives of ease, shielded from the world, removed from all possible hardships or satisfactions, they exist like imported animals, caged from all except their like, in an atmosphere with a regulated temperature, surrounded by keepers whose duty it is to see that they do not escape or come to harm. . . . The disuse of an organism which has potentialities for action inevitably means degeneration.[56]

"Riches," Nearing declared, "leads those who are rich toward physical and spiritual death," with dire implications for the larger society. This decay of the dominant class led "the community toward the social death that is a necessary product of parasitism";[57] while on the one hand "poverty starves initiative," on the other hand "riches surfeits it," and "both, in the end, destroy it."[58] He minced no words when he spoke to the well-to-do, claiming that

we have assumed that we are the keepers of our brothers and yet we employ the millions of men and women in industry and pay them wages which in a great many cases will not purchase even the bare necessities of life. . . . We cast a shadow, and in that shadow men and women suffer and die. It is our sin. We are to blame. People are poor because we make them poor. . . . We are the masters. We have the advantage of knowledge, of culture, of wealth and power. We have the talents of stewardship, and down there in the mire there are millions of our fellowmen who have not had the culture, education and opportunity.

"It is our responsibility, we who own the property, who have culture and opportunity," he reminded his listeners, "we are the only ones who are in a position to work out a solution."[59]

The dominant class in society was clearly the problem, but that class, Nearing was convinced, maintained the power of cultural control, and he therefore found solace in the belief that the decadent rich existed "only in sufficient numbers to act as a warning to their virile fellows, of the abysses which life may hold for the well-born."[60] If there was a "spirit of revolt" in the air, Nearing was inclined to view it not as a revolt of the masses but rather as a revolt of the masters, whereby "even the exploiters—the masters—are leading revolts against industrial and social injustice." He noted the examples of "Tom L. Johnson of Cleveland, a past master at the game of getting rich,"

"George W. Perkins . . . reared in the citadel of exploitation," "Joseph Fels . . . multimillionaire," and "Rockefeller, Stokes, Patterson, Gifford Pinchot." While hardly as illustrious, Nearing might have included himself, for to some degree he identified himself among those of privilege who offered counterhegemonic possibilities to the dominant social order.

These "revolting masters" were "representatives of a great movement of dissatisfaction among the masters of capital"; they were "among the very men who have profited most by the system of society against which they protest." Believing that reform was possible in what was becoming an ever more desperate situation, Nearing's faith rested in the hope that "the revolt of the masters is deep-seated and widespread." Only then would the dominant class return to its position of public duty and enlightened leadership that was its destiny: "When the masters and beneficiaries question, and even condemn, is it any wonder that the spectators take sides against a grotesquely unjust system of wealth distribution."[61]

While Nearing preached a jeremiad of doom, he always spoke too of hope in the promise of regeneration:

> Let no one argue that because historic civilizations have, without exception, developed economic parasitism, therefore economic parasitism is a necessary accompaniment to the development of civilization. No such black prophecy is reflected in the pages of the past. History contains, at most, a warning, which those who would learn do well to read.

This was a warning to the wealthy to live up to their civic ideals. He reminded them that his view of economics was no radical departure but simply the goal that the "civilization of the West has marked . . . plainly." "It aims," he claimed, "at universal opportunity" with "no thought of equality, but . . . a very strong sentiment in favor of equal chances for men and women of all social classes." The well-to-do should return to the virtues of productive labor and recognize that Western civilization "has been erected upon the theory of the validity of effort."[62]

Beneath the compilation of facts and statistics presented as objective evidence was an argument that was as much ethical as economic. Nearing wanted the dominant class to reform itself to reverse what was emerging as a historic separation between individual liberty and cooperative association, thought and action, leisure and labor; to eradicate economic distinctions based upon earned and unearned income. This, however, was not a sterile intellectual issue of economic analysis. It was a matter of morality.

# The Morality of Riches

## Chapter 3

THE themes of the decadence of the rich and the moral decay in riches were located in American cultural history as well as social and economic facts. A deeply rooted tradition of republicanism in American political thought viewed history as illustrating the degeneracy of ancient republics as their citizens lost sight of their most precious liberties in the haze of corrupting wealth and luxury. The ideas that "increasing luxury constitutes an increasing social burden"[1] and that "wealth is meaningless and sterile"[2] pervaded Nearing's thought throughout his life. "History teaches," Nearing noted in 1913, "pretty conclusively, that there never was a social group . . . which did not fall victim to social decadence. [Ancient republics] rose one by one to positions of wealth and power, became corrupt and decadent, and then fell easy prey to some virile, conquering people. Social decadence is commonplace in history."[3] The key question for Nearing and for other progressives was whether "any such doctrine appl[ied] to the United States?" Would the historical conditions just beginning to emerge offer a way out of the cul-de-sac of republican degeneracy? Could the republican virtues of self-disciplined civic duty be revived in a highly individualistic society amid economic abundance?[4]

Nearing shared a progressive view of history that saw eighteenth- and nineteenth-century American liberalism departing from the ideal of republican virtue in defining independence by the principles of possessive individualism and transforming the ideal of a cooperative commonwealth based upon a common good into an unrestricted struggle in a free market. By the early twentieth century, Nearing maintained, the social consequences of economic competition had become increasingly unacceptable, and the dream of civic humanism welcomed the discarding of the old system despite its achievements. The evolutionary optimism of progressive theories of history revealed new developments that would overcome the crisis of republican history. For Nearing, modern economic developments, cooperative productive enterprises, interdependence, and abundance, all of which offered universalized leisure and control of the environment, made the ideal of personal independence within an organic life a real possibility. Nearing, as we have seen, argued that this ideal could be achieved if economic abundance was distributed widely and the industrial order humanized; more important, he believed that if these reforms were to be effective, America would have to undergo a transformation in values, returning to the classical notion of republican citizenship dedicated to a search for the public good.

When Nearing argued for social change that could "be made only through the effective expression of a feeling of social responsibility," he drew upon a rights–duty dualism, emphasizing the importance of positive rather than negative liberty, duties rather than rights. "Rights," he declared, "are always accompanied by duties." Just as social interdependence had replaced individual independence as the modern condition of life, Nearing argued, a corresponding change was necessary whereby positive liberty would accompany negative liberty as an ideal. "Each right is accompanied by a proportionate responsibility," he believed, and "men who have a right to choose have also a duty to fulfill, and this right and this duty are inseparable."[5] "The slave alone is free," he explained; "his master dictates his life; never once is he called upon to make the choices upon which his future depends; but the freeman is bound, unless liberty be interpreted in terms of license, to render an account of his every act. Since he is his own master, he must answer for his own conduct."[6] Freedom in modern society was not something simply to be cherished but to be vigorously exercised. This conception of social responsibility meant redefining not only the meaning of freedom but also property rights and the role of the state.

Nearing outlined an economic republicanism based upon "four basic democratic concepts—equality of opportunity, civic obligation, popular government and human rights." "Citizens of a democracy," he claimed, "must assume the responsibilities of citizenship under the pain of missing its benefits." In such a society, "the important values are human values; the great rights are human rights." No longer would an active government be seen as threat to liberty since "a people's government can know only one duty—the service of those who support it." Since the ideals he advocated had been "sound as tests of political democracy," then "perhaps they may be equally useful in testing the democracy of industry." "The real fight for liberty of opportunity at the present time," he explained, "centers about the economic world." It was "there that the next battle for liberty will be won or lost."[7]

---

The logic of the new republicanism led to the belief that in a democratic society a reorientation of individual initiative toward social responsibility relied heavily on education as the key to social change. John Dewey expressed this belief when he stated that "education is the fundamental method of social progress and reform."[8] Thus educational reform was heavily debated in the Progressive Era, and Nearing detected "revolutionary activity in every field of educational endeavor."[9] Nearing's interests frequently turned to the issues of education and reflected the importance of education in the process of social change.[10] The focus on the problem was two-sided: the reform of education to prepare the individual for life in an organic, interdependent, highly industrialized society and the reform through education to foster intelligent political action.

Nearing's approach to education began with the evolutionary view popularized by Herbert Spencer—that the purpose of education was to assist the individual to adjust to the changing circumstances of life. He would cite Spencer approvingly to the effect that "the object of education is a complete living" and claim that "a perfect educational system would prepare those participating in it to live every phase of their lives, and to derive from life all possible benefit."[11] But the notion that humanity could only adjust to evolutionary development reflected a harsh determinism under which reform was futile. To draw on Spencer yet make his educational philosophy acceptable, Nearing next turned to Lester Ward's conception of universal human capacity for knowledge, along with the claim that it was the purposeful human mind that made society dynamic and reform possible. Ward's "great scientific affirmation" was that "society is full of capacity,—latent, unused,—because of the lack of opportunity for its development."[12] It was the duty of progressive thinkers to place "before the public in a striking unanswerable way, the facts of human capacity and the possibilities of adjustment."[13] This view was egalitarian, democratic, and highly optimistic. Education was the key to progress.

Reform had to begin with the educational system itself. Under the modern factory system, "apprenticeship has vanished from modern industry," which meant that it now fell to the schools to assume the functions of teaching the preparation for life. "As a means of preparation for these thousands of different pursuits," Nearing wrote, "the school system in most cases holds out merely a traditional form of classical education which . . . fails to give . . . any ground work for the special line of industry in which he is to spend his life-work."[14] The new age demanded a "new basis of education" whereby the "ideal education is that of the three 'H's',—the education of the Head, the Hand, and the Heart."[15]

In addition to John Dewey and Randolph Bourne, Nearing wrote approvingly of the school system of Gary, Indiana, as a model of the new education.[16] In his book *The New Education*, Nearing explained that the Gary plan "aims at the education of the whole child. . . . In no school that I have visited did I find a more conscious effort to unite the mental and the physical, hand and head, and vocation and recreation, in one complete system."[17] Under the ideal of the new education, "the school prepares for life—in fact, it not only prepares for life, it is part of life," he noted, "a life with wider boundaries and greater depths opens, bringing with it a greater chance for service."[18] The schools "are the laboratory for our democracy."[19] And it was "through the agency of the public school," he believed, "that the social conscience can and will be aroused."[20]

An "effective education" founded upon "the vision of a trained intelligence"[21] emphasized the organic nature of modern circumstances and prepared the individual for social duty. The schools, Nearing wrote, "have thus far been content with the teaching of individual morality, but it now devolves upon them to instruct in social morality." "The time has come," he claimed, "when the community is prepared to regard social responsibility on a much broader, saner basis."[22] The public school system presented "practically the only organization which can be depended upon to develop and evolve a . . . feeling of social responsibility in the body politic."[23]

Here was the link between education and social reform—public opinion. Nearing believed that the basis of the new civilization was already apparent and that "the will of an aroused public opinion alone seemed to be lacking." There was only one way for public opinion to reflect a sense of social responsibility, and that was through education. Making this connection, he wrote that "popular education, soundly based and wisely given, will lead ultimately to the development of a public opinion on all vital questions."[24] Believing that social problems were "remedial through the awakening of the public conscience," he envisioned "the development of a more widespread and deeper feeling of social responsibility through the education of the public conscience."[25]

It was just a short step from the development of public sentiment on social responsibility to "concentrating public opinion in the form of legislation."[26] The goal of reforming public education was "to prepare men and women for social action, and social action will be expressed in the form of wise legislation."[27] This link between thought and action, education and legislation, was critical to the health of democracy. "Social responsibility," Nearing wrote, "may be strongly felt by an overwhelming majority, yet in the absence of legislation, crystallizing social responsibility, the feeling of the majority has no effective means of expression."[28] His optimism extended beyond a belief in the benevolence of human nature to a faith in the processes of popular government. He claimed that "the primary necessity is a thinking population."

> A thinking population can be created only through a good system of education. If men and women think, they will act. If they think wisely, they will act wisely, and in a democracy the test of the wisdom of thought is the wisdom of action. . . . The action of a democratic people can rise no higher than the public enlightenment. Enlighten the public and enlightened action will inevitably follow.[29]

Appealing to the public conscience was a way of solving the ills of democratic America with more democracy. Nearing noted that "public opinion furnishes a phase of social control which is entirely new and which is the longest step taken toward a popular form of government."[30] A public opinion awakened to the virtues of social responsibility and civic duty was not, however, an end in itself; it was the means to overthrow existing social arrangements and habits of thought. It was not incidental that Nearing mentioned "the necessity for some radical expression of public disapproval."[31]

▬▬ A further expression of this ennobling republicanism emerged regarding the role of American women in the new abundant society. Nearing noted "the fact that women have capacity, but have failed to play a part in the affairs of the world because of lack of opportunity."[32] But now women had opportunity, and how they used that opportunity had significant consequences for the future of the nation. He advocated a liberating vision, yet his feminism was carefully proscribed. He not only detested barriers to opportunity placed before them but saw women in the midst of economic abundance falling prey to dependence, or "sex parasitism."[33] His feminism was hardly a vision that would transcend the confining cult of domesticity; it was more accurately a metaphor for the dilemmas faced by all Americans under new economic conditions.

Nearing explained that "the revolution in the home together with the breakdown of tradition, and the establishment of educational facilities, has reshaped the environmental influences acting upon women until they are presented, for the first time in centuries, with a wide opportunity to choose the pursuits to which their lives shall be devoted." The important question that followed was "what is involved in this possibility of choice?" He provided the answer by contrasting the "social conditions in Rome,—the greatest republic of antiquity, with the United States,—the greatest republic of modern time."[34] In the history of Rome, a complete transformation had taken place whereby "wealth had increased" and "women and men alike" had achieved "boundless leisure" by becoming dependent upon the labor of slaves. Romans were faced with "a life of social usefulness or one of selfish luxury." The women of Rome, he claimed "were called upon to make this fundamental choice between selfishness and social action; between indulgence and service." Roman women chose "childlessness, idleness, luxury and dissipation." The result was republican degeneracy. The point of drawing on this history, Nearing explained, was that "the same choice that confronted the women of Rome is confronting the women of the United States today." "Will the American woman," he asked, "choose Selfish indulgence or Social Service?"[35]

This, of course, was a question faced not only by women but by men; it was a question faced by all Americans of "the income class" to whom this choice was a reality. Women were facing it anew; they could avoid errors made by men in the past. Speaking not only of women but of all Americans, he declared that the "freedom [they] have gained through recent social changes and the significance of their consequent choice, constitutes one of the profoundest and at the same time one of the most inscrutable problems in American life." "The women of the United States are free to choose," he wrote; "what does their freedom involve, and what will follow from their choice?"[36]

The American woman had achieved great opportunity "with her emancipation," yet with "each new opportunity" came "the necessity of choice." Women might, "like the women of Rome, choose selfishly" and live a life free "from care and responsibility." "Well-to-do" women could choose "lives of idle dependence . . . devoting their lives to that social will o' the wisp mistakenly called Happiness." Women who took this course had to know "that they are taking more from society in sustenance than they are returning in service; that they are parasites, supported by the workers of the nation."[37] He hoped that they would choose social responsibility and recognize that "with rights . . . come duties, and if they regard duties as irksome, women will find that there is a thorn for every rose."[38]

Women, he hoped, would assume "their share of the responsibility of the nation,—bearing and rearing healthy, noble sons and daughters, administering worthy homes, occupying leading positions in industrial, educational and philanthropic ventures; utilizing their time wisely; choosing socially and not selfishly."[39] This was not, however, a vision only of women's goals for social advancement; the problems faced by women would clarify the dilemmas of freedom and social responsibility in the modern age. In the new society of abundant economic wealth, the choice had to be made to direct it "into any channel that promises high returns in human service." "Twentieth Century American society," he preached, drawing on the biblical dictum invoked by the Puritan John Winthrop in 1630, "is a city set on a hill, a candle on a candlestick; the whole world is regarding our progress."[40]

In part, this vision of women's emancipation was based upon the faith that "armed with new power through the assumption of civic rights, women will, in time, assert their independence of masculine dominance and assume their true position as one organic factor in modern society."[41] Yet it was more fundamentally enhancing the Victorian cult of domesticity rather than departing from it. "The advancement of women means her individualization," he explained, and "only the woman who is a human being, with the power and freedom to choose, may teach the son of a free man. . . . The mothers of America are prepared to teach their sons and daughters because they have been taught to think the noblest thoughts and to do the strongest things."[42]

Updating the belief that the woman was the moral core of the home and the source of moral training for the nation,[43] Nearing found that "the direct responsibility for ethical conditions and social economics is placed upon the shoulders of women."[44] "Perhaps," he claimed, "the whole future of the Republic lies within the realm of 'woman's sphere,' for it is there that the new generation is born and reared."[45] According to this ideology of the home, "the family is engaged in that highest of all human occupations—the manufacture of souls."[46] The emancipation of women meant that they would fulfill their duties in the home, but they could do so only if they became "independent and self-sufficient individuals."[47] While there were "two alternative occupations open to women: first, motherhood, and second, some form of industrial pursuit," and neither was exclusive of the other, it was "motherhood," he stated, that was "by far the most important occupation of the two."[48]

These views were apparently shared by the woman Nearing married, Nellie Marguerite Seeds, who collaborated on Nearing's most important work on women, *Women and Social Progress: A Discussion of the Biologic, Domestic, Industrial, and Social Responsibilities of American Women* (1912), a book they wrote together during a trip to Europe during the summer of 1911.[49] She was the daughter of a realtor in Germantown, Pennsylvania, a graduate of Bryn Mawr, and an Episcopalian who enlisted in the fight against child labor. She was at the University of Pennsylvania at the same time as Nearing, taking a master of liberal arts degree in 1910 and a doctorate five years later. Sharing not only an academic life but a reformist faith, they were married in June 1908. Rexford Tugwell recalled their

> suburban house. There I learned what a family was like whose interests were mainly intellectual. I learned that scholarly affairs need not be merely retreats for stolen moments; they could be ordinary daily occupations. For Nellie (Seeds) Nearing, Scott's wife, no less than he, was caught up in the general movement of those times for change and reform.[50]

While Nellie Nearing seems to have shared her husband's beliefs about women's emancipation, she may also have found it difficult to reconcile the paradoxical goal of greater achievements outside the home while maintaining a traditional role at the center of the domestic sphere. Her doctoral thesis on "education and fecundity" suggests that she questioned the logic that advanced education for women led to enlightened motherhood. Concerned with whether the "increase in higher education of women" had "any effect upon fecundity," her evidence revealed that "the proportion of women college graduates who marry" was approximately one-half that of noncollege women.[51] She would marry, and the Nearings had two children—John, born in 1912, and Robert, an adopted son born in 1914. The Nearings would try in their home to live out their feminist ideal of enlightened motherhood as the cornerstone to the development of virtuous republican citizens.

▬▬ The values associated with social responsibility not only had republican roots but were strongly reinforced by Christian traditions. Republican and Christian influences merged in what was a new "social gospel" movement that focused on the ethical responsibility of the dominant groups in society and the social implications of theology. Charles Hopkins found that this "new movement probably obtained its greatest impetus from those enlightened conservatives who strove to reconcile the truths of Christianity with the new science, and to reorient Protestant ethics to the needs of a newly industrialized society."[52]

Drawn to the writings of Walter Rauschenbusch, one of the leading minds of the social gospel movement, Nearing was in full agreement with the idea "that faith without works is dead."[53] He was part of a scientific community in the early years of the twentieth century that came out of a profoundly Christian culture and retained traditional doctrines of Christianity as they embraced the new science. Of the New Testament he wrote that he "believed it to be one of the most valuable books within the reach of the social scientist."[54] Most important for the social scientists who sought a moral response to economic problems was the accommodation of religious and scientific concepts that produced three closely related ideas and laid the basis for purifying the faith and finding social application for ethical teachings. First was an emphasis on the Old Testament as the law of social relations and the New Testament as the practical application of the teachings of Jesus; the developments of social science would apply the teachings of the Gospels to modern society. Second, the purposelessness of natural selection could be criticized at the same time that evolution was accepted as a synonym for development consistent with divine purpose and the millennial faith in the kingdom of heaven on earth. Finally, an organic view of society, emphasizing cooperation and solidarity, was reinforced by belief in the brotherhood of men; social divisions would be bridged through recognition of a common creation.

With this Christian version of harmony and brotherhood in particular, a fresh emphasis on the social aspects of Christ's Second Commandment stressed the need for the leisure class to fulfill its obligations to humanity. Social responsibility based upon Christian imperatives extolled a system of production and distribution in which all moral income was earned and all shared equally in the fruits of their labor. Nearing's thought was infused with these advanced religious conceptions, and he insisted that political and economic reforms had to be accompanied by moral reform. He admitted to having "always been interested in the church" and "in preaching, because I have regarded the preacher as having the hardest job in the community."[55]

In all aspects of his life, powerful Christian beliefs informed his thinking, making him as much a prophet as an economist.[56] As he absorbed the progressive philosophies of experimental social science, when he turned to James, it was not the philosopher he evoked but the New Testament apostle.[57] When writing on the task of science, Nearing cautioned against inferring that "speculative philosophy and religion have no place in the scheme of things." These fields were "ever broadening" and "still direct the work of science, suggesting and leading into untried fields."[58] His deep religious sensibility, or what Tugwell called his "moral radicalism," remained inescapably a part of his assumptions.[59] This habit of moral judgment was symptomatic of basic social and moral teachings that took the spirit of the New Testament as the essential guide to human action and belief. Science provided knowledge of what man could do but not what men should do. For free will to operate beneficently, worthy values were required for guidance. "In all things," he claimed, "some guiding principles must exist."[60]

These were found in the remnants of nineteenth-century liberal religion, what Nearing called "Social Religion—a religion of love, fellowship, brotherhood, and social service."[61] He arrived at socially responsible "guiding principles" by adhering to a system of ethics that would instruct the individual's conscience. For Nearing, "two elements—an individual and a social,"[62] were apparent in the practice of social religion. The individual component was a "belief in the innate goodness of men. . . . Hence no matter how concealed, there is, in each person, that divine spark called conscience—a soul." The social aspect, revealed through the "modern investigation" of social science, had "established beyond the possibility of doubt that the causes of poverty and misery are not personal but social."[63] Nearing saw his role not only as an investigator of modern society but as a teacher working "for the liberation of the individual soul."[64] Social religion, in attempting to transcend the moral crisis of industrial capitalism, offered a solution that united social science with spiritual values by connecting moral teachings to economic and social facts.

Recognizing the "need for a new birth of religion,"[65] he believed that the orthodox church ethic of otherworldly personal salvation was the greatest obstacle to moral reform. The new faith sought to remove Christianity from the church and was critical of conventional Protestantism. Nearing believed that the modern church had failed to promote a social reformation, although in the distant past it had been a church of the masses. "The church during the Middle Ages," he explained, "and in fact down to the opening of the 19th century, focused and expressed the popular feelings of social responsibility."[66] With the coming of industrial capitalism and the ethic of individualism, Christ's teachings had been "misrepresented and misused," with the result that they "have never been put into practice."[67] Now that the church had become influenced by the wealthy to promote an ethic of individualism, "the influence of the church has been seriously restricted and its power of control over the population has been greatly lessened."[68] It was on this basis that Nearing rejected "the institutionalizing of the Christian church," claiming that it was "entrenched behind great ramparts of theological dogma"; it was "judged by its fruits, and so often is that fruit tainted with the bitterness of theological dogma."[69]

The alternative was to universalize the faith in order to revive it as a moral foundation for social change:

> The Scribes and the Pharisees understood their theology thoroughly. . . . They had the letter of the law but not its spirit. . . . This condemnation of the Scribes and Pharisees is not, however, a condemnation of all theology. Jesus lay down his

doctrine in unshakable terms. "Love thy God," said He, "and thy neighbor as thyself." That is the extent of Jesus' religious theory. . . . Our belief in God is demonstrable only through our belief in man. . . . Our faith, in short, will be tested by our works.[70]

If the church "wishes to live up to the ideals of its founders," he declared, "it must cease dogmatizing and in pursuance of Jesus' example, it must preach, heal, and teach."[71] In order for organized religion to "maintain a social religion," the church would have to "stop sacrificing mankind on the altar of . . . iron-bound creeds."[72] Faced with the church's betrayal of its mission in its failure to promote social reform, Nearing drew on the spirit of the Gospels to advocate a practical Christianity of works as well as faith.

He stated this conviction most forcefully in his *Social Religion: An Interpretation of Christianity in Terms of Modern Life* (1913). He explained that when "confronted by certain facts, Jesus said and did certain things. His followers, if confronted with similar facts, should, if they be what they profess to be, imitate his words and deeds. Such imitation would constitute, for the Christian, a Social Religion."[73]

For religion to be "a vitalizing force," it would have to "face and master the situation." "A social religion," he claimed, "would prove such a force."[74] Whereas in the past people waited "a thousand years in order to realize a promised millennium," it was because "a group suffering from constant deficit could not hope to realize their heaven on earth."[75] Now, with control of the environment and an abundance of economic goods to provide leisure, "heaven on earth" was "a possibility that may be immediately realized."[76]

Organicism, legitimized by the religious conception of brotherhood, found expression in a belief in solidarity, cooperation, and social responsibility. The brotherhood of man could be realized in an organic society with its interdependent relationships. Declaring that "we are the sons of God," Nearing went on to explain that it was "not as an individual, but as a member of a progressive society, the believer in Social Religion makes effective his belief by an insistence on social justice."[77] What, then, according to his theological considerations, were the causes of the economic maladjustments he had discovered through social science? "Why," he asked, "is a system of distribution tolerated which fails to give to every family a living wage?" The answer was readily apparent: "It is because we do not really care to apply the Christian doctrine of brotherhood to the affairs of daily life."[78]

The "doctrine of brotherhood" and the belief in practical religion, the application of the Gospels to everyday life, was the basis upon which Christianity converted all economic and social problems into moral ones. It was on this basis, too, that the study of economics became the expansive enterprise of studying humanity in terms of a social self. Yet no purely scientific investigation would be able to solve the problem of the distribution of wealth without some generally accepted principles of social justice and responsibility. Social science could not provide ethical standards. Nearing adhered to the view that all economic questions were essentially moral questions, noting that "there must be some guiding idea behind analysis and criticism, else their best efforts lead nowhere beyond the desert of skepticism and disillusionment."[79] He spoke of "prophetic ones who see in the materialism of their science a faint recollection of the spirituality of all things."[80] "Behind all human purpose, in its larger scope," the economist found "the conservation of . . . spiritual values, which are the highest values that man thus far has learned to measure, truth and justice and mercy are the real measures of worth." All Nearing's hopes for economic adjustment, for social reform, for America's progress, were found in "an optimism based on science and belief, and leading to virile effort."[81]

His optimism for the realization of a Christian society expressing the moral values of the Gospels, however, rested largely upon his message reaching the dominant class. "You and I," he declared, "share in the benefits of the maladjustments which exist in our society. . . . We share the benefits and we are socially responsible for their continuance."[82] To "fully understand Jesus' Social Religion," he asked that they "recollect His attitude toward social problems": "The smug, self satisfied conceit of a superior social class is an abomination to Him."[83] He arraigned his own class just as Jesus had denounced the "Scribes and Pharisees who, engrossed in selfish pursuits and satiated with their traditional righteousness, were playing havoc with the lives of human beings over whom they had acquired or inherited power." This, he admitted, was a serious indictment, yet it was "richly merited, for those men, born leaders of God's chosen people had betrayed their trust; had cast aside their obligations to the society of which they formed so essential a part; and, in riotous living, and meaningless word bandyings, squandered the substance of the nation on the one hand, and debased its religion on the other."[84] "I wish," he pleaded to his leisure-class audience, "you would put side by side the social ethics of the New Testament and the game which has as its object the establishment of the maximum inequality in your favor. . . . There is no such thing as harmonizing Christian ethics with getting rich, and the system that works on that basis is in direct opposition to all the teachings of Christ."[85]

As with all jeremiads, Nearing's *Social Religion* concluded with the hope of salvation and regeneration. After leading his readers "through the valley of the shadow of living death," the "night" of poverty and human misery, he claimed that "the night is far spent, the day is at hand and already we behold a new dawning."[86] Hope rested upon the firm belief that "a spirit of religion dominates the American people"; they "long to serve."[87] Economic investigation revealed clearly that "we are a wealthy nation; we can afford to pay living wages; we are an enlightened people; . . . we are a far-seeing nation."[88] Religion and science merging into an ethical economics would become the salvation of industrial capitalism.

▬ It is important at this point to turn to "speculative philosophy," a field that Nearing saw as expanding its horizons while offering an important basis for economic and social reform. The philosophic movement contributing an essential element to his economics as the system suited to experimental social science was pragmatic philosophy. He caught pragmatism from all sides, whether from Patten, who, as noted earlier, discovered that the new movement in philosophy paralleled and reinforced the new economics, or from the general influence of this social philosophy on the economic and social thought of the day. Pragmatism was part of the intellectual milieu of his age—as Morton White has argued, by 1912, "pragmatism was already a national password"[89]—a philosophy that tore down the ossified walls of determinism to offer a vista of a relativistic, open-ended, pluralistic world, a world that offered a degree of human freedom and choice, a freedom that was more meaningful socially than individually, and a concept of free will that strongly implied a tendency toward action. As a philosophy of the new science, pragmatism also offered a method, a technique for analyzing means conceived as becoming rather than being, with truth as a process of discovery but not discovered. This conception of flux meant that all study of man was historical and all truths were relative and knowable only when tested in experience. Patten's "tests," which applied only under current conditions and based on the known facts of the time, were as follows: "The economic tests are prosperity, peace, and cooperation, the physical tests are efficiency, vigor, and longevity, and the emotional tests are service, public spirit, and missionary zeal."[90] Nearing's tests were similar, if not so baldly stated, as he absorbed the new philosophy of social progress.

The pragmatic method as a tool of social science appealed to Nearing as a technique of economic analysis. Consistent with the pragmatic view, Nearing upheld "the scientific attitude" or "turn of mind that scorned prejudice, resisted dogma, or experimented enthusiastically." This method would lead to "the intelligent direction of social processes" since man's current activities were so fluid that "they could be shaped and directed by properly trained hands and minds."[91] His economics were conditioned by a commitment to the pragmatic contention that knowledge was experimental and changing and that truth was discovered in practice. After reading a contemporary work on pragmatism, Nearing noted its meaning as "a philosophy whose main contention is that true ideas are working ideas, and that truth itself, like a creed or a belief, is simply a working valuation of reality."[92] Elsewhere he remarked that "the past has made its contribution, and has died making it. For the contribution the present is grateful, but it must steadfastly refuse in its own name, and in the name of the future, to be bound by any decree of the past which will not stand the acid test of experience."[93] Social reform would be tested and judged "in relation to the freedom it affords for the development of the individual" and "could best be measured by its effectiveness in providing its citizenry with the incentives and opportunities to broaden and deepen and strengthen the spirit of man."[94] Pragmatism provided a method of analysis of the means for social progress, the end of which was a new individual whose freedom and self-awareness would flourish and whose originality and uniqueness would be nurtured through the ideal of cooperation.

Nearing looked to the pragmatic attitude for the principles of its method and techniques of analysis. He could quote Dewey approvingly regarding method; "'Science is, after all, a matter of perfected skill in conducting inquiry—not something finished, absolute in itself, but the result of certain technique.'"[95] While experience could be tested only in the context of a commitment to certain principles and common values, a scientific method lacked the values capable of determining the ends toward which change should be directed. Nearing clearly differentiated between techniques for testing means and those for determining ends. Because science and the pragmatic method were capable of the former but not the latter, Nearing was never so enthusiastic about pragmatism as his mentor. Science could guide investigations of society, but it could not provide values. Those had to come from another source. For Nearing, values were provided by a social religion rooted in the Gospels. His deep religious sensibility allowed him to turn to pragmatism for technique, but in a universe that was "neither absolute nor arbitrary," ideals and purpose were supplied by practical Christianity.

# The Strenuous Life

## Chapter 4

THE awareness of a need for a moral regeneration of society arose in part from an analysis of capitalism that emphasized its contribution to cultural decay and moral atrophy, as well as its creation of a sense of the futility and meaninglessness of daily existence. Economic developments produced "ennui, dilettantism and parasitism," Nearing contended, circumstances whereby individuals had "become devitalized."[1] He recalled many years later that industrial capitalism led to "superficial living," "purposeless lives," "a sterile life pattern" so narrowing and devitalizing human experience that he longed for real possibilities of authentic experience.[2]

As a substitute for the decline of authentic experience, Nearing sought a vitalizing social force as a solution to physical and spiritual enervation.[3] Even in his youth, he responded to this sense of devitalized existence and tried to recover its intensity by subscribing to the program of "physical culture" offered by the fitness advocate Bernarr McFadden. Nearing read his magazine and was "a devotee of his good health formula: plenty of exercise, fresh air and sunshine, a simple diet, and fasting."[4] The belief that America produced wasted lives, devoid of the possibility of purposeful existence, lay beneath the surface of all Nearing's economic and social analysis, leading Joseph Freeman to remark that "behind many of his political beliefs was the anterior conviction that wealth, luxury, riches, surplus, destroyed a man's initiative."[5]

In the Progressive Era, there was a heightened sense of the need to address this crisis before physical and moral vitality further degenerated and to offer solutions for revitalizing the energies of man toward constructive ends. A common remedy was to invoke martial virtues as a cure for the ills of American society, a way of renewing national vigor. Veblen observed "warlike prowess," an "attitude of emulative ferocity," "the predatory temperament," and "the martial spirit," which the leisure class used to "foster a manly spirit" allowing the individual to "assert his manhood."[6] Someone like William James, who sought in national service "the moral equivalent of war," admired the reinvigorating function of military experience, its ability to "redeem life from flat degeneration." "Does not," asked James, "the worship of material luxury and wealth, which constitutes so large a portion of the 'spirit' of our age make somewhat for . . . a certain trashiness of fibre?"[7] The problem, said James, was "summed up in Simon Patten's words, that mankind was nursed in pain and fear, and that the transition to a 'pleasure-economy' may be fatal to a being wielding no powers of defense against its disintegrative influences." While he saw virtue in the "military ideal of hardihood and discipline," he refused "to speak of the bestial side of the war-regime" and considered "only the higher aspects of military sentiment." In other words, he hoped that "the martial type of character can be bred without war" and that "strenuous honor and disinterestness abound elsewhere."[8]

This was not the case with one of the strongest advocates of "the strenuous life," Theodore Roosevelt, whose summons for invigoration extolled aggressive nationalism, strenuousness for the sake of strenuousness, and a turn to vigorous physical activity on a world scale. Yet he too admired the man "who has those virile qualities necessary to win in the stern strife of actual life." Roosevelt declared that "we cannot . . . be content to rot by inches in ignoble ease . . . sunk in scrambling commercialism; heedless of the higher life, the life of aspiration, of toil and risk," and he complained of "the timid man, the lazy man, the man who distrusts his country, the overcivilized man, who has lost the great fighting virtues, the ignorant man, and the man of dull mind, whose soul is incapable of feeling the mighty lift that thrills." Echoing the Progressives' lament that modern civilization offered only a deadening existence, he called "not for the life of ease but for the life of strenuous endeavor."[9]

For Nearing, the strenuous life meant an appeal to the well-to-do to recognize the moral and social implications of an economics based on earned and unearned income. This was not simply the principle of the immorality of idle habits imparted by the apostle Paul in the Gospels that "the man who will not work shall not eat." If the dominant classes would adhere to the values of productive labor, they would benefit from its vitalizing virtues and become reinvigorated. If the values of the dominant class included a belief that man deserved the fruits of his labor, the leisure class would no longer be isolated from real life, inhibiting social progress and leading the way to national decay. The only true, moral form of wealth was derived from productive labor.

A worthy society "is built upon labor," he remarked, "its processes are continued and its wealth is recreated by labor. . . . The well ordered society will encourage work. It will aim to develop enthusiasm, to stimulate activity."[10] The wealthy not only deprived themselves of the broad range of creative and moral fulfillments offered by the experience of productive labor, but in appropriating surplus wealth, they robbed the workers of the fruits of their labor. The problem lay with the propensity for material acquisition by the leisure class; its "desire for things," he surmised, "lies at the bottom of the hurry and turmoil of American life." But this was a false pursuit leading "to naught save vanity and the vexation of spirit." The fact was that "a great gap—a gulf . . . yawns between modern life and personal contentment."[11] Unless the wealthy "climbed out over the foothills of a belief in salvation through the possession of things," they would find that "their lives are barren."[12]

So in addition to a transformation of economic values, the solution Nearing offered in *Reducing the Cost of Living* (1914) was to pursue the vitalizing practice of "the simple life." To remedy the malady of the dominant class, he prescribed "an individual remedy for the high cost of living" that included each person "simplifying his life, curtailing his wants, serving himself wherever possible, and spending the income which he receives more efficiently." This was an antidote of vigorous living "that may be applied with particular advantage by the well-to-do."[13] Christian moralism and pragmatism were neatly assimilated into a view of life that incorporated the essential value of creative intelligence in human experience with a notion of "salvation through effort." "Salvation lies in doing, which is another term for growing or unfolding. Men derive the greatest beatitudes from a life of achievement. The blessings of the world are showered upon the head of him who does the world's work. It is not yet time to sit peacefully down and wish for the happiness of the millennium."[14] For Nearing, vitality and purpose would survive only in a society that satisfied man's spiritual needs and offered meaningful values. Such a transformed society defined labor in terms of human fulfillment rather than the accumulation of wealth. His moral equivalent turned to the "instinct of workmanship" as the "basis of industrial morality," noting that "the soul of sound industry lies in the pride a man feels in his work."[15]

It is worth noting that while Nearing did not make the appeal that James did to the military for the recovery of ideals essential to a revitalized existence, their correctives were in the end similar. To counteract civilization's barrenness while avoiding un-Christian strenuousness, both offered vigorous productive labor that would vitalize the individual and provide a service to society. James envisioned conscripting "our gilded youths" and sending them "to the coal and iron mines, to freight trains, to fishing fleets in December, to dish-washing, clothes-washing, and window-washing, to road-building and tunnel-making, to foundries and stoke-holes, and to the frames of skyscrapers."[16] Yet when he had considered the problem of strenuousness earlier and thought about it in terms of "the old monkish poverty-worship," he asked whether "voluntarily accepted poverty" might be a means to "the strenuous life." Christian renunciation of "material luxury and wealth" could "make for heroic standards of life" for the "so-called better class." Poverty "*is* the strenuous life. . . . When one sees the way in which wealth getting enters as an ideal into the very bone and marrow of our generation, one wonders whether a revival of the belief that poverty is a worthy religious vocation may not be 'the transformation of military courage.' " He thus envisioned a "spiritual reform" based upon the "idealization of poverty."[17] Finally, James saw that his solution to the strenuous life also had political advantages, offering a degree of freedom to escape forces of conformity and passive consent to dominant values: "Think of the strength which personal indifference to poverty would give us if we were devoted to unpopular causes."[18]

Strenuousness for Nearing did not end with a robust physical life, but included "mental vigor" and "virile ideas." There had to be strenuous ideals to guide the strenuous life. Nearing found these in Christian morality and service, a strenuous Christianity. His notes under the heading "the spirit of revolt" among the drafts of his autobiography included a long quotation from Walter Rauschenbusch's writings, which read in part:

> The Kingdom of God would evoke the spirit of battle and the finest temper of sport. Indeed, the Kingdom of God is the greatest fight for which men ever enlisted, and the biggest game that was ever played. The odds are always against you. It is just as if a lone little eleven on the gridiron should see the whole crowd from the bleacher pouring down from the field and lining up against them. Yet you know in your soul that you are bound to win, for God is playing on your side, and God has unusual staying powers. All who have ever fought for the Kingdom of God know that there is a strange joy in it. The memory of one good fight for freedom or justice gives a thrilling sense of worth for a life-time. There is even the stern sense of humor as you watch the crowd rolling down on you and you wait to be trampled on.[19]

Strenuousness for Nearing had enormous intellectual significance. It emanated from an intense adherence to self-culture, conveying a stern self-reliance. It addressed a fundamental cultural contradiction between individual autonomy and social improvement. The intensity with which one lived drew together one's inner spiritual life with an impulse toward active existence. There was a completeness to a self-reliant life if it was authentically lived. There was in fact, as the passage above conveys, an urge toward combativeness, an air of the valorous in solitary confrontation. One is reminded of Emerson's comments on Thoreau: "There was something military in his nature, as if he did not feel himself except in opposition. He wanted a fallacy to expose, a blunder to pillory, I may say required a little sense of victory, a roll of the drum, to call his powers into full exercise."[20] Looking back from his later years, Nearing decided that there were "two kinds of people in the world: those who yearn for a soft sensuous life, and those who would revel in a hard life of decision and struggle." A strenuous life and a strenuous mind active in "the struggle toward the ideal" would "develop the bone and sinew of body, mind and spirit."[21]

■■■ The strenuous life Nearing envisioned included a idealization of country life reflecting the antiurban bias of progressivism.[22] The basis for the moral economy of a society built upon the values of productive labor would be found in self-sufficient country life offered as a strenuous antidote to a deadening urban-industrial America. "The city dweller," he explained, "is confronted by fearful odds." "The confining restraint of city life overwhelms his spirit, giving him, as it does, the sense of restraint and lack of vision. Against these coercive forces that hedge about the freedom of the city man, he cries out in vigorous protest."[23]

While "the pressure of city life is intense and the resulting nervous strain takes a heavy toll of strength and energy," the country "is the very opposite of city life." The solution to the life of "weary, overworked city dwellers" was "the charm of country life, the love of experiment." In the country one could live a strenuous life; the country "affords every opportunity for the development of vigorous manhood and womanhood." The country life was "more real" and provided "the best physical and spiritual health." "Around those who live in the country there is the wonder of real things and the beauty of nature in all its perfection. There is the inner strength that comes from producing what the world is needing. . . . There is an intimate touch with the fundamental things of life."[24]

Country life was a synthesized life, integrating head and hand, mind and body, life and work, in an organic, vigorous life where "hard work" made "strong determined men." Referring to this ideal as "the homestead spirit," he noted that there were "two parts to homestead making. One has to do with making a workplace; the other with making a living place."[25] The simple ideal he held out to the well-to-do envisioned a movement "back to the land"; "the hope of the well to do lies in a new vision of life." Turning to country life would end the parasitism of the dominant classes, instilling vitality and fostering the values of independence, service, and democracy. "The movement back to the land," he believed, was "in its essence, a protest against the intricacies and complex relationships of a society in which men have become so interdependent that they feel the yoke of enforced cooperation pressing upon them."

He recognized that the reformers whose hopes for progress praised the interdependence and cooperation made possible by industrial capitalism had failed to take account of inherent power relationships and the fact that interdependence had become a situation of unequal dependence. The entrenched divisions in society revealed mutual interdependence as merely illusory commonality, no longer expressing an authentic common good but fostering destructive self-interest in the name of social cohesion. Instead of the producers' being coerced into a form of service to the nonproducing class, "the chief cause of satisfaction that men and women find in rural life is freedom from servility and independence of service." Service as it existed in rural life was "likely to be independent and democratic." A simple life of strenuous activity "expresses the demand for self-service," and "the problem of simplifying life and reestablishing personal service is a problem of the well-to-do." Back to the land "means back to a complete life."[26]

▬▬ Nearing experimented with a simple life, going back to the land where he could practice the principles of vitalizing labor, as a single-tax community, Arden, Delaware, where he summered from 1906 to 1915. Life at Arden "minimized theory and emphasized practice, both individual and social," he recalled; "there was a reality and completeness about it that was satisfying and uplifting."[27] Choosing a simple way of life in the Progressive period was not seen as regressive but consistent with the spirit of the times. As one back-to-the-land advocate proclaimed in 1910, "We label our most progressive movements with a contradictory word of retrogression." "We have come to realize," he continued, "that 'back to the land' expresses a wish to advance." A simple way of living, another remarked, "does not necessarily . . . consist of doing without, but rather in the proper use of things."[28]

Arden began in 1900 as a village colony south of Philadelphia, founded by the sculptor Frank Stephens and the architect William Price, and financed largely by the millionaire Joseph Fels. Its goal was to make art a vital part of life, and the means to that end was to create an environment in which art could flourish. So the founders turned to what Stephens called "the religion of Henry George."[29] As one historian of Arden has noted, "The founders of Arden had as their aim not only the building of a small working model of the single tax, but likewise the development upon such a foundation . . . of a real living handicraft movement, which should become a vital part, and an influence in the community."[30]

The practical operation of "the Arden enclave" was a land system under which the trustees of the community held title to the land. The system "recognizes the right of all to use the earth." Arden also instituted a "tax system which does not penalize industry, business or thrift, and does not give premiums for land monopoly or speculation"; it granted "full women suffrage"; it was "the first community in the United States to elect officials by Proportional Representation"; it instituted a "banking system based on character, not 'collateral' " and "never issued bonds or granted exclusive privilege or monopoly"; and it claimed to be "a center for the study of the international language of Esperanto."[31] The activities of the community were divided into ten "gilds," including music, lectures, theater, pageants, athletics, language study, and economics, which Nearing headed.[32] Most important to the ideals of the founders was the "Arden Craft Guild," which adhered to the beliefs of "the great English craftsman and prophet, William Morris, that it is 'right and necessary that all men should have work to do and which shall be worth doing, and be of itself pleasant to do, and which should be done under such conditions as would make it neither over wearisome nor over-anxious."[33]

It was the principled activity and organic life of Arden that drew Nearing and others. For an annual fee of $13 he rented a lot, which he cleared, and then "hand built a small but livable summer house" and "laid out a garden."[34] His neighbor Upton Sinclair preferred to live out of a tent and rent Nearing's cabin in the winter. Sinclair described Arden as "a charming place about twenty miles from the big city, with many little cabins and bungalows scattered on the edge of the woods."[35] For Nearing, life in Arden meant taking produce to the Saturday town market, playing roles in the town theater productions, and participating in collective building activities, making for "a real triumph of community enterprise." One Ardenite recalled, "What a stimulation you gave the minds of the younger generation—asking callow adolescents such startling questions as 'what are you doing to justify your existence.' "[36]

He also "attended all town meetings" where lively debates between single-taxers and socialists drowned out a vocal minority of one, the town anarchist. While Nearing admired Henry George's writings as marking "an epoch in the development of economic thought," he believed the practical application of the single tax to be a failure.[37] But when some Arden socialists tried to win Nearing to their side, one of them, Ella Reeve Bloor, remembered that "Scott at that time refused to be labeled."[38] The socialist Sinclair found Nearing to be nothing but "a mild liberal, impatient with my socialist theories."[39] Nearing did not go to Arden for partisan struggles—Arden offered a cooperative social environment conducive to individual regeneration and salvation. "The first and most compelling appeal of country living" in Arden was "bread labor in contact with nature."[40]

During this period of strenuous living, Nearing first tried a purely vegetarian diet, something that would become a lifelong pattern. Vegetarianism in the Progressive Era expressed both a religious orientation and an optimistic confidence in scientific progress. Christian physiology explained the human body as God's temple, making physical purity not only a moral duty but a prerequisite for social purity. Consistent with millennial notions, physical health blended with ethics into a form of strenuous Christianity suitable for resurrecting full vitality in the individual so that he or she would be fit for efficient service. The scientific optimism associated with strenuous vegetarianism emerged from a reaction to social Darwinism and the belief that voluntary human action could effect evolutionary development. These vegetarians found that they could take control of their own evolution by cultivating the physical vitality necessary for the nervous and mental hardships of the modern environment. Vegetarianism became a tool of evolutionary advance.[41] Nearing's religious and scientific sensibilities led him to practice health reform as if it were the duty of self-improvement. "The foundation of success in life," Nearing proclaimed, "is rugged health. . . . Most of the men and women who have done the important things have had strong constitutions and a world of surplus physical energy."[42] Nearing's experiments with a vegetarian diet were a compelling complement to the strenuous country life at Arden as well as a small individual effort toward Progressive change.

Arden was also the kind of place to which the leisure class would go to redress the difficulties of urban-industrial society. The strenuous life of simplicity had a wide appeal among those who sensed the deadened quality of modern existence. While Sinclair would look back to his days in Arden and recall a community founded by people "who were sick of the grime, greed, and strain, and fled away to a legend, the Forest of Arden,"[43] the Arden ideal was less an escape than a compensating remedy. Nearing recalled it as "pleasantly adventurous and recreational," a "vacation area" where he had the "opportunity to combine country living, professional work, bread labor, and rewarding association."[44] Arden was a subcommunity where a vigorous challenge to the dominant values of industrial capitalism was nurtured in the cultural realm of leisure activity. Behind the purposeful activity of Arden, and the simple life in general, was an attempt by Progressives to create standards for the domain of leisure that had emerged amid the economic abundance of industrial growth. Nearing's concern with "the relation between vacations and efficiency"[45] led him to view leisure activity as a way to counteract the disintegrative forces of economic developments by providing "for the higher things of life . . . spiritual valuation."[46] "Leisure is a universal right in a society that boasts an economic surplus. The great things of the world are done in leisure time. Leisure is not idleness, but opportunity to follow personal desire, unrestricted by any exigency or routine requirement. Leisure affords the opportunity for that spontaneous expression which exemplifies personal development."[47] A decade before the Lynds would study the leisure habits of Americans and find the cultural terrain debased by capitalist standards—what they called "the long arm of the job"[48]—Nearing tried to reserve the domain of leisure as a corrective to "the grosser, harsher forms of the livelihood struggle."[49]

The fact that the strenuous life was an ideal not for complete living but more correctly for strenuous leisure has led some historians to conclude that it was disabled by inherent tensions and contradictions. The argument is made that a retreat to the land meant a temporary escape that not only maintained the social order but promoted social change in a restricted and limited way. But to argue that these were naive reformers overlooks the evidence that there was in Progressive America sufficient cultural openness for groups who did not consent to the dominant values and enclaves where the creation of alternative values were nurtured. Arden served as a countermeasure to remedy the stress and distress of the day, and when Nearing recalled that he "summered at Arden and . . . wintered and taught in Philadelphia," the public and private, professional and domestic spheres formed a continuous whole in a dynamic open system where the creation of alternative values remained a real option. Although only "a vacation area . . . merely pleasantly adventurous and recreational,"[50] Arden provided a "taste of a well-rounded life" through the regenerative possibilities in the cultural realm of leisure activity.[51]

━━ In addition to his association with Arden, Nearing also spent six weeks each summer from 1912 to 1917 as a member of the Chautauqua summer-school faculty. The institute and its idyllic lakeside community in upstate New York were a popular and nationally prestigious Protestant middle-class vacation spot offering a summer respite from the tensions of urban life. It offered the leisure class a vacation with a purpose, if not in terms of physical strenuousness, then as a place for mental vigorousness, for uplifting intellectual and moral development. The original Chautauqua began as an institution for religious instruction, and while it retained a moral and religious purpose well into the twentieth century, its program expanded and diversified to include scientific as well as theological subjects.[52] It was a place where William James found that "sobriety and industry, intelligence and goodness, orderliness and ideality, prosperity and cheerfulness, pervade the air." This "sabbatical city," which James likened to "a serious picnic on a gigantic scale," embodied "all the ideals for which our civilization has been striving."[53]

For five years, Nearing and his family joined in this leisure-class recreation of intellectual strenuousness. It was not uncommon for Nearing to teach two classes and give a lecture in a single day. The large audiences he drew attested to his reputation as "an expert on economics and a writer and lecturer of ability" as well as the personal appeal of his "youthful appearance"; "a young man of slight build, not above medium height, with light hair, a complexion somewhat brown, with considerable color, and clear blue-grey eyes and a frank, pleasant expression."[54] Nellie Seeds Nearing, described as "a public lecturer and writer," also spoke on such subjects as "Women and Democracy" to the Chautauqua Equal Suffrage Association.[55] At Chautauqua, Nearing participated in the strenuous life of the mind essential for fortifying civic virtues in the leisure class. He had the opportunity to take his message to the source, to point out the road to social salvation to the well-to-do.

In his lectures to Chautauquans, Nearing took it upon himself to preach the virtues of a strenuous life to the leisure class, those he referred to as "the men higher up." "The world," he told them, "is seeking salvation" and depended on "men of energy, vigor, enthusiasm, and vision."[56] Addressing the subject of "the simple life," Nearing told his audience that "the well-to-do have been led by a will-o-wisp called the 'possession of things.'" For them, "the simple life is fraught with uncounted possibilities"; "the simple life lies in the pursuit of those things which are worth pursuing."[57] "Wealth," he lectured his economically secure audience, "leads to inactivity, . . . defective social intelligence, defective concepts of the things around about, narrow ruts of life, lack of initiative and ambition" and "isolates the rich man from all but the crawling, whining crowd."[58]

Scott Nearing, 1910. Courtesy of Robert Nearing

Nellie and Scott Nearing, en route to England in 1911. Courtesy of Robert Nearing

Nellie and Scott Nearing with sons Robert and John in Toledo, Ohio, May 1916.
Courtesy of Robert Nearing

When Nearing tried to convince his listeners of the revitalizing virtues of reducing the cost of living by going back to the land, his critique of riches did not sit well with some Chautauquans. Confronted with questions following his lecture, the daily paper reported, "It seemed as if many of the audience had come there with the intention of trying to get Dr. Nearing to retract some of the things he had said about extravagance among the middle class." Nearing, it seems, "remained firm that there is a great deal of extravagance among the people who have not had to face the problem of the necessities of life." Responding to his questioners, he asked: "What will be the results if we keep up the present conditions of luxury and emulation?" Pressing for redistributive remedies centered on the distinctions between earned and unearned income, he advised that they "adopt some measures to take away from the luxuriously living class the things which they have in excess of the necessities of life."[59] While at Chautauqua, it seems, Nearing was a messenger sent to the enemy camp, and while the Chautauquans liked the messenger, they appeared at times to resent his message.

His lectures at Chautauqua often presented a critique that could be construed as lamenting the very thing in which he was participating. While he might appreciate the intellectually redeeming qualities of Chautauqua, its comfortable isolation from the hardening struggles of life could easily create a paradox for the socially sensitive. William James, who had gone to Chautauqua in 1896 to lecture on education, found that the purpose of the place was "to redeem life from insignificance." Yet the community was "unbalanced," there was the "absence of human nature *in extremis*," it offered nothing but "flatness and lack of zest." He complained that "this order is too tame, this culture too second-rate, this goodness too uninspiring." Chautauqua represented "an irredeemable flatness . . . coming over the world" where "bourgeoisie and mediocrity, church sociables and teachers' conventions, are taking the place of the old heights and depths and romantic chiaroscuro." He hoped for "some sort of fusion, some chemical combination among these principles, for a life objectively and thoroughly significant to result." He left Chautauqua wishing for "something less blameless and more admiration-worthy."[60]

Invoking the hardiness of strenuous living, Nearing's critique of the leisure class amounted to much the same sentiment. Yet it appears that he had great hope that the lives of the well-to-do could one day be lived with purpose and social responsibility. He was optimistic that "the men higher up" would provide civic leadership and bring about what he told a Chautauqua audience was needed: "a radical readjustment of some of the most fundamental economic and social relations."[61]

One woman who went to Chautauqua in 1917 to attend Nearing's classes later turned him into the protagonist of a number of her novels, offering a remarkably straightforward portrayal of his person and beliefs. Helen R. Martin was so enthusiastic about Nearing's talks that when she returned to her home in Harrisburg, Pennsylvania, she persuaded her husband to go for a week to listen to him. Martin was a moderately successful writer of novels that dealt primarily with the improvement of young women and is remembered too for her less than flattering caricatures of the Pennsylvania Dutch.[62] Although she was a feminist, a campaigner for suffrage, and a socialist, the publication of her *Fanatic or Christian?* (1918), which portrayed the corruption of both business and the church, was received with dismay. The copy of that book she gave to Nearing was inscribed to him as "the hero."[63]

In *Fanatic or Christian?* Nearing's somewhat larger-than-life character is assumed by one David Phelps who is a "well-to-do lawyer . . . about thirty-five years old." "His big, rather raw boned figure, usually relaxed and lounging, suggested a somewhat formidable amount of force and reserve. His face, clear-cut and intellectual, expressed virility without sensuality. In repose his countenance was serious and aloof; but when he smiled it softened and broke into twinkling kindness and humor."[64] Phelps' key concern is religion and social change. At one point he is queried about the perception that he does not believe in Christianity, to which he replies, "But I do, that's the trouble. I really *believe* in the love and brotherhood that Christ taught. The Church doesn't. . . . Really Christianity is great stuff if we'd only try it."[65] His theories, he claims, "were taught by Jesus two thousand years ago, being only the Gospel of brotherly love." Later in the novel, Phelps concludes that "a just appreciation of the whole situation" in American society must recognize that "so long as the present economic order exists none of us can wholly escape it. It is social reconstruction, not individual martyrdom, we want."[66] Martin further injects Nearing into her character by having him declare that "the man who is ready, for the sake of the progress of the race, to stand up against the jibes and jeers of those who wish everything to remain just as it is (because things as they are are comfortable for them) must have the hide of a rhinoceros—or the vision of a Jesus—or the brass of a Bernard Shaw! As I think I've got a tiny bit of all three, I'm in for the fight."[67]

While Nearing reappears in other novels in different guises, the themes remain the same; he represents most forcefully the ideals of Christianity, the reason and enlightenment of social science, a critique of the moral menace of riches, and hardiness in the struggle for the right. In *Maggie of Virginsburg* (1918), Nearing is portrayed as the teacher Henry Butz, and in *The Church on the Avenue* (1923) as an Episcopalian minister, the Reverend Clement Calloway. Denouncing "great riches," Calloway claims that "far from being a means by which we may best serve humanity, [they] are much more apt to destroy us—incapacitate us for real service, which is first, last and always personal and spiritual service." A sermon Calloway delivers echoes the views Martin could easily have heard from Nearing as she sat in the crowded amphitheater at Chautauqua:

"The aims of those who would socialize our government are humane, as the aims of capitalism are not; they are therefore nearer the Christian ideal. Human fraternity, not selfish antagonism and rivalry, is the expression of the true Christian spirit. A socialized government would compel bad men to act like Christians, as capitalism now compels Christians to act like selfish robbers! In a society organized on the basis of brotherhood, Christian ideals would for the first time have a chance of being realized . . . serving the common good instead of exploiting it."[68]

If we are to take Martin's characters as an accurate portrayal of Nearing's beliefs, then at least for her, and presumably for others, his message was plain. Whether its challenge to the dominant values was popular among the leisure class was another matter. For the Chautauqua gentleman who found Nearing's views discomforting while "intensely interesting, even if you don't believe all he says," it may not have been at all settled whether he had been listening to a fanatic or a Christian.

# Social Adjustment

## Chapter 5

WITHIN the organic unity of all things, personally and socially, the elements of economics did not amount to a coherent whole unless there were deeds to match analysis. In Nearing's case, all economic discussions were paralleled by suggested programs for reform so that economic thought formed a continuum with social action, or as Nearing put it, "Action without thought is as bootless as thought without action."[1] There had to be some practical application of scientific analysis to society, measures he grouped under the label *social adjustment*. Under adjustment schemes, theory could be translated into practice, allowing for a new ethical economics of redistribution to be tested in the experience of social reality. The meaning assigned to adjustment was often somewhat vague. While at times defined as "the process of securing welfare," it could also designate "the science of molding institutions." What the term social adjustment always included in its meaning was a focus on the social group and a belief in evolutionary development. There was a "common goal" of "welfare and universal opportunity" to strive toward, "a common philosophy of life in which all may share,—the philosophy which places the interest of the group above the petty self-interests of the individual."[2]

Nearing contended that "the object of Social Adjustment is the provision of universal opportunity,"[3] but that this was inhibited by a system built upon unearned income where opportunity for the minority was achieved through exploitation of the majority. The goal of universal opportunity also suffered for lack of the proper kind of environment through which it was available. This environmentalism found reinforcement in antideterministic evolutionary assumptions of continual change, gradual but inevitable, so that to "adjust" meant in large part to redirect or encourage the direction of evolution. Because evolution was unending, Nearing's notion of adjustment was always future-oriented, so that the individual in the present found himself subordinated to the future society. Social adjustment, then, was not intended to prescribe one remedy for the present and for all time. It was a dynamic concept with broad goals and wide-ranging forms of application.

Finally, social adjustment found expression through the state. While Nearing valued individuality and decentralized government, he also recognized that individual expression was already dangerously inhibited by concentrations of capital. The national government was the only force powerful enough to combat this threat. So he was faced with "one of the most difficult of modern questions—the question of the relationship of the government to the individual; and the extent to which the individual should rely upon the government for support." The state, he claimed, "exists as a means of enhancing the general welfare of the community," and when possible, this responsibility "should be left to local authority." However, when confronted by the power of industrial capitalism, "no one should hesitate about turning to larger governmental authority in cases where the smaller has failed of its purpose."

Governmental activity was not a constraint on individual freedom "since many of the services upon which life now depends are performed by the government in an entirely non-despotic fashion." Americans had become convinced "that there are things innumerable which the government can do far more effectively than the individual."[4] This belief was a central theme of progressivism, and Nearing's conception of adjustment relied heavily on the beneficence of the positive, active, powerful state. Only in this context could he find that "the science of social adjustment has occupied the most prominent place in American thought." In Progressive America he found that "the country has been swept . . . by a whirlwind of legislation directed toward the adjustment of social institutions to human needs."[5] The possibilities for adjustment were virtually limitless.

━━ Nearing's enthusiasm for adjustment reached its furthest extreme with his interest in controlling the outcome of heredity through the practice of eugenics. His interest in heredity emerged between 1911 and 1913, amid growing popularity among educated, white, Protestant, middle and upper-middle classes for discussions of hereditary forces and their national implications. The eugenics movement reached into all areas of American social, political, and academic life, influencing social scientists like Patten, who maintained a long-standing interest in the issue. He wrote on the topic in *Heredity and Social Progress* in 1903 and would write in 1912 that "the science of eugenics tells us how to proceed. . . . In this field a social appeal can be made fully as strong and more effective than in any other field."[6] The widespread optimism for social advance through eugenics was revealed in the 1910 essay on civilization that appeared in the new eleventh edition of the *Encyclopedia Britannica,* foretelling "the organic betterment of the race through the wise application of the laws of heredity." While in London in 1911, Nearing made a point to visit not only Toynbee Hall, the settlement house, but also Francis Galton's eugenics laboratory at the University of London.[7] Nearing's concept of eugenics was, claimed Tugwell, "the logical outcome of the economics of reform, the sociology of race improvement and of governmental institutions devoted to social welfare."[8]

In Nearing's most systematic discussion of eugenics, *The Super Race: An American Problem* (1912), the cardinal point was that "the object of Eugenics is the conscious improvement of the human race by the application of the laws of heredity to human mating." Drawing on the pioneering work of Galton, which stressed inheritance as the key to evolution, and the studies of Charles Davenport, the leading American eugenicist, Nearing denied a basic antagonism between heredity and reform, claiming that it was consistent with social change. The promise of eugenics was that it would supersede the evolutionary determinism of natural selection by directing biological evolution toward a chosen goal. Maneuvering among the debates between environmentalists and hereditarians, Nearing found that "ability and defect may be the result of heredity through the germ cell," or it could be attributed to the "environment through training, or they may be caused by both." The key factor was that "in any case, they are not the product of chance."[9] While Nearing believed that "the environment shapes the man," the more important point was that "equally, the man shapes the environment." Yet manipulation of the environment as a means of overcoming the determinism of eugenics was not all that was possible; there was room for conscious hereditary choice.

He contrasted "natural selection," which "is unconscious, occurring in the course of struggle for existence," with "conscious . . . artificial selection."[10] Human choice allowed for the rational control by man over the natural forces of evolution; to the "progressive thinker," these were "merely forces which must be utilized or counteracted in the work of human achievement." Choice employed successfully in the name of hereditary control could forever destroy the notion of the determinacy of natural laws. An abundant society with universalized leisure provided "an opportunity for free choice." The core belief of Nearing's eugenics was that "the twentieth century citizen is free because he makes efficient choices" and that "the continuance of his freedom depends upon the continued wisdom of his choices." Eugenic choice, with its freedom from hereditary determinism, was "America's distinctive opportunity."[11]

We know that Nearing insisted that choice was not only one's right but also included duties beyond the self. In his writings on eugenics, this conviction emerged again in the notion of the social responsibility of the individual to act in the best interest of the larger community, or as it was conceived at the time, the race.[12] When Nearing discussed voluntary choice in a program of "race building through wise mating" he focused on a positive approach to eugenics. Yet while couched in the innocuous language of the importance of "training for eugenic choice," so that voluntary eugenics would succeed, his approach to eugenics again reveals his class bias. Positive eugenics was a means through which the dominant classes could lead the way to a "super race." Nearing offered voluntary "assortive mating as a moral duty for the highly endowed."

When his positive approach to eugenics overlapped with a negative one, his Progressive vision lost sight of humanitarian goals. While he claimed that compulsory eugenics—to "eliminate defect by preventing procreation"—was "but a part, and by far the least important part of the eugenics programme," he nevertheless favored the "denial of parenthood to those who have transmissible defects," even if "such a process works individual hardship in the present." In the case of negative eugenics, the government could be relied upon for "a series of legislative enactments [to] prevent the mating of the hereditarily defective." With scientific single-mindedness and unbalanced moral consideration, he noted that only through segregation or sterilization of those with hereditary defects "could the scum of society be removed, and the source of social contamination be effectively regulated."[13]

The emphasized connection between social standing and defectiveness found popular expression in fears of a Malthusian dysgenic nightmare—that the superior classes had limited their population and civilization was being overrun by hereditary degenerates who propagated freely. Nearing noted the "birth-rates of different parental groups" and the fact that "in violation of [evolutionary] law, the population of the United States is increasing most rapidly from that group which is least fitted to transmit social worth to the coming generation."[14] What Nearing called "reversed selection" Theodore Roosevelt, a popularizer of eugenic theories and their racial and imperialistic importance, decried as "race suicide."

Nearing, significantly, took issue with Roosevelt's notion of race suicide and his call to the dominant stock to reproduce more abundantly. Nearing's position, rather than indicative of an attack on racist eugenics or the imperialistic tendencies of Roosevelt's claims, reveals the environmentalist limits of his eugenic ideas. The goal of eugenics, he claimed, was the quality of human beings, not their quantity. Those whom Roosevelt denounced as "race murderers" were "in reality race saviors, for, acting in accord with the dominant evolutionary tendency of modern civilization, they are disregarding quantity and seeking to insure quality."[15] "*Conscious* limitation of the birth rate" was a democratic triumph through which all were "free and equal" to limit the number of their children and thus raise their standard of living, creating improved circumstances for child rearing.[16]

Nearing's interest in the topic of eugenics was enthusiastic if brief. His last writings on the subject appeared in 1916.[17] One could speculate that

Nearing retreated from the harsher realities of the regimented reform, inequality, racism, and morality devoid of humanity implied by eugenics. He may have come to agree with the view taken by a reviewer of *The Super Race* that it erred in its "trustful optimism" and that cold rationality and antideterminism had fostered unintended dehumanization to such an extent that "only a sophisticated academician who has wandered far from life in her first intentions could so confuse his values."[18] While there is no evidence conclusively indicating the reason for his loss of interest in eugenics, there are more persuasive suggestions in the fact that the program for hereditary improvement was always intended as a minor, if revealing, aspect of his vision of progress.

Emphasizing that "the Super Race is the produce [*sic*] of heredity, of the social environment, and of individual development," he was careful to add the disclaimer that "eugenics alone will not suffice."[19] The science of eugenics always had to be coupled with the shaping of the environment and the molding of social institutions. The key to understanding his eugenics is that environmentalism always assumed predominance over heredity; "the average man," he stressed, "is largely made by his environment,"[20] and "a congenial environment is necessary for the perfection of any hereditary talent."[21] Genetic improvement through selective mating was viewed as a Progressive goal, "yet, reared in an unfavorable environment," eugenic advances "cannot produce their highest results."[22] In the end, eugenics was "not the most effective" method of social reform; he favored "education rather than eugenics."[23]

▄▄▄ If concern with selective choice in the bearing of children was untimely, not so with the raising of future generations. Through his writings and his tenure on the Pennsylvania Child Labor Committee, Nearing became widely known as a champion of the highest ideals in the development of youth. Child labor was both an economic and a social issue, but more important, it was a moral issue wherein ideals were being crushed by the dead weight of material advance while the future was being inherited by the weak and devitalized, their virtues stunted. "The child who is working," Nearing maintained, is "not developing intellectually, may be degraded morally, and is apt to be stunted physically."[24] Child labor destroyed body and soul.

There was more at stake in the issue of child labor than morality or vitality, as Nearing would later learn. Crusading to remove children from the labor market also meant assaulting a source of cheap unskilled labor in high demand in factories owned by some of the most prominent members of the community. In self-defense and belittling his critics, Nearing observed that "into the child labor problem, with its peculiar setting, and its broad interests, enters the 'Child Labor Reformer,' 'the Fanatic,' the 'Deluded Social Agitator,' emphasizing the human side of industry."[25]

Child labor deprived the child most immediately of "play, the chief guardian of youth"—a significant loss because it was during play that free will and social morality were nurtured. "The basis of character," Nearing contended, "is the will, and at no time does this function of the mind have so free a scope as during recreation."[26] Free will meant, as it did in Nearing's concept of freedom, not simply unbounded autonomy but "self restraint," "cooperation and group action."[27] "Out of play develops a social morality, having at its basis the full recognition of the relation of the individual to the co-operating group in which he belongs."[28] "Morality and play" were inextricably linked in the development of a "group morality" essential for social responsibility. So it was that Nearing could approvingly quote G. Stanley Hall's *Adolescence* that "play at its best is only a school of ethics" and deplore the fact that "the working child . . . lacks the group instinct."[29] Child labor "deaden[ed] the very instincts that lead to effective group action" and promoted the "premature decay of moral fibre."[30] "The child who gets no chance to play loses the opportunity for the moral development play affords,"[31] he concluded: "Work denies to the body of the growing child its complete development, and curtails the growth of his moral faculties."[32]

For Nearing, it seemed that the child was the victim of a mortal battle between the industrial workplace and the values of humanity. The child "of twelve or fourteen who stands at a machine . . . for eleven hours a day is not growing through expression, but is being narrowed by an unvarying, monotonous impression."[33] Instead of "enthusiasm, play and life," the child laborer experienced "grind, monotony and degeneration." During youth, Nearing argued, there were "two forces constantly at work, the one calling the child to higher ideal of life and growth, and the other tending to brutalize him for the sake of a few dollars which his unformed hands will earn." "All the future," he continued, "is conditioned on that struggle; if the forces of the ideal conquer, the child will develop through normal channels into a fully rounded man; if the forces of the dollar win, the child's life is set and hardened into a money-making machine."[34] The "standardization" of unskilled factory work made it hopelessly "monotonous and deadening," and eliminated the possibility of the development of vigorous, virtuous citizens.[35] Ideals would be overwhelmed by materialism.

Because the ideals most damaged were those nurtured in the republican home, the child-labor problem was a national emergency. Child labor, Nearing warned, "helps to destroy family life." The children who worked did "not participate in the duties and pleasures of home life." Since the home was the place where republican virtue was cultivated, "if national integrity is to be preserved," the home must "be maintained at a high standard. . . . The standard of the community can be maintained only by maintaining a high standard of home life."[36] Concern with the development of virtuous republican citizens led Nearing to affirm that "a condition precedent to high type of citizenship is protected in childhood."[37]

The solution of the child-labor problem lay in "eliminating the causes which send children to work." He found that there were "two primary forces which are sending children to work,—family necessity and an uncongenial school system."[38] He outlined the problem as follows:

> 1. The wages of the average workman are so low as to preclude the possibility of his bringing up his family without some outside aid. This is often secured by sending the children to work.
> 2. The school system with its ancient curriculum, rigorous discipline, and low paid, inexperienced teachers, is heartily detested by the average boy, and probably by the average girl, who take the first opportunity to escape from its monotony and confinement to the freedom of work.[39]

The state had a role in solving these problems, but not through legislation, which served as "a primarily negative, coercive instrument." School reform was best addressed through "increased public interest and increased appropriations." The problem of an inadequate standard of living was another matter. Here Nearing reasoned that child-labor legislation and compulsory-school laws combined to "deprive the family of anticipated income." Why, then, shouldn't the government "in some justice, make some restitution in the numerous cases where family income is insufficient to meet family needs." A nation with an increasing "social surplus" was better "prepared to keep its children away from monotonous toil." The state's role in solving the problem of child labor was clear: "If it is socially advantageous that every child should be thoroughly educated, it would seem socially just that the government make some return to the needy family of such a child while education is being supplied."[40] Nearing's solution to the child-labor problem went far beyond attempts to regulate industrial practices and protect the socially disadvantaged. Social adjustment implied more than the term suggested; modifications were not enough. Nearing was interested in a fundamental transformation of economic and social relations.

▬▬ Dorothy Ross has suggested that Progressive social scientists who wanted to conceal the political implications of their work employed scientific euphemisms such as *adjustment*.[41] Whether this explains Nearing's choice of terminology is worth considering. He was critical of standard programs of Progressive reform and made it clear that the solution to many of the "problems of value and distribution" were to be found in a radical economic transformation.[42] His disenchantment with the leading approaches to social reform led him to conclude that "while often inspired by the loftiest motives, the reformer fails sadly in method."[43] He had little faith in the efficacy of "reform agencies" such as "unions, reform movements, and reforming societies" because they were "disconnected and in one sense spasmodic. They aim at securing fragmentary advances in various directions without laying any foundation for them in social consciousness or social intelligence. . . . Their results have been measurably but not fundamentally beneficial. . . . As methods for securing adjustment, they are negligible factors."[44] Attempts at reform by the wealthy were particularly hollow, and even at its best, philanthropy by "the well-to-do group in the community" merely indicated "an incomplete feeling of social responsibility." It was important not to overlook the fact that "the funds which are provided for philanthropic purposes often represent the incomes from life- or health-destroying industry."[45]

When Nearing searched for alternative approaches to addressing social problems, he found that "the recent growth of Socialism is one of the most important phenomenon of modern times."[46] Here was a larger program of social and economic change that could be achieved democratically. The socialist "demands a reorganization which he proposes to effect through the use of the ballot."[47] Socialism, he discovered, seemed consistent with his own economic analysis as "an organized protest against the present system of distributing income, coupled with an organized effort to establish a new system, whereby income may be more rationally distributed."[48] Socialism "is now a factor to be considered in any statement of political tendencies."[49]

When Nearing considered the possibilities of socialist reform, he began by pointing out that "there are many different forms of socialism."[50] The form he could not uncritically accept was what he called "Marxian or State Socialism." Nearing meant by this a restricted sense of the term, a specific definition that associated socialism with all-pervasive theories of economic determinism and control of the economy through collectivist state action. In terms of theory, he was careful to note that "the question of socialism" was "first of all a question of fact." In other words, no theory of socialism could account for newly evolved historical circumstances; those that claimed to were simply false "panaceas." In the same way that he disapproved of natural-law theory of laissez-faire economics, he noted that the rule for the economist approaching the theory of socialism was that "the spirit of science requires the individual to confront all issues in a frank, open-minded way, with an entire willingness to accept the logical conclusions derived from things as they are."[51] He was adamant that "there is no great theory which can be applied to human society en masse."[52]

One feature of socialism that he was not willing to accept was rigid socialization of capital. More acceptable was the view that "those things that can be privately managed, with a maximum advantage to the community, must be left under private control," while "those things, on the other hand, that under private control, might become a menace to community welfare must be publicly managed in the interests of all."[53] Pointing out the limitations of socialism defined with uncompromising rigidity, socialism in a broader sense—recognizing economic redistribution, cooperative social relations, growing economic independence, and the need for the limited exercise of state control in economic activity—could prove a promising alternative. Nearing argued that while it was "unlikely that the doctrines of State Socialism will be carried out in their entirety," it was "equally likely that they will be applied in a modified form to the solution of many pressing problems."[54]

He indicated the promising aspects of socialism in his textbook, written in 1908 under the encouraging guidance of Patten. There he pointed out that it substituted "a social control of the annual income of society, in ways that it deemed best to aid the social end" in place of classical economic theories of distribution. He further noted contemporary circumstances indicating that "municipal ownership and operation is not a dream of the theorizing socialist, but a business proposition based on the concept of the greatest efficiency to the consumer at the smallest possible cost." The socialist, he contended, "believes that in many ways society has outgrown the institution of private property. . . . In attacking the institution of private property, it should be borne in mind that the socialist opposes private ownership of land, natural resources and the tools of production only. . . . He believes that the tools of production are . . . means of life [and] should be held in common."

Furthermore, in the political atmosphere of the day, socialism stood in "marked contrast" to its rival political alternatives. Theodore Roosevelt's "square deal," he claimed, "accepts the present organization of society but asks for fair play." A position of "government regulation," soon to be the cornerstone of Woodrow Wilson's New Freedom, stood "for a destruction of all monopolies in order that under the law of competition just prices may obtain." The "Single Taxer would restore social justice by abolishing all private monopoly in land and natural resources," while the "programme of social work . . . seeks to improve the environment that each individual may ultimately have equal opportunity." Only the socialist came "forward in opposition to the whole present order of industry" and declared "that there is no cure for our modern ills unless we uproot the capitalist system of production and put in its place state cooperation, thus entirely destroying the competitive system which each of the other programmes accepts."[55] This assessment may explain why he voted for Eugene V. Debs in 1912.[56]

Yet for this very reason, socialist political positions were not widely accepted. Even though the Socialist party platform had, Nearing said, called for "many specific forms of adjustment, its policies have not been such as to put these demands into practical form." Socialism could not be accomplished "with public opinion in its present condition." Until the necessary "intellectual revolution" was accomplished, Nearing suggested, the socialist should consider two courses of action "by which he may ultimately reach his goal of the complete socialization of industry." He advised that socialism would benefit from some of the key aspects of what he called "the programme of social work." Social work incorporated a social morality while advancing the expression of individuality. He admired its ultimate aim—"a social democracy in which there shall be an equality of opportunity for everyone to reach the highest development of which he is capable"—and he valued "the religious nature of the appeal that it makes" to the organic ideal of "universal brotherhood." While he recognized that "the desire to supplement the work of religion may seem presumptuous and the programme too large for successful execution," he was forceful in his conviction that at the core of any "broad constructive programme" there had to be a deeply moral justification.

Socialism would also benefit by abandoning "some of its older traditions of substituting at every point state action for that of the individual." In the socialism he saw taking shape in America, he detected a process of "conciliation going on." The "possibility of the social 'individualist' and the individual socialist" was "the result of the growth in social consciousness" as well as the realization by socialists that "in the past they often misread human psychology by allowing no room for the expression of individuality." He was hopeful "that public opinion will ultimately come to be much more unified on many of the economic questions involved in socialism." The "socialist of to-day," he observed,

> seems to be more individualistic than his predecessor, while . . . the man who still styles himself an individualist, has become more and more a socialist. The force of this statement can be felt by comparing on the one hand the works of such socialists as Marx and Engels with those of H. G. Wells of England and John Spargo of America, and on the other hand, the works of such individualists as Herbert Spencer with Professor Clark, or men of the type of President Roosevelt.[57]

Finally, there was even "a measure of unison" regarding the belief "that improvements are made through evolution rather than through revolution. . . . The pages of biologic and social history are written in terms of slow change."[58]

Socialism had a specific meaning. It was a theory that had to evolve if it was to remain pertinent in the face of changing social and economic circumstances. Without being dogmatic, it would be based on the principle of limited government activity to protect opportunity and ensure the expression of individuality. It would eliminate exploitation by favoring productive labor and earned income while eliminating unearned income; workers were entitled to the fruits of their labor. And it would embrace a notion of freedom based on social responsibility, rooted in the religious notions of human brotherhood and organic solidarity. It was a socialism that aimed at liberating man from the bonds of economic necessity so that the ideal and not the material would be the main concern of life. This was a socialism not only suitable to American conditions but the kind of adjustment imperative to America's economic, social, and political advancement. It would be achieved gradually and peacefully, and democratically, dependent upon a revolution in the minds of men.

Socialism, then, was the answer to the problem of community, and it offered in part a solution to the difficulty of social organization. More important, it was the basis of a community ideal that asserted the creation of a viable moral unity to match the economic interdependence of the industrial process. His notion of community envisioned new potential in associations bringing acceptable integration of individuals into working wholes, offering a liberation from individualism in a union of self and society, head and hand, ideal and material. His community ideal exceeded the physical collectivism of socialism and focused on the corresponding consciousness of community as a spiritual whole. If the transcendent community was to materialize to match the organic solidarity of society, the individual would need to realize a greater sense of common purpose and shared values.

The realization of this new consciousness relied on shaping public opinion; the problem of moral unity was a problem of knowledge and communication. The channels of communication used to shape public opinion were vast and expanding, offering seemingly unlimited prospects for persuading individuals of the necessities of community and the morality of fellowship and duty. There was a unifying power of communication to distribute to the public infinite information and argument as the basis for an enlightened public opinion. Socialism offered an ideal that brought life into an intelligible whole, revealing a moral unity and the harmony of society, regenerating civic life.[59]

For Nearing, the way toward finding a concrete expression of the transcendent community was the university. The university was a moral model of the ideal community. Education was the key to cultivating the new consciousness; an educational revolution would change the social conscience. In emphasizing "the importance of trained thought," Nearing stressed that "schools are among the most vital of all social institutions, and teaching is one of the most important of social activities."[60] The teacher maintained a critical intellect in the belief that free inquiry would result in the unity of all knowledge, and he or she also preserved the institutions of higher learning as citadels of moral values and democratic freedoms. As Nearing put it, "The teacher is a sentry—an outpost in the realm of ideas," and education was "the salvation of the community."[61] The institutions of higher learning were the springboard for larger social transformations. In the universities, knowledge could be organized synthetically, connecting disparate parts into an integrated whole so that ideas would give unity and direction to life. But more than this, the university meant applied knowledge; it was a link to the larger community. "Teachers," said Nearing, "are not isolated occupants of academic chairs."

> No matter what the class room opportunities may be, the sphere of the teacher does not end there but passes into the realm of group living. . . . The teacher must teach the truth in the classroom. The teacher must also teach the truth in public. The teacher thus becomes the leader of thought; the community authority in matters of great community concern.[62]

The disinterested pursuit of truth did not mean the pursuit of knowledge for its own sake—that scientific study was free from values, that the scientist was cloistered and isolated. The study of social science assumed not only application but ethical convergence. Nearing explained that "every teacher of social science requires some system of values with which he can measure the importance of events and of courses of action."[63] In promoting the moral convergence and practical application of thought, the university as an institution had become more effective than the church for advancing the transcendent community; the teacher became "a high priest—a missionary of the finest things in personal and social life."[64]

Socialism became a metaphor for the potential of cooperative spirit, providing functional concepts of community. It was an ideal through which to cultivate a social identity that would give concrete form to the transcendent community. Finally, pursuit of this ideal left the teacher facing "a terrible responsibility and a mortal conflict" as the transcendent community confronted society and the teacher encountered pressures for intellectual conformity. "The issue," for Nearing, "is fundamental": "Either the teacher is a hireling of the established order, who is receiving a fee to act as its apologist or champion, or else the teacher is a servant of the community and as such is bound to take whatever stand the exigencies of his position demand."[65]

▬ From 1915 to 1917, it is possible to detect a subtle but important shift in Nearing's thinking. His critique became more strident as he grew impatient with the reform potential of privileged groups. In a revealing debate with Clarence Darrow early in January 1917, Nearing affirmed that democracy was the key to solving the social ills of America. He took the position that "popular control of public affairs . . . of all the affairs on which all of the people depend, would mean the elimination of unearned income and the substitution of an economic interdependence for the old economic independence." He no longer had faith in his own class, "the exploiting class, the owning class, the unearned income class."[66] "Their economic advantage is the direct outcome of the repressive coercive activities of vested interests."[67] He looked instead to raising the popular standard through the expansion of democracy.

"Economic democracy" would "enlarge opportunity; give broader freedom, pick out more geniuses, permit more people of talent to display their abilities and utilize them in the interests of the rest of mankind." With an enlargement of democracy, the common man would act in the way Nearing had previously hoped the dominant classes would behave. "Either you must run your public affairs by a class, picking the leaders of each successive generation from that special class, or you must run your public affairs by the community, for the community, picking the leaders of each generation from the community." Turning away from his hope in the virtuous leadership by the socially privileged, he rested his hope on expanded opportunity allowing the common man to develop his talents and intelligence for the social good. This was the hope of American progress.[68]

But Darrow argued that Nearing had miscalculated the masses' enthusiasm for moral enlightenment and social justice. They were not, he said, independent of the values and attitudes of the dominant groups in society. Democracy was not going to be a force for social progress. He warned Nearing to be wary of "the collective wisdom of the common herd" for whom democracy meant merely "promiscuous and indiscriminate voting." Darrow asked

Nearing to consider who "the people" were and how they went about formulating their opinions. Only if they exhibited a tendency toward enlightened thought and were immune to the invidious emulation of the dominant values could democracy cure the ills of the world. This, Darrow suggested, was not the case. The masses were "not interested in science, philosophy, logic, government." Their lives were filled with "baseball games, the movies, saloons, the churches, and they read the newspapers." They were mostly eager to consent to the political economy of industrial capitalism and to conform to the dominant values in society. By placing his faith in democracy, Nearing's hopes for a social transformation counted on "the common people who live an automatic life, who hold conventional opinions, who fear change; who are moved by the common things and nothing else." This, said Darrow, was a false hope.[69]

A similar critique of Nearing's conception of democratic socialist adjustment emerged when his *Poverty and Riches: A Study of the Industrial Regime* (1916) was reviewed in the *Intercollegiate Socialist* by Randolph Bourne. Bourne's primary criticism was that Nearing's analysis did not adequately account for the superior power of capital. The struggle between the rich and the poor, he posited, was hopeless unless some definite course of action was offered. He further chided Nearing for his belief that the public, if presented the facts, would see right and do good. "To set poverty and riches helplessly confronting each other, with a vague ideal of industrial democracy and for the neutral 'public' is not encouraging," argued Bourne. What Nearing neglected was the power that capital had to influence the values of the same public he was contending for.

Bourne commended Nearing for "performing invaluable service in the way of arousing a public to criticize industrial institutions that they usually take for granted." He was, said Bourne, a "promising case, but he is still in the intellectual bogs." Nearing's eclecticism left "no definite impression on the mind of any point of view, except a vague and obvious need of 'doing something.'" His was a "radicalism that does not eventuate in sound socialist economics." "What we must do," argued Bourne, "is to view the class struggle as fundamentally a conflict to socialize the economic surplus, which now, because of superior power, is directed to the reward of capital, instead of to the community as a whole."[70]

━━ By mid-decade, the contours of Nearing's intellectual development had clearly taken shape. Bourne and Darrow did not find what they were looking for in Nearing largely because Nearing had forged a set of ideas that adhered to worthy principles more than social reality. Faced with enormous social decay and economic dislocation, Nearing, like other Progressives, imagined tremendous potential in human nature to do good and fervently believed in the power of intelligence to guide action. This boundless idealism frustrated his critics and led Nearing into hopeless, even dangerous illusions, whether the belief that the wealthy would behave contrary to their self-interests, that democracy would inevitably lead to social justice and moral enlightenment, or that the state could be trusted to carry out benevolent hereditary control.

A key feature in the development of Nearing's thought was its fundamental convergence of social science and religion, what John Dewey identified as the "via media between natural science and the interests of morals and religion."[71] Amid the heady optimism of progressivism, Nearing expressed no doubts about the fragile coherence of this intellectual position. Yet its weaknesses were readily apparent and would leave him intellectually and professionally vulnerable. The secularity of his version of social religion eroded the moral authority he had hoped to salvage. At the same time, it tainted his economic analysis as unscientifically sentimental. The vacuous intellectual coherence that Nearing found in the ideas of Ruskin, Morris, Marx, Veblen, Patten, and others was precisely what irritated those, like Bourne, who hoped for a genuine alternative system of thought.

# Intellectual Repression

## Part Two

# Academic Asphyxiation

## Chapter 6

IT APPEARS that even as Darrow and Bourne addressed the weaknesses of Nearing's thinking, Nearing himself was becoming reconciled to the fact that his social vision was no nearer to becoming a reality than when he first formulated his youthfully optimistic views. The unbounded enthusiasm for American progress had by 1913 given way to "a troubled, questioning, partially disillusioned, unrestful, discontented age" with "unbelief, distress, perplexity."[1] Disenchantment set in as he saw his belief in an organically unified society crushed by destructive economic divisions.

His hopes for brotherly love were shaken by the discouraging specter of conflict, hate, and fragmentation. He wrote in 1915 that

> perhaps the United States has not yet reached the point where an open breach may be expected between those who receive service income and those who receive property income. Certainly the crisis in the conflict has not yet come. Nevertheless, one who has watched the developments of the past few years—who has followed the labor movement in its larger phases [Lawrence and Paterson], who has given an ear to the undercurrents of socialist thought and syndicalist agitation, cannot help feeling that the United States is moving towards the crisis at breathless speed.[2]

The "spirit of protest," he observed with dismay, "grows in intensity"; he could foresee nothing but "impending conflict."[3] He sensed a new urgency for dramatic social adjustment; without it, he feared, "sooner or later, conflict will arrive."[4]

Something more than pious platitudes was required, and he counseled "the necessity for transferring power from the few who have it to the many who need it."[5] Alarmed and disillusioned, he concluded that "there can be no considerable readjustment of income values until the preeminent position of property is overbalanced by some social action."[6] Faced with such ominous threats to his view of the American ideal of progressive advance, his mission was revitalized. But to some, he was preaching dangerous ideas.

Nearing, it seemed, was at the epicenter of alarming opinions that were sending shock waves through the Wharton School and into the respectable society of Philadelphia. His student, Rexford Tugwell, recalled that in 1911 "the exegesis of fundamentals [orthodox economic theory] was still emphasized more than the criticism or departure from them. This was changing; the criticism was getting sharper year by year." Tugwell had "the widespread impression that most of my teachers were growing desperate in their opposition to the degenerative forces they inwardly believed to be so powerful that they might prevail in spite of all efforts to expose or to reform them. Something had gone very wrong, but they were not able to say where or when it had occurred or what was likely to come of it."

Boldly, fearlessly, even recklessly, Nearing's economics vigorously assailed the moral outcome of the unearned income around him. This, however, said Tugwell,

> was causing the widespread disapproval of reactionary Philadelphians, for if one establishment attitude was more marked than any other, it was the desire to escape from unpleasant reality. All the less defensible results of free enterprize had to be concealed or ignored. Probers beneath the gloss so carefully protected by the press and pulpit were naturally regarded with abhorrence. . . . A certain number of Wharton alumni wanted to be rid of [Nearing]. . . . His teaching was regarded as an affront to the tradition so well represented by the University's trustees and administrators.

Nearing probed into dangerous territory and found himself in confrontation with the dominant class of Philadelphia and its institutions. Nearing, Tugwell knew, "was in trouble and thus [I] was awakened to the dilemma of the American liberal patriot."[7] Nearing found that he "was on the way to [becoming] 'an enemy of society.'" "If I succeeded in practicing my rules of social conduct, and persuading the oncoming generation to do likewise," he said, "I would disturb the establishment or even help disrupt it."[8] For Nearing, the ideal of freedom meant not only that he had a right to dissent but that it was his social duty to do so. He was testing his ideals in experience. Only then would he know their worth.

━━━ When Nearing joined the Wharton School faculty in 1906, the school faced a financial crisis brought about by its meager bequests upon Joseph Wharton's death.[9] The university was forced to appeal to the state for funds as never before. Ties between the governing board of the university and the state had been brought closer in 1903 when Judge Pennypacker, a longtime trustee, had been elected governor.[10]

These links of financial dependence also came in the wake of long and bitter struggles between Philadelphia's political and financial establishment and professors at the Wharton School pressing for municipal reforms. "Gas wars" flared from the late 1890s through the early years of the next decade over municipal management of the city gasworks. While Wharton reformers provided economic analysis to show that the public would be best served by management of the works in the hands of a professional civil service removed from the corrupting influence of the legislature, the city's business interests and their political allies backed a private corporation, the United Gas Improvement Company (UGI), which won a thirty-year lease from the city council.[11]

Vested interest in UGI translated into a loss of interest among Philadelphia's establishment for the reform schemes of the Wharton professors. One faculty member, who saw vividly the wealth and power of Philadelphia's upper class crush all notions of civic ideals, bitterly complained that "in those very classes that should furnish leaders in our own civic life, we are waging the conflict between private interests and public welfare which usually rests in the triumph of the former."[12] It was no wonder that Lincoln Steffens concluded in 1903 that "other American cities, no matter how bad their own conditions may be, all point with scorn to Philadelphia as worse—'the worst-governed city in the country.'"[13]

The university and the city were in a period of transition and turmoil. The faculty members of the University of Pennsylvania found themselves by 1911 faced with new men in power. The appointment of the new provost, Edgar F. Smith, a political and moral conservative—Rexford Tugwell described him as "a reactionary of the most mulish sort—even in religion"[14]—coincided with the need to secure new sources of funding. It was well known that Smith was on intimate terms with politicians of the city's corrupt Republican machine. While one historian of the university noted that his connections and the influences they brought were "generally considered harmful,"[15] few could overlook the fact that the state's two-year appropriation in 1911 was the highest ever made to the university.[16] Smith also made it clear to the faculty that reform might not be in the best interest of the university; he asked three Wharton School teachers to consider carefully "what business have academic people meddling in political questions? Suppose, for illustration, that I, as a chemist, should discover that some slaughtering company was putting formalin in its sausage; now surely that would be none of my business."[17]

New influences on the university were felt in other ways too. While only two additions were made to the board of trustees in the years from 1903 to 1910, in the following year nine appointments occurred. In 1910 and 1911, the board added six businessmen, one politician, one corporation lawyer, and the brother of a political leader of the state. In 1911, fully one-third of the board was composed of members added that year.[18] The *Alumni Register* explained that "the Board from end to end is one which any great financial or railway corporation might well be proud to call its Board of Directors. . . . The members of the Board who stand as an active force along educational lines are in the minority."[19] They represented, one faculty member maintained, "the ruling social, financial, and political class in this city."[20] "It is to be observed," the *Register* reported after the 1911 state appropriation, "that certain men, whose affiliations with the dominant regime in the state are close, have recently assumed a responsibility for the university."[21]

Meanwhile, the Wharton faculty carried on an active program of reform. Nearing recalled that he and his colleagues "were a rising generation of progressive thinkers, young people who . . . were beginning to recognize domination by big business over not only the pocketbook of the country, but the mind of the country."[22] Nearing's influence was felt not only on campus where he taught the largest class in the Wharton School, the introductory economics course required of all freshmen, but at a time when Pennsylvania ranked among the states with the highest number of working children, he also gave speeches throughout the state "to women's clubs and other organizations where people had no idea there was such a thing as child labor," condemning the exploitation of children. "The University authorities," he said, "thought I should confine my activities to the classroom and should not speak in public."[23] Nearing was warned: "You have been trying to wipe out child labor and poverty. These things have always been and always will be. Take up some work that will let you get somewhere. Besides, such talk hurts the University."[24]

Almost immediately, the university administration attacked the activities at the Wharton School. Coercion took a number of forms. Nearing and two other young instructors at Wharton were denied promotions despite their professional and educational achievements and the favorable recommendations of their peers and the Academic Council of the university. To pressure the faculty in general to refrain from intellectual and social progressivism, the trustees held up funds for the school.[25] The Wharton School dean in 1911 was James T. Young, who in the twilight of his tenure, found that public statements on controversial issues endangered the school and could no longer be tolerated. For the young instructor of economics, Scott Nearing, this was further indication that pressure would be brought to bear on members of the faculty who held unorthodox views and engaged in public activities off-campus. The pressure was not subtle; on one occasion Dean Young called Nearing into his office and said, "Mr. Nearing, if I were in your place I would do a little less speaking about child labor."[26] At another time, after Nearing had accepted an invitation to speak at a local Unitarian church on "Social Religion," Young and Patten interceded, advised that the meeting be called off, and got him to agree to refrain from public lecturing for one year.[27] Nearing assented, or so it seemed.

While he toned down activities that would antagonize the university administration, it amounted to little more than waiting for the appointment of Roswell Cheney McCrea, a student of Patten's and professor of economics at the school since 1911, to replace Young as dean in 1912. This appointment coincided with a major university reorganization that not only abolished the requirement of Greek, representing the ascendancy of the new social science curriculum and the decline of the disciplines of past traditions, but also gave greater independence to the separate schools within the college, including the Wharton School. This was viewed as a great victory for the Progressive forces on the faculty.[28] Dean McCrea began his tenure by declaring his belief that "as capitalism increases, misery and unemployment and low wages increases until there is some sort of social action."[29]

With Wharton's newfound autonomy and a like-minded dean at its helm, Nearing returned to his activities as a public economist. Yet neither he nor others were unwary of the consequences. According to Tugwell, "Even a freshman could know that Scott's promotion had been retarded, that a certain number of Wharton alumni wanted to be rid of him, and that his teaching was regarded as an affront to the tradition so well represented by the university's trustees and administrators." He "began to understand that an important issue was coming up having to do with the fabric of our university society and the limitations of our theoretical freedoms."[30]

Tensions simmered throughout 1912 and came to a boil in the spring of 1913, when the state was again to determine university appropriations. An influential group of alumni began a campaign against Nearing, voicing their opposition through the official *Alumni Register*.[31] While under typical circumstances the views of the alumni body could be largely disregarded since it was their loyalty more than their power that determined their influence, at the university the alumni were enmeshed with the "interlocking directorate" and became the voice of the trustees.[32] Because a large group of influential alumni had "more or less close professional, business, or personal relations with the trustees"[33]—and one trustee had announced, "We have arrived at the opinion that professors are the most dangerous class in the community"[34]—the alumni were taken seriously. The alumni periodical raised the issue of "academic freedom" in March 1912, conceding that while "it is a serious problem for a liberal university to decide to what extent its liberal tone should be confined," it condemned "the spread of doctrines that are hostile to civilization which the advancing world has accepted and recognized."[35]

Again, in September, it came out even more forcefully, warning that "we must not unduly value the opinions of over-zealous individuals founded upon that which is contradictory to fundamentals and merely a matter of local or passing expediency."[36] In late July, the state appropriation to the university, with a better than 50 percent increase over the previous one, was signed by the governor. However, six days later, instructors at the Wharton School, Nearing among them, were sent official notices that their appointments were for one year only and that they would expire if not renewed. The Wharton School faculty accepted this action as indicating the intent of the board of trustees to remove Nearing and perhaps others at the end of the 1913–1914 academic year.[37] A showdown loomed.

━━ In late December 1913, the annual meetings of the American Economics Association, the American Sociological Society, and the American Political Science Association all adopted identical resolutions supporting the principles of "liberty of thought, freedom of speech, and security of tenure." Each organization formed a committee to merge with that of the others into a "Joint Committee on Academic Freedom."[38] Out of this joint committee would emerge a year later the American Association of University Professors.[39] "The direct cause" for the simultaneous adoption of the resolution, according to the reformist Philadelphia *North American*, was the "efforts of reactionary trustees of the University of Pennsylvania to inaugurate a systematic elimination of progressive teachers."[40] Provost Smith responded by calling the professor's organization "a waste of effort." "I do not believe in muzzling any member of the faculty," he declared, but added, "I do believe, however, that no man may go too far."[41]

The alumni, too, took note of professors "forming a 'union' to force the right of free speech and to maintain the security of their positions under all circumstances." They acknowledged that there was talk on campus of faculty "cowardice in surrendering to the views of the trustees and rich benefactors in their teaching." But they went on to denounce "the mania for making laws to reform the universe" based upon "economic fallacies" and applauded the trustees for standing "firm for sound thought and guarded education . . . against the whims of popular fancy."[42] The storm center around which all this controversy swirled was Nearing. While a number of trustees denied a newspaper report in early January that there were deep tensions at the Wharton School and that Nearing might be dismissed, Dean McCrea stated, "There is no question about the open hostility toward Dr. Nearing . . . on the part of certain interests."[43]

Those close to Nearing's troubles at the university saw the attacks against him as emanating from Joseph Grundy, a wealthy wool manufacturer and powerful Republican politician from Bristol. Nearing and Grundy had been at odds for some time, largely over legislative efforts dealing with child labor that Nearing, as a key figure of the state Child Labor Committee, actively supported. Grundy, on the other hand, had emerged as a leader in the fight against passage of child-labor legislation.[44] Nearing then caught Grundy's ire when late in November 1913 he preached a sermon on child labor in a Methodist church in Morrisville, a town in Grundy's native Bucks County. As Nearing always did, he addressed the issue of child labor in economic terms that were inextricably of moral and public concern. This convergence of meaning was powerfully reinforced and given symbolic social sanction by the setting itself. It was too much for Grundy, who had not only his economic beliefs challenged once again by his nemesis but his ethics as well.

Nearing was confronting the moral basis of the economic order. "Grundy and his fellow executives in textiles and other industries," Nearing explained, "were convinced that private enterprize was almost divinely ordained, that the state must not interfere lest property be endangered."[45] The day following Nearing's "sermon," the Bristol *Daily Courier* carried an angry editorial castigating the minister of the church who had invited Nearing. Addressing itself to the "*quasi*-religious service," the editors noted that Nearing was "at war with the entire order of civilization."[46]

Nearing responded to the editorial by writing to the owner of the paper, who replied that he thought it best that he bring Nearing "into closer touch with some industrial facts than you have been in the past." The economic facts were, said the owner, that "the prosperity of this borough depends upon free and unhampered operation of its industries. . . . You have seen fit to single out a man with whom I am more or less closely in touch as a type of what you are pleased to call industrial iniquity. I refer, of course, to Mr. Joseph R. Grundy."[47] The newspaper's proprietor closed by inviting Nearing to meet with Grundy, an invitation Nearing accepted in a letter in which he explained that he had not criticized Grundy specifically but the economic order generally. "Personal blame does not attach for the present situation," he replied. "No individual is responsible." "Yet as a society," he went on, "we are collectively responsible if we fail to use the means at hand to readjust living and working conditions." No one was more interested in the prosperity of the state than he was. Nearing's "definition of prosperity, however, includes the welfare of the people of Pennsylvania, and not the welfare of the selected few."[48] Nearing and Grundy met and talked over their differences. While Grundy's animosity would remain submerged for a time, he would have the last word.

Nearing's public activities and his economic views had become intolerable to the university officials by early 1914. Provost Smith, undoubtedly speaking for the trustees, requested that Dean McCrea instruct Nearing to cease speaking on the subject of child labor. Nearing also found himself openly assailed in the press when the president of the Manufacturers Club criticized him in a Philadelphia newspaper.[49] There were rumors that the state legislature was to tie the university's appropriation to Nearing's dismissal.[50] The alumni kept up their attack and in their report on the Wharton School expressed concern over "the course of economics, which deals in a measure with the distribution of wealth."[51] Nearing, however, was not without his supporters. Other members of the university faculty sensed threats from the trustees, and a public campaign in support of Nearing and the others was launched in progressive city newspapers by faculty, students, and some alumni. In February, Nearing wrote to a friend that "we have a splendid little nucleus here, however, which is up and alive . . . when they go into a scrap. It is a good place to be."[52] Ultimately, the board of trustees decided to promote two controversial assistant professors to the rank of professor and Nearing and one other faculty member to assistant professor. Trustee minutes recorded that "the usual order of business was suspended and the board proceeded to ballot upon the nomination of Scott Nearing"; he was promoted by a vote of nine to five.[53] "The recent conflict at the University of Pennsylvania," claimed the *New Republic*, was "highly significant" because "what looked like a determined raid upon certain teachers in the Wharton School . . . collapsed immediately under the return fire of publicity."[54]

But significantly, the new assistant professors received with their notification copies of a bylaw warning them that their appointments were for one year only, to be renewed only upon further notice. Assistant professors in 1914 had received no such notice from the trustees. The true intent of the trustees and the meaning of their seemingly incongruous decision to promote professors who were problems for the institution was made clear in the October issue of the *Alumni Register*. Identifying Nearing by name, an editorial, "Free Speech Again," explained that

> a man's sense of fairness teaches him that he should not compromise the institution of which he is a part. By employing him, the University places her reputation in his hands. He becomes in a sense her spokesman. The realization of this fact should have, and probably always have [*sic*], a sobering influence. Morally, the man who joins an institution thereby relinquishes his right to complete freedom of speech. If the occasion should arise in which he thinks outright speech of a kind to embarrass the management of the institution, is of greater importance than his connection with the institution, he should at once resign his position in it.

The "University's answer" about how to rein in recalcitrant professors was clear: Coax them under control by bringing them into the institution, and their affiliation would serve to prevent them from publicly addressing controversial issues. Accepting academic careers included consenting to limitations on academic freedom. Of course, the trustees had kept their options open in the event that their strategy failed. If Nearing would not consent to institutional conformity, the door was open to him first to resign, and if that did not come about, they could ultimately dismiss him by not renewing his appointment.[55] As one member of the board explained, Nearing's promotion was expressly meant as "an appointment on probation."[56] The same alumni editorial concluded: "By all means expound radical doctrines, but do it so that they do not over-top those of a more conservative character. . . . The established order of society has an underlying philosophy. . . . The university cannot afford to maintain a school that over-develops the radical tendencies."[57] Nearing's teaching and his on- and off-campus activities would come under intense scrutiny over the course of the coming year. Both his ideals and his livelihood were on the line.

By the fall semester, Nearing's situation at the University of Pennsylvania had attracted national attention as an infringement on academic freedom.[58] Again the issue was simmering on the campus, and as it did, Nearing came to focus his thinking more clearly on his own role and the meaning of teachers' freedom. At the annual convention of the American Sociological Society late in December, he participated in a discussion on restrictions on the scholar's freedom and in a revealing dialogue appeared to exempt himself from the problem of enforced conformity in the academy.

No one could miss the personal nature of Nearing's remarks when he declared that "the vital issue involved in the freedom of teaching concerns itself very little with the aggressive, determined man who is constantly courting difficulty, and is constantly extricating himself from the situations which his impetuosity creates. He has something to say; he feels called upon to say it; and he answers the call with vigor and energy." The "real issue regarding freedom of teaching," he continued, "lies in an entirely different direction." Those who carried out their mission with integrity were "in the minority of any college faculty" and could "be counted upon to take care of themselves even in the face of serious difficulties." Much more common were the educators who "would speak frankly if they dared, but the sacrifice involved in speaking is too great. The name of these men is legion in the American college work, and their plight is pathetic in the last degree."[59] The commentator following Nearing was E. A. Ross (a man who fell into the category of Nearing's minority), who concurred with his observation that "academic asphyxiation is much more common than is generally realized. . . . The dismissal of professors by no means gives the clue to the frequency of the gag in academic life."[60] Included as part of the society's annual meeting was the issuing of a report by the Joint Committee on Academic Freedom and Academic Tenure, followed by further meetings and the ultimate organization during the first days of 1915 of the American Association of University Professors (AAUP). John Dewey stood as its president, backed by a coterie of charter members that included thirty-two members of the faculty of the University of Pennsylvania—Patten, Young, McCrea, and Nearing among them.[61]

━━━ It was not long before Nearing found himself embroiled in controversy again, this time over an issue that went right to the core of his ethical economics. The business elite of the city, including many of the university trustees, had sponsored the evangelist William "Billy" Sunday for a four-week crusade in Philadelphia. Sunday had been recruited for a religious revival that brought him to the university a year earlier when Provost Smith presided at a university service led by the minister.[62] His present campaign began early in January, but it appeared that his wealthy promoters, not evangelical in their worship, had more in mind than moral uplift. A union official of the Amalgamated Association of Street and Electric Railway Employees pointed out that a three-year struggle for higher pay had reached the critical juncture where a strike was possible, and the charge was made that Billy Sunday was brought to Philadelphia not for the purposes of revivalism but to avert a strike.

One person familiar with the labor situation in the city claimed that "there is league to enforce peace in Philadelphia. It is financed by the millionaires. 'Billy' Sunday is the best strike breaker the country has produced, and they are willing to pay him for strike-breaking. These men whom I know personally on the 'Billy' Sunday committees are the most conservative men alive." There was going to be a strike, he explained, but the Rapid Transit Company would benefit if Sunday was enlisted to avert labor unrest by preaching to the workers that the this-worldly gain in wages should be forsaken for the afterlife. Sunday, he maintained, "asks what difference it makes whether you get $2 or $5 a day, so long as you are only to be here twenty years or so and in hell an eternity."

The union secretary agreed: "Undoubtedly 'Billy' Sunday was brought here to deflect their attention from hours and pay to the world hereafter."[63] A local minister explained why the business interests promoted Sunday. "Business was taught that religion was profitable," and "a better understanding has developed between the church and big business. . . . These are the things that cause business men to rally around Mr. Sunday and consider him a good investment for the individuals, cities, or business."[64]

This was enough to provoke Nearing. Not only was his religious ideal being debased and corrupted by this minister, but Sunday also degraded the university ideal since the business interests with university connections were the ones promoting him on the campus. Sunday referred to Provost Smith as "an old friend,"[65] and Trustee George Wharton Pepper, a high-Anglican layman, was particularly enamored of the preacher. "It requires all the deep religious earnestness of a man like Sunday," he announced, "to rescue revival phraseology from an offensive materialism."[66] When Sunday came to campus, it was arranged that he speak to the entire student body in a huge assembly where he was warmly greeted by Smith and Pepper.

For Nearing, Sunday's presence was further evidence that the social elites, who were in a position to promote progress and civic ideals, had abandoned their leadership role. "The very best people" of the community were responsible for turning the "American way" away from its founding ideals toward "the determination of businessmen to hold down wages and push up profits."[67] Nearing went public with his disgust for the crusade on the first day of February with an open letter to Billy Sunday in the newspapers. He asked Sunday:

> Is not the world beginning to realize that today the most sinister crimes against the ideals of Christ's religion are committed by the system of industry for profit—a system which pays wages so hideously low that if the poor were made spiritually and morally perfect they would still be abjectly poor?

He pointed to Sunday's dictum: "Would you inspire them with the true spirit of Christ?"

> Interpret your doctrine of salvation in terms of modern life! Would not Jesus, if he were face to face with a multitude of ten-dollar-a-week men, feed their bodies

before he attempted to save their souls? . . . Look around you and ask yourself what salvation means here.

The city is filled with unemployment and poverty; multitudes are literally starving; thousands of little children toil in the city's factories and stores; its workers, a third of a million strong, have no workman's compensation law for their protection. Meanwhile the railroad interests which control the hard coal fields are reaping exorbitant profits; the traction company extracts the highest fares paid by the people of any American city; the manufacturers, entrenched in Harrisburg, are fighting tooth and claw to prevent the passage of up to date labor laws, and the vested interests are placing property rights above men's souls.

These "monstrous offenses against humanity—this defiance of the spirit of Christ's gospel"—existed in the very city where Sunday preached his message. This, however, was only half of Nearing's letter, and didn't touch the heart of the problem.

And further: The well-fed people, whose ease and luxury are built upon this poverty, child labor and exploitation, sit in your congregation, contribute to your campaign funds, entertain you socially, and invite you to hold prayer meetings in their homes.

These are they that bind grievous burdens on men's shoulders, that make clean the outside of the cup and platter—the devourers of widows' houses, against whom Christ hurled his curses.

Make no mistake! The chief priests, scribes and Pharisees of Philadelphia will never crucify you while you deal in theological pleasantries. Has it occurred to you that their kindness is a return for your services in helping them to divert attention from real, pressing worldly injustice to heavenly bliss?

Nearing demanded that Sunday turn his "oratorical brilliancy for a moment against low wages, overwork, unemployment, monopoly and special privilege,"[68] and turn his own advantages toward the benefit of the impoverished in the defense of truth without cowardly fear of retribution.

Nearing also reacted against Sunday's crusade by attempting to counter the values foisted upon the students by the "interlocking directorate." He brought his own preacher of a sort to campus in the guise of a national labor leader. Inviting Samuel Gompers, the president of the American Federation of Labor, to the campus stirred the ire of the authorities again. In the wake of the faculty's pushing the union idea among their own rank and file with the formation of the AAUP and with the labor unrest in the city, the provost would have none of Nearing's insurgency. In a heated turn of events, Smith refused to allow the student Civic Club to use any university facilities for an address by Gompers, whereupon the outraged students formed a "Free Speech Club" and hired a hall off-campus. There the labor leader addressed them on the principles of "freedom of speech and freedom for the pursuit of truth." The students were further incensed when they discovered that their posted announcements for the lecture had been torn down. No doubt the university authorities were equally enraged to find that Nearing had taken his classes off-campus to hear Gompers's talk.[69]

▬ Nearing's off-campus activities were becoming increasingly controversial; "no one," claimed a trustee, "likes itinerant lecturers." Yet, it was as much Nearing's classroom teaching, according to Tugwell, that was the "real cause" of his troubles. Tugwell recalled one lecture in particular aimed at a discussion of the theory of consumption. To illustrate his point, Nearing went right to the social facts; he pinned a double-page spread of a city newspaper to the bulletin board, which in photographs and print reported on an extravagant dinner given by Mrs. E. T. Stotesbury for the socialites of Philadelphia. The newspaper account revealed, claimed Tugwell, "a lavish, absurd, even an outrageous performance." And Nearing "placed it precisely in a world still tolerant of child labor, unemployment, slum dwellings by the hundred thousands, and, in that very winter, actual cold and hunger within the proverbial stone's throw from the Stotesbury mansion." This was not simply a lesson in economic theory but a lesson in morals and social salvation. Nearing knew, as did his students, that Edward Townsend Stotesbury was a powerful city and statewide businessman and Republican politician who sat on the board of trustees of the university. Furthermore, it was known to all that Stotesbury's son was sitting among the students. The alumni would angrily denounce this method of classroom instruction "by certain inquisitorial examinations into the social conditions surrounding the homes and families of the students." Yet the students, whether because they hungered for moral enlightenment or because they were conscious of the risks Nearing took by such a presentation, broke into a prolonged ovation at the end of the class.[70]

He took other risks, too, some that he had consciously avoided taking earlier. In the spring of 1915, Nearing came forward as one of the few faculty members who supported the re-formation of a chapter of the Intercollegiate Socialist Society (ISS) on campus. The ISS was the brainchild of Upton Sinclair, who founded the organization in 1905 with the object of promoting "an intelligent interest in Socialism among college men and women by the formation of Study Chapters."[71] It emerged at a time when unorthodox economic and social theories were discouraged on college campuses yet also a time when students enthusiastic for progressive reforms were eager to challenge established ideas. This, of course, created tensions, since the more common view of the ISS was that it was "an amazing attempt to corrupt the Americanism of students throughout the country."[72] An ISS chapter first formed at the University of Pennsylvania in February 1908 after struggling against administrative opposition. At its founding meeting, the campus chapter totaled thirteen students, who elected Guy Nearing, Scott's younger brother, its president. Yet, in a clearly embarrassing situation where the brother of the chapter president was a member of the faculty "known to be a sympathizer," the "faculty took such action as made it advisable for this member of the chapter to withdraw."[73] Not only did Guy Nearing step down, but the chapter had to contend with the provost's denying permission for prominent Socialists to come to the campus and speak to the organization.[74] "Socialism," claimed

Guy Nearing's successor, "has only penetrated college walls by sheer force of worth." The members of the ISS had found that their learning about socialism quickly raised the question of the right of teachers to teach unorthodox views. "We are beginning to see," he continued, "what the effect of this wholesale education under the present capitalist system will be. . . . As long as the machinery of production and distribution remains in private ownership, education alone will not better the condition of humanity one bit."[75]

The University of Pennsylvania chapter of the ISS ceased actively functioning in late 1913, only to be revived by the beginning of 1915. By April, a new chapter had been formed, with Nearing's endorsement.[76] Whereas precautions had been taken years earlier to avoid even the suggestion of association, he now courted it openly. And he did it at a time when the ISS was particularly concerned with the tendency of "heresy-hunting" in the universities. An editorial in the *Intercollegiate Socialist*, the publication of the ISS, during the winter took notice of Nearing's comments at the American Sociological convention and the formation of the AAUP, wondering if "the black-coated proletariate" was "becoming class conscious."[77]

Nearing was also testing the limits of intellectual freedom through his writings. His major scholarly work of the year, *Income*, which appeared in the spring, was a carefully argued and forcefully presented discussion of earned and unearned income with its consequences for distribution and social progress. While *Income* scrupulously avoided mention of socialism, even less advocacy of socialist economics, Socialists and conservatives alike understood its message.[78] A reviewer for the *Intercollegiate Socialist* called it "a most valuable contribution to the arsenal of the Socialist and social reformer."[79] Nearing also continued to write for the popular press, with one change in the magazines to which he contributed. In the spring his articles appeared for the first time in the *International Socialist Review*. Even these did not explicitly embrace a Socialist position, dealing instead with "The Parasitic Power of Property" and "The Impending Conflict."[80] Denouncing the "immortalization of capital," these pieces were above all concerned with the ethics of capitalist economics. A member of the "interlocking directorate" told Nearing in the late spring that the status of university teachers was secure but added, "We will give you young fellows plenty of rope. You will hang yourselves."[81] As if to declare his intellectual independence from the pressures for conformity of thought at the university, Nearing laid his ideas and principles on the line and waited to see whether ideals or pecuniary interests were at the core of the institution, education, even American society.[82]

It looked as if a lynching party was being promoted by the combined forces of the alumni and the trustees. Some saw it coming and tried to spare Nearing. One Wharton faculty member confided, "You have made a fine contribution here. Some of us would hate to see you go, but things are getting tough and you might as well face it." This friend had used his influence in high places to get Nearing a Department of Labor job in Washington at better than triple his teaching salary. Nearing politely refused, explaining, "This is my post. I stay here. Teaching is my job."[83]

The alumni mounted an attack that turned increasingly virulent as the academic year came to an end. In its January issue, a *Register* editorial pronounced its view of "the professor's calling."

> The members of the profession, especially those whose subjects deal with those economic, financial, statistical, or legal principles which underlay the practice of government, should carefully avoid a participation in exciting or controversial questions of the moment. . . . The life of a professor is led apart from practical affairs so as generally to preclude the formation by him of a sound judgement on questions that are pressing for a definite solution.[84]

An editorial the following month focused on "public utterances" by faculty members, claiming, "We deprecate the recent frequent appearance in the public print of members of the University's faculty upon controversial subjects . . . because such appearances have a tendency to estrange an important element of the community from the University."[85] A member of the faculty should not "submit himself to solving intimate social and economic problems," a second editorial, "Professors as Public Servants," declared, since such issues were "steeped, no doubt, in local politics and calculated to arouse popular passions and controversy."[86] Since Nearing was in charge of the freshman course in economics at the Wharton School, there was no mistaking the target of the assertion that "the bizarre and radical theories advanced by enthusiastic young instructors are likely to have a poor effect upon freshmen."[87]

By April, the alumni committee of the Wharton School urged the dismissal of faculty members who "tended to arouse class prejudice" and whose studies, according to the committee, seemed to reach "fallacious conclusions." The committee placed itself on record "as squarely opposed to the use of the fair name of the University as a vantage for utterances foreign to the scheme of its teaching and ideals in education, and recommends that where such members of the teaching staff are not willing to subscribe to its policies, their services should be dispensed with."[88] A report issued by the committee in May specifically addressed concerns over "the course in Economics, which deals in measure with the distribution of wealth."[89] The directors of the alumni adopted these recommendations and in their report to the trustees suggested dismissing faculty at the Wharton School who were "not willing to subscribe to its policies."[90] The May issue of the *Register* reported that "the question of so-called academic freedom, which is puzzling the authorities of all the universities and colleges, is claiming a large share of the thought and attention of the board." This was evident in a letter by a trustee published in the same number that supported the recommendations of the directors and again called attention to the wayward beliefs harbored in the Wharton School, which were "entirely inconsistent with Mr. Wharton's well-known views and in defiance of the conservative opinions of men of affairs."[91]

The turmoil at the university once more had gained the attention of the editors at the *New Republic,* who found it "in the midst of a moral crisis." "The conflict in Pennsylvania" they found "peculiarly grave" and "supremely significant" in that "it reveals within our universities a conflict between intellectual repression and freedom of speech, between plutocracy strongly entrenched and democracy not yet conscious of itself."[92] "A heresy hunt will probably be started at the Wharton School," they warned, with the result that "a particular brand of economic teaching will receive a certificate of orthodoxy. . . . For the next few months the Wharton School will be worth watching."[93]

By mid-June, the semester had ended, and Nearing and his family had moved to Arden for the summer. Then a call came from Nearing's secretary at the university: she read him a perfunctory letter from the provost informing him that his appointment as assistant professor had expired and that he was "directed by the trustees of the University to inform you that it will not be renewed." Although university authorities acted as if this were a routine matter, it was far from ordinary. Nearing was the only one with a favorable recommendation from the faculty to be refused appointment. Quite simply, Nearing explained, he had been "fired without previous notice, without charges, without a hearing, without recourse, from a job that I held for nine years."[94]

# The Dred Scott
# of the Teaching Profession

## Chapter 7

WHEN the board of trustees had met at the end of the semester, a motion had been made to rehire Nearing, but another member of the board raised the question of Nearing's liability to the university, which was ultimately determined to be a serious enough problem to invite dismissal. There had been a good deal of discussion at the meeting; clearly, the trustees were somewhat apprehensive about what they were considering. It was late in the year, and because they had not made their decision earlier, perhaps to avoid protests from faculty and students, they left Nearing with little chance of finding employment elsewhere for the coming year. They voted to arrange payment of Nearing's salary for a year after his severance from the university, but since this could be construed only as an admission of the nefarious character of their actions, they voted not to have the salary provision recorded in the minutes of their meeting.[1]

The trustees also agreed that they would maintain a protective silence about Nearing's dismissal. Yet this silence was slowly pierced. It became known that the fight against Nearing had been led by a trustee who was general counsel for the United Gas Improvement Company and others, including E. T. Stotesbury and George Wharton Pepper.[2] Pepper discussed the issue of free speech without direct reference to Nearing, but the association was unmistakable. If free speech meant "the unrestricted right of a teacher to adopt any method he pleases for the propagation of any views he happens to hold," he explained, "then I could not bring myself to advocate such license in the University or anywhere else." What seemed to offend Pepper most were Nearing's moral views. He continued: If "free speech means the right to proclaim views not discordant with the ethical sense of the community" then he supported the principle, but not "if a man might feel himself justified in advocating a disregard for moral principles regarded by the rest of us as fundamental."[3] A typical response was to explain that Nearing was not re-employed because "in the discharge of my duty as a trustee," a board member "believed that the good of the service and of the University required [it] and because of professional utterances in the university, unbecoming of a teacher and against the best interests of the institution and its student body."[4] A less evasive answer came from one trustee who admitted that Nearing was a problem because "he advocated the ruthless redistribution of property."[5]

It had emerged that Nearing's economic and religious views were the cause of his removal. As Clyde Barrow has explained, "The concepts of laissez-faire economics and public morality were so intertwined in the minds of Philadelphia businessmen that what began as a dispute over Nearing's 'economic fallacies' in advocating the abolition of child labor ended with the trustees accusing him of religious heresy and immorality."[6] Finally, it seems that Nearing had to go because Joseph Grundy had had enough of his child-labor agitation, and through his political ties had held up the university's appropriations to pressure the trustees to force Nearing out.[7] This was in no sense simply an internal university matter.

Dismissal from the university "came as a shock" to Nearing, "but not as a complete surprise."[8] From Arden his wife claimed that they had "been expecting it for seven years." She also refuted the notion that Nearing was an atheist or that he believed in "Socialist doctrines."[9] Nearing immediately returned to Philadelphia, turning his attention to orchestrating a public opinion campaign, which was less an attempt to pressure reinstatement than an effort to educate the public on the issue of academic freedom. He sent out "about 1500 envelopes addressed to the newspapers of Pennsylvania, the leading papers of the country, the press associations, associates in other universities, and to influential individuals all over the United States."[10] To the Socialist Rose Pastor Stokes he wrote:

> Dear Comrade,—
> For a week we have had daily publicity; next we need the weekly papers, + in another 2 weeks the monthlies such as the Review of Reviews, Current Opinion, etc. + the bulkier magazines. There is no way of making a dent in this fight except through public opinion. If you know any editors, emphasize to them
> 1. The impersonal, organic nature of the issue.
> 2. The issue between plutocracy and democracy in University control.[11]

Nearing was determined to let the trustees know that independent minded teachers like himself "did not propose to be hanged without a tussle."[12]

The *New Republic* deplored "the brutal dismissal" of someone whose economic theories were, the editors claimed, "not very new and not very terrifying." The action of the trustees—"black reactionaries"—produced "the picture of a University in which the power is in the hands of a closed corporation of men financially interested in the perpetuation of certain economic doctrines." Yet this "dramatic event" also threw the whole subject of academic freedom "open to public discussion." "The issues here," maintained the editors, were "as vital as any in American life, because the Universities are coming more and more to focus the thought of the nation. . . . They cannot do the work if they are governed by stupid rich men or stupid politicians."[13]

Left to speculate about the trustees' intentions in the face of the seemingly incontrovertible facts of the case, many Wharton professors discerned a threat to the teaching profession. Dean McCrea informed the provost of "deep concern among members of the Wharton School faculty."[14] One faculty member saw Nearing's situation as representative of the damage administrative regulation exacted upon the teacher's professional status. "Scott Nearing," he proclaimed, "has become the Dred Scott of the teaching profession. . . . His experience has become a case, his treatment a precedent that menaces the teaching profession." He angrily denounced the tendency toward "controlled freedom" and the prevalence of attempts at "smothering radicalism." If the lesson to be learned, he continued, was that "men of mental and moral independence must of necessity stay out of the universities," then the professor would "degenerate into a kind of high-class deferential butler."[15]

A professor of psychology at the university, Lightner Witmer, was so outraged by the actions of the authorities that he devoted his summer to analyzing the case and producing *The Nearing Case: The Limitations of Academic Freedom at the University of Pennsylvania by an Act of the Board of Trustees*. Witmer could not ignore the question of "whether public service corporations and politics inspired the Trustees' actions" and surmised that "back of the Nearing case is the problem of financial support and the question of administrative control." Witmer had no affinity for Nearing's "economic views nor . . . some of the methods which he employs in placing them before the public." But the principles at stake in the case made "differences of opinion and method . . . immaterial." The conflict exposed by the case, he asserted, was "a part of the universal struggle of democracy against aristocracy. An essential feature of the democratic form of government, whether in state or university, is tolerance of opinion." He felt compelled to write about the dispute because it touched not only Nearing but all other professionals at the university who could fall under the accusatory specter that they were "virtually employees of a few representatives of inherited or acquired wealth in the city of Philadelphia."[16] A professor in the history department at the time of Nearing's troubles, in an official history of the university written many years later, found in the firing "indication of a disparaging attitude of the

Administration toward the faculty" at a time when the relationship between the two "was a rising issue."[17]

While Witmer concluded that "the issues are much more complicated than the mere fact of dismissal would seem to indicate," the fundamental areas of controversy centered on religious and economic issues that challenged the dominant values of the "interlocking directorate." According to one trustee, prior to Nearing's termination the provost had received four letters complaining of his "ecclesiastical heterodoxy."[18] When Tugwell attempted to assess the "hidden causes" behind the firing, he could not help but acknowledge that by doing much of his speaking before church groups, Nearing had offended the ethics of one man in particular, George Wharton Pepper.[19] Pepper claimed it was "generally recognized that Doctor Nearing not only antagonized industrial orthodoxy, but orthodoxy in other fields, social and religious."

Pepper had made his religious views widely known in the city and at the university. In a book published in 1915, he wrote that in "Christian theory there are really no such things as secular and religious education. . . . Subtract God and you get—not secular education, but no education at all." Witmer noted the "antagonism of certain religious convictions to modern scientific methods and to efficient social organization" in statements by Pepper such as, "We include nowadays among subjects studied in the universities many courses with high-sounding names which are scarcely more than opportunities for instructors to express their individual views upon the great problems of life." Thus it was beyond question that Nearing's version of "social religion" would infuriate a man who believed that "the teacher who interprets all of life in terms of brotherhood is responsible for leading the student to forget God." Pepper's role in the Nearing case prompted Witmer to "put the friends of intellectual freedom and new knowledge on guard against the kind of religion which joins with wealth to grasp at power in the name of charity."[20] But for Nearing it was too late, and Tugwell was resigned to believe that the trustee "had been acting in the interest of his clients and associates rather than of Christian principles."[21]

One trustee who revealed publicly that he had voted to retain Nearing at the university reported that he had been charged with "economic heterodoxy, rather than of ecclesiastical heterodoxy."[22] The attacks upon Nearing were made, he asserted, "not because of his views upon religion, but because he attacks the aggregations of associated capital; attacks made because associated capital knows that its aggression upon economic rights of the people is nefarious and cannot stand against adequate presentation of the demands of the people."[23] Behind assaults on Nearing's economic and social views were always the charges of "socialism" and "radicalism." One professor at the university dismissed accusations of the extreme nature of Nearing's beliefs, claiming that "his attitude toward general economic and social questions . . . seems to be much that of the other teachers of the same subject in our and in other universities and colleges, his suggestions for reform are just such as are being made every day."[24] Another writer blamed what he called "the 'Billy' Sunday crowd" for Nearing's dismissal because they were "the men who regard as Socialist all who see injustice and wrong in the present economic order of things." "They consider Scott Nearing a Socialist, though he is not," he insisted: "They are men who see only through corporate eyes."[25]

Nearing had never expressly identified himself with socialism (even as he came to write for Socialist publications) whether in theory or politics, although he recalled that he "was in sympathy with the Socialists and did what I could to help them build a Socialist America."[26] Yet, even if he avoided commitment to the movement, Socialists found that they could claim him for their own. As early as 1911, a reviewer in the *International Socialist Review* maintained that Nearing's *Wages in the United States* was "a book of first importance to Socialists" and that "the Socialist movement of America should be congratulated that this volume issues not from one of its own editorial sanctums but from the Department of Economics in that most conservative and respectable of American Universities."[27] In his books, and presumably in his courses, Nearing discussed the Socialist program in a dispassionate manner, as he did all other economic programs and theories, indicating its merits and weaknesses. It was not until after his firing that he explicitly addressed his relation to socialism.

In October he shared a stage in Brooklyn, New York, with the Socialist party leader Morris Hillquit to take the affirmative in a debate against a pair of opponents on the question "Should Socialism prevail?" After opening the discussion by defining socialism as "the collective or community ownership and management of the social tools of production," he immediately went on to quote from the New Testament. Then, on the role of the government in promoting reform and progress, he declared:

> I subscribe to the doctrine of Thomas Jefferson that "that government governs best, which governs least" provided you add to that dictum the statement that a sufficient amount of government must be provided to safeguard the welfare of the majority of the people in the community. We need not more government, but sufficient government.

As Nearing continued, it became clear that he had not come to the debate as one promoting socialism—that it *should* prevail—but rather as a keen observer of American society reporting his analysis—that it *would* prevail. "The people who are making socialism inevitable," he asserted, were the "people who control . . . our public and municipal utilities, our railroads, our iron and coal mines, our oil wells—and who cannot control their own greed." Because the dominant classes guarded their own profits above all else, democracy was breaking down under "the strain of too much wealth and power vested in irresponsible public hands." "These people," he emphasized, "are the people who are making socialism as inevitable as it is." Before he closed, he reminded the crowd that "I am not a Socialist, I am not a member of the Socialist Party, but a student of economics," and he warned them that "Socialism does not promise everything." But "neither does capitalism."[28]

▬ In the aftermath of Nearing's dismissal, interest in his case received international attention from those who saw it as justified and those who perceived, as one put it, "the death of American scholarship."[29] The trustees found support from the leader of the National Civic Federation (NCF), an organization formed to promote social reform on a national scale but in such a way as to prevent restrictions on the abuses of big business from turning into radical solutions.[30] Founded in 1905, the federation promoted such programs as business–labor cooperation in the form of conservative unionism, an approach Eugene Debs claimed would take labor "by the hand and guide it into harmless channels."[31] The NCF was dominated by big businessmen who stood in active opposition to what they considered to be their greatest threat, socialism.

Officially, the federation undertook public and private campaigns to halt the spread and destroy the influence of socialism, although it acknowledged that its attempt to influence public opinion "must be skillfully and tactfully carried on" since socialist ideas were "held and preached by many persons who are quite sincere" and "held in high regard by the public."[32] The founder and moving spirit behind the NCF, Ralph Easley, was particularly concerned that "the sensational and misleading stuff put out over the country by Socialist writers has done a great injustice to many fair-minded and humane employers,"[33] and he abhorred the emergence and spread of groups like the Intercollegiate Socialist Society that disseminated Socialist doctrines.

Shortly after reaction to the trustees' actions had risen to a crescendo of criticism, Easley wrote to the trustee John C. Bell, a Philadelphia Republican and attorney general of the state, backing the board's decision and adding that he was "getting up some material on the matter myself and will send you a copy when I have it ready." He assured Bell that "if some of your friends will go through Scott Nearing's writings they will find plenty of reasons why he should have been kicked out of the university long before this." Easley reassured the trustee that "there will be no trouble to prove that Nearing is a socialist and a man whose utterances are of such a character as to make him unworthy of being connected with an institution like the University of Pennsylvania."[34] Heartened by Easley's blessing, Bell thanked him for his "valued suggestions and approval of our action." "I am sure we did what was right," he confirmed; Nearing "was undesirable, not to say intolerable."[35]

When the chancellor of Syracuse University publicly granted that Nearing had been "properly dismissed" since "the terms of professional service are made to conform to the treasurer and the board of trustees or overseers," John Dewey, president of the AAUP, denounced this " 'hired-man' theory of the status of the American College Professor." "If the governing boards of universities" endorsed such a notion, they would "drive from their institutions all men of ability and backbone, and retain to teach the youth of the country only weaklings in mind and character." He warned that "no self-respecting teacher who has spent his life in study of a topic would willingly retain his position a moment under such circumstances." Furthermore, Dewey underscored the consequences of this crude censorship for the teaching of beliefs subscribed to by the dominant culture. He quoted an editorial from the New York *Evening Post* to the effect that "the silencing of a single radical professor would perceptibly lower the value of everything that might be said by a hundred professors who stand for the established order."[36]

Randolph Bourne, writing in the *New Republic*, asserted that the Nearing case raised the question "Who owns the universities?" It was "clearly a case of old tradition against new science, the prejudiced guesses of corporate officials against the data of a scientific student of economics." At the root of the problem lay a "determined autocracy" composed of "men ignorant of collegiate business and little interested in educational policy." Yet the "new view of the place of the university in the community" was one of "public intellectual and scientific service." Because "the issues of the modern university are not those of private property but of public welfare," Bourne asserted, "irresponsible control by a board of amateur notables is no longer adequate for the effective scientific and sociological laboratories for the community that the universities are becoming." Professors like Nearing, who maintained "a dynamic and not purely academic interest in social movements," were "an asset for the whole community."[37]

In one of its first and most important investigations into infringements on academic freedom, the AAUP involved itself in the case because in a broader sense it was "not directed solely or most significantly, against the individual teacher affected." Rather, the investigative committee maintained, it was "directed also against the local faculty as a body, and against the academic profession at large," since it represented "an instance of lay intervention in what is essentially a professional question." "The removal of Dr. Nearing," their report stated, "had aroused an unprecedented measure of interest and concern among both the academic and general public, and in other countries as well as our own." The evidence led the committee to conclude that Nearing's dismissal "was unmistakably based upon objections to the character of Dr. Nearing's social and economic teachings." This, said the AAUP, "constituted an infringement of freedom of teaching."[38]

▬ In September, returning students rallied to Nearing's cause and presented the administration with a petition signed by fifteen hundred students asking for his reinstatement. The Wharton faculty, meanwhile, demanded that Nearing be given back his job, and they raised the equivalent of a half-year's salary for the deposed professor to give him time to devote to the campaign.[39] There was no escaping the fact that the university was deep in crisis. Since June, the Wharton faculty had wondered "whether or not we are to regard Mr. Nearing's dismissal . . . as a precedent for possible future action on the part of the Board of Trustees?"[40] One professor reported "serious dissatisfaction and dissension within the university and without." The university, this faculty member asserted, had "been humiliated in the public view." The result of the action by the trustees was that "younger members of the faculty are shaken in their sense of security and allegiance to the university; older professors are perplexed and dissatisfied."[41] Nearing observed that the "consequences were almost as far reaching for the University as for me."[42] There was a mood of impending exodus among the faculty, but Nearing opposed anyone's leaving. "The University does not belong to the Trustees," he told his colleagues, "it belongs to you, its teachers, and to its students. That the Trustees have an essentially undemocratic power and have used it irresponsibly does not warrant you confirming them in it. You must think of your students and of the university's mission."[43]

Provost Smith also recognized the destructive effect the Nearing case was having on the university. To avert disaster, he persuaded the trustees to reassure the faculty that there would be no reoccurrence of the events of the previous June. By the end of the year, they had adopted a series of changes in the bylaws that set procedural guidelines for appointments and promotions, placing responsibility for the removal of professors in the hands of a committee of nine faculty members, with final say remaining with the trustees. The university rulers had arrived at a managerial concept of academic freedom that focused singularly on the procedural issues of tenure and university governance.

While some saw this as a great victory at the university and an advance for colleges across the country, even an admission of fault by the trustees, it did not prevent some of the best minds from forsaking Nearing's entreaties and quietly withdrawing to potentially more secure settings where they could advance their professional careers.[44] It was only a matter of time before J. Russell Smith, professor of geography and industry, and Dean McCrea accepted appointments at Columbia. Rexford Tugwell, a young instructor in the midst of his doctoral studies, went to the University of Washington to finish his degree because he could not stay "where betrayal was tolerated." There were other resignations, mostly by those, not coincidentally, who had once proudly endorsed public advocacy as the "Wharton School Eight."[45] If any solid proof were needed that the trustees had not mended their ways and were not ready to abandon their oppressive practices, it came when the axe fell on the originator of Wharton's intellectual insurgency, Simon Nelson Patten.[46]

In spring 1917, with the United States on the brink of formally entering the Great War, a peace group in Philadelphia had scheduled David Starr Jordan, president of Stanford University and a staunch pacifist, to speak at a local theater. They approached Patten to chair the meeting, which he agreed to do. On the evening of the talk, Patten went to the theater to find it surrounded by police and was told that the meeting had been forbidden. Patten had just reached the age of sixty-five, normally the age of retirement, yet the trustees by custom extended the tenure for distinguished members of the faculty. In Patten's case, apparently because of his alleged pro-German leanings, they refused to continue his contract, releasing him from the university.[47] A Philadelphia newspaper suggested that the antiwar association was not the cause but simply a pretext the trustees could use to dispose of Patten. They had been "gunning" for him for some time because he was the "fount and origin of the doctrines against the vested interests." It was impossible to "deal with the Nearings," the paper determined, "until you have reckoned with the teacher of the Nearings."[48]

Years after the event, the cantankerous pundit H. L. Mencken worried about the legacy of Nearing's dismissal. All told, it seemed, he said, "to cast a glow of suspicion over the whole of American political economy, at least in so far as it comes from college economists." He held no brief for Nearing, thought him "wrong in his notions," and identified his own "convictions and instincts . . . all on the other side"; he voiced his concerns "not as a radical, but as one of the most hunkerous of the orthodox." But he could not ignore that "a troubling question keeps floating in the air, and that is briefly this: What would happen to the learned professors if they took the other side?" What if Nearing had "gone in the other direction" and "defended child labor as ardently as he denounced it and denounced the minimum wage as ardently as he defended it"? In other words, Mencken wondered, "to what extent is political economy, as professors expound it, a free science?" Nearing was not thrown out of the university, claimed Mencken, "because he was honestly wrong, or because his errors made him incompetent to prepare sophomores for their examinations; he was thrown out because his efforts to get at the truth disturbed the security and equanimity of the rich ignoranti who happened to control the university, and because the academic slaves and satellites of these shopmen were restive under his competition for the attention of the student body. In three words, he was thrown out because he was not safe and sane and orthodox."

In the aftermath of the Nearing case, Mencken was uneasy about "the professors of economics who had *not* been thrown out." "Who will say that the lesson of the Nearing *debacle* has been lost upon them? . . . And who will say that . . . their arguments against Nearing's so-called ideas are as worthy of confidence and respect as they would be if they were quite free to go over to Nearing's side without damage." Few professors would be "sent to the block," as Nearing was, "yet all would have to contend with "plenty of pillories and guardhouses on the way, and every last pedagogue must be aware of it." Mencken would have had less anxiety over the validity of the "orthodox" economic and social beliefs he adhered to if he could rest assured that intellectual freedom guaranteed their solid underpinning. "I should be a great deal more comfortable in those convictions and instincts," he confessed, "if I were convinced that the learned professors were really in full and absolute possession of academic freedom."[49]

▬ Nearing's case was not the first, or the last, infringement on the ideal of academic freedom. But it occurred at a time in American history when the university was in the process of being transformed into its modern structure. Faculty dismissals occurred with increasing frequency, predominantly among professionals whose inquiry led them to question and sometimes challenge the prevailing economic order.[50] Following the most infamous turn-of-the-century academic freedom cases, trouble escalated. In 1915, the year Nearing was fired, there were at least eleven significant complaints of infringements of academic freedom.[51] Nearing's case became the most notorious, because of widespread publicity and the fact that it was one of the first cases investigated by the fledgling American Association of University Professors.

In one respect at least, Nearing's situation was different from previous cases.[52] Unlike his predecessors, he resisted pressures for intellectual conformity, eschewing the model provided by Richard Ely in 1894 of consciously retreating from radicalism through an opportunistic strategy of survival and advancement. Nearing refused to heed warnings and invoked the principles of academic freedom, which recently led one writer to claim that Nearing was "the first professor fired from an American university for his radical beliefs and activities."[53] More important, Nearing's firing clarified for many the meaning of academic freedom and the changing role of the university in society. His discharge, wrote one commentator who echoed the views of others in 1916, "has brought the discussion of academic freedom in American colleges to the very forefront" and "involves a contest for the privilege of expressing one's convictions regarding the very foundation of the present economic system, not only in the classroom but in public."[54]

Academic freedom, it was increasingly acknowledged, was under assault as the modern university emerged dependent upon the wealthy, the state, and the market. As religious denominations gradually released their hold on the universities by the late nineteenth century, "secular" wealth, whether from endowments or taxpayers, was welcomed to fuel the massive expansion of the modern university. This affected the composition of the institution's administrative leadership and its concerns.[55] The university would have to maintain an aura of respectability and genteel politeness, which often meant deferring to the powerful and reputable elements in society. Yet more and more, the values of the administration and the limits of respectability came to be strained through the bars of the dollar sign. The wealth that had been a boon to institutional expansion now seemed to threaten the university's ideal of free and open inquiry. Academic freedom became an issue less of educational theory and more of institutional structure.

Fear that these new influences on the university threatened free inquiry figured heavily in critiques of the university. Nationally organized professors of the nascent American Association of University Professors in their first statement on academic freedom in 1915 declared that "it is the first essential that the scholars who carry on the work of the universities shall not be in a position of dependence upon the favor of any social class or group."[56] And during the war years, the issue of conformity of thought only heightened the concerns of corporate domination. Reflecting on "the idea of a university," Randolph Bourne lamented "how frankly the American university has become a financial corporation, strictly analogous, in its motives and responses, to the corporation which is concerned with industrial commodities. . . . Under trustee control the American university has been degraded from its old, noble ideal of a community of scholarship to a private commercial corporation."[57]

Similarly, Thorstein Veblen lashed out at the business-minded "captains of erudition" who were corrupting the scholarly mission of the university and the pursuit of pure knowledge. Nearing's case, he claimed, was simply evidence that

> a wise academic policy, conducted by an executive looking into the fiscal interests of the university, will aim not to alienate the affections of the large businessman of a ripe age, by harboring specialists whose inquiries are likely to traverse these old settled convictions in the social, economic, political, or religious domain. It is bad business policy to create unnecessary annoyance. So it comes about that the habitual munificence of the captains of industry who have reached their term will have grave consequences for that range of economic science that is occupied with matters on which they hold their convictions.[58]

When John Dewey detected strains upon the university ideal as early as 1902, he too had observed that "the financial factor in the conduct of the modern university is continually growing in importance, and very serious problems arise in adjusting this factor to strict educational ideals." While he conceded that "money is absolutely indispensable as a means," he feared that it was subverting ideal ends and fostering a pernicious "academic materialism." Thus, a "new type of college administration has been called into being by the great expansion on the material side," with the effect that "this machinery tends to come between the individual and the region of moral aims in which he should assert himself." But, he claimed, this "academic materialism" would "not be so threatening were it not for its association with the contemporary tendency" toward specialization with its specialization of scholarship.[59]

In Nearing's case, his economic and moral radicalism led to a questioning of his professional conduct and the quality of his scholarship by his peers. For many of his academic colleagues, taking the role of a public intellectual and injecting questions of morality into economics threw into question the standards of professional objectivity. When Edwin R. Seligman, the conservative economist from Columbia University and chairman of the AAUP Committee on Academic Freedom queried prominent scholars on the merits of Nearing's case, he found an underlying questioning of Nearing's professional stature. Seligman himself had doubts about Nearing's "scientific merits," which were defended by Jacob H. Hollander, a professor of political science at Johns Hopkins University. A professor of economics at Harvard University, B. M. Anderson, replied to Seligman that from his understanding of the case, it was Nearing's talk on child labor that was the cause for his dismissal, but he added that his "unscientific methods" were indeed dubious. From a professor of economics at Indiana University came the opinion that "the fact that the victim is a somewhat garrulous and perhaps intemperate young man is unfortunate, but this does not change the situation materially." Even among his colleagues at the University of Pennsylvania the question of Nearing's professionalism was raised, which was interpreted by some of Nearing's opponents as a pretext for attacking him. When Dean McCrea was called before a subcommittee of the trustees, he conceded that Nearing was "impulsive" and had "not been so tactful as he might be." And in reply to a trustee's question whether Nearing was not wanting in "professional gumption," McCrea answered: "I think that is about it."[60]

Thus, Nearing's situation at the University of Pennsylvania was complicated by the fact that the educational structure of the modern university was centered on the simultaneous emergence of an administrative bureaucracy providing organizational efficiency to the large institution and the professionalization of scholarship that organized, structured, and contained knowledge.[61] While this created tensions within the university as administrative control was challenged by an increasingly professionally conscious faculty that insisted on greater power in university management and enlarged freedom of inquiry, there were also internal tensions in the new culture of professionalism. Heightened standards of scholarship and claims to scientific authority allowed scholars to declare the university an inviolable refuge from outside infringements on their intellectual pursuits. At the same time, pressing social problems were reduced to scientific and technical terms so that controversial issues were removed from the public realm and organized into isolated professional spheres, further contributing to the cultural fragmentation of American life. The vast majority of these new men of knowledge, observed one critic, "by training and temper, are inclined to view their function as that of transforming information rather than as the training of critical, inquiring minds, eager to go wherever arguments might lead them."[62] Tensions arising from economic dependence and centralization that lead to claims of authority and power placed the professor in the tenuous professional-employee role and played a central role in Nearing's dismissal. Yet, a contributing factor was that genuine academic freedom was eroded by professionalization that sought to segregate, contain, and regulate ideas. Nearing was caught within and finally devoured by these larger tendencies.

▬ Although it was a summer of turmoil, Nearing spent the usual time at Arden and on the Chautauqua circuit. At Chautauqua, he lectured on the theme of "the schoolhouse as the nucleus of social organization." "We are trying to make a government by discussion," he contended; "we are trying to bring our citizenry together to work out the problem." The "schoolhouse" could serve as "the center of community discussion," he claimed, because it maintained "an advantage unique in the community: it is non-sectarian, non-partisan." "No other community institution comes in that class," he argued: "It is the natural place where the people should assemble." It was "the logical council chamber for the community," the heart of a democratic society. Educational institutions served as "the people's council chamber," as "the place to secure the truth . . . through the conflict of differences, not through the agreement of likes." "We must have our public opinion molded," he declared, not "thru political bosses or wealth control, but from freedom of expression from the common people."[63]

At the end of the summer, Nearing sold his cabin, left the Arden colony, and tried to pick up the pieces of his educational calling. Freed from the university, he lectured when asked, as he did early in October before a Hartford, Connecticut, community club. On that occasion he spoke on "Public Opinion and Academic Freedom," informing his audience that "the economic interests are among the most powerful that influence public opinion." If public opinion was "to be effective in the long run," it "must be intelligent." This could happen only if the educational system allowed for the free exchange of ideas. "The logical place for the development of this intelligence," he maintained, was in the schools.[64]

By the time the semester opened at the University of Pennsylvania, he had accepted the request of the Social Service Corporation in Baltimore to give a course of six public lectures on present industrial conditions and problems, entitled "The Industrial Regime," dealing with the tension between "industrialism and human well-being." Unlike the authorities at the university who had recently pushed him out, the corporation directors—a "community committee made up of some fifty social workers and representatives of civic improvement associations, labor unions, city and state departments, public and private schools, and churches of all denominations"—found the deposed professor an appealing choice. He drew large crowds from the middle class of the community. The Baltimore lectures offered an opportunity to continue his educational work without the constraints of institutional conformity.[65]

He also found what would become a more permanent institutional home in the Rand School of Social Science, an educational facility endowed by a wealthy socialite with progressive values founded in 1906 in New York City and operating with the "very definite object—that of providing an auxiliary or specialized agency to serve the Socialist and Trade Union movement of the United States in an educational capacity." It would "offer an opportunity for studying the principles, purposes, and methods" of the Socialist movement, providing "instruction and training along lines calculated to make them more efficient workers for the Cause." The Rand School maintained close ties with the Socialist party, but the administrative control of the school fell under the auspices of the American Socialist Society and remained independent of party influence. It was from the Rand School, too, that the Intercollegiate Socialist Society carried on its activities. These "two important institutions," Hillquit noted, promoted the "cultural activities of the Socialist movement."[66] Among those who had taught at the Rand School by 1916 were Hillquit, Charles A. Beard, Franklin H. Giddings, John Spargo, and Lester Ward. By the time Nearing began teaching at the school, it had earned the reputation as "the Workers' University of America."[67]

His affiliation probably says more about the expansive nature of the Socialist movement and the open cultural space for alternative values in American society than any shift in Nearing's pedagogical or political thinking. Because the teaching methods employed by the school were specifically, "modern and non-dogmatic,"[68] he could without contradiction teach without intellectual constraints at a socialist institution just as he had taught uninhibited for years at a capitalist one. Even as an instructor at the Rand School, he believed fervently that no teacher should "go out and propagate for this or that sect." "I do not believe any school teacher has a right to do it. I do not believe that he should dogmatize. . . . This is not scientific."[69] What began as occasional lectures at the school would later turn into a regular teaching assignment. But in the fall of 1915, Nearing taught only one course, The Human Element in Economics.

His activities at the Rand School remained peripheral to his role as a public economist primarily because he had accepted a position at the Toledo University as professor of political science and dean of the College of Arts and Sciences. His colleagues at the Wharton School had tried to use their influence to get him a position at the University of Wisconsin and at Columbia, but neither institution expressed any interest. Toledo had actively sought Nearing, and it was a far cry from Pennsylvania.[70] First, it was a municipal university with a public service ideal. Its president described it as an institution whose function was "to develop intelligent, efficient citizens, and as a branch of the city government its function is to place at the disposal of the city the services of its experts in so far as those services can be utilized by the municipality or by its citizens in their endeavors to improve the social or civic life of the city."[71] Furthermore, Nearing recalled, "its trustees were appointed by the Mayor of the city and were representatives of the major interests in the town: the Chamber of Commerce, the Central Labor Union, the professions." Only the "business group" opposed his appointment.[72] An editorial in the local press early in October welcomed Nearing to Toledo, declaring, "The biggest thing the Toledo University has is freedom. . . . Dr. Nearing can express whatever views he has, suggest any progressive reform he believes in, and there will be no reactionary, medieval brained trustees attempting to muffle him." Nearing introduced himself to the citizens of the city the following week with a newspaper article explaining the "Grave Faults of the Wage System."[73]

Had his economic views remained the only potentially controversial issue, he might have stayed at Toledo for some time. He went to Toledo "with hope and real enthusiasm . . . welcomed as a progressive social scientist."[74] Yet by 1916, a presidential election and events overseas combined to make the Great War an American problem. Although Nearing's "strongly anti-war and pro-peace" beliefs had been well known at the University of Pennsylvania, they appear not to have played a part in his dismissal.[75] And even as he tried "during these years of spectacular military conflict," as he wrote in late 1915, not "to forget the increasing economic turmoil that is interwoven with present day existence,"[76] the war wreaked havoc on his hopes for the achievement of his social philosophy—and on his academic career.

# Free Speech

## Chapter 8

FOR those who believed that a society founded upon the brotherhood of all men presupposed the principle of peaceful human relations, the war in Europe caught many American social reformers, including Nearing, "completely off guard." The war, said John Dewey, "seemed remote and unreal, and the American public reacted with incredulity and exasperation."[1] "War in July 1914," Nearing recalled, "had surprised, horrified, and dismayed me." Including "peace" as an explicit issue in a larger program of social advancement had the immediate consequence of piercing the vague abstractions surrounding the academic-freedom debate, laying bare the issue of the role and ideal of the university in American society. It further had the effect for Nearing of vividly confirming the fact that not only had the wealthy and well-born chosen self-interest over civic responsibility but that the dominant classes were compelling acceptance of their values. In the end, the American experience in the Great War revealed that the United States had "become a nation . . . squandering its rich economic and political heritage in frantic efforts to mark out and destroy all who stood in the way or even questioned its mad race to affluence, conquest, power, and destruction. . . . The significant wreckage resulted in the abandonment of the American dream and the replacement of American idealism."[2]

By the time Nearing had arrived at Toledo in January 1916, the issue of peace was unavoidable. Wilson had announced early the previous November his plans for military expansion, and he had set out the following month in a cross-country "swing around the circle" to sell his preparedness program to the American people. What began for Nearing as a test of his university ideal and the exercise of academic freedom would dissolve under the burden of free speech in the defense of peace.

Nearing might also have been emboldened in his pro-peace advocacy, and in his social activism generally, since he came to Toledo University, in part, because of its commitment to the concept of a "municipal university." Here was an institution of higher learning that stressed the development of responsible citizenship and gave the university a vital role to play in the community.[3] The Toledo *Blade* in an editorial the previous summer had thrown its support behind this new concept in education since it would serve to make experts in the university available to public officeholders. "This is where the Toledo University can develop its great usefulness," claimed the paper: "It can be the curator of experience, saving new municipal officeholders from errors of the old. It can be a storehouse of technical knowledge, to be drawn upon liberally."[4] The university encouraged a public function for its faculty and offered an atmosphere of open inquiry unencumbered by limitations imposed by the business class. Its nine-member board of trustees, appointed by the mayor, consisted of four attorneys, two businessmen, two representatives of labor, and one physician (who was not only sympathetic to Socialist ideas but had been instrumental in bringing Nearing to Toledo). It was, explained Nearing, "a different university": board "members were appointed by the Mayor and confirmed by the City Council, so that the University of Toledo was a much more democratic institution than the institution of Pennsylvania."[5]

Yet the notion of a municipal university was controversial in its novelty. While political pressures cultivated by progressive forces in the city were responsible for the new institution, paid for with tax revenues raised from the citizens of the community, there remained forceful opposition to this educational experiment. From the beginning, advocates for the municipal-university ideal were also supporters of their new nationally prominent professor, so that Nearing's fate became linked to that of the institution. None of this, however, was troubling at first. On the contrary, a local editorial in December heralded Nearing's arrival, claiming that "Toledoans love radicals—if they have the backbone to make their radicalism real, vital and workable"[6]—precisely what Nearing had attempted at Pennsylvania.

▬▬ With a burst of energy, he threw himself into the Toledo community as the embodiment of a public academic. He was first and foremost a teacher, but his teaching was not restricted to the campus. In his first public appearance early in January, he spoke at the First Congregational Church of the Reverend Allen Stockdale, "a liberal clergyman," according to Nearing, "known and respected for his progressive stand on public issues."[7] His subject for the occasion was "The Kingdom of Man." Stressing the role of the church in modern society, he urged not only that the church become a force for denouncing social wrongs but that the congregation should reject any preacher who turned his back on social problems under pressure from the wealthy. "The public," Nearing claimed, "is interested not too much in the Kingdom of God as we hear enough about that, but in the kingdom that will teach it how to live 24 hours a day and about infant mortality and its causes."[8] Nearing's church talk was the beginning of a continuous series of lectures on pressing social issues presented to a full array of community organizations. Furthermore, the Toledo *Blade* opened its pages to Nearing for a series of articles on "The Industrial Problem." And when the Toledo Public Forum was created to discuss important public questions, a university trustee was named its chairman and Nearing its secretary. One *Blade* writer noted that Nearing "stands out as a man with 'punch' in his vitalized American message."[9]

Perhaps his warmest reception came from the Central Labor Union (CLU). He spoke before the CLU often and immediately championed its cause.[10] In a speech before the union in mid-January, he asked the workers to take an interest in the university. For this to happen, of course, the university would have to accommodate itself to the needs of the laboring class, so Nearing offered evening extension classes for the union members. But to bridge fully the distance separating the common man from the university, he proposed that "if organizations find it impossible to come to the university, then perhaps, we can take courses to you." "If a number of glass blowers are interested in a course on philosophy, perhaps we can arrange to offer that course in the headquarters of the local. If Toledo University is to be a municipal university it must meet the needs of the majority of Toledo people, who are the working class."[11]

It was also before the CLU in late January that Nearing attacked Wilson's preparedness plan. Yet it was clear to Nearing that the fight over preparedness was merely a part of an already existing struggle between capital and labor, a battle over the control of public opinion and a test of the university ideal. So when he spoke against military expansion, he asked the workers to "begin in the schools to educate your children for liberty, truth, and justice; then you will have solved the problem of the fight between capital and labor." And while he denounced Wilson as a "tool" of the wealthy, he was more concerned that the schools not become such "tools" themselves. He asked his audience to "take any school board in the country and see who comprises it." "The members are solid businessmen who have been successful in their community and their business. Go through any of the schools and you will not find a teacher who will dare to speak against the present order of sordid gain. They measure life in profits, not in truth, justice and equality of brotherhood."[12]

Just as the dominant classes had defiled the institutions of higher learning and thus threatened democracy by corrupting public opinion as an instrument for social progress, they were now undermining the people's government by promoting militarization to increase profits and protect their investments. The fight against preparedness was a fight for the American mind; at stake was not only the university ideal but the meaning of democracy.[13] It was not long before Nearing spoke at a series of meetings promoted by the Anti-Preparedness Society, and in a speech to a local PTA he asserted that the program of preparedness he supported was not one that emphasized rifles but one that stressed intelligent citizenship.[14]

Preparedness served to focus Nearing's concerns upon an enlightened democracy, and his attention remained fixed foremost on the question of academic freedom and its larger implications. In a lecture given early in March, "The Teacher, the School and the Democracy," he maintained that the country now faced a "crisis" of democracy and that "the duty of the school," as "the guardian of truth," was to teach "the truths of history," "the possibility of man's power over nature," to "give a vital meaning to citizenship" and to "inspire the pupils to rise to those standards of citizenship." The teacher under such circumstances "must teach the truth in the classroom" and "also teach the truth in public" because "he is the logical person to speak with authority on public questions." The university, then, would resemble a "missionary society," "not for any narrow propaganda; not for any special brand of truth, but a missionary society which stands for the very highest, noblest and best things that have ever been thought; that have ever been said and have ever been done."

Central to Nearing's argument was the belief that a key feature of the present age was "the titanic struggle for the control of public opinion." He told his audience that after "the campaign of muckraking and exposure" whereby "public opinion was aroused and the very existence of the plutocracy threatened, . . . then the plutocracy began as never before, to control the channels of public opinion." It was possible, he claimed, to "sum up the whole struggle between plutocracy and democracy in that struggle for the control of public opinion." The principle of academic freedom stood as a bulwark against the control of public opinion; it was simply the ideal of free speech at the place where it was most needed to preserve enlightened citizenship. Hence, he concluded, "the future of the Democracy hangs on the guarantee of free speech."[15]

▬▬ While Nearing continued his campus and public activities unabated—he even spoke to an Intercollegiate Socialist Society chapter in New York on "The New Economics and Socialism"[16]—by March, when a decision was due from the board of trustees on which of the faculty would be retained for the following year, Nearing again found himself at the center of controversy. There were already hints of problems by early February when a *Blade* editorial complained of "his running amuck."[17] Then the Toledo Real Estate Board opened an attack on Nearing, calling for his removal from the university.[18] This was perceived by some as an assault on organized labor and by others as an attack on the structure and purpose of the university. The CLU quickly and vigorously came to his defense, one member declaring that "the owning class is leading every effort to drive Prof. Nearing out of the University because the professor recognizes there is an owning and working class and preaches this to the workers." Pledging to oppose any attempts to "railroad" him out of Toledo, the union member concluded that "it is the time for organized labor to champion the cause of Scott Nearing." The union went on to adopt a motion notifying the mayor and the university trustees that "if Nearing is kicked out, we'll kick you out."[19] Those who headed the university, in a move some suspected was an attempt to avoid a fight over Nearing that might have threatened the institution itself, met in a closed session and rehired him for nine months with a provision that his contract would be renewed for three years. Even as defenders of Nearing and the school seemed to have succeeded in defusing the conflict, all knew the opposition to the institution could emerge again when a tax levy was introduced before the city council.[20]

Suddenly opposition to Nearing arose from another sector of the community. While in Cincinnati early in May, Nearing had stated during a speech that "the phrase 'freedom and justice for all,' as recited by the innocent children" was "humbug" and "that we are putting misstatements in their mouths when we ask them to repeat the words." "The Flag," he declared, "belongs to the capitalists, and why should you fight for the capitalists?" Immediately local patriotic groups assailed Nearing, denouncing his statements as unpatriotic and disloyal. The local chapter of the Sons of the American Revolution launched an investigation and reported to the membership that his speech had done "harm and injustice to the city and country in many ways." They urged "the taking of any steps that may be necessary to secure the discontinuance of such teachings by those occupying places of responsibility and profit in any branch of government." Similarly, the Toledo post of the Grand Army of the Republic resolved that "it seems impossible that the city of Toledo would employ a man as a public educator who makes statements . . . which insult the flag of our country."[21]

In the midst of the furor over his "flag" speech, Nearing spoke before the local chapter of the National Association for the Advancement of Colored People on the anniversary of the birth of John Brown. Welcoming Nearing as a "hero," the president of the chapter asserted that "colored people do not share the opinion of those who denounce Professor Nearing because he may have said that freedom and justice for all do not exist in this country. They have good reason to know that freedom and justice have not been universal." Significantly, Nearing's comments had a deeply personal ring to them as he spoke with the defiance of a martyr. Honoring Brown, he lectured on "The Man and the Message," contending that "all great men have been misunderstood." Yet, "the world needs brave men." He continued: "When the majority of a group have one idea and an individual in the group has another idea, it is inevitable that the individual is going to be licked. John Brown knew it; Jesus knew it. Yet they delivered their message." One suspects that Scott Nearing knew it too.[22]

That same month, the American Association of University Professors met in Philadelphia and reported the results of their investigation of the actions of the trustees at the University of Pennsylvania that led to Nearing's dismissal. Nearing may have sensed his own situation at Toledo enhanced by the finding of "an infringement of freedom of teaching," or the investigation may simply have confirmed his belief that the university was under assault by the dominant class in its attempt to control public opinion. The report probably carried little weight at Toledo University, in part because Nearing was the only member of the association at that institution.[23]

Furthermore, the findings of the organization in no way represented a unified voice on the threats to academic freedom. When Nearing debated the noted economist Edwin R. Seligman of Columbia (who had chaired the AAUP Committee on Academic Freedom and convened a special committee to investigate Nearing's case at the University of Pennsylvania) at the Brooklyn Institute of Arts and Sciences on the question "Have American Universities Academic Freedom?" he faced a professor who had determined that there had been very few deliberate attempts to limit academic freedom. Yet Nearing forcefully disagreed. "I know of scores of University Professors who teach what they do not believe and I want to say that the man who teaches what he does not believe is prostituting his intellect." "If any university professor dared to teach what he believes," he concluded, "and if what he believes is contrary to the economic interests of the university that employs him, he would speedily be dismissed."[24]

As Nearing returned for another summer to Chautauqua, questions of war and peace loomed large in the national political debate since the country was engaged in the turmoil of the election of 1916. After covering his right flank the previous year as an advocate of preparedness, the president had now become fully converted to the political potential of fusing the peace issue to the ideals of progressive democracy.[25] It was a period of vigorous intellectual debate in the United States, a time of vibrant activity by groups and individuals of myriad opinions. At Chautauqua, Nearing gave the first lecture in a symposium on "The Defense of the United States" where, it was claimed, "every possible viewpoint of the preparedness proposition would be presented."[26] In it he reiterated all the themes that had pervaded his economic analyses, but this time he placed the questions of redistribution, morality, American ideals, industrial democracy, and responsible leadership in an international perspective. "The theory of my address on the subject," he said, "was the same as the theory that I had been working out for a number of years."[27]

"We are urged to prepare," he began; "it has become a national shibboleth. The question before the American people is whether we are going to prepare for war or for peace. On that answer rests the argument for militarism or for pacifism." He continued:

I do not believe in Protection, Prosperity and Preparedness, yet I believe I am an American. I believe in the Principles upon which this country was founded, if I read history correctly; liberty, justice, and right. . . . Protection, Prosperity and Preparedness is the morality of the pigsty where you are fattening porkers for winter hams.

So long as capitalists are out to exploit another country it means war sooner or later. . . . The germs of war lurk in international competition for business. . . . War at home or war abroad is due to the same trade diseases. . . . You don't have to go to Berlin to find Prussianism. You need only go to the coal fields of Colorado or West Virginia or to the Steel Mills of Pittsburgh or any other great industrial district. . . . War is the conflict for economic advantages.

If this country would eliminate war we must set a certain standard of intellectualism; clear out special privilege; check economic competition . . . give the working man exactly what he earns; and tell those taking rent, interest, and profit without labor to go to work. Democracy must be extended so that the leaders of industry may be elected as are the political leaders.

The United States faces the duty and the sacred opportunity of bringing about industrial freedom in this twentieth century as it showed to the world a new political freedom a century and a half ago, and thus remove the germs of war.[28]

He asked Chautauquans to consider the question "What is America?" It was not, he told them, "a territory," or "a set of institutions," or even "a geographic boundary." It was "a thought, a concept," "a body of ideals and ideas." Therefore, the preparedness issue should center on the problem of "how are we to defend these ideas and ideals?" While the answer seemed to be that "we will defend the United States with an army," he said, "we should not do this, because democracy means the broadening of life, increase of life." Progress, he maintained, would succeed only "by one of two means, competition or cooperation." Clearly, the process of social advance was as important as its result. Competition meant "rising by means of climbing up on some one else," whereas "cooperation is the means of progress . . . making all of us richer in order that we may each get richer."[29]

His analysis of American militarization appeared that summer in a pamphlet entitled *The Germs of War: A Study in Preparedness*. In it he repeated his conclusion that "the modern war is a business proposition," that the dominant class of economic exploiters had engaged in "a campaign of misrepresentation" to sway public opinion, and that Americans should "begin the work of true preparedness—for life, joy, hope, and the future."[30] He also saw the preparedness campaign as signifying an uncompromising "struggle between militarism and democracy," whereby the country would choose either "militarism," with its "despotism, vested might," "oppression, tyranny and injustice," or democracy's "liberty, equality and fraternity." He advocated a preparedness turned inward, "defending American ideals." "The real question," he claimed, "is whether the most threatening enemies of American ideals are in Berlin or New York." And if Americans were deeply concerned with the defense of their democracy, then why the conflicts at "Lawrence? Why Paterson? Why Little Falls? Why West Virginia? Why Colorado? Why Youngstown, and the copper strikes, and the clothing strikes, and the machinist strikes?" The answer was that "the grinding tyranny of unlimited industrial power" had "aroused the American people to revolt." His examples of social unrest were "not a picture of a democracy, of opportunity, of liberty, and of justice." It was "the story of exploitation, and hopeless, intolerable human degradation." He emphasized that at the root of preparedness were also those things that threatened democracy and that the problem was not with Germany. "Those unspeakable conditions of American life that may be met with in every great center of industry, commerce and finance," he concluded, "are the product of that same system of exploitation that we are now patriotically preparing to defend in its policy of foreign aggression."[31]

Throughout the fall and winter months, Nearing repeated and refined this message in the classroom, in public speeches, and in the press. And he drew mounting criticism for his peace position, no doubt because he remained consistent in his pacifism, even as events seemed to push the country ever closer to intervention in the European conflict. His Chautauqua lectures sparked a controversy in Toledo, since it was reported that he had said in a discussion of preparedness that when he found "a church in Toledo that preaches Christianity, I will attend that church."[32] At an evening lecture course, he told his students that "Americanism must not be confused with material well-being, not even with personal safety" and that it was "a hope, a faith, a conviction, centering in an ideal for the human race."[33]

In a *Blade* article in early January, the president of a local welding and manufacturing company assailed Nearing, claiming that he doubted "the value of socialism as preached by Scott Nearing." Labeling him "Mr. Socialist Agitator," the businessman denounced his tendency "to stir up trouble and class-hatred."[34] Undeterred, Nearing told a peace meeting in February that "there is more danger to national integrity in a $10-a-week wage, than in the Kaiser's army" and that "there is no such thing as a sufficient provocation for war. Should we fight for capitalist traders?"[35]

By early 1917, hopes for peace were quickly slipping away, and anti-preparedness proponents were swiftly shifting their ground as Germany resumed unrestricted submarine warfare. Wilson, in less than a month, put "peace without victory" forever behind him and broke diplomatic relations with Germany. The swift march of events and Wilson's dramatic reversal threw advocates of peace into disarray. Peace groups not only found themselves faced with a new and more desperate situation but also found their ranks quickly thinning. The ones who remained, those whom Merle Curti referred to as "the uncompromising pacifists," discovered that they were no longer a legitimate or tolerated voice in discussions of America's foreign policy.[36]

Opposition to Nearing peaked on March 8, 1917, at a patriotic meeting held at the city's Memorial Hall. The purpose of the rally, sponsored by the Commerce Club, was partly to arouse support for the president's war policy and partly to denounce pacifists. Nearing was singled out as the foremost target for their indignation. A Toledo attorney speaking to the crowd declared that Nearing headed the pacifists, adding, "I don't know who brought this discard [from the University of Pennsylvania] to Toledo, but it is time for the trustees to get rid of him." A local minister, challenging Nearing to "a debate or fight on the question of patriotism," said, "God forgive me, men, if it is un-Christian, but I feel tonight like taking him from the nape of the neck and hanging him to the nearest tree. I am not a Christian tonight. I am just a patriotic citizen of the United States." On his way to a speaking engagement in Detroit the next day, Nearing was asked to give his view of patriotism, to which he replied, "Patriotism is love of one's country which means the people of one's country. It is best shown, therefore, by helping to raise the standard of living and improve social conditions among those people." From Detroit he wired the president of the university, submitting his conditional resignation: "I hereby tender my resignation from the faculty of Toledo University, the same to take effect whenever the board of directors feel that my retention is detrimental to the best interests of the University."[37]

He explained that his action resulted from the fact that he was "hampered in his work by the element clamoring for war between the United States and Germany."[38] More to the point, he would force the university officials to decide specifically whether they accepted his activities, and by extension the ideals of the university. The trustees' actions this time (unlike those at the University of Pennsylvania), could not be excused as some routine matter of disposing of a hired hand. Those who administered the university, and the people of Toledo, would have to decide the nature of that institution. He placed the responsibility in their hands. If they maintained their ideals, they would retain Nearing. If not, he would go. His fate was linked to the university ideal that he believed in so strongly.

In a "letter of explanation" on March 10, Nearing publicly disclosed his convictions:

> My utterances on the question of pacifism and patriotism have led to the storm of criticism that has been directed against me and against the University. . . . I believe in democracy and the brotherhood of all men. No community can endure which ignores the Golden Rule, the basic law of social life—"Each for all, and all for each." . . . I am opposed to [militarization] because I believe that the dearest liberties of democracy must be sacrificed in the process. . . . I oppose militarism because I believe that it stands for the brute in human nature, and that if we adopt it the democracy is doomed. . . . They that take the sword shall perish by the sword. It is only those who are willing to overcome evil with good that attain the full promise of manhood. . . . I revere the government that represents democracy. I honor the flag that stands for liberty and justice. So strong is my

feeling on this point that I resent seeing my government turned over to an irresponsible burocracy [*sic*], just as I resent having the flag, which is the symbol of our democracy, used to cloak special privilege and shameless exploitation.

"Militarism," he explained, "is the madness of the past—dragging us down and destroying us." Instead of succumbing to atavistic irrationalism, "the spirit of brotherhood and good will among men is the voice of the future, calling us to a higher plan of life than humanity has ever known." It was "to that future," no matter what the consequences, he declared, that "I dedicate my life."[39]

The board of trustees responded to Nearing cautiously. On March 11, they met but took no action on his resignation. Instead, they appointed a committee to investigate the charges against Nearing and ascertain "where the true interest of the university lies."[40] They would meet again in a month. In the meantime, Nearing's fate, and that of the university, embroiled Toledo in heated controversy. The *Blade,* earlier a Nearing supporter, claimed in an editorial that attacks on the university were "all due to Scott Nearing," who "may be the Moses his pacifist friends declare him to be, and yet be a heavy burden on the University." Concluding that Nearing would have to be sacrificed in order to save the institution, the paper found that "the University is back where it was seven or eight years ago. . . . As long as Nearing stays at the University, the School will be under fire." To the trustees, the paper advised, "Let him resign." It also counseled that "free speech is not involved. . . . It is the peace and the future of T.U. and the community at stake."[41]

Others disagreed. A mass meeting of more than five hundred supporters of Nearing was held to declare that the real issue in the matter was free speech. Numerous groups, including the Toledo Rationalist Society, petitioned the trustees to retain Nearing. Students at the university attested to Nearing's popularity and held street meetings in addition to circulating their own petition whereby they obtained over fifteen-hundred signatures in support of their beleaguered professor.[42] When the investigating committee questioned two students about Nearing's alleged Socialist teaching, both denied the accusation. Yet Nearing's most forceful backing came from labor: An editorial in the *Union Leader* maintained that "Nearing is fast becoming the idol of workers and has proven himself to be a fighter throughout. . . . He is doing good work and men like him are few and far between."[43] The Machinist Union gathered two thousand signatures protesting acceptance of Nearing's resignation. And a CLU official testified before the board that "a fake issue was being raised by Nearing's opponents to get rid of him" and that "organized labor feels that when a university professor is prevented from expressing his private opinions outside the classroom that it was throttling free speech."[44]

Nearing in the meantime was "pretty well satisfied that I cannot talk peace and retain academic connections, which seems rather anomalous in a democracy."[45] In late March, he spoke at Ann Arbor, Michigan, to between three and four hundred students who turned out to hear his lecture but ran into difficulties securing a place on the campus for him to speak.[46] With the Toledo trustees weighing the evidence of their probe into Nearing's views and activities, he stepped up his activity in one of the few remaining active antiwar organizations, the American Union Against Militarism (AUAM), and began attending meetings to shape its policy.[47]

The AUAM, formed shortly after the beginning of the war, was led by those who explicitly linked the war with a threat to their work for social reform. For the first years of the war, the AUAM campaigned against preparedness and for American neutrality, and grew to such an extent that it became one of the foremost opponents to Wilson's military expansion. Always with a concerned eye on the domestic reform movement, its members increasingly came to view the struggle over preparedness and war as an extension of the familiar domestic battle between special privilege and the people.[48] They came to believe that they faced a "conspiracy of class and press" and that preparedness was fostered by those of "hereditary wealth and influence," the "masters of privilege," the "big employers and monopolists." One leader of the group warned that "such men are using the preparedness campaign as an excuse for preaching the sanctity of American industrial absolutism."[49]

In the AUAM, he found an organization that expressed for the most part his own analysis of dominant class hegemony and the need to link antiwar activism with activism for sweeping social reform. When Roger Baldwin, then a local representative of the AUAM in St. Louis, heard Nearing speak for the union, he recalled his "very sharp and didactic and positive way of expressing himself in an almost strident voice. . . . There was always that ring of self confidence and assertiveness. . . . It was not hard to feel that he was almost a religious figure, almost a preacher."[50]

On April 11, the board rejected Nearing's resignation by a vote of five to four, with two attorneys and two businessmen on the board voting to accept it. Like the board and the community, the investigating committee had been divided in its recommendations.[51] One member had urged that the trustees accept the resignation since "Nearing has pulled the university into his own storm center." Another member supported Nearing, asserting that even though he disagreed with the professor's pacifism, "it is not within the province of our board to say what things should be said or advocated by our idealists or higher educators."[52] By a narrow margin, the board backed Nearing and the principles of academic freedom and free speech. Yet at the same time they protected themselves by adopting a resolution presented by the Citizens Patriotic League, pledging their "unfailing loyalty to the United States and confidence in our government, and . . . enjoin[ing] upon all those who serve the University in any official capacity, the necessity of faithful support of our government."[53]

The reason that questions of loyalty and conformity of opinion dominated the meeting was that four days before the trustees met to decide their action on Nearing's resignation, the United States had declared war on Germany. Resisting intense pressures to consent to American intervention, the AUAM immediately came out against the declaration of war, Wilson's proposals for conscription, the suppression of alleged disloyalty, and taxation to finance the mobilization. In the week following the vote on his resignation, Nearing, as the secretary of the Toledo branch of the AUAM, tried to invigorate the organization with a membership drive. He sent Toledo citizens applications for membership along with a letter stating: "We need the active membership of every person in Toledo who is opposed to militarism in the United States, who believes in the maintenance of free speech and free assemblage, and who is anxious to see that the plutocracy which worked so hard for this war, pays for it now. We want you to work with us against despotism and plutocracy and toward industrial democracy which must be built up in the United States after this war."[54]

Just a week after the trustees had voted not to let Nearing resign, they met again to consider the renewal of contracts for the coming year. Nearing had been told of the agenda for the meeting. A trustee explained to him: "I am attorney for the Toledo Chamber of Commerce. . . . They have directed me to introduce a resolution at the next meeting of the Toledo University trustees, ending your connection with the institution."[55] With two of his supporters absent, a resolution to dismiss Nearing passed by a vote of four to three. Of the entire faculty, only Nearing's services were dispensed with, and the pay of every other professor and employee of the university was increased.[56]

Whereas his firing from the University of Pennsylvania had raised the issue of academic freedom, his severance from Toledo University over opposition to preparedness and American entry into the European war broadened the issue (and removed it from the educational structure) to freedom of speech. By the time his confrontation with these institutions of higher education had ended, he came to view the issue less as free inquiry or constitutional guarantees and more as the freedom afforded to a free people when public opinion was controlled and regulated by a dominant group in society. The destruction of his university ideal focused his thinking on the relationships between politics and the economic realm and between the state and civil society. Because of his concern over the shaping of public opinion, he explicitly raised the question of consent in the democratic process, hence the deeper meaning of American freedom.

▬▬ While he believed as strongly as ever, as he stated in a debate on the question of military training in the schools, that "in the school, of all institutions, we have the opportunity of putting across a kind of training that will prevent future wars,"[57] there was no looking back. Thereafter, he devoted his attention to peace work. At an AUAM meeting in late April, Nearing drafted a letter to be sent to Congress to be introduced as war measures. He stated that the group did not intend to criticize the president and that they had changed their focus from preventing war because the nation was already at war. But he opposed conscription and declared that no profits should be made from the war. The group proposed first that Toledo would open an office to receive voluntary contributions from the wealthy. Second, the government would confiscate all railroads, land, utilities, and other property needed for the war effort. Additionally, no individual would be allowed to receive an income of over $150 a month, and if between the ages of twenty-one and sixty, no one could receive income during the war unless he or she worked to earn it. If the United States was going to war, then it should be a war that would effect a social transformation at home, eliminating class domination and exploitation, instituting an economy based upon earned, and eliminating unearned, income.[58]

Even as he presented these demands, there was nothing to suggest to him that he, or any other advocate of peace in time of war, commanded a hearing any longer. He recalled that even "for weeks before the second of April, freedom of speech had been restricted throughout the United States." With the country at war, "freedom of assemblage was denied in numerous instances," and "halls were refused to citizens when they mentioned the word 'peace.'"[59] Already a Kansas City club had canceled one of his peace talks, and late in April peace groups in Toledo were notified that they would no longer be allowed to rent the hall that they had customarily used in the past. By May, the mayor of Toledo, with some misgiving, barred the AUAM from using the municipal Memorial Hall. When the group did find a meeting place nearby, Nearing was off at a national meeting of the AUAM, but his wife was present and spoke until a small riot broke out and the police intervened. Nearing found that those who had enthusiastically welcomed him to Toledo just sixteen months earlier now closed their doors to him and denounced his activities.[60] In an event symbolic of the change that had occurred, the Reverend Stockdale, whose church Nearing had spoken at in his first public address in the city, used his Sunday sermon of April 29 to tell his congregation that "Scott Nearing should shut up and stay shut up." While there was a time when the issues of war and peace were legitimate topics for discussion, "when the country is thrust into war it is no time to preach disloyalty or to talk dissension. Men who do are guilty of treason. They are traitors."

The following Sunday, Nearing and others stood outside Stockdale's church and distributed a leaflet Nearing had written, "The Right and Duty of Free Speech." It consisted of two parts, the first dealing with religion, in which he asked Stockdale:

> You come before the community as a preacher of the doctrine of Jesus, who spent the active years of his life teaching and practicing the gospel of brotherhood, love and peace. . . . Should Jesus have said no more after the Scribes and Pharisees discovered that he was stirring up the people? Would you have advised Paul to hold his tongue in spite of the light which he saw on the road to Damascus? . . . The point is so clear—so plain! All of the traditions of your

religion proclaim, so eloquently, that a man must speak the faith that is in him. . . . I am one of many who hold this faith,—that good alone will overcome evil; that only love will conquer hate, and that most men will do right if they get half a chance. I believe that the race must be saved through cooperation, fellowship and service.

"I have so much faith in mankind," he exclaimed, "that I desire to see these ideas of brotherhood tried out here and now." If he were to follow Stockdale's advice "and hold my peace, I should stand before the world as a coward, and before my conscience as a moral prostitute."

The second half of his leaflet dealt with the question of democracy. "Look at the matter from another side," he implored: "As a citizen of a democracy, I see things happening which, I believe, threaten the foundation of the Republic. I have reached the conclusion that we are running rapidly toward militarism and that militarism is social suicide. . . . I am in a minority. It is still my right to raise the issue. Nay, more, it is my social duty to use the knowledge that I have acquired at public expense to defend the institution of democracy. . . . Democracy rests on free discussion." In sum, "the builders of your religion recognized the moral obligations to speak out," and "the founders of the American Republic insisted upon the civic necessity of public discussion."[61]

After his dismissal from Toledo, and in striking contrast to the aftermath of his firing from the University of Pennsylvania, few came to his aid or defended the principles of academic freedom and free speech. This time, the AAUP did not investigate his case. In part this was because, as one historian has written, "as a group American professors were among the most enthusiastic supporters of the war."[62]

Only a week after the United States entered the war, the editors of the *New Republic,* in an attempt to answer the question "Who willed American participation," arrived at the conclusion that intellectuals, and academics in particular, had led the country into the conflict. Over twenty cases were reported of professors whose termination was related to their lack of support for the war, including not only Nearing, but, as noted early, Patten.[63] The AAUP remained silent until 1918 when it issued its "Report of the Committee on Academic Freedom in Wartime," claiming that war "gives rise to new problems concerning the rights and obligations of free speech."[64] Significantly, the AAUP retreated from its principled 1915 report on academic freedom to such an extent that the editors of the *Nation* maintained that the association had not only withdrawn from its initial defense of academic freedom but that its report "jeopardizes the very concept of a university."[65]

In wartime, the AAUP decided, professors' views could legitimately justify their termination, and in fact, that academics were bound by special restrictions beyond those imposed on ordinary citizens by the state. And whereas the earlier report enunciated a principle of professional review, the association now endorsed public prosecution and supervision by laymen.[66]

Coming from an organization entrusted to defend professors and uphold standards of professional conduct and academic ideals, it was a mighty capitulation. "The most ardent adherents of the warlords," wrote Nearing to a friend, "are the preachers + the professors."[67]

The war, Nearing acknowledged, brought on "catastrophic changes in my life."[68] All he had believed in so deeply was thrown into question. In his youth, he recalled in his autobiography, he had been "loyal to the United States, to its articles of faith . . . loyal to its purposes and to its institutions." The United States had "been a progressive, creative force in the world." "Not until the preparedness campaign," he wrote, "and the United States entrance into the European war in 1917, did I seriously question the American or Western way of life."[69] His belief in the free discussion of ideas as the cornerstone of an enlightened democracy dissolved in disenchantment as the classrooms, the public forums, the church pulpits, open-air meetings, lectures, and the popular press were closed to him and others who dissented from the dominant beliefs.

In 1917, Macmillan, his publisher for nine years, dropped him from its publications list and remaindered his books. And while he went to Chautauqua that summer, it would be the last time he would be invited to lecture there. What had been a open "era of self-criticism" was now "cut short by the 1914–1918 war."[70] He was "on my own, in deep water, swimming against a tide of conformity, intolerance, fear, hate, and organized violence."[71] He realized that it

> was not too late to turn back, confess the error of my ways, ask pardon for past misdeeds, join the war party, whoop it up for the allies, buy liberty bonds and plunge with the herd into the maelstrom of the European War. Or I could do what some of my associates eventually did when they went to Washington and took government jobs, hoping from their privileged positions to push social reforms in which they were interested.

He wondered "what had happened" to the "formula" of his university ideal—to "seek out the facts, teach them to the rising generation, build them into the life of the community." War, he found "tore the formula to bits." "Under intolerable war pressure," he saw that "American liberals and radicals were bending, conforming, rationalizing, surrendering." "The United States of my youth," he despaired, "was slipping from under my feet and vanishing from my sight."[72]

# The Great Betrayal

## Part Three

# For Democracy and Peace

## Chapter 9

"THE war or American promise—one must choose. One cannot be interested in both."[1] This severe but unavoidable destiny of antithetical consequences, wrote Randolph Bourne, resulted because the war produced a situation requiring profound moral and intellectual choices. When faced with these alternatives, America was led to war, and Nearing sided with American promise. He understood that "war drags human beings from their tasks of building and improving." "Peace, progress, prosperity . . . inquiry, education, legislation, reconstruction, improvement betterment. . . . Now in the Era of the Great War, all such ideas were obsolete."[2] As the war precipitated difficult choices, it also sharpened analysis.

The key question focused on why America was at war, why she had squandered her promise. The answer for Nearing was that the dominant classes in American society had abandoned their cultural role and the ideals of their heritage, had thrust their values on the citizenry through the control of public institutions, and had corrupted the country's democratic ideals. America was at war because of a great betrayal. It all came down to "organized mendacity." "The mighty ones—the masters in the land—the favored, trusted leaders of American public opinion," he declared, had "turned militaristic." "Consciously, deliberately, with premeditation and malice aforethought, they lied to us! The shepherds of the flock, the bishops of men's souls, the learned ones, the trusted ones . . . they betrayed us. . . . We had trusted them all and most of them betrayed us."[3]

America was at war because of an economic system that had put enormous wealth and power into the hands of a privileged few, or in the political and social vernacular of the times, the plutocracy. By the "American plutocracy," Nearing "meant the small group of men who exercise the authority in affairs of economic, social and other forms of American life."[4] The "great menace to the liberties of the American people," he claimed, came from "the growing power of the plutocracy, the growing power it was gaining through the war."[5] The war was, at bottom, "a business proposition."[6]

The economic system of industrial capitalism had released "a great competitive struggle from which the final appeal was the appeal to arms."[7] Through international conflict, "the American Exploiters are to continue their system of exploitation; they are to take the surplus secured by this exploitation."[8] The war was a situation with "wider implications": it was an opportunity for the plutocracy to strengthen its position and the economic system through which it secured its power. Nearing believed "that the members of the capitalist class as a rule would prefer war to the disestablishment of capitalism."[9] Thus, he "tried to show how the economic control of the country, of the resources, and of American life is manifesting itself all through the social structure."[10]

Only in understanding this hegemonic control would it be possible to explain why the country entered the war and why the United States had descended "into a condition of social disorganization which today approaches economic anarchy and social ruin." An economic system that allowed for the "complete domination by big business of American public life"[11] created the circumstances

> so that the small group of people in the United States who own the essential jobs, resources, transportation, manufacturing, financing and merchandising, the small group which owns the essential jobs owns the jobs of the majority, own the product and own the surplus created by industry. Now, given [their] ownership and the economic means of livelihood, the rest naturally follows: That is, the control by the plutocracy of the machinery of society. For example, the newspapers depend on their advertising, the wealth owners advertise in the newspapers and therefore the newspapers are likely to do what the wealth owners want done. . . . That is not bribery, that is not corruption, it is just a pervasive influence that always goes out, goes forth and controls, it is the influence that naturally comes from those circumstances.[12]

This hegemonic control was "in part instinctive and unorganized, and in part it is intelligent and organized." Among the privileged in society there was "an instinctive cohesion of wealth," a "class consciousness" expressed in "economic control through ownership and emotional control through sympathy and intellectual control through conscious organizations." Yet Nearing believed that "most of this influence is unconscious influence—and you get newspaper men, lawyers, preachers, all of what we call the professional class, reflecting the spirit of control."[13] The means through which this process of influence and control succeeded could be "summed up in one word, 'Acquiescence.'"[14] The individual consented "automatically, instinctively or semiconsciously,—but he does it."[15] No matter the precise means by which it was exerted, the result was that "this control was very complete." It had "been extended to include newspapers, colleges, churches, and other forces that shape public opinion, as well as the machinery of government."[16]

Nearing's analysis emerged naturally out of his own experience of confronting university administrators, painfully revealing the relation between culture and power in American society. At Pennsylvania and Toledo, he discovered that cultural control transcended the bounds of ownership and nonownership, of religious and ideological ties; it derived nonetheless from distinctive economic interests and control over the society's predominant means of production. He saw a class interest coalesce that subordinated other, potentially conflicting interests.[17] Now, with the war, the control by the plutocracy of the instruments of the state—"the machinery of government"— was perhaps most damaging to democracy. For the plutocrats, wrote Nearing, "their public institution is the capitalist state, and their rule is perpetuated by the manipulation of its machinery."[18]

This analysis, that "the business interests, through their control of the economic surplus have dominated the commissions and have used the machinery of the political state as the instrument for further exploiting ventures,"[19] was shared by others and captured in Bourne's classic statement that "war is the health of the state."[20] Thus, wrote Nearing, "militarism and democracy are contradictory terms. Militarism stifles democracy." "The citizens of democratic America were forced into war without their consent."[21] The state, as such, was not democratic, but was used by the ruling class to subvert democracy and protect vested interests. The war and the control of the state were rooted in a problem of economic control.

If America was to achieve her promise, if the country was to live up to its political creed and offer people true freedom, this stranglehold of economic control would have to be broken. A society built on exploitation and competition and dominated by a minority of wealthy privileged individuals meant that "the economic conditions of life determine all the conditions of life."[22] Under the hegemony of the plutocracy there remained "the simple fact of economic determinism—the influence of the livelihood struggle upon the conduct of individuals and society."[23] Because he saw that "economic forces are fundamental," he believed "that economic change must precede, or at least accompany every form of social change."[24] He was not concerned with economic determinism in a Marxian sense of historic inevitability; rather, he saw the "economic control, economic restriction, economic coercion"[25] of the plutocracy and wanted to eliminate it.

While he acknowledged that "the economic factor is usually the major factor in controlling public affairs," he realized that "economic emancipation does not include all aspects of freedom" and that "many other chains remain to be broken." The problem was that "the man fighting for bread has little time to 'turn his eyes up to the eternal stars.' The western cult of 'efficiency' makes no allowance for philosophical propensities." He hoped that "men everywhere may be able to participate in that unending search after love, beauty, justice, truth—the highest of which humanity is capable"—and be given "the opportunity to have a well made body, an enlightened mind and a soul eager to embrace the glad, radiant beautiful message of the life-spirit."[26] "All these things lie outside the realm of economics, yet none of them is possible for the mass of mankind until there is established a system of economic life that will provide the necessaries upon which physical health depends, together with an amount of leisure sufficient to enable a generation to find itself."[27]

Had "the mighty ones—the masters of the land"—been faithful to their trust, they would have led their fellow men into a future of American promise and true freedom. Instead, according to Nearing, through treachery, fraud, and deception they had led the country astray, amassed great wealth through exploitation, and placed the people in a situation of "economic slavery." As for the common man, "in order to get a living he throws aside freedom and culture and enters the shop. . . . So thoroughgoing has been the deadening influence of this economic order on men's thinking, that the workers themselves accept, as a matter of course, full warehouse on the one hand and starvation on the other."[28] Even before the plutocrats looked to advance their economic control through the war, they had committed a great betrayal. But the war tended to clear away obstructions and clarify one's view, and in times of war, as Bourne said, one must choose. Nearing chose not to collaborate with the betrayal or consent to the plutocracy's rule.

Through the Socialist party, the People's Council of America for Democracy and Peace, and other antiwar groups, he took up the fight for "liberty, justice, freedom, leisure, culture" and went into opposition to the coercive control of the dominant class. In doing so, he broke ranks with his own class, uprooting himself from the cultural soil he once shared with the masters. And because of his dissent, he found himself the target of those who tried to enforce wartime conformity in the name of patriotism, loyalty, and Americanism. The choice was clear: "Behind modern wars," he contended, "lies the predatory power of vested interest and the plutocratic authority against which the American people must wage their fight for liberty."[29] While "the war has defined the issue sharply, the same thing happened during peace times. . . . On the one side are the American people; on the other side are the American profiteers."[30]

▬ Not only did the country face a national crisis, but for the intellectuals there arose a crisis of social philosophy. Among those who championed the liberal values of progressivism there had been widespread acceptance of the philosophy of pragmatism with its open choices, its focus on means and ends, and its method of determining social values through their consequences once tested in experience. Nearing too, as discussed earlier, had flirted with this Progressive social philosophy. As Jane Addams noted, "Every student of our time had become more or less a disciple of pragmatism."[31] When the great teacher of this instrumental philosophy, John Dewey, found cause to support America's war effort on pragmatic grounds, many reformers were dumbstruck. To Joseph Freeman, a student of Dewey's at Columbia, it seemed terribly incongruous that Dewey "signed a declaration of 'absolute and unconditional loyalty' to the government in its war against Germany, although as a pragmatist he professionally disavowed the absolute and the unconditional."[32] For someone like Randolph Bourne, who became Dewey's most scathing critic, his idol's position on the war suggested "a slackening of his thought" and "the inadequacy of pragmatism as a philosophy of life in this emergency."[33]

For Nearing, the adequacy of pragmatism lay in strict adherence to its method. The critical dilemma was that it had to resist absolutes while arriving at principles to guide action. Those vital principles became a combination of pragmatic results and religious moral virtues. Paradoxically, pragmatism would work if it rejected the absolutes imposed by militarism and war while rigidly adhering to values of choice and cooperation. Jane Addams also faced this dilemma of appearing intransigent while trying to rescue nondogmatic philosophy for the pacifists. "On the subject of war," she found herself "forced into an unequivocal position." And when the pacifists stood firmly for principles of peace, she explained, "we slowly became aware that our affirmation was regarded as pure dogma. We were thrust into the position of the doctrinaire, . . . although, had we been permitted, we might have cited both historic and scientific tests of our so-called doctrine of peace."[34]

The crisis pacifism caused for pragmatism was central to the crisis of ideas in this period. Many had to resolve the dilemma of social philosophy posed by the war silently, while a few key thinkers construed pragmatism to support opposing positions on the war. Like most, Nearing did not enter directly into this debate. Yet his resolution of the crisis of pragmatism is better understood if the fundamentals of the opposing arguments are briefly explored.

Dewey was not in any sense a militarist, and in the years before the United States entered into the war, he found no cause for devising a pragmatic justification for armed conflict. When Wilson asked Congress to declare war, Dewey, like others, faced an untenable set of alternatives. He recorded that an "immense moral wrench involved our passage from friendly neutrality to participation in war."[35] Furthermore, even as he supported the war effort, he lamented the repression of free discussion, denouncing the demands for "conscription of thought."[36] Yet it was pacifism more than anything else that forced Dewey to lay his philosophy on the line. He felt that "the pacifists wasted rather than invested their potentialities when they turned so vigorously to opposing entrance into a war which was already all but universal, instead of using their energies to form, at a plastic juncture, the conditions and objects of our entrance." Pragmatism had to be realistic, claimed Dewey, and in order to be effective in shaping reality, it had to resist the dogma of pacifist resistance and make itself available to shaping the forces of change. "Because the professional pacifists were committed to the idea that anything was better than our getting into the war," he contended, "their interest in general international reorganization had no expression."[37]

In answering Dewey, Randolph Bourne drew upon a distinction between "realistic pragmatists" and "genuine pragmatists."[38] Dewey was of the former group; the latter classification was reserved for those who opposed the war on the basis of the pragmatic fundamental of choice. Bourne acknowledged that Dewey's

> argument follows the well-known lines of his instrumental use of intelligence for the realization of conscious social purpose. The conscience, he implies, if balked by an unpleasant situation, is futile unless it attaches itself to forces moving in another, and more desireable, direction. Dissatisfied with the given means or ends, one chooses another alternative, either a new end to which the means may be shaped, or a new means to effect the desired end.[39]

The problem was that "in applying his theory to the war situation," Dewey ignored "the fact that it is exactly in war that alternatives are rigorously limited. Is not war perhaps the one social absolute, the one situation where the choice of ends ceases to function?"[40] Again and again, Bourne would point to the fact that with war one "lives no longer with a choice of alternatives": "Once you accept war, there is no choice but to be shoved along the line of inevitable with which war is organically bound up. . . . War is just that absolute situation which is its own end and its own means, and which speedily outstrips the power of intelligence and creative control. . . . You have precipitated an absolute where mastery is a mockery."[41]

"Nothing is so disagreeable to the pragmatic mind," wrote Bourne, "as any kind of absolute." But war was "as near an absolute, coercive social situation as it is possible to fall into."[42] Since the pacifists—"they are genuine pragmatists and they fear any kind of absolute"[43]—who "challenge the entire force of the nation" were "automatically crushed out," this meant that "in wartime, one's pragmatic conscience moves in a vacuum."[44] The realistic pragmatists, Bourne suggested, "seem to have forgotten that the real enemy is War rather than Imperial Germany."[45] The absolute of war also meant that "we are passing out of an era when it was good form to be a dissenter," when "one made no pretense to thinking unless they were open-minded, hospitable to heresies."[46] Pragmatism, when defiled in the name of war, said Bourne, "no longer works" because "the contrast between the idea that creative intelligence has free functioning in wartime, and the facts of the inexorable situation" is "too glaring." He was left wondering "why this philosophy which has no place for the inexorable should have adjusted itself so easily to the inexorable of war."[47]

Nearing also had to grapple with this crisis of social philosophy. In the first instance, what Bourne called the "inexorable of war" instituted aggressive nationalism, precluding the ideal alternative of community cooperation and human brotherhood. Nearing believed that "a comprehension of any social theory" involved "a reasonable freedom from prejudice and preconception,—that is, an open mind."[48] He also recognized the unifying nature of war, yet he wanted fellowship instead of national hatred and stated, "Is it not a more difficult and more desireable thing that all Americans should put partisan prepossessions aside and draw together for successful prosecution of peace."[49] But "the conditions which demand this common action for the common good," he asserted, were contradicted by war and "not confined to war times." The dogma of militarism was found in "oppression, tyranny, and injustice . . . despotism, vested might." "The militarized nation," he wrote, "forgets 'liberty,' 'equality,' 'justice,' and 'fraternity.'" And the absolute of war would destroy the values of progress, since "the conflict between militarism and democracy is a conflict to the death."[50]

"Democracy," Nearing contended, "signifies free choice."[51] Echoing Bourne's assertion that the problem was not some distant nation but war itself, Nearing wrote: "Worse than the self-destructiveness of militarism is its denial of everything held most precious by the disciples of democracy." He envisioned "a world made safe for democracy" through "effective opposition to [its] real enemies,—the plutocracy in any land."[52] The absolute of war prevented the possibility of a democracy of social cooperation. "Militarism is the sway of organized might," Nearing explained, while "democracy is the cooperative activity of fellowship and brotherhood."[53]

Equally disturbing was the issue of conscription, which seemed to symbolize the negation of pragmatic reliance on choice. As Dewey described it, "Conscription did not originate the crisis in moral experience, but it brought it acutely to a focus."[54] Free will and voluntarism, creative intelligence guiding social progress—all this lay wasted by "established involuntary servitude."

> The free people who accept militarism accept the death warrant of their most precious liberties. . . . There is no longer any choice. All of the people—the peace-men and war-men alike, must prepare for war. . . . A democracy expects that its citizens will act only after mature consideration and discussion. The very spirit of militarism makes both consideration and discussion impossible. . . . The soldier does not think, nor does he choose—he obeys.[55]

This "conscription of conscience" was "a menace to fundamental democratic life," creating "a three-fold slavery. First of all, it is slavery of the body; again, it means slavery of the mind, and in the third place, it involves the slavery of the soul."[56]

How could this pacifist resolve the crisis of pragmatism? His approach was twofold. Pragmatism provided an important method for achieving social progress through experiments in social experience judged by their consequences. Whether an experiment succeeded, according to Nearing, was determined by the increase in individual freedom. Thus, "the history of social institutions," he said, "is a history of social experiment—of community progress through trial and error."[57] Progress was achieved "whenever in a community changes are made that increase enlightenment," "that increase the freedom of the individual. . . . Any change which enlarges man's vision of life—which enables him to broaden or deepen his life experience—is 'social progress.' "[58]

Yet even though "we may judge social activity in relation to the freedom it affords for the development of the individual," he found this method lacking a "system of values,"[59] "some system of values" with which one could "measure the importance of events and of courses of action."[60] Effective pragmatism needed certain values—as became apparent in wartime, the values of cooperation and choice—in order to advance freedom. It could operate within certain values, but it could not create those values; it was a philosophy that told men what they could do but not what they should do. What was missing in social philosophy was a "synthetic concept," a "view of the whole of life."[61]

In Nearing's mind, any useful social philosophy needed prerequisite moral values. Nearing found these moral values in religion, although less and less in Christianity alone. Even though Roger Baldwin noted that Nearing "was through with organized religion although he hung on to nominal Christianity until the world war," Rexford Tugwell recalled that at Chautauqua in the summer of 1917, "Scott told me with a wry smile, that in an assembly dominated by preachers and actually organized for the advancement of Sunday School teaching, he, not a professing Christian at all, was by now the only defender of such an obvious Christian principle as pacifism."[62] He searched widely for a system of values, turning to Eastern religions, spiritualism, virtually any form of cosmic religiosity; he claimed that "the most important single activity of man is the time he spends in contemplation of the cosmos, whatever form that contemplation might take."[63]

Religion in the form of ethics would provide moral values for progressive social philosophy. "If you take the teachings of any of the great, ethical leaders of the world," he explained, "and put them into practice, they would make for social progress."[64] Pragmatism alone simply lacked the moral values to make it a synthetic philosophy. When Dewey died in 1952, Nearing recalled that

life for Dewey was practice. There were no principles, only tentative generalizations. Life was fragmented into trial and error experiments. There was no recognizable whole. What concerned humans was the parts—the day to day problems.

An acquisitive, competitive life-pattern, reaching its optimum expansion between 1870 and 1910, needed this pragmatic philosophy to justify its shoddy, sterile opportunism. William James in the previous generation and John Dewey in the present supplied the philosophical justification for dealing with every problem by itself and the Devil take principle.[65]

According to Nearing's analysis, cultural control by the plutocracy had extended to social philosophy itself, and pragmatism had simply accommodated the demands of the dominant values. Between social science and religion, Nearing steered a narrow course. He bowed to pragmatism, believing that "means and ends are inescapable aspects of every human enterprize," yet he wanted to rescue pragmatism with moral values: "If we succeed in elevating the ethical and moral level . . . we will have scored an important success at the outset. . . . At any given moment it is the ethical and moral standards enunciated and followed by the elements that compose the body social which determines ethical and moral levels upon which society operates."[66]

━━ The "plutocratic class," those "who control community affairs because they own property,"[67] had engaged in a struggle to win the minds of Americans through a kind of indoctrination achieved by means of deception. In one instance, the key ideas of pragmatism had fallen to distortion, and vital social philosophy became mere "opportunism," the ruling class using propaganda to sway public opinion in support of its interests. Before the war, Nearing had opposed any manipulation of truth, declaring that he was "not a propagandist, if by propaganda" one "means narrowness, sectarianism, dogmatism."[68] Yet, by mid-1917, it became clear to him that war propaganda and government repression were preventing public discussion of peace proposals.[69] The necessity to counter the one-sided views of the plutocracy led Nearing to advocate oppositional propaganda. The "great task of reaching the masses of the people" could be achieved either "through organization or through propaganda . . . usually combined in some degree." The most potent "avenues of propaganda" were "political organizations" and "propaganda organizations" through which "information will be passed most rapidly."[70]

He believed that "there must be inaugurated a widespread propaganda the object of which will be to get the facts and their implications to the people: the facts regarding the disintegration of the present order; regarding the possibilities of a new society; regarding the next steps that are necessary for its establishment."[71] When he joined antiwar groups, it was for "propaganda, organized for the discussion of public policies."[72] "Propaganda," he claimed, "to be effective, must consist of a well-ordered summary of facts . . . put in a form that can be easily understood by the average man, and distributed in such a manner that it will reach the public."[73] To maintain an uncorrupted public opinion, he would have to counter the influence of the dominant class. The propaganda he advocated, like that of the plutocracy, was unmistakably one-sided, but it was intended to achieve just the opposite effect: he wanted to tell the public all of what they were not being told by the ruling class. "The main point of view," he explained, "that I believed in above all other things" was "the truth. That is, I believed that most of the people were not getting the truth and I believed . . . they should have the entire truth which was not being set forth and stated to them." It was his "responsibility, to tell them the truth" by "presenting one side of the general situation."[74]

Nearing advocated a propaganda that consisted of a "type of coercive signalling." In "our age of high tension," he said, "we have to interfere, and to coerce [the common citizen], and to impose our ideas upon him." For example, he believed that "the country should propagandize against war as it should against disease and against poverty." In a world where the free flow of ideas was restricted and the public mind controlled by a "plutocratic class," Nearing contended that "propaganda has a value in education." "The kind of independent mind that I should like developed," he stated, "is not the isolated mind, but the mind that can meet the questions which press for some kind of answer."[75] Whereas he advocated propaganda not to impose dogma but for enlightenment, the hollow logic he applied could just as easily be used to justify the plutocratic distortions he criticized.

Convinced of the need to counter the ideas of the ruling class through oppositional propaganda, Nearing began to ally himself with groups opposed to the war. One such political organization was the Socialist party. On April 7, 1917, in a planned meeting, the Socialist party met in an emergency convention in St. Louis to formulate a war program. Even though the United States had already entered the war, an overwhelming majority of the delegates supported opposition to the war and the statement that the congressional declaration of war was "a crime against the people of the United States." The majority report pledged "unalterable opposition" to the war, maintaining that it was a capitalist's war and would crush democracy. The Socialists' plan for action included public opposition to the war, opposition to conscription and restrictions on freedom of speech and the press, "consistent propaganda against military training and militaristic teaching in the public schools," "widespread educational propaganda to enlighten the masses as to the true relationship between capitalism and war," and international working-class solidarity, among other demands.[76]

While not yet a member of the party, Nearing joined in a "symposium" published in the April–May issue of the *Intercollegiate Socialist* on "Socialists and the problem of war." When asked whether Socialists and others should oppose entrance into any international wars, he replied, "I believe all socially minded people should oppose entrance into war because war is probably the most disintegrating of all social forces. The best substitute for war that I know of is economic and social justice, intra-national as well as international." As for whether opposition should continue, even after the country had declared war, Nearing evoked the spirit of Thoreau and the "duty of civil disobedience," maintaining that Socialists should "refuse consistently to go into something in which they do not believe." As for constructive measures Socialists should pursue in wartime, he proposed that they "fight for free speech, free press, and other forms of civil liberty." "Fundamentally," he contended, "they should keep constantly in mind the necessity for social and economic readjustment which will make war impossible."[77]

Although Nearing was clearly sympathetic to the antiwar position of the

Socialist party, as he had been to its economic program, he hesitated to join its ranks. He shied away from party affiliation because he believed that party dogma and Socialist doctrine would interfere with the open-ended inquiry of his teaching and economic study and he "did not want to be a teacher with a doctrine, unable or unwilling to face new situations." It was for this reason that he "had joined no political party, because as a student and teacher I wanted to follow where the search for truth led."[78] But when he reached the conclusion that the truth was inhibited by the plutocracy and could be presented only through educational propaganda, the party became an attractive organization for promoting countervailing ideas. On July 1, 1917, he joined the Socialist party, explaining that he "did not join before that time because I taught school up to that time and I believed that a teacher should not be a propagandist."[79] With the country at war and the public culture controlled by a ruling class, he now seemed to propound the contradictory belief that the teacher of truth had to undertake dutifully the necessary evil of propaganda.

Of course, joining the party meant more than propaganda for the sake of resistance. It was a way for Nearing to espouse and promote long-held beliefs and values. He recalled that it was for "ethical" reasons that he "became a socialist in order to plan and work for a cooperative social pattern that will give maximum opportunity for human life at its most constructive and creative levels."[80] He thought of the party as a moral force; he was not interested in theory and political strategy but conceived of the party in ethical and cultural terms, as a way to impart alternative values. The reason he became a Socialist, he explained, was because he was interested "in destroying . . . economic division lines. . . . I believe that the only way to destroy these barriers and make international life a reality [is] to give to those who work the full product of their labor." Therefore, "as a socialist," he said, "I approve of the confiscation of all forms of property which enables one man to live without work on another man's labor, and that includes the liberty loan or any other form of bonded indebtedness." As a Socialist, he was first of all, "an internationalist."

> That is, I believe in the brotherhood of all men. In the language of the Declaration of Independence, I believe that all men are created equal, and that they have certain rights to life, liberty, and the pursuit of happiness. . . . I believe in the Brotherhood of Man.[81]

As the party of organized antiwar opposition, the Socialist party became for Nearing the embodiment of nondoctrinaire political theory able to promote counterhegemonic moral and social values.

■■■ Following America's entry into the war, Nearing threw his support behind the Socialist party, but he gave most of his energies to another antiwar propaganda organization, the People's Council for Democracy and Peace, a group that emerged during the summer of 1917 as the most prominent antiwar force in the country. Early in May, Nearing had signed a call for the First

American Conference for Democracy and the Terms of Peace.[82] It was at a huge Madison Square Garden rally launched by the conference that the People's Council was conceived. Speaking at the assembly, the pacifist Rebecca Shelley claimed that Congress in taking the American people to war without their consent ceased to represent the will of the people; therefore, it was time for the American people to form a more democratic government. The function of the council, she explained, "would be to work for the repeal of the Conscription Law, to combat all violations of the Constitutional Rights of citizens, to urge an early and democratic peace on the terms announced by the Russian government, and to let the American people know that there is a definitely constituted body through which the democratic forces of the country can express themselves."[83]

Those who enthusiastically endorsed and organized the People's Council formed a broad spectrum of the Left. They were predominantly moderate socialists, antiwar Progressives, and pacifists. Joseph Freeman, who joined the People's Council, reported that "Socialists, wobblies, anarchists, liberals and pacifists of every kind crowded into the old Madison Square Garden."[84] A resolution passed at the conference provided for an organizing committee to be formed "to organize a permanent delegated People's Council."[85] A Second Conference on Democracy and the Terms of Peace was held early in July in Chicago, preparing for a third conference in early September to call together officially the First Constituent Assembly of the People's Council.[86]

Nearing had joined the organizing movement early. Before the United States had entered the war, he "believed that we should keep out of it. After we got into the war, I believed that we should get out of it with as little damage as possible."[87] Immediately he prepared an outline for the organization of the council, envisioning it as a national organization bringing together all the antiwar forces in the country and cooperating closely with the Socialist party.[88] "There were three different purposes," he explained: "the first one was to secure a statement of peace terms, of war aims; the second was to preserve civil liberties; the third, was to safeguard economic standards and rights."[89] "The theory of the People's Council as I understood it was that the Liberal and Radical elements of the country should get together and express their opinions in coherent form just as the banking and business houses of the country had gotten together in the preparedness campaign and expressed their point of view."[90] Later that year, speaking at St. John's Evangelical Church in Louisville, Kentucky, Nearing told his audience:

> We would like to see the time when every city in the United States, the labor unions, the Socialist locals, the I.W.W. organizations, the single taxers, and every other group who are working for fundamental democracy, will be represented on a central council, a local people's council of delegates from these different groups, discussing the local problems, the national and international problems, running in open forum, maintaining a paper, keeping in touch with the national organization and with the other organizations throughout the coun-

try. We look to build upon a method by which the democracy can convene together just as the plutocracy get together through its chambers of commerce. We look to establish a common meeting ground, a common basis, a common clearinghouse for the democracy of the country. We would like to bring the forces of democracy in America into a unit they have never known before so that our political and economic rights may be reasserted and reestablished and maintained.[91]

The People's Council was not simply an antiwar organization. It was an attempt to put into practice an alternative form of democratic government, a deliberate effort to counter the economic and political organization of the plutocracy in the name of conserving and promoting America's democratic heritage. To succeed, it would first have to struggle for the mind of America, against the plutocracy's control of public opinion. The primary purpose of the People's Council, according to Nearing, was "propaganda." It was "organized for the discussion of public policies."[92]

Even though the demands for peace, protection of American liberties, and economic justice were moderate proposals, and despite the fact that the composition of the movement was complex, the People's Council increasingly came to be seen as a Socialist organization. Ostensibly it was not part of the Socialist party. Efforts were made to emphasize that membership in the council did not commit anyone to socialism.[93] Even Nearing was apparently concerned that the openness of the People's Council could not be curtailed by any doctrine. When he became chairman of the organization, he accepted only on the understanding that the council would work for "industrial democracy." When asked if that meant socialism, he replied, "No."[94] A council bulletin stated that

> The People's Council has no selfish interests to serve. It is not a Socialist movement as some claim. It is not a labor movement. It is not the organization or organ of any class or classes of citizens. . . . We are trying to help workingmen and save the plutocratic rich from the consequences of their own folly in amassing great fortunes which . . . endanger the free institutions of their country.[95]

Yet there was no denying that leaders of the Socialist party were influential in the People's Council. Roger Baldwin, who served on the council's organizing board, described it "as essentially the anti-war agency of the Socialist Party, a united front that embraced all the left."[96] The Socialists, he claimed, "were the most daring of the anti-war crowd; they dominated the People's Council; it was not officially socialistic but the party furnished most of the steam."[97] It was, in fact, the overwhelming similarities between the Socialist party's antiwar program and the People's Council's demands that appealed to Nearing because of their counterhegemonic possibilities.

One aspect of the People's Council that differed from the policies of the Socialist party and went to the heart of the council idea, pushing the People's

Council further to the left of the party, was its emphasis on plans for restructuring society based on the Russian Workingman's Councils that emerged with the February Revolution. In Russia, the overthrow of the Czar left the country essentially without central government but with a provisional government and the Petrograd Soviet of Workers' and Soldiers' Deputies, which called upon workers and soldiers to select delegates to the Soviet. Pro-war liberals reviewed the events in Russia with enthusiasm since they seemed to legitimize Wilson's view that America was fighting a war that would end autocracy and make the world safe for democracy. But the antiwar Left focused primarily on the Petrograd Soviet, the radical counterpart to the provisional government, and secondly upon its war aims; the Soviet became a model of pure democracy and peace.[98] Joseph Freeman recalled that "we looked upon Russia as the earth's most crucial area. That country had taken socialism out of books, pamphlets and meeting halls and was trying it out in real life."[99] The Soviet's call for quick negotiated peace on liberal terms was exactly what the American antiwar forces had been demanding of the U.S. government. For those like Randolph Bourne who suspected that America had gone to war for profits and not to advance democracy and peace, the question raised was whether "it is the political democracy of a plutocratic America that we are fighting for, or . . . the social democracy of the new Russia?"[100]

For those who formed the People's Council, the Russian Revolution became a forceful inspiration and the Petrograd Soviet a model for their organization.[101] They "hoped that our People's Council will voice the peace will of America as unmistakably and effectively as the council of the workingmans' and soldiers' delegates is speaking for Russia."[102] Russia became a symbol of what they wanted in America; it reinforced the notion that the war resulted from an unjust social order and that a ruling class could be overthrown and society democratically reorganized in the name of the majority—the workers. The organizers of the People's Council drew from the Russian experience the lesson that international peace would come only with genuine democracy. It wasn't that the world had to be made safe for democracy but that democracy would make the world safe. "The time has come," Nearing emphasized, "for the American people to follow the example of their Russian comrades. To throw aside the barbarisms of modern industrial society, to destroy economic parasitism, to annihilate all of the social institutions which enable one man to live upon another man's labor."[103] In the Russian mirror the antiwar forces saw their own democratic ideals.[104] As Max Eastman, another People's Council member, explained, "What makes us rub our eyes at Russia . . . is the way our own theories are proving true."[105]

Even though the People's Council found vindication for its goals in Russia, other peace groups viewed such emulation as creating an opening for charges of foreign influence, thereby attracting unnecessary criticism and hostility. Following America's entry into the war, the American Union Against

Militarism had ceased opposing the administration and the war, and concentrated its efforts on influencing the shaping of the postwar world. The AUAM almost immediately became divided over endorsement of the People's Council. One of its founders feared that affiliation with the council would be interpreted as sponsoring an alien government policy.[106] The AUAM was having internal problems as well. As soon as Congress enacted the Selective Service Act, Roger Baldwin, a key figure in the AUAM, created a "Bureau for Conscientious Objectors" and brought Nearing on its directing committee.[107] Baldwin's new agency divided the leadership of the AUAM. While a majority of members approved of it, others objected on the basis that "we cannot combine an aggressive policy against prosecution of the war with an aggressive policy for settling it through negotiations and organizing the world for democracy."[108] The majority who supported the bureau were also sympathetic to the People's Council.[109]

The bureau and the council increasingly split the AUAM over the course of the summer. In August, a crisis arose over whether the AUAM would participate in the national People's Council conference scheduled for early September. Lillian Wald, speaking for the old guard of the organization, thought that peace efforts were being endangered by Baldwin's bureau and threatened to resign if the AUAM endorsed the People's Council. While the AUAM stood for "the reflective thought of those opposed to the war," she claimed, the People's Council represented "impulsive radicalism." Norman Thomas, not alone in belonging to both the AUAM and the People's Council, saw that the only distinction between the two organizations was that the former was a middle-class and the latter a working-class movement.[110]

Yet Wald drew another distinction. Those who led the council, she claimed, had no connections with established institutions that could be politically and socially effective during the war, and for that reason, neither did they face a threat to their institutions when resources were withdrawn under the accusation of radicalism. The council was promoted by those she labeled "free lancers," who were not "disciplined by the torture chamber method" of trying to effect social change without accommodating themselves to the militarism of the ruling class.[111] The vote to send delegates to the People's Council convention effectively divided and weakened the AUAM. All that remained was for the board to vote in September to have the bureau and its parent organization sever all connections. With the destruction of the AUAM, the torch of peace activism was passed almost exclusively to an increasingly contentious People's Council, with Nearing at its head.[112] "For a brief period," wrote Nearing, the People's Council "had the reputation of being the focus of national anti-war activity."[113]

As the People's Council rose in prominence and visibility, it found itself faced with efforts to silence its oppositional views. While the national government took steps to pressure antiwar groups, state and local authorities rushed to prevent radical activity, and the People's Council became a primary target.[114] The council had planned to hold its national convention in Minneapolis, but before any delegates had arrived, a hostile press had caught wind of the convention and denounced the pacifists as "pro-German." Because of adverse publicity, the organizers were unable to rent a hall or even land on which to erect a convention tent. Finally, the governor of the state issued a proclamation prohibiting the People's Council from assembling in Minnesota.[115] Those delegates who had already arrived in the city, including Nearing, met informally in their hotel while a new convention site was sought. Among them was a Justice Department infiltrator who found it difficult "to get the names and all the particulars about many members," because "the Council is very suspicious of anyone who has not a previously bad reputation." The agent, however, did report on Nearing, who, he claimed, "is very popular and DANGEROUS for he is looked to as being very wise."[116]

Having given up on Minneapolis, council representatives were prevented from entering Hudson, Wisconsin, and Fargo, North Dakota, before eventually being promised protection in Chicago. While the mayor of the city defended the council's constitutional right to assemble, the governor of the state tried to persuade the mayor not to allow the meeting. Meanwhile, approximately two hundred delegates opened their convention on September 1. But the meeting was broken up and some members arrested when the governor ordered the city's police chief to close down the convention. The delegates retired to their hotel to continue their work and returned to the hall the next day since the mayor had promised to restrain his police force. Outraged, the governor called out the National Guard and ordered them to Chicago. In a flurry of activity, the delegates hastily completed their business before the troops arrived.[117] While clearly the repression faced by the People's Council confirmed the argument it was making about the failure of democracy at home, it found itself less able to make its case before the American public.

This was due less to harassment by local officials than a concerted effort by the federal government to silence the council. Early in August, when President Wilson received a complaint about People's Council mail being held up, he confessed that he didn't "even know what the People's Council of America is."[118] The postmaster general, in turn, was advised that the council was "rapidly establishing branches throughout the country" and that "every class of people opposed to the Government in the war appear to be very rapidly connecting themselves with this organization, with the hope that it will be the great force to paralyse the activities of the Government in the war."[119] The postmaster quickly informed Wilson that the council was "doing much harm to the Government in the present crisis."[120] Consequently, "approximately four thousand letters and three thousand circulars have been . . . withheld from dispatch."[121] The council had caught Wilson's attention. By mid-August, he referred to it as "for the most part a bad a mischievous lot."[122] By the end of the month, he told his cabinet that the council was composed of "eminent cranks and others who have sense in normal times."[123]

The federal government would go to great lengths to silence the People's Council, even indicting Nearing in March 1918 for violating the Espionage Act by writing an antiwar pamphlet. Yet well before that, the government was involved in an intense propaganda war with the People's Council. Much of the council's program, whether its peace proposals or its restructuring of economic and political life, was aimed specifically at the American labor movement. Out of fear of this radicalizing effect and the need to keep the labor movement on a conservative course and behind the war effort, an alliance was formed between conservative labor, business, and the government to oppose the People's Council. Thus, during the summer of 1917, the AFL's Samuel Gompers and the National Civic Federation, under the auspices of George Creel's Committee on Public Information, formed the American Alliance for Labor and Democracy. Financed and controlled by the federal government, the sole object of the alliance was to counter council propaganda and persuade American workers to support Wilson's war program. In its propaganda war, it distributed over 1,380,000 pamphlets to combat the People's Council's program.[124]

Not only did the alliance hope to steal the thunder of the People's Council by holding its national convention in St. Paul at the same time that the council had planned to meet, but it helped to poison the atmosphere for the council. In late August, George Creel wrote to a war loyalist in Minneapolis to inform him that the People's Council was "made up of traitors and fools, and we are fighting it to the death." Creel instructed him to "have patriotic societies and civic organizations pass resolutions condemning the People's Council as Pro-German and disloyal. . . . Get a good committee together and go around and see all the newspapers and see to it they get the point of view and action that I am giving you now." He closed with the instructions to "tear this letter up."[125] The alliance conference, according to the attorney Frank Walsh, a pro-war defector from the Socialist party, was a great success. Yet his participation in pro-war alliance with the ruling class angered Nearing; Walsh had betrayed his conscience, his civic duty, and the country's democratic ideals. In a letter to Walsh, Nearing wrote: "You knew about Paterson and Ludlow. You knew who was behind them. You know that these same forces are throttling democracy in America today—in the name of liberty in Europe. . . . You are lending your name and your influence. The plutocrats are using your power to rivet the chains. How can you do it?"[126]

# A Good Propagandist

## Chapter 10

THE People's Council struggled through the fall of 1917. It had emerged as the predominant antiwar organization yet at the same time was responsible for splitting the antiwar forces and causing the disintegration of the AUAM. Although it was revitalized by the October Revolution and the rise of the Bolsheviks in Russia—with the slogan of "All Power to the Soviets"—the council, and Nearing, came under increasingly harsh suppression.[1] Under these conditions there arose the problem of how to carry out educational propaganda to create a revolution in the minds of men when nearly all avenues of communication were closed to those who opposed American war interests. It became apparent that propaganda through political organizations offered a protected refuge from repression, a somewhat autonomous field for divergent ideas. Political action by the Socialist party could symbolize not only a restoration of democracy but a means of countering the dominant ideas in a legitimate social arena. By late fall of 1917, Nearing had come to look favorably upon the electoral possibilities of socialism. At the national convention of the Intercollegiate Socialist Society, he hailed the prospects of the Socialist party in the 1918 elections, claiming that "the November, 1918, election will be the first big opportunity of the Socialists." It was the task of the party leaders to be "good propagandists" and "to educate people."[2] Grasping this opening to forward oppositional ideas, Nearing became a candidate for the party, running for Congress in the Fourteenth Congressional District of New York City.

146

The election of 1918 surged through lower Manhattan with an intensity greater even than the usually rousing and animated campaigns there. The Fourteenth Congressional District found its incumbent congressman, Fiorello LaGuardia, back from leave from Washington to fly a warplane in Italy, challenged by Nearing, who in March faced federal indictment under the wartime Espionage Act. Events of the past year, both at home and abroad, made for a volatile campaign. The district teemed with open-air meetings, constant canvassing, rallies, parades, and massive demonstrations, day and night. Nearing addressed thousands of enthusiasts daily; met workers in their shops at noon; in the evening held house meetings of fifty to seventy-five voters, often women; and sometimes addressed "as many as four or five of these meetings nightly, in addition to hall meetings in his own or other districts."[3]

The life of the election pulsated through the streets, spurring lively outpourings.[4] At a major event toward the end of the campaign, a debate at Cooper Union, the crowd came close to rioting. Members of the audience shouted angrily at the speakers; they hissed at their candidate's opponent with a chorus of protests; the candidates screamed back over the roar; parts of the crowd surged forward toward the platform, then in the direction of their rivals in the audience; and always the cheering was hysterical when their man could magically match moment with message.[5] Election events allowed active expression of alternative ideas by both the candidates and the public. Campaigning offered a vital autonomous sphere of vibrant politics.

Yet if this diffuse political culture of the Fourteenth District rose to the occasion of the election event, it also expressed a unique meaning and significance at a time when "public meetings were generally broken up," as Nearing recalled: "Free speech was quite generally denied, and the freedom of the press was very seriously curtailed."[6] To struggle, agitate, discuss, and dissent publicly now meant, claimed one Socialist, facing "mob violence and legal terror."[7] Indictments and prosecution against those who spoke or wrote against the war were increasingly commonplace.[8] Newspapers were harassed, offices raided and mail opened; even the specter of deportation was raised. In New York City, so many dissenters who took to the streets to protest the war were jailed that the *Call* mused whether the prison on Blackwell's Island might request a local Socialist party charter.[9] By the time of the 1918 election, the various public forums through which the people of the district actively expressed their politics were directly threatened as never before.

It was under these conditions that the political campaign emerged as the best remaining forum for public discussion and struggle. Through the arena of electoral activity the Socialist party could put before the public a national platform opposing the war, the very thing, said the *Call*, that "has brought restrictions on our Constitutional rights of freedom of speech, press and assemblage, which are not only unnecessary, but which menace the whole future of democratic institutions and individual liberty."[10] Nearing, in his speech accepting the party's nomination, declared to his supporters: "I shall go to Congress in your name, opposing the present Democratic administration because it passed and enforced an Espionage law and other similar laws under which the rights . . . guaranteed by the Constitution, have been abridged and denied."[11] The *Call* claimed that "the Socialists stand for true Americanism," that it was they who were "fighting for the fundamental rights of Americanism," and that "never was there so little for the old parties to take up . . . never was the line of cleavage between them and the Socialist forces so manifest."[12]

▬ Although the political calendar of 1918 did not officially begin until July, attention to the congressional election had been heightened well before that time. With LaGuardia having left for Italy early in the fall of 1917, serious discontent in the district focused on the fact that he was not acting as the representative of the people of the fourteenth if he was out of the country. In December, the Women's Peace Party of New York gathered over three thousand signatures on a petition under the banner "Let's Be Represented," urging Congress to hold a special election in the district.[13] While the petition was delivered, it was stalled, and eventually the movement faded. Yet electoral activity was clearly seen as a legitimate sphere for voicing opposition.

By midsummer, the *New York Times* urged its readers not to forget their soldier and congressman LaGuardia, "the most worthy and indefatigable herald of the Government's Democracy."[14] The *Times* also applauded the federal arrests of Socialists and offered some additional advice: "Comrades, don't talk in public too much. . . . Why get into jail when you can stay out?"[15] At a meeting of the Central Committee of the Socialist Party of Local New York on July 13, Nearing was nominated "by a large vote" as the candidate to run in the Fourteenth District.[16] Meanwhile, the pro-war, pro–100%-American National Security League warned Democrats and Republicans of the need to unite for a "war Congress." The Fourteenth District, it feared, was one of five districts in the city that might go Socialist. Since the "increase in the 1917 antiwar Socialist vote over 1916, as shown by the assembly votes, was 61 per cent," the league called for agreement on "coalition candidates." By the end of July, the executive committees of both the Republican and Democratic parties had agreed on fusion nominations, including LaGuardia's.[17] For the first time in the Fourteenth District, the Socialist party faced a fusion candidate.

During the month of August, the *Call* published the "National Socialist Party Platform," which included demands for Constitutional protection of civil liberties and the end of censorship by the postmaster general.[18] These demands had real meaning for the people of the fourteenth. Before April 1917, every major Socialist newspaper in New York increased its readership, yet within five months of America's declaration of war, all the leading Socialist publications had been suspended from the mails at least once.[19] Those who read the papers learned of widespread attacks on the rights of American citizens. There was the famous "Mooney Case" and the passing of his second execution date on August 23. About this man, who had been convicted of throwing a bomb at a San Francisco Preparedness Day parade in 1916, the *Call* wrote: "For [American Labor] the whole fabric of justice and democracy seem interwoven with the fate of Thomas J. Mooney." During this month, the papers would also inform the people in the fourteenth of the convictions and sentences in Chicago of Big Bill Haywood and ninety-three other members of the IWW for conspiracy to interfere with the war program.[20]

The papers made these national acts of "legal terror" real to the people of the fourteenth. Yet they did not read only about the trials of others. The terror was going on all around them. A group of Russian immigrants on August 23 threw leaflets, written in both Yiddish and English, from the upper story of a building two blocks south of the district to protest the recent dispatch of American troops to eastern Russia. For this act they were arrested in the street by soldiers, had their papers seized, and faced brutal treatment at police headquarters.[21] On August 31, a massive protest occurred against the government seizure of "2,000,000 pieces of literature and correspondence" and the fact that "300 organizations and individuals" had been "subjected to [post office] department interference."[22] A primary target of the mail seizure was the Socialist party, which was charged with attempting "to raise a $1,000,000 fund for use in the Fall political campaigns throughout the country."[23] Making the world safe for democracy was having serious repercussions for the people of the fourteenth.

By September, the *Times* declared that LaGuardia's nomination "certainly shows the spirit of the country today, how the people are all united to bring this war to a successful and speedy termination."[24] Nearing, it claimed, "will have no chance of being elected."[25] The Socialist party, in the meantime, appealed for funds and support. "These times are serious," it warned. "We have reached a point in public life that tests men's hearts. Our papers are denied mailing privileges, our meetings are suppressed, our speakers are arrested."[26] LaGuardia wrote his campaign manager to ask that "if you have any campaign posters made . . . by no means use any pictures of me in uniform."[27] Nearing was in Cleveland to meet with the Socialist leader Eugene V. Debs the day before Debs went to trial following his arrest on June 30 for allegedly violating the Espionage Act.[28] Debs would be convicted later in the month, and in response the *Call* commented:

> In defense of the guarantees of the federal Constitution, the Socialists stand almost alone today. These guarantees have been the distinctive features of the republic that have attracted millions to our shores. They have been regarded as peculiarly American, and in this sense the Socialist party is distinctly an American party.[29]

While Nearing was identifying himself with the right to dissent freely without recrimination, LaGuardia was doing what he could not to be unduly identified with the war and its consequences in the district.

The shock of the abridgement of civil liberties and the democratic rights of free expression continued to reverberate throughout the fourteenth. In September, the trial of the editors of the radical *Masses* magazine took place in the city.[30] In October, Congress passed the Deportation Act as an amendment to the Immigration Act, a threatening measure to a largely immigrant population by any standard.[31] Another New York trial in October resulted in the conviction of the Russian immigrant Jacob Abrams and four others in the case involving the leaflets thrown from the building just south of the district.[32] Late in October, a great uproar ensued over the violent stabbing of a campaigner for Socialist candidate Congressman Meyer London.[33] The threats to liberty that the Socialists had warned were imminent became realities during the campaign.

While LaGuardia remained in Italy until late October, Nearing commenced a vigorous campaign. He first faced the people of the fourteenth at a ratifying rally on September 11. The *Call* enthusiastically reported that "Nearing shook to their depths the souls of a thousand men and women" as he outlined the principles of the Socialist party and his own campaign platform. He presented a statement of principles in favor of international socialism organized to oppose capitalism, recognition of and assistance to the Soviet government, steps toward a democratic peace, and industrial democracy. Furthermore, he took the position "that the producing classes of the United States take over the machinery of production and declare their independence of Big Business, just as our ancestors in 1776 took over the machinery of politics and declared their independence of royalty." He also attacked the current administration for attempting to "terrorize a free people into silence on public questions of the greatest importance."[34]

Because of the climate of repression, Nearing claimed, the campaign could not be carried out as strictly a speaker's campaign. The Socialists would have to find other ways to get their message across.[35] There would be weekly leaflets, written by Nearing as letters to the people of the fourteenth, beginning with his widely distributed letter of acceptance.[36] "When you send me to Congress," he told the people of his district, "I shall go as a representative of the producing class; as a spokesman for American Socialism and industrial democracy . . . as an opponent of capitalism in every form, including private capitalism, state capitalism, the state control of private industry, and every other scheme that permits one man to live, without working, upon the work performed by a fellow man."[37] Some of these leaflets were translated into Italian and Yiddish to reach the mixed immigrant groups that made up the fourteenth. Nearing also used the *Call* in his campaign to get across the Socialist message, and his workers distributed two to five hundred copies daily in the district.[38] The campaign, claimed the *Call*, was "peculiarly a campaign of literature and canvasses."[39]

Even the Yiddish theater, which functioned "as educator, dream maker, chief agent of charity, social center, and recreation hub for the family," according to one of its students, became a forum for political expression during the campaign.[40] George Bernard Shaw's *Mrs. Warren's Profession* was staged in Yiddish as a benefit performance for the Nearing campaign. The play, said the *Call*, was meant to "bring the people the message of social significance," and between acts Nearing took the stage to deliver his own message.[41] Finally, Nearing relied heavily on the Rand School as a forum for his Socialist message, spending six Thursday evenings lecturing on "The Economic Conflict" and twelve Saturday mornings teaching a course entitled "Current History."[42]

Even though Nearing expressed fears that public speaking would be curtailed during the campaign, he was constantly stumping in the fourteenth and in nearby districts. He spoke to large crowds that set, according to the *Call*, "new marks for size . . . and enthusiasm"; he arrived at halls "filled to overflowing"; he was "speaking nightly, and the response [was] unprecedently large." At one meeting the *Call* reported: "To say that the house was packed does not convey any adequate idea" of the size of the audience.[43] Louis Waldman, a Socialist candidate for the New York Assembly, recalled introducing Nearing to a crowd of "about five thousand people" in his assembly district early in the campaign.

> "Toledo University," I said, "may not want Scott Nearing, but we welcome him to the Second Avenue University of the Open Air." They cheered for several minutes. . . . Young, vigorous, and with an engaging personality, Scott stepped forward to receive the acclaim of his new "students" in this open air assembly, students who came back to listen to him for many weeks. . . . Instead of the crowd dwindling—which is usually the case at a street meeting when the hour grows late—by the time he was through his audience had swelled to a number which police estimated to be over seven thousand.

"There, under the stars," Waldman wrote, "we pleaded with thousands of men and women, black and white, Americans and Irish, Poles, Russians, Scandinavians, Jews, for comradeship, understanding, friendship, democracy."[44]

Nearing's campaign came to focus largely on economic concerns, and he clothed his politicking in discussions of the exploitation of the worker, the loss of economic equality, economic rights, and equal opportunity. Through a succession of weekly letters, he set forth his views on "Profiteering," "The High Cost of Living," and "Who Owns the United States?" Profiteers made money, he explained "at the expense of other people," and "the profiteer is in his glory when war is declared. . . . The profit system enables a few to grow rich from the labor of the many."[45] Moreover, "since the outbreak of war . . . prices have risen with terrible speed" while wages lagged behind. "But the war," he told the voters, "is not the cause of the increase in the cost of living." It merely "hastened a process that was well underway when the war broke out."[46] He pointed out to the people that they were "living in a city where more than nineteen people out of every twenty . . . do not own their own houses—how much less do they own their jobs!" The factories, stores, and banks, he contended, were "in the hands of less than five per cent of the people of New York. . . . The people of New York are about as close to owning their own city as the Russian people were to owning Russia under the Czar."[47] The election choice, he said was clear-cut:

> The Democrats and Republicans stand for profiteering. The Socialists oppose it. . . . The old parties stand for capitalism; stand for the high cost of living; stand for the increasing exploitation of the wage earners which the high cost of living necessitates. The Socialist party alone is out with a remedy for the increasing cost of living.
>
> The Republican and Democratic Parties in the Fourteenth have united their forces to maintain the established order. . . . The Socialists want the producers of America to own and control America.[48]

To a crowd of more than three thousand who gave Nearing, said the *Call*, "a reception such as few other Socialists ever received in this city," he delivered the text of one of his weekly letters. The theme was "patriotism." "The time has come," he claimed, "when we Socialists must make known our definition of patriotism." He read aloud the second paragraph of the Declaration of Independence and asked, "What does it mean? It means that in America we still have a right of free speech, press and assemblage; it is for that that we are fighting." Neither the postmaster general, "nor the Democratic Administration," he went on, "means to me the highest ideals in life." The United States, he explained,

> was established to guarantee economic freedom, equal opportunity and civil liberty. . . . To every true American devoted to liberty, justice and equal opportunity is the heart and soul of patriotism. . . . The true American . . . is loyal to liberty, justice and the common rights of mankind. . . . Our loyalty in America is loyalty to all that is grandest and best in American traditions and American life.[49]

Democracy had to begin at home, he asserted, but "better no America than America in chains."[50]

At a gathering in his district he told an audience of two thousand men, women, and children of the "necessities of peace." "As we approach the end of the war," he said, "we socialists are coming out to demand the necessities of peace." These were "bread, work, enlightenment, liberty and happiness."[51] The world was through with the "abominable capitalist system," he told a Sunday-afternoon audience later in the month; it was time for a "new economic system." The watchword of Nearing's political discourse was "industrial democracy." He advocated a system composed of men and women endowed with economic citizenship and not merely political rights. "Political citizenship means very little," he told the crowd, and "we shall have no economic citizenship until we have the right to select everyone in the shop, from the employer down."[52] Without economic rights, he claimed, neither did the worker have true political rights in the full expression of democracy.

As election day approached, campaigning went on sixteen and eighteen hours a day, with regularly scheduled meetings every noon and night.[53] Kate Richards O'Hare—out of jail while appealing her conviction under the Espionage Act—assured a Sunday gathering for Nearing that it was the Socialists who would preserve civil liberties; Max Eastman, the editor of the *Masses* spoke in support of the candidate; "Helen Levine, dramatic soprano," sang for the crowd; and Art Young drew political cartoons.[54] The Irish Americans in the district held a ratifying meeting in support of Nearing, and for the first time in twenty years, when the Amalgamated Clothing Workers of America endorsed a candidate, they supported Nearing, contributing to his campaign fund.[55]

Nearing became known affectionately as "the professor," whose trademark in the campaign was to arrive at a platform with books and a folding blackboard that he would use to instruct his audience.[56] LaGuardia, in contrast, symbolized the man of action. When he landed in New York on October 28 to face a flock of reporters eagerly awaiting his arrival, he was decked out in army khaki decorated with stripes and medals, and he expressed confidence that he would win the election.[57] Told of Nearing's indictment, he responded by saying that the "question of patriotism must not be introduced into this campaign."[58] But the temptation quickly became too much, and the next day he told a cheering crowd that it was his "patriotic duty" to oppose the candidacy of a Socialist.[59]

He threw himself into the campaign with desperate energy. Echoing Nearing, he focused on the wage earner's grievance. "You're getting a little more money than you used to," he told one of his audiences, "but your real wages have been cut in two. A dollar today buys you less than what it bought you in 1914." If this was what the Socialists were saying, he claimed, that was fine, but he wanted to go to Congress because he could bring about the needed changes better than the Socialists.[60]

Fusion campaigners saturated the district in the final days of the election to argue that "the Socialists are all right in what they want, we all want it . . . but the Socialists attack the government and point out its faults. They want too much at once. While we believe in Socialism we can't stand the Socialists."[61] The fusionists, reported the *Call*, "have sent speakers to the West Side to profess Socialism, but to discredit the Socialists themselves."[62] No doubt, this was an easier task for LaGuardia—who had originally joined the Republican party because he "could not stomach Tammany Hall"—than it would have been to defend the fusion ticket.[63]

In the debate that climaxed the campaign, over three thousand people jammed Cooper Union to hear the candidates. Separating Nearing and LaGuardia was a pillar upon which was engraved Lincoln's words: "Let us have faith that right makes might, and in that faith let us to the end do our duty, as we understand it."[64] LaGuardia opened the debate voicing his opposition to war but claimed that he "went to war to fight against war, in order to end war. I don't think we can end war by merely talking against it on East Side street corners." This, however, only precipitated a chorus of protests. LaGuardia continued, not attacking socialism but pointing out that Socialists throughout Europe had supported the war. He then attempted to discredit the Socialists as pro-German and disloyal, nearly causing a riot. Everyone was on their feet, the crowd completely out of hand. It was fifteen minutes before order could be restored.[65]

When Nearing's turn came, he repeated the principles of socialism and his position on the war. He questioned LaGuardia on contributions to his campaign from Rockefeller, United States Steel, and J. Ogden Armour—profiteers all. And he pointed out that the issue was only incidentally the war itself.

> My opponent harps on war. He doesn't seem to realize that the war is practically over and that the end of the war is only a matter of a few days. When he or I go to Congress, we shan't be confronted by war matters, but matters of peace, of reconstruction. The War is practically over. But the war between plutocracy and the worker continues. . . . The old world is passing and a new one is being created.[66]

LaGuardia closed the debate claiming that the Socialists, and Nearing, professed only a dream. The Russian Revolution, he claimed, was a failure and an example to the American people that socialism as the Socialists preached it was not a practical reality.[67] He concluded by claiming: "I can't debate this man. I understood he was a professor of economics. It's a mistake—he's a poet."[68]

The Socialists lost the election in the fourteenth to the fusion ticket, but Nearing almost doubled the 1916 portion of the Socialist vote.[69] When the ballots were counted, LaGuardia received 14,523 votes to Nearing's 6,214.[70] Nearing's campaign followed a pattern in the city where promising Socialist candidates lost their races to coalition forces. For Crystal Eastman writing in the *Liberator*, a publication that typically found elections and politics somewhat preordained, the "amazing" increase in Socialist votes merely demonstrated "once again that the Socialist Party is only incidentally a political institution, it is something that politicians cannot understand, a deep-rooted faith and thoroughly understood intellectual conception which must grow because it satisfies the vital desires of real human beings."[71]

Nearing showed little interest in political analysis, largely because he saw an electoral approach to socialism less as the immediate achievement of power than as the foundation for social transformation. Roger Baldwin noted that because Nearing knew "he could not be elected, he used the campaign as an opportunity for educational work."[72] "Elections," Nearing explained just after the results were in, "are but incidental to the big thing—educational propaganda to make the worker develop his common sense and intelligence."[73]

---

# The Great Madness

## Chapter 11

NEARING'S opposition to the war indicted the American plutocracy for breaking faith with the people by betraying their trust and disgracing their democratic legacy. Conversely, he personified a revolt against the masters, leading the country to social transformation, betraying the dominant creed as well as the power of the ruling class. His activities thus became suspect, and he was found to be an enemy of society by the "plutocracy." Under a wartime statute broadly interpreted to include political dissent as an obstruction to military objectives and therefore treasonous, Nearing became the target of heavy surveillance, a raid on his home, and finally indictment and trial by the federal government.[1] Ostensibly, Nearing had violated the law by writing a pamphlet entitled *The Great Madness: A Victory for American Plutocracy*, which was published and distributed through the Rand School under the auspices of the American Socialist Society.

Nearing was seen as a threat, but seemingly less for what he said or for the specific pamphlet for which he was charged; by silencing Nearing, the government could also strike at the People's Council as well as the Rand School and the Socialist movement. The actions against him confirmed his belief that the plutocracy would go to great extremes in stifling democracy to protect its interests. It also affirmed the necessity of establishing and working through institutional forms outside the dominant culture in order to effect social change. Finally, the government's actions validated his belief that the antiwar forces and the Socialists were the true defenders of American ideals; the "radicals" were the conservators of American democracy.

Agents from the Justice Department began surveillance of Nearing early in July 1917.[2] The federal government viewed his antiwar agitation, and particularly his involvement in the People's Council, as a possible violation of the third section of Title 1 of the Espionage Act, enacted on June 15, 1917:

> (1) Whoever, when the United States is at war, shall willfully make or convey false reports or false statements with intent to interfere with the operation or success of the military or naval forces of the United States or to promote the success of its enemies (2) and whoever, when the United States is at war, shall willfully cause or attempt to cause insubordination, disloyalty, mutiny, or refusal of duty, in the military or naval forces of the United States, (3) or shall willfully obstruct the recruiting or enlistment service of the United States, shall be punished by a fine of not more than $10,000 or imprisonment for not more than twenty years or both.[3]

At the end of the month, an informant was sent to cover the Chicago convention of the People's Council.[4] Nearing's activities were watched with increasing frequency through the month of August and continued when an agent went to Minneapolis to report on the first national convention of delegates of the council.[5] While Nearing was suspected of seditious activity, none of the surveillance had produced incriminating evidence. Immediately following the aborted convention, Nearing returned to Chautauqua to finish what would be his last summer on Lake Erie. On September 18, federal agents conducted a raid on the IWW headquarters in Toledo and, in the first domestic raid of the war, on Nearing's residence. His secretary had apparently been alerted to anticipate the agents' visit, met them courteously, and assisted in locating material. They inspected "a mass of lectures and memoranda used by Mr. Nearing in connection with his educational work," according to the agents' report, and after making "a very thorough search of his office and his home from the basement to the attic," they confiscated "a number of files, correspondence, lists of names, publications and various other matter." These they sent off to authorities in Cleveland and Washington for careful inspection; again nothing incriminating was found.[6] To Nearing, the "invasion of the premises of a private citizen by the agents of the government" was proof "of the morbid, nervous sensitiveness of the authorities."[7]

Nearing was watched even more closely after this raid, but it appears that the People's Council was as much the target as Nearing. Agents apparently hoped to find the council's activities in violation of the law through its spokesman. A council event became a sure way of conducting surveillance on Nearing. Agents attended his speeches in Detroit, Rockville, Chicago, and Boston, where one agent took notes while Nearing delivered a talk to Simmons College women on the lawn and sidewalk in front of the school.[8] An agent attended this latter meeting so that, he reported, "if anything is done or said which is considered a violation of the Espionage act, suitable action will be taken." Yet the agent had to concede afterward that "Mr. Nearing did not say anything for which he could be held criminally accountable."[9] On November 22, the People's Council offices in San Francisco were raided with a warrant authorized by the attorney general.[10] Only days later in Duluth, when Nearing addressed a People's Council meeting and declared "We want peace and we want it now," police broke up the meeting and arrested him. A federal agent was on hand to question him while he was incarcerated.[11]

When Nearing spoke in Louisville, Kentucky, early in December, a Justice Department agent was there to record his denunciation of the plutocracy and the country's "invisible government."[12] A stenographer recorded an entire talk, "Profiteering during War," that Nearing gave in Boston in January 1918. There he told his audience that "the papers are suppressed" and that "people are unable to express themselves." Claiming that the People's Council was having "one awful time" carrying on public discussions, he added, "I don't know how we have gotten through the time since last September but we are still at it." "We do care that we cannot get these facts [about the present situation] across to the American people and educate them . . . and try and develop an intelligent public opinion in the United States."[13]

When he spoke in New York, agents were there. One informant overheard a woman remarking to Nearing that she was being watched by the Secret Service, to which Nearing replied, "Then you have joined the ranks of the respectables, as all respectable people are being watched by the Secret Service."[14] Surveillance continued in Providence, where an agent was one in a crowd of eight hundred who listened to Nearing's talk, "Socialism and What It Is."[15] At a lecture given in Philadelphia on "Richness," the agent present recorded that Nearing "made indirect sneering remarks about the Government." Nearing also told the audience that "the Government has Department of Justice agents any place where socialist meetings are held. There might be one here now."[16] While surveillance may have been difficult to conceal, it is unlikely that Nearing knew that the government's search for incriminating evidence had extended to the seizure and opening of his mail.[17]

■■■ By February, the Justice Department had seemingly discovered the offensive evidence they had been searching for. After an attack on Nearing's pamphlet *The Great Madness* by the American Defense Society in the New York *Tribune* early in the year, the Justice Department focused on it as incriminating material.[18] Although it had been published in September 1917 and had gone through two editions of ten thousand copies each, only by February 1918 did federal officials determine it "clearly a violation of the Espionage Law, being a frank description of the war as a capitalist scheme."[19] The Justice Department official noted that "while it does not expressly urge anyone to refuse military service or other help to the United States, the implications are toward a mass fight against the war." Because the pamphlet was "absolutely frank, open and direct . . . it is a fair surmise that Nearing knew he was violating the law and intended to do so."[20] The department forwarded all its files on Nearing to the U.S. attorney in New York, with instructions that "it is the personal opinion of the Attorney General . . . that the Nearing pamphlet 'The Great Madness' presents a prima facia case of matter violating the Espionage statute."[21] It still remained, however, for agents "to investigate when, where and by whom this pamphlet has been distributed throughout the country."[22]

That investigation easily led to the New York Rand School of Social Science, run by the American Socialist Society. By the time the Rand School had published and distributed the pamphlet in September 1917, Nearing had become a regular instructor.[23] In the meantime, the school had become increasingly suspect since its staff and administration were closely allied with the Socialist party and its antiwar manifesto. Furthermore, as with *The Great Madness*, the Rand School had undertaken an effort to publish material critical of the corruption of democracy by the wealthy in America and the protection of moneyed interests through the war.[24] By the time the Justice Department focused on Nearing's pamphlet, he had become the most sought-after lecturer at the school, teaching the most popular course, "The Human Element in Economics," which filled the auditorium with a thousand students, according to the school's bulletin, while another thousand had to be turned away.[25] Clearly, Nearing was a cornerstone of the school by 1918, and his prosecution would be a blow not only to the People's Council but also to the American Socialist Society and its educational institution.

Two separate four-count indictments were handed down in New York against Nearing and the American Socialist Society, the first on March 21 and the second on May 13. In sum, they charged that Nearing and the ASS had in writing and publishing *The Great Madness* separately violated, and together conspired to violate, Section 3 of the Espionage Act and the Selective Service Act. Immediately, a "Scott Nearing Defence Committee" was formed to mount a legal challenge to the indictment. Nearing was released on bond and continued his antiwar activities unabated, but for the time being within the realm of political activity, running for a congressional seat for the Socialist party. The Justice Department refocused its efforts. The attorney general was informed by the district attorney in New York "that the case is somewhat weak" and that the New York office was "anxious to have all possible information which will show previous seditious activity by Nearing."[26]

Even though Nearing claimed that he took the title of his pamphlet from a speech by President Wilson in which the president claimed that with war, "madness has entered all things," *The Great Madness* was only incidentally about the war; it was an attack on the American plutocracy.[27] While it decried conscription, censorship, the Liberty Loan, and militarism—all war-related to be sure—the war had come about because, wrote Nearing, "the plutocracy welcomed the war . . . because it meant a chance to get a stronger grip on the United States."[28] The plutocracy had used its position of privilege and economic power to live off the labor of others and to control the channels of public opinion as well as the machinery of politics. Contrary to its claim that the war was fought to safeguard democracy, "the American plutocracy," claimed Nearing, "was no more interested in establishing democracy in Germany than they were in establishing democracy in the United States."[29] He identified strongly with Randolph Bourne's "brilliant article" despairing of the betrayal by American intellectuals, especially the pragmatists, in throwing their efforts into the war. In *The Great Madness* he quoted from Bourne's "War and the Intellectuals" to the effect that "it was the least liberal and least democratic elements among whom the preparedness and later war element were found. . . . The intellectuals, in other words, have identified themselves with the least democratic forces in American life."[30] In going to war, Nearing charged, America was "throwing morals and ideals to the wind."[31]

Nearing's counsel, Morris Hillquit, attempted to have both indictments thrown out. On August 1, District Judge Learned Hand issued an opinion overturning two counts of one indictment but letting all others stand.[32] He judged the indictment in error only in that it charged Nearing and the society with writing and publishing the pamphlet with the intent to cause insubordination or obstruct recruiting. "The pamphlet in question," Hand summarized, "undertakes to show that America's entrance into the war was the result of capitalist intrigue."[33] But, he continued, "the political measures which the author recommends as remedies do not involve any disobedience to existing law; they consist of political agitation by discussion and in the press, 'capture' of the schools, 'industrial and political solidarity,' 'the elimination of all profit from industry,' 'equal opportunity and justice for all.'" Thus, while "there is nothing in the pamphlet" that Hand "understood to constitute any counsel or advice to obstruct the draft or become insubordinate," the author and publisher's purpose remained entirely within the range of permissible public discussion.[34]

This, however, was a technical point, since previous cases had set forth "an added measure of criminal liability" under the Espionage Act, so that Hand ruled that "there is language which, taken broadly, can be made to mean that the author is liable if he merely knows that his words will so result" in obstruction of enlistment. Hand let the bulk of the indictments stand, rejecting Hillquit's argument that "to prosecute those whose propaganda is directed towards the repeal of [the existing order] involves a perpetuation of that order, whether right or wrong, since it chokes the opportunity for any expression of opinion that might in the end change it."[35]

Between the time of the indictments and the trial in February of 1919, the Justice Department kept up its surveillance of Nearing while it also searched for additional evidence with which to prosecute him. Agents watched him throughout the country. Hoping that Nearing would say something blatantly seditious, the Justice Department advised a wary police chief in Schenectady, New York, not to prevent Nearing from speaking.[36] Agents interviewed Provost Smith at the University of Pennsylvania about Nearing's alleged socialism but were told that it was not the reason for his dismissal.[37] From Toledo University, government officials received a copy of a report covering Nearing's dismissal from that institution.[38] An agent and stenographer even posed as newspaper reporters to attend a dinner given to raise funds for Nearing's defense.[39] In June, the San Francisco office of the People's Council was again raided, this time surreptitiously and without a warrant, the agent reporting that he had "seized a great many letters and the entire membership list of the U.S."[40] Furthermore, in July, arrangements were made with the telephone company to eavesdrop on the phone lines of the council.[41] And while Nearing ran for Congress, agents followed his campaign route.

On one occasion, two agents arrived at a closed Socialist party meeting in the Fourteenth Congressional District only to be denied admittance because they weren't party members. When they insisted on entering and tried to force their way into the hall, Nearing intervened and provided the two men with chairs at the front of the audience so they could be sure of what he said.[42]

▬ At his trial he also wanted to make his views clearly understood, this time to a jury. From February 5 through February 19, he took the stand in his own behalf, and as Joseph Freeman recalled, he "apologized for nothing, retracted nothing."[43] Nearing and the ASS were tried on a four-count indictment, two for alleged conspiracies and two for violations of Section 3 of the Espionage Act. According to one observer, Nearing was

> just the scientific investigator who had arrived at the true diagnosis of a social sore and was telling his patients. . . . Nearing did not care about the trial. He answered everything directly, without hesitation, almost belligerently, and the more involved and captious the question, the more straightforward and pugnacious was the answer. . . . He stood by everything he wrote, he took back nothing . . . palliated nothing, and reiterated everything he had written with added emphasis.[44]

He answered questions about the St. Louis antiwar platform of the Socialist party and his affiliation with the party; he expounded at length on the meaning of socialism. Reading large portions of *The Great Madness*, he presented the jury with his critique of the American plutocracy. He explained the purpose of the People's Council and his role within it; he lectured the courtroom on the aim of the Rand School and its educational importance. Although the war had ended by the time the trial took place, he told the jury that he regarded "war as incident to the economic struggle, and the economic struggle as fundamental and continuous." "If we are going to have democracy in the world," he testified, "we have got to begin at home and have it at home." The working class, he contended, "had to keep on, during the war and before the war and after the war, in preserving their own standards and safeguarding their rights." The struggle to establish "industrial democracy," he claimed, was "a problem that goes on continually with the wage earner."[45]

The trial was highlighted by Nearing's final address to the jury. Facing a possible twenty-year sentence, he defended himself by telling the jurors, "I have been a student of public affairs. I am a Socialist. I am a pacifist. But I am not charged with any of these things as offenses." "By convicting me for writing this book," he said, "you convict me for public discussion . . . for an expression of my opinions." Emphasizing his long-held belief that "citizenship involves duties as well as rights," he explained that he wrote *The Great Madness* "because I felt that as a teacher, I had a certain obligation to the community." "I have been throughout my life as consistent as I could be. I have spoken and written for years, honestly and frankly. . . . I stand before you today as an advocate of economic justice and world brotherhood, and peace among all men." He was, therefore, an advocate of "industrial democracy" because "if democracy means anything, it means that the majority of the people control the conditions of their own lives." In this he was not claiming "that the socialists have the entire answer," or "that the socialists when they come into power . . . will dispose of the problems of all the world." But, he explained, "we are solving the problems of production and are able to . . . solve the problem of distribution."[46]

When the United States entered the war, he told the jury, he "saw what I believed to be a great menace to the liberties of the American people, namely: the growing power of the plutocracy, the growing power it was gaining through the war." This was a problem in which he was "profoundly interested" since he had come "to the belief many years ago that with the resources of America and the opportunities in America we could have a very much finer and much higher standard of life here than we actually have." Yet over the years, "we have seen a gradual widening chasm between those who possess the necessities and those who do not." Rather than being justly charged with fomenting insubordination and disloyalty, Nearing explained that "no person is more anxious than I to have a well-ordered, well-conducted society, but I do not believe that it is possible to maintain order in society where one man or one group of men living without labor, luxuriously, and another man, or group of men, in spite of their most earnest efforts, are unable to provide their families with the necessities of life." He believed, therefore, that "the only way in which we can have justice in the world is to have economic justice."[47]

Before the case went to the jury, the judge, upon a motion by counsel for the defendants, dismissed the first two counts of the indictment, agreeing that there was insufficient evidence to establish a conspiracy. After thirty hours of deliberation, the jury returned its verdict; Nearing was found not guilty for writing *The Great Madness,* but the American Socialist Society was found guilty of violating the Espionage Act for publishing the pamphlet.[48] Nearing recalled years later that "the government did not care so much what sentence I got; they wanted to win the case. Their prime aim was to stifle and dispose of opposition to the war."[49]

▬ Immediately the focus of the case shifted to the Rand School, and its attorneys challenged the decision. On March 1, 1918, the judge who had heard the case refused a motion to dismiss the verdict on the basis of its inconsistency. Nearing, the judge surmised, had been acquitted because "in indictments for crime, where human beings are jointly tried with corporations, the human interest naturally centers around the living individual," while "the corporation is a sort of abstraction"; and whereas "the human being may lose his liberty if convicted," the worst thing the corporation could suffer was a fine.

Furthermore, he claimed, Nearing's "personal history and career were such that he had never failed to do by direct appeal what, from his point of view, he thought he ought to do." But that in no way invalidated the verdict against the ASS. In fact, the judge was reassured of the proper legal basis of the decision by two Supreme Court decisions—*Schenck v. United States* and *Debs v. United States*—handed down after the trial. From the *Debs* decision he quoted Justice Holmes to the effect that "the main theme of the speech was Socialism. . . . With that we have nothing to do, but if a part of the manifest intent of the more general utterances was to encourage those present to obstruct the recruiting service, and if in passages such encouragement was directly given, the immunity of the general theme may not be enough to protect the speech."[50] On March 21, the American Socialist Society was sentenced to pay a fine of three thousand dollars. The society appealed the sentence, but the higher court upheld the decision on the grounds that "the jury might believe that Nearing did not write these harmful views with the intent of obstructing the recruitment and enlistment service of the United States, and at the same time believe that the Society did print and distribute them with that intent."[51] Upon final appeal, the Supreme Court refused to review the case, and on October 19, 1920, the society was ordered to pay the fine.[52]

While the verdict was a blow to the Rand School, it did not cripple it. But almost immediately further attacks against the school began. In March 1919, the New York State Legislature voted to spend fifty thousand dollars to investigate radical activities in the state and started its investigation by focusing on the Rand School. On June 21, the state committee under the chairmanship of Senator Clayton R. Lusk, the "Lusk Committee," raided the Rand School as part of its investigation. Approving of this action against the school, the *New York Times* claimed that the Rand School "has taught hatred and class discrimination, and under our too tolerant laws has been allowed to go on without interference."[53]

To the American Socialist Society it became apparent that the attack against Nearing had simply been "the first attack" in what was emerging as the "most persistent and determined attack yet made upon a Socialist and labor educational institution in the United States."[54] "Education," claimed the Socialist party in a resolution adopted at its National Convention in 1920, "is the keynote to the ultimate emancipation of the working class." "But it is a special kind of education, one that enables the workers to see through the evils and shams of the present social and economic order, that is of value. Fully aware of this, capitalist interests have made strong attempts to destroy institutions like the Rand School."[55] Taking its case to the public, the Rand School published a record of Nearing's trial not only "because of the defendant's lucid exposition of the philosophy of Socialism," Morris Hillquit wrote in the introduction, "but also because it presents an authentic record of an American political trial."[56] The attack on the Rand School, said the society, was conducted by "the same interests [who] fought labor seventy-five years ago" and now "controlled the public schools," seeing to it "that the teacher who tells the truth about the conflict between labor and capital ceased to be a teacher."[57]

The Lusk Committee tried repeatedly to curtail the operations of the school. After its attempt to put the school into receivership was thrown out of court, the committee tried to annul the charter of the American Socialist Society. When that too was dismissed by the court, the committee attempted to strike at the school through legislation. In its report to the legislature in March 1920, it recommended that laws be enacted whereby all teachers in New York would be required to take a loyalty oath and, with the exception of religious schools, that educational institutions be licensed by the New York Board of Regents. Under this requirement, the regents would have to be "satisfied that the instruction proposed to be given will not be detrimental to the public interest." Eventually, legislation was passed to implement these recommendations.[58]

Nearing continued on the faculty at the Rand School through 1923. The school itself limped through the 1920s, a mere shadow of its former self. Nearing's wife had been the associate director of the school, but resigned in 1925, stating that there was no longer any interest in classes on socialism and that resources were lacking to teach other courses.[59] Yet the demise of the Rand School—and the repression Nearing had encountered generally—could only confirm the notion that discussion of public issues vital to democracy was being stifled and controlled in the United States. And because of that fact, Nearing would continue his activities to counter the influence of the plutocracy. "All through my life," he had told the jury at the close of his trial, "I have been interested in preserving the institutions of democracy."

> That has been one of the things . . . that seem to me fundamentally important. . . . I have been a student of the institutions, standards and ideals of American life. . . . I have been profoundly interested in seeing a certain thing done in the United States: I wanted to see liberty first, because I believe liberty is fundamental in society; then I wanted to see justice.

It was these things to which he had devoted his life and for which he would continue to struggle; he foresaw a dark future for American liberty and a long fight to come. He saw "ahead of us in our industrial life, exploitation, widespread, by the masters of those who work for them." "The outlook in America," he contended in 1919, "was not bright. . . . There are clouds on the horizon. I believe America is in peril and I believe that the danger lurks within. And I believe it rests primarily in our unfair and unjust distribution of wealth, and the income of the country." Because he stood opposed to this degeneration of America's democratic freedom, he declared to the jury:

I want to say to you that I want to see America free. I want to see liberty, opportunity and democracy here, as well as in every other country on earth. As long as America is not free, you are not free and I am not free.

"We belong to the body of this citizenship," he instructed the jurors, "and we suffer in common with it, and we benefit in common with it."[60]

# Every Man His Own Radical

## Chapter 12

AMID the turmoil of the war Nearing found sanction for his recusancy and legitimacy for his actions in the writings of the prophet of nonviolence, Count Leo Tolstoy (1828–1910). Tolstoy, claimed Nearing, offered "one powerful line of argument against war," unmasking it as "a logical product of competition and exploitation."[1] Tolstoy had shown that "the whole system of landlordism and capitalism" was supported by "violence and armed force" and that "the source of the war motive lies in the economic struggle between men." Military life, wrote Nearing, "made a deep impression on Tolstoi's mind"—as did militarism profoundly offend Nearing—"the routine and coercion, as well as the sheer brutality of military activities offended and outraged him."[2]

Nearing spread Tolstoy's gospel through courses he taught at the Rand School and in a collection of the sage's writings he edited under the title *War, Patriotism, Peace* (1926). He selected essays that denounced organized religion and official patriotism as "false doctrine" and advocated a return to true faith and conscience so that man would be "free from that lie in which we are all brought up, and which is given out to us as divine."[3] Patriotism was "immoral," Tolstoy had said in one of the essays Nearing chose, because "instead of recognizing himself as the son of God, as Christianity teaches us, or at least as a free man, who is guided by his reason,—every man, under the influence of patriotism, recognizes himself as the son of his country, the slave of his government, and commits acts which are contrary to his reason and his conscience."[4] To fulfill our social morality, Nearing quoted Tolstoy to the effect that

> we need no images, no relics, no divine services, no priests, no sacred histories, no catechisms, no governments, but on the contrary, a liberation from all that— because only the man who is free from those fables which the priests give out to him as the only truth, and who is not bound to other people by promises to act as they want him to act, can treat others as he wishes to be treated by them.[5]

Finally, there was tragic verity in Tolstoy's observation that "no one speaks or knows of these heroes of the war against war, who are not seen and heard by anyone, who have died under rods or stinking cells, or in oppressive exile, and still to their very last breath remain true to the good and to truth."[6]

Already by the late nineteenth century, Tolstoy had been brought to Americans' attention—largely through the efforts of William Dean Howells in his "Editor's Study" columns for *Harper's Monthly* from 1886 through 1892— and the power of his social philosophy as well as his religious pacifism caught the imagination of important social reformers and peace advocates, some of whom even made the pilgrimage to Yasnaya Polyana. The Russian's ideas became a mirror for assessing American ideals. Many, like Howells, who were questioning their values soothed their social guilt through Tolstoyan sympathy for the suffering of the common man. They found strenuous revitalization in a moral vision that encouraged deeds that would lend moral authority to their words. They read in Tolstoy not only of the corruption of materialism and the parasitic nature of the nonworking rich but of a social solution in brotherhood as a moral force and work as service to humanity.[7]

Nearing claimed late in his life that with the onset of World War I, he "turned more and more to Tolstoy as my counsellor and guide."[8] When his social vision was shattered by the destruction of war, he was increasingly drawn to Tolstoy's thoughts on nonviolence. At the same time, the war served to intensify a strong interest in Tolstoy's highly individualistic radicalism. Yet his attraction to Tolstoy preceded and transcended issues of war and peace. Nearing identified strongly with the activist side of Tolstoy's life—consciously putting ethics into practice; breaking with organized religion to raise himself to a higher level of spirituality; turning to the simplicity and abstention of a healthy rural existence with a vegetarian diet and manual labor; denouncing property, wage slavery, and exploitation; and in nonresistance to evil, suffering surveillance, censorship, and suppression by the autocracy. It was the postresurrection Tolstoy Nearing evoked in his own life, the philosophical, religious prophet who renounced his privileged status and his property, discovered revitalization in a peasant existence, turned away from material gain toward higher pursuits, and tried to live according to uncompromising moral principles. Most important, the aspect of Tolstoy's life that attracted Nearing was the notion that the power to shape the future lay with the cultivated classes who were also the ones in need of reform, that it was the privileged who would lead the revolt by providing a model for others.

In struggling against his own social class and its domination of social institutions, Tolstoy fought for a concept of freedom whereby man would create a producer-oriented society and be released from the grip of economic necessity to reach a higher level of spiritual existence. For Nearing, it became increasingly apparent in postwar America that the antithesis of a producers' society had emerged in a consumer culture that expressed the culmination of entrenched capitalism. Nearing's concerns over issues of work and leisure in this new culture were similar to those echoed by the Lynds in their 1929 study of Muncie, Indiana. A social psychology of possessions, Nearing wrote, paralleled a notion of production whereby "job owners seek profits" and "do not stop to ask whether human beings are growing or shrinking up under the pressure of the new economic order." It was "profitable to put men into specialized jobs, tending automatic machines," which created jobs of "dull, deadening monotony." When the worker was "pressed into the mould of the automatic machine beside which he works," he ceased "to stretch his facilities."

And because "the monotony of the work [was] deadening," it kept the workers "diverted in their leisure hours and help[ed] them to forget." In order to escape their devitalized life on the job, they turned to the consumption of a sensationalized press, to sports, to alcohol, to movies, and to cheap automobiles. The result of this new culture of consumption was that "human life was modified and reshaped through mass work, mass life, mass recreation, mass education and regimentation, and mass thought." "The new life experiences, with their corresponding habits, have created a new type of human being,—the mass man, the proletarian,—the coerced, narrowed, routineered, plaintive, soul-hungry, ignorant, overstimulated, industrial worker."[9] This mass society enforced a "necessity for conformity," "an intellectual abdication," resulting in "prejudice, bigotry, mental atrophy and social decay." There was a resigned "smugness and self-satisfaction of the ordinary American community, convinced that what it has is the best on earth."[10] The political consequence of this mass society meant that while "theoretically, the United States is a 'free country,'" in reality "the people there enjoy an unusually narrow range of political thought."[11]

In contrast with America's consumer society, a "producers' society" would make each individual "the arbiter of his own economic destiny."[12] As one concerned with the wholeness of life and individual independence and personal growth, Nearing, like Tolstoy, directed his attention to the organic relation of work and leisure. "Work and blessedness," Nearing declared, "go together." Work should "inspire" and call "creative imagination into play." Yet, the work of an industrial society did not "gratify the instinct of workmanship." "Most modern jobs," Nearing declared, "are intolerable in their endless, unvarying monotony."[13] "The machine threatens to inaugurate a new slavery—a slavery of the individual worker to routine, mechanical production, a slavery of the community to an irresponsible, self constituted industrial plutocracy."[14] Consistent with Tolstoy's prescriptions, he advocated "joyous, blessed work . . . work that calls for initiative, spontaneity, intelligence, judgement, enthusiasm."[15]

Furthermore, "an emphasis on production rather than accumulation" would also mean that "the primary aim of a producers' society would be leisure rather than goods—an opportunity for expression rather than an increase in the amount of possessions." "One of the greatest tasks" of the producers' society would be "the education of its citizenship in the effective use of leisure."[16] This would be a "new leisure" leading to "a high social standard"; "leisure must be more than free time, if it is to be of value," Nearing claimed. "It must be a leisure of energy as well as a leisure of hours."[17] Thus, "the growth of the individual, in a modern community, depends, in large measure, on the way in which he uses his leisure."[18]

Capitalist hegemony kept the workers entrenched in economic struggle for a livelihood centered on acquisitions. Thus, it was "one of the logical products of a stratified or class society [that] the lower classes seek to ape the upper classes, while the latter engage in a mad scramble to determine which shall set the most grotesque standard of social conduct."[19] Only if released from this economic struggle would one's "best energies . . . be liberated for the pursuits that are dictated by personal desires rather than social coercion." Then "the individual will be free in the highest sense of the word—free to be himself."[20] Nearing was refuting a purely materialist notion of human freedom, claiming that "economic emancipation does not include all aspects of freedom. Many other chains remain to be broken." One's "holy aspirations"—"that unbending search after love, beauty, justice, truth"—were located "outside the realm of economics, yet none of them is possible for the masses of mankind until there is established a system of economic life that will provide the necessities upon which physical health depends with an amount of leisure sufficient to enable a generation to find itself."[21]

Like good Tolstoyans, "the citizens of a producer's society will therefore teach to their children, and will practice an abstemiousness in the midst of plenty—a withdrawal from possessions—in order that the body may have enough, but not too much, and that the spirit may be freed from an undue weight of things." They would then achieve "an enrichment of life, which they realized could come only through understanding, tranquility, and inner growth." This was "the application of the highest ethical principles to economic life, and is the course of procedure that man's most elemental sense of justice demands."[22]

Tolstoy's greatest influence, according to Nearing, was in his challenge to "the moral foundations, the property and class assumptions, privileges and institutions of a competitive, acquisitive society." Tolstoy "went beyond precept and protests by trying to live his own concept in a society which not only rejected his moral and political assumptions but branded as criminal those who tried to put his beliefs into practice." Nearing caught the parallels of their lives when he noted that "Tolstoy fought the social system under which he lived and of which he was a beneficiary," and "besides denouncing the system, he tried in association with other like-minded people to abolish the system entirely and to put something better in its place." For Tolstoy, as for Nearing, "a veil was lifted from his ruling class blindness," revealing "the thin social veneer of an exotic class structure which rested upon and was supported by the underprivileged, exploited, oppressed mass of Russian peasants and industrial workers." Tolstoy was one who had "turned against his class," and like Nearing, "he was struggling against himself and his own position."[23]

Undoubtedly drawing on the Russian Socialist G. V. Plekhanov's characterization of Tolstoy as a "repentant nobleman"—meant as a critique of Tolstoy's socialism—Joseph Freeman described Nearing as a "penitent nobleman." According to Freeman,

> Nearing developed a social morality which held that it was difficult for a man to sit down in a starving group of people and eat to satiety without offering them a share. This Tolstoyan philosophy was essentially an appeal to the Christian "conscience" of the well-to-do; it was akin to the self-abnegation of the "penitent nobleman" whose "revolutionary" morality stressed surrender by the idealistic bourgeois rather than acquisition by the realistic proletariat.

Nearing, said Freeman, "lived his life literally, renouncing all personal comfort, and preaching the gospel of the new world with the intensity of a Savonarola."[24]

▬ Like Tolstoy, Nearing would remain always the teacher. Even as a freelance teacher, he saw it as his civic responsibility to continue to educate the public. He thus remained deeply concerned with the problem of how public opinion was shaped. When he was invited by the Liberal Club at Clark University in Worcester, Massachusetts, to speak on March 14, 1922, he chose to address the question of "The Control of Public Opinion in the United States." His lecture drew a receptive crowd of some three hundred students, citizens of the city, and a handful of faculty members, including the renowned social scientist and ex-president of the university, G. Stanley Hall.[25]

Nearing began his address by noting that whereas "the nature, creation and operation of public opinion" was poorly understood, Americans generally admitted "the dominant position and supreme importance of public opinion in a democracy." In order to understand the "system of social control through the operation of public opinion," Nearing turned the audience's attention to Thorstein Veblen's *Theory of the Leisure Class*, which indicated that "the governing group is that which possesses the majority of the property of the country, and it attempts to create a public opinion justifying this possession, and its uses and advantages." Nearing contended that

> a dominant group, through suggestion and contagion, are able to create the governing ideas and motives, and to shape the current public opinion to their

own uses. . . . The problem of public opinion in the United States, then, resolves itself into a consideration of the methods whereby the leisure class is able to control public opinion, and the chief types of machinery through which it is created, as well as the channels through which it flows.

One institution controlling public opinion, Nearing explained, was the press; another was the church; also, he suggested his audience consider the law, in which "the economic philosophy of wealth has come to dominate."

Finally, he focused his discussion on the institutions of education and their role in shaping and controlling public opinion. "Education," he asserted, was "also adjusted to the task of creating a philosophy of justification of great inequalities in wealth in the community." To support his claim, he drew upon the results of the Lusk Committee, noting that "in New York State no teacher in the secondary schools can advocate any change in any form of government existing in any part of the world, even by peaceful means." Much the same was true in higher education, he claimed, again drawing on Veblen: "The higher education, as Professor Veblen has shown in his *Higher Learning in America,* has also come to reflect the philosophy of the present-day business man." "With the growth in the size of the modern institution of higher learning the problems of administration have become so multifarious and exacting that they exceed the capacity or inclination of the scholar," he continued. "They are being given over in a continually increasing number of instances to businessmen, or to educators who have demonstrated the administrative qualities of the business man."[26]

Unbeknown to most of the audience, Wallace W. Atwood, president of the university, had slipped into the back of the lecture hall just in time for this discussion of university control by vested interests. Atwood had come to Clark in 1920 from Harvard University, where he had been a professor of geology, yet as one of his colleagues commented, "I suppose Clark thinks it is getting a geographer and an educator; Clark will find it is getting neither."[27] In fact, ever since his arrival, the university had been in turmoil. The faculty found their position undermined when Atwood was hired by the trustees of the university without their consultation. The university then underwent a major academic reorganization under the new president, again without the prior knowledge or advice of the faculty. Thus, the atmosphere was already poisoned when the students of the Liberal Club secured Atwood's approval to have Nearing speak— although the president made clear he did not approve of Nearing's views. After only five minutes of listening to Nearing excoriate university administration, Atwood reached the conclusion that the lecture was "disgusting."[28]

As Nearing read aloud from Veblen's study (Veblen happened to be Atwood's brother-in-law), Atwood approached the president of the Liberal Club, ordering him to stop the lecture. The shocked student was then grabbed by the shoulder and marched up to the lecture platform as Atwood announced that the meeting was dismissed. A startled Nearing stopped his speech to ask a student on the platform, "Who is that guy?" An equally astonished audience tried to comprehend what was happening as Atwood repeated his decree. Still unsuccessful, the president finally ordered the janitor to turn off the lights and threatened to summon the police.[29] Slowly, the disgruntled crowd dispersed, some pausing to speak to Nearing, as did one professor who shook his hand and said, "I am glad to have a chance to have heard your address. I am humiliated that this should have happened in this university."[30] The tragicomic quality of the incident was reflected in the comment one student made to Nearing, who was invited to complete his lecture in a nearby fraternity. "To think of it!" said the student. "You were just telling us how college presidents behaved when one of them appeared on stage and put on his act. Did you hire him to do it?"[31]

The "Nearing incident" at Clark, as it was known, had serious repercussions at the university. It became an incendiary event that brought all the underlying tensions over questions of faculty control and academic freedom into the open. The student body took the offensive against the increasingly defensive president. A number of demoralized faculty members resigned and went elsewhere to teach, and the suicide of one teacher was attributed in part to the unrest. The incident also caught the attention of the American Association of University Professors, which launched an investigation not into violations of academic freedom but as a case study of "the recent history of this one institution" in the hope that it "may perhaps contain something of instruction for officers and teachers in other universities."[32]

Atwood's actions also attracted the attention of the local press and community groups, which largely applauded, as the Rotary Club put it, "his patriotic stand against radical propaganda." *The Nation*, however, condemned not only the president but the people of Worcester. By breaking up Nearing's lecture, it claimed, the president simply obtained "an immediate and convincing demonstration of the truth of his words." "The City of Worcester," it continued, "not only proved how easy it is for the established order to get assistance from college, church, and press, but it showed how simply those forces can lead the average citizen by the nose."[33] The *New Republic* was equally disturbed, commenting that "in the long run, a college president must make his choice between an honest, troublesome faculty, and one that is complaisant and worthless. He must choose between a student body of rebellious, mettlesome youngsters and ones too spineless to care."[34] Nearing was left to make sense of this bizarre event in the perspective of his previous academic dismissal. He noted soon afterward that "had the exigencies of the war been the real cause of academic coercion, with the winning of the war the coercion would normally decline and ultimately cease." "As a matter of fact," he concluded, "it has done no such thing."[35]

▬▬ In Nearing's analysis, the incident at Clark was not at all unusual. It was simply another instance of the control, and closing-down, of the channels of communication in the United States by those who maintained economic dominance. The irony of the situation was that during the 1920s "science and technology developed important new means of communication," yet "at the same time the control of the communication channels passed more and more completely into the hands of the oligarchy." "As each new channel of communication demonstrated its effectiveness," he claimed, "it was grabbed up by the monopolists and used as one more device for reaching the public ear, holding the public attention, and washing the public brain." Finding himself "face-to-face with an oligarchy which owned or dominated all of the most effective channels of communication,"[36] he determined that radical social transformation could only emerge autonomous of the central institutions of capitalist culture. Countering the dominant influence of the ruling class meant in part creating alternative institutions. Yet to be freed completely from restraints that would hinder open discussion and social progress might also require an anti-institutional solution. As he explained in his lecture to the students at Clark University, "There are two modes of activity open to those who desire to break down this domination of public opinion by the vested economic interests." One was "the road of action in organizing movements to create a new social order." The other was "the approach of the social philosopher, who studies the existing order, reveals its weaknesses and injustices, and indicates the desireable path of reform." Most desirable would be the "effective development of thought and action contrary to the vested interests."[37]

Beginning with his dismissals from academia, Nearing realized that he was temperamentally and intellectually unsuited to institutional life. He had felt "confined to classroom routine," the "routine of a restricted schedule." Thus, "escaping from the class room limitations" proved to be "an exhilarating experience." He experienced the "unutterable delight of having barriers suddenly removed and of discovering that one is master, enjoying the absence of restraint" while "weighed down at the same time by the same sense of responsibility" to his fellows.[38] Regarding his attitude toward institutions and social advancement, he often quoted one of the "finest passages" from Walt Whitman's *Leaves of Grass*:

> I hear it was charged against me that I sought to destroy institutions;
> But really I am neither for nor against institutions; (What indeed have I in common with them?—Or what with the destruction of them?)
> Only I will establish in Manhattan, and in every other city of these states, inland and seaboard,
> And in the fields and woods, and above every keel, little or large, that dents the water,
> Without edifices, or rules, or trustees, or any argument,
> The institution of the dear love of comrades.[39]

On February 12, 1922, Nearing debated the Reverend John Haynes Holmes in New York City on the question "Can the Church Be Radical?" Nearing, taking the negative side of the argument, applied his analysis of institutions to the Church, claiming that "the Church is not radical . . . the Church has not been radical" because "it has stood with the vested interests against the rights and liberties of the people. . . . It stands thus today on capitalism." The Church, he contended, was "exactly like any other social institution" in that "it places a premium on conformity."[40]

In fact, he declared, "you dare not commit the functions of radicalism to any institution, Church or otherwise." He warned that "the moment you have hired a representative, a creed and bricks and mortar, you have fastened the shackles of conservatism permanently on that institution." Once established, an institution will "stand by the present order . . . whether your institution be a Church, an educational system, a political party, or a trade union." Even though he did not believe "that any educational institution can be fundamentally radical," he did exempt the Rand School from his argument. There was "one thing that differentiates it from the Church, and that is that it is not part of the present social order." Otherwise, his analysis of institutions held. "I don't believe the Socialist Party can be consistently radical. I don't believe the Communist Party can be consistently radical, and I don't believe that the Soviet Government of Russia can be consistently radical."[41]

This analysis did not "lead to blackness and despair." For those who believed "in the fundamental reorganization of the present social life," there was but "one course and only one course to pursue . . . to study and to think and to observe and to draw our conclusions and to hold our faith high and clear and keep our ideals uncontaminated, and when the time comes act—*we*, not the Church, not the institutions, but *we* must act."

> Every man his own radical, every man his own thinker, every man his own ideals, every man his own understanding and his own actor when the time for action comes—that is the only way for radicalism. That is the only basis upon which the present order of society will be changed.

This, he claimed, was "not doctrinaire individualism"; it was "not saving your own soul." It was, however, a Tolstoyan appeal to the individual conscience for moral authority. "Every man must be his own radical," he implored. "If you want to be radical you have to do it yourself."[42]

# What Can the Radical Do?

**Part Four**

# The American Empire

## Chapter 13

AS THE Great War slowly receded into the past, Nearing saw that it had been the "supreme contradiction" that "Christian civilization" was "preaching peace and good will on the one hand and on the other paying its most glowing tributes to those who have been most effective in organized destruction and mass murder." "What more conclusive evidence," he asked, "could be found of the Marxian contention that prevailing institutions express, not the ideas of some pre-existing social code, but the economic and political needs of the dominant economic class?"[1] The war left him "an outcast,"[2] "an involuntary exile from the social pattern into which I had been born."[3]

He was in a paradoxical situation, full of both doubt and determination. Disillusioned, he was hardened for further social struggle. Early in the 1920s he observed that "uncertainty and a sense of futility have gripped the world" and were manifested "in unrest, disillusionment, the abandonment of ideals, opportunism, and a tragic concentration on the life of the moment, which alone seems sure."[4] He seemed to speak for the multitudes and for himself in a debate with Clarence Darrow when he claimed that the masses had "tried the present system" and that "it has turned to dust and ashes in their hands."[5] Faced with such a crisis, he questioned his personal role. In his autobiography he recalled being faced with the question "Where did I belong?" He saw himself as "an outcast, sure enough, separated by a formidable barrier from most of my fellow Americans." Standing outside of and in opposition to the dominant values of industrial capitalist America, he wondered if he was "a Don Quixote, tilting against windmills?"[6]

He found himself "in a new incarnation," he explained. "In a very real sense I felt as if I had been born again."[7] His confrontations with the institutions of capitalist culture and wartime coercion "converted" him "from a citizen of the United States, proud of the title and the honor it implied, into a citizen of the world." He was "ashamed to . . . admit association" with America; "the alienation," he claimed, "is complete."[8] He was a victim not simply of the war; there were deeper forces at work. America's wartime experience, he said, "was the episode that had led to such catastrophic changes in my life, but it was not only the war." The war worked to illuminate for him more serious problems. "The war," he maintained, "intruding into the way of life to which I had become accustomed, gave me a totally new perspective."[9]

With this "new perspective," Nearing left behind the study of the distribution of income and his conception of capitalism as a problem of industrial America. Capitalism had more than national implications; it manifested imperial characteristics. America had assumed the features of an imperialist empire. As Nearing explained this shift in focus, he noted that he began his career with "specific studies [of] the distribution of income in the United States." Then the war "compelled me to enlarge my scope of studies" and "pushed me into new aspects of social science." He moved "boldly out of my academic specialty—the distribution of income—into a new and far larger field," the study of "war, revolution, imperialism and civilization." "My distribution study had centered on the economy of one nation—the United States." "The new study of war, revolution, imperialism and civilization bypassed nationalism with its nagging problems and spread across the entire field of social history."[10]

Nearing could easily shift his analysis of unearned income to a conception of economic surplus, reorient his conception of the American plutocracy to a universalized view of a ruling class in all industrialized societies, all of which reinforced his belief that war was a feature of capitalist economics. He concluded that "the organizing of nations for war came into present-day society with the present industrial system."[11] Just as a plutocracy had emerged in the United States out of inequalities in the economic system and exercised a dominating control over society, in an international perspective, "the industrial revolution made financial imperialism the inevitable flower of an economic system based on special privilege and organized for the few for the exploitation of the many."[12] In his first book following the war, *The American Empire*, Nearing stated that "certain liberal American thinkers have taken the stand that the incidents of 1917–1918 were the result of the failure of the President, and of certain advisors, to follow the theories that he envisioned, and to stand by the cause that he had espoused." The problem with this liberal analysis, he claimed, was that it tended to "overlook the incidental character of the war as a factor in American domestic policy."[13]

"The entrance of the United States in the war," he contended, "brought to the surface" certain "factors of American life that had been evolving unnoticed, for generations." America had been revealed as an imperial empire with "conquered territory; subject peoples; an imperial, ruling class, and the exploitation by that class of the people at home and abroad." The industrial revolution had created an "imperial class" in America, and along with "these economic changes" came "political changes." The political traditions of "the American Republic," he noted, had "been thrust aside." "Above its remains towers a mighty imperial structure,—the world of business. . . . That structure is the American Empire."[14]

The lament accompanying this analysis exposed this imperial structure as "wholly inconsistent with the traditions of American life." Imperial competition eventuating in war brought with it abrogation of free speech, free press, free assemblage, due process, and conscription—all "activities directed specifically to the negation of those very principles of liberty which have constituted so intimate a part of the American tradition of freedom." The "contrast between the promise of 1776" and the twentieth-century reality, he said, was "brutal in its terrible intensity." He questioned how it was "possible to harmonize the Declaration of Independence with the subjugation of peoples and the conquest of territory," since "the letter and the spirit of the Declaration of Independence contradict the letter and spirit of imperial purpose." This imperial structure, Nearing asserted, stood "upon the spot where many of the founders of the American government hoped to see a republic." Assenting to this American empire meant accepting the fact that "a vast gulf lies between the inspiring promise that a handful of men and women made to the world in 1776, and the fulfillment of that promise that is embodied in twentieth century American life." The loss of "liberty," he claimed, "is the price of empire."[15]

Nearing's analysis in *The American Empire* was heavily influenced by the work of J. A. Hobson, the radical British economist who had written the influential, pioneering *Imperialism: A Study* (1902). He agreed with Hobson's interpretation of the economic basis for imperialism. For Hobson, obvious causal links existed: the process of industrial consolidation, class domination, the production of surplus, financial imperialism, and eventual conflict. He also promoted the idea of development away from national economic rivalry and toward a "world federation" and "internationalism," and he called for "social reform" focused on the workers, since "trade-unionism and socialism are . . . the natural enemies of imperialism, for they take away from the 'imperial' classes the surplus incomes which form the stimulus of imperialism." A gradualist, like Nearing, Hobson proposed a nonviolent movement toward a harmonious world order.[16]

Hobson's solution to this problem of surplus was to advocate policies allowing full consumption within nations. To achieve this, he offered a program of taxation of unearned income, thereby promoting redistribution of wealth and greater consumption. But having moved away from the belief that

American capitalism was but a national economic system in need of redistributive adjustment, Nearing implicitly rejected Hobson's solution to the problem of surplus. Nearing was no longer convinced that surplus could be disposed of for the social good under a capitalist economy. That "major assumption is historically incorrect," he would later claim; "the conquest over nature lulled us to believe that an equal conquest over social forces was at hand, and having learned to produce we could learn to distribute."[17]

Nearing also departed from Hobson's study in viewing imperialism as a natural result of capitalism. He did not endorse Hobson's explanation for the development of imperialist empires in which the British and Roman empires were compared, describing imperialism as a universal social system guided by "laws." For Nearing, unique features of imperialism emerged out of the specific circumstances of modern industrial capitalism. Finally, contrary to Hobson, Nearing found that capitalism was not something in need of reform, but instead had to be surpassed. Only then could imperialism come to an end and America escape "the slow and terrible decay and dissolution that sooner or later overtake those peoples that follow the paths of empire." Capitalism would pass on to something else, "a new cycle of development."[18]

While the present course of empire meant ruling-class domination, the intensification of international rivalries, and eventually another war—"because the present system of competitive capitalism makes war inevitable"[19]—there were also the examples of challenges to capitalist imperialism in British labor and, more significant, the emergence of Soviet Russia. His view of British labor echoed that of the Socialist party, that the labor movement in the United States had more in common with its British counterpart than with the Soviet experience. While the Russian Revolution was initially the idol of the Socialists, Nearing explained that the Socialists gradually took "it for granted that the labor movement in the United States and Canada will follow the lead of the British Labor Movement" in adopting "an 'evolutionary' policy."

For Nearing, although British labor appeared "a formidable affair,"[20] the Russian model seemed to embody exactly the kind of change assumed under the economic classifications to which Nearing ascribed. In a class at the Rand School, he taught that "on November 7, 1917, all the workers of Russia proclaimed an industrial democracy." They took over the means of production, "declared an end to unearned income," and created a "democratic form of economic organization." The Soviet example drew a "fundamental distinction between those who work and those who exploit."[21] In this way, the Russian Revolution "was directed against capitalism in Russia and against imperialism everywhere," he wrote in *The American Empire*, focusing "the eyes of the world upon Russia, making her experiment the outstanding feature of a period during which the workers were striving to realize the possibilities of a more abundant life for the masses of mankind."[22]

Nearing hoped that trade unionism and socialism would negate capitalism and imperialism, that worker-controlled production would eliminate the economic surplus and erase conflict. This was an alternative path to a new world order.

> The workers of Europe have come to the conclusion that the world should belong to those who build it; that the good things in life should be the property of those who produce them. . . . The right of self-determination is the international expression of this challenge. The ownership of the job is its industrial equivalent. Together, the two ideas comprise the program of the more advanced workers in all the great imperial countries of the world.

This held true, Nearing surmised, for America too since "these ideas do not originate in Russia, and they are not confined to Russia any more than capitalism is confined to Great Britain."[23] "The way out" of the cycle of empire and destruction was for American workers to follow the course of the European proletariat and the Soviet Union's "dramatic assault upon capitalist imperialism." The "struggle between capitalist nations is incidental," he contended; "the struggle between the owners of the world and the workers of the world"—"between capitalism and socialism"—was fundamental. Only victory by the workers and the achievement of socialism could preserve the "promise of America."[24]

While Nearing saw in the Russian experience an ideal version of the kind of economic and social change he already advocated, he was selective about how much of the Soviet model he was willing to adopt. This was particularly true regarding the Marxian theory underlying revolutionary action in Russia. While Marxist analysis confirmed his belief that "the life and thought of a period quite naturally reflects the productive and social system then existing,"[25] he rejected the identification of socialism with any underlying dogmatic dialectic. His version of socialism resisted elevating any abstract propositions to the level of eternal truth while overlooking the need for ongoing empirical study and the necessity of voluntary action in understanding social change. He remained averse to the invisible hand of the classical liberal's political economy and to the inevitability of Marx's dialectical philosophy of history. Recognizing that the purpose of social revolution was to create new values and new social institutions, he emphasized the need for personal action and commitment while rejecting the economic determinism of dialectical materialism.[26]

■■■ As his new perspective of the world and social change came into focus, Nearing was faced with the critical question "What can the radical do at the present time?" He answered that the "social radical has three jobs": "First is to show why the existing order is unworkable—not that it is unworkable, but why; the second is to show the possibility of a more workable system, and the third is to show how it may be secured and established."[27] This was the program of action that Nearing set out for himself and that determined the tasks that would guide him through the troubled 1920s.

During the early years of the decade, Nearing devoted himself to traveling, studying the social facts, lecturing, writing, and teaching at the Rand School. In 1921 and again in 1922 he toured the American West to observe the labor movement and social circumstances.[28] These trips, and another late in 1924, took him not only west but south to Mexico, where he could view the labor situation outside the United States. Mexico, it seems, had a special fascination for him, possibly because it gave him the colonial perspective of American imperialism but also because Mexico served as a mythical land of real, vitalized life. The poverty was unmistakable, yet, he explained, there was "another side of Mexican life" that was "intensely colorful."[29] On the train from Mexico City back to the States, he chose to ride in the cars where the masses rode, the second-class "segunda," instead of in the luxury of a Pullman car. He talked to fellow passengers of the political situation in Mexico, the labor movement, and religion, but it was the common people who fascinated him. In a letter to his son Robert, he claimed that he had "written this much only to prove that the real romance and interest of life are after all in Segunda and not on the Pullmans." The "moral of the tale is obvious. The next time you start for the border (or anywhere else in Mexico) substitute the humanity and variety of Segunda (real) life for the superficiality and vapidity of the thoroughly respectable and sophisticated Pullman horde."[30]

When not away "taking stock of American labor" or experiencing the moral idealism of "real" life, Nearing made his home in Ridgewood, New Jersey, near his wife's family. Nearing's home became a magnet for leftists who escaped the city to revitalize their radicalism in rural New Jersey. A sampling of visitors gives an indication of the diversity of radicals with whom Nearing associated: James Cannon (a future Communist), Walter Liggett (editor of the New York *Call*), Algeron Lee (director of the Rand School), David P. Berenberg (a centrist), Henry W. L. Dana (a pacifist), Ralph Chaplin (the Wobblie poet), Carl Hassler, Harry F. Ward, Solon DeLeon, Louis Lochner, Lewis Gannett, Rexford Tugwell, Charles Garland, and of course Roger Baldwin. The *Masses* cartoonist Art Young left his name in the guest book along with a "self portrait of feet before a roaring fire." The young Margaret Mead, whose parents were friends of the Nearings, came "for introversion." And the artist–Communist Robert Minor expressed his hope "that the Nearing family will be in on the Dictatorship."[31] At Ridgewood, Joseph Freeman observed, "Nearing was a methodical worker; he budgeted his time for each day, and planned his work ahead for years to come." In the cellar of the house were "rows and rows of files, boxes of steel and wood, card catalogues and folders and notebooks of all kinds in which he kept his material as he gathered it. Here every book and article that interested him was outlined, and plans were plotted for books to be written in the future."[32] He had seen the present, and it needed work.

▬ All Nearing's activities were aimed at fulfilling the radical's social role as he saw it. "In the first place," he explained, "the most essential thing . . . to do is to make a clean-cut issue . . . as to what is the matter, what changes are desireable, and how those changes should be brought about." When he resumed teaching at the Rand School after a six-week tour of the West in November 1922, just as his book *The Next Step: A Plan for Economic World Federation* came off the press, his thought and activities were focused on defining the primary role of the radical in America.

*The Next Step* took Nearing beyond the problem of imperialism and looked ahead to establishing a world order in which capitalist imperialism and the conflict associated with it would be ended. In this study, which Freeman referred to as "an attempt to clarify the aims of socialism and at the same time to supply a workable solution" and Tugwell said presented "a rational and . . . particularly well ordered plan of march upon the promised land," Nearing tried to solve "the vexing questions arising out of the production and distribution of wealth" on a world scale.[33] He began by pointing out a contradiction of capitalist imperialism: as international competition increases, international solidarity grows. Undoubtedly it was an odd "contradiction" that "this interdependence has been intensified under a system of society that deified competition." Nonetheless, this conclusion provided "a means of co-operative living." The economic changes that had "established a world fellowship" were not "of the kind about which utopists had dreamed, but one growing out of the exigencies of world interdependence." It was "not because of any sweet reasonableness but because the pre-emptory demands of existence leave . . . no choice."

Interdependent economic activity made possible "the organization of a producers' society." He was presenting "an idealized picture, subject to an infinitude of modifications . . . a general design which is intended to place the whole subject of economic reorganization on a plane where it can be discussed as a matter of practical social science."[34] He offered a "plan for a world producers' federation" designed "with the object of placing all power in the hands of the producers."[35] *The Next Step* revealed Nearing's thought to be consistent with what one historian has called the "community internationalists," those who looked toward international organization with a vision of a natural community of organic unity that could embrace all the world with a morality of fellowship. The community internationalists focused their attention on social and economic remedies that would foster a sense of organic solidarity, and they rejected governmental or institutionalist solutions that conceived of the world as atomistic and competitive, bound together by legalistic arrangements, formal treaties, and leagues. One of the key problems for the community internationalists was war, since war destroyed the human community.[36] War had laid waste Nearing's earlier faith in the organic solidarity of American society that had been the cornerstone of his university ideal. Whereas he found he no longer had a place in American society, he could find membership in a world community that was infinite, ideal, and not tied to any organized institution.

It was in this sense that Nearing proposed a plan for world federation as an alternative to other proposals for postwar international organization. In particular, Nearing opposed legalist structures such as the League of Nations and the World Court. The League of Nations, he argued, was a failure because it was "a political and not an economic document. . . . The League, as a means of world organization, was destined, from its inception, to pathetic failure. World economic life is an established fact of such moment that it must be reckoned with in any scheme for social rebuilding."[37] Distinguishing between those who favored the World Court and those whose view he shared, he noted that the former did not want "a world controlled by workers and equalization of economic opportunity, but the danger of revolution reduced, law and order established." "What we are interested in," he said, "is seeing a world constituted in which men and women are living together and working out their problems on a world scale." Those in favor of joining the World Court were "interested in the preservation of rationalism and property; we are interested in seeing the human race as a cooperating group."[38]

He lashed out at the League of Nations as "a political arrangement between the allied and certain neutral nations" that contained "no important economic provisions" and was "intensely antidemocratic."[39] The league was "the last stand of capitalism—the last obstacle in the way of the economic emancipation of labor." It could not "bring world peace" since "the causes of modern war are economic. These causes the League Covenant, as it is drawn, ignores entirely."[40]

> The League of Nations is the logical political expression of international capitalism just as the bourgeois state is the logical political expression of national capitalism. . . . The League of Nations will come at the behest and under the control of the most reactionary forces in the capitalist world. It will be a league of bankers, diplomats, manufacturers and traders. Its function will be the preservation of capitalist society with all its monstrous inequities.[41]

He advised labor and Socialists to shun the league and its false shibboleth of liberty. With bitter sarcasm, he asked whether imperial America was "going to extend to the other portions of the earth the liberty of Everett, Ludlow, Bisbee and Lawrence? The liberty of Bill Haywood, Tom Mooney, Kate O'Hare and Eugene V. Debs?"[42]

In his plan for international economic federation, Nearing drew on the political model of the United States and the economic model of the Soviet Union. His selection is significant. The new world would have a political federation similar to that of American federalism, yet it would dispose of economic capitalism. The economic order would be based on the "experiments in workers' control" in Soviet Russia while avoiding "*economic bu-*

*reaucracy,* involving the concentration of economic authority in the hands of a centralized group."[43]

"The structural organization of the world producers' federation," Nearing explained, "would be similar to that of the United States of America or that of the Russian Federated Soviet Republic."[44] From the Soviet experiment he arrived at the notion that the "organization of producers into groups corresponding with their occupations lays the basis for world thinking and world federation."[45] And from the model of the United States as "an association of sovereign states," he devised a plan for the "organization of a producers' society" where "local initiative will be preserved; self-government in economic affairs must be assured, and the activities of the world must be federated in such a way that all economic problems will be brought under . . . a world parliament composed of representatives elected by the workers in various producing groups" forming the "central authority."[46]

Having presented this economic plan for world federation, Nearing noted that "if there is to be an organization of economic society that will function successfully and autonomously, the knowledge on which the decisions affecting economic policy are made must be public property." Because this was not possible under the controlling plutocratic hegemony, "there must be inaugurated a widespread propaganda, the object of which will be to get the facts and their implications to the people; the facts regarding the disintegration of the present order; regarding the possibilities of a new society; regarding the next steps that are necessary in its establishment."[47]

▬▬ Thus, turning to the third task of the radical, Nearing advocated "propaganda," which, he explained, was "the most important one for the American radical at the present time. For the time being, and for a long time to come, the job of the radical will be an educational one." Educational propaganda could be pursued in "the field of journalism," "the field of the arts— painting, literature, the drama," and in "the field of political action, which is now a method of propaganda."[48] Nearing took up the task of propaganda in his teaching; his writing; subsidizing the Left through the American Fund for Public Service; organizing the Federated Press, an alternative labor press service; and an attempt at promoting radical art.

He continued his teaching at the Rand School and even attempted publishing a regular newsletter in the spring of 1919, which was alternately called *Scott Nearing's American Letter* or *Scott Nearing's Article Service*.[49] What concerned him most was the problem of "the control of labor education." Formulating "a real proletarian culture" that would "finally throw upon the shoulders of the industrial worker the responsibility for controlling his economic destiny" required preventing the ruling class from "dominat[ing] the educational activities of the workers." He was interested in institutions like the Rand School that were "financed by the workers, and that are avowedly . . . engaged in the struggle for a new social order."

While he maintained that "there were more of these institutions before the war,"[50] he was still able to gather students into study groups, like the one he led in the spring of 1925, which met once a week either at the Rand School or at the Socialist party headquarters or in a Communist party office. In this class, the students and their teacher attempted to formulate "the laws of social revolution."[51] Even though his teacher was not a member of the Communist party, one young party initiate, Whittaker Chambers, attended the course "more," he said, "to observe the mind of Scott Nearing at work than for the sake of anything it might work on." He recalled that most of the students "were engrossed less by the law of social revolution than by Nearing." He vividly remembered Nearing "in front of the room, from time to time slapping into his mouth and chewing with audible energy handfuls of whole oats which he poured from a candy bottle that he always carried with him."[52]

Nearing's educational propaganda included continued study of American imperialism and resulted in *Dollar Diplomacy* (1925), which he coauthored with Joseph Freeman, the young radical he had met at the American Civil Liberties Union. *Dollar Diplomacy* differed from *The American Empire* primarily in its objective case-study format; it focused neither on theories of the development of imperial systems nor on alternative paths to a nonimperial future. Dollar diplomacy was defined as "the growth of the United States economic interests abroad, and the diplomatic and military support accorded them by the Federal Government." Their study had but two aims: "to indicate how far the United States is following an imperial policy, and . . . to suggest some of the outstanding characteristics of United States foreign policy." As Freeman explained, "The book itself did no more than 'expose.' We deliberately avoided carrying the facts to their logical revolutionary conclusions." Their study was wholly descriptive, mainly a documentation of the imperial stage of American expansion and its variety of forms. It was, claimed Freeman, "essentially a liberal, not a Marxist analysis; we did not illuminate the class characteristics either of the imperialist or of the colonial countries, or show the relationship between the two in light of the general development of capitalism."[53] After "initial publishing obstacles," *Dollar Diplomacy* was well received as a scholarly study and became the best known of Nearing's books on the subject. "Nevertheless," Freeman recalled, "we had a sense of void; we felt that we had made only a crude step toward a revolutionary study of American imperialism."[54]

It is worth noting that Nearing published *Dollar Diplomacy* through a small Left-oriented publisher in New York. Ever since being dropped by Macmillan in 1917, he had published his works either privately, as with *The Next Step*, or through the radical press, houses such as Vanguard Press, International Publishers, Social Science Publications, or through the Rand School. According to Nearing, the mainstream capitalist press would not touch books dealing with topics such as American imperialism. This made the left-wing presses absolutely essential for carrying out a program of educational propaganda. But it also meant that the channels for communication were limited and that there was difficulty with getting one's ideas across to the masses. He gained a wider audience through writing for popular magazines, but again he found himself restricted to the periodicals of the political Left and again to a narrowed audience. He wrote for an array of newspapers and magazines spanning the American Left: the New York *Call*, the *Liberator*, the *New Masses*, the *Daily Worker*, *Revolutionary Age*, *Advance*, the *Nation*, *Modern Quarterly*, *Labour Monthly*, *Labor Age*, the *Communist*, and others. In one instance, an essay on the state of Pennsylvania that he subtitled "A Study in Godliness and Economic Determinism" was rejected by the *Nation* because it "lacked grace"; the New York *Call* published it in its Sunday magazine. In another instance, an article on wages and the standard of living was rejected by the *Saturday Evening Post* since "it did not leave a good taste in the mouth" and the magazine needed "to get and keep advertizing." "Writing for anything but Left magazines," Nearing found, "was next to impossible."[55]

Under circumstances of closed communication, it became critically important to preserve and promote those channels that remained open. It was with this purpose in mind that Nearing became involved with an unusual effort at funding radical causes through philanthropy. This mostly forgotten trust, which subsidized a wide array of leftist causes in the 1920s, began in 1920 when Charles Garland, the twenty-one-year-old son of a railroad financier, decided to give up his inheritance. He made it publicly known that he believed that the wealth was not his since he did not earn it, and furthermore, he wanted to put it to public use. Garland had been greatly influenced by Tolstoy and was determined to live a simple hardworking, abstemious life, making a living from the soil by his own labor. He was faced with the problem of how to give away more than a million dollars to socially progressive public causes as quickly as possible.

When Roger Baldwin heard of Garland's dilemma, he jumped at the opportunity and drew up a trust that would "finance all sorts of leftist and pioneering causes, nonpartisan and unconventional, to do what no established foundation would dream of touching." Garland signed off to this American Fund for Public Service, as it was named, and went off to live the simple life on a farm; he did not join the trustees. Baldwin assembled the board of the fund, entrusted with dispensing what quickly became Garland's millions in the boom market of the 1920s. Baldwin chose for trustees "a mixed group, intentionally mixed to box the left compass." They included, in addition to Baldwin, the civil libertarian, "a socialist, Norman Thomas; William Z. Foster, later a communist, then an unclassified Red; an errant leftist, Scott Nearing; a trade unionist, Sidney Hillman; a lawyer, Morris Ernst; a couple of liberals, Freda Kirchwey and Lewis Gannett; an ex-iww, Elizabeth Gurley Flynn; a negro, James Weldon Jones," and a handful of others.[56] What this diverse group shared, according to Baldwin, was a "common anti-capitalist outlook, our faith in the workers to build up a new political and economic power to replace capitalism."[57]

Nearing emerged as the persistent voice advocating the promotion of individuals and organizations that carried on the task of educational propaganda. He proposed funding that would advance work in the area of "American imperialism," "the field of labor research," and "the field of labor education." In April 1924, he put forward a five-year program for the fund in which he called for "consistent educational work looking to the establishment of a new world order." His program, he explained, was "based on the assumption that what is most needed in the United States at the moment is a carefully worked out and consistent propaganda for economic and social emancipation." Cognizant of divisions within the Left, divisions that undoubtedly emerged within the board itself, Nearing noted that "if the Fund is to participate in this work, it must do so educationally without commitments to any of the factional or partisan groups that are aiming to bring about the results."[58]

Consciously avoiding the exercising of control through moneyed power, the board declared its "refusal to dictate . . . the social policy of any organization" that received funding. This, they claimed, "would be an improper and dangerous use of power." The board announced in April 1923, after six months of operation, that the fund had given away over $25,000 and lent over $100,000 "to radical and labor organizations." Money was given outright to a number of causes, including the Rand School; the United Mine Workers, "District No. 2, Cresson, Pa., for the relief of destitute families on strike"; and to the National Association for the Advancement of Colored People in New York City "for the campaign for the federal anti-lynching bill." Loans were made to the United Mine Workers, Brookwood Labor College, the New York *Call*, the Labor Defense Council, and others. These were typical of the fund's activities. Baldwin claimed that "we went heavily into . . . newspapers, periodicals and books [and] backed the new experiments in labor education." Enterprises such as Vanguard Press were established with initial capital outlays by the fund. During the 1920s, according to Baldwin, the American Fund for Public Service subsidized "almost a hundred enterprises of pioneering character directly or indirectly related to building up the power of the organized working class."[59]

One organization the fund supported was the Federated Press, an "example of a subsidized Left communication channel," established by Nearing and Louis Lochner after the war. The Federated Press emerged in 1921 out of the *People's Council Bulletin*, which Lochner and Nearing had produced while with the People's Council for Democracy and Peace. It was conceived as a news service that would "bring about a closer contact between the liberals and the labor movement itself," with the purpose of defending "the principles of the freedom of the press against the forces which seek its destruction." The Federated Press put out its own newspaper, the *Federated Press Bulletin*, and drew upon the People's Council form of organization, proposing a "league composed of locals—local councils" that would gather news. It stated in its bylaws that "being unable to obtain unbiased news service from the existing press associations," its editors would "unite in a mutual and co-operative organization for the collection and interchange of intelligence" relating to labor.[60]

---

In June 1921, one observer writing in the *Nation* declared the Federated Press "the most important of all forces at work during the past year in welding the detached and inadequate labor papers of the country into a common structure, and in creating a public to support it." It was, he argued, "the first international news service to come into existence" and "by all odds the most hopeful . . . of any development in American journalism within a generation." It claimed to be "a cooperative press association which gathers news from all countries, interprets it from the working-class point of view, and distributes it to many newspapers in America and overseas." Like the composition of the Garland Fund's board, the editors of the Federated Press represented varied positions on the political Left, "and they agreed to a new policy free from dictation of any faction." At its height, it distributed news releases on a daily basis to more than one hundred subscribers in the United States and abroad. Nearing initially served as associate editor and later became a correspondent, as did his wife and others such as Paul Hanna, Frederick C. Howe, Anna Louise Strong, and Carl Sandburg. With the help of the Garland Fund to sustain it, the Federated Press struggled through the 1920s providing the Left and the labor movement with news the capitalist press ignored.[61]

Surprising to some but consistent with his devotion to the task of educational propaganda, Nearing expressed an interest in art in the early 1920s. Joseph Freeman, who traveled in literary circles, was pleased with Nearing's new interest but found that "his aesthetic views, like his politics, were a blend of puritanism and socialism." After viewing an art show, Nearing wrote Freeman "a tirade" against the exhibit, asking, "How could painters waste their time and effort on flowers and richly gowned ladies in the face of the 'titanic struggle for existence that is gripping the masses.' "[62] Nearing rejected the notion of art for art's sake and thought of "art and literature" as "avenues of propaganda" for "reaching the masses of the people."[63]

It was in this vein that the poetry of Ralph Chaplin, the incarcerated editor of the IWW newspaper *Solidarity,* caught Nearing's attention. He personally went to see Chaplin in jail, and through his efforts Chaplin's prison poems appeared in 1922 as *Bars and Shadows* with an introduction by Nearing.[64] He was particularly impressed with poems like "Mourn Not the Dead."

Mourn not the dead that in the cool earth lie—
Dust unto dust—
The calm, sweet earth that mothers all who die
As all men must;

Mourn not your captive comrades who must dwell—
Too strong to strive—
Within each steel-bound coffin of a cell,
Buried alive;

But rather mourn the apathetic throng—
The cowed and meek—Who see the world's great anguish and its wrong
And dare not speak![65]

For Nearing, Chaplin represented both an intellectual persecuted by the dominant class and a prophetic voice in the struggle for a new society. Chaplin faced a twenty-year sentence, not as the court claimed for interfering with the conduct of the war, but rather, said Nearing, because he was "against the present economic order, of which the world war was only one phase."[66] Referring to Chaplin, Nearing argued that "it is the protesting brain that counts for the most in the long run; it is the departure from the established order that makes progress possible."[67] The strength of the new order could be gauged not only by the "solidarity of its organization" or by "the efficiency of its propaganda" but by "the tone of its art." Chaplin's poems were "a contribution to the propaganda and the art of the new culture."[68]

Nearing seems also to have been attracted to the unmistakable religious spirit of Chaplin's poetry, a proletarian millennialism rooted in an international, even universal, class struggle. In the IWW Chaplin found sanction for his religious search for solidarity with the disinherited, in this case class solidarity. As one student of the IWW has noted, it "often violently opposed all forms of organized religion [and] frequently derived its critique of capitalist America through a radical, prophetic, interpretation of Christianity."[69] Nearing commented that for Chaplin and his fellow Wobblies, "the task of freeing humanity from economic bondage took on the aspect of a faith, a religion . . . with zealous devotion. They had seen a vision; they had heard a call to duty; they were giving their lives to a cause—the emancipation of the human race."[70] "The spirit lying behind" Chaplin's poems, Nearing said, "is the spirit needed in the United States now." "At no time have we been more devoted to mere material things; we need men and women to tell us there is something in life. This man Chaplin sees liberty and freedom as great ideals for which to strive."[71]

▬ Nearing had already committed himself to educational propaganda through political action when he joined the Socialist party during the summer of 1917. The question of the purpose and goal of political action was one that would haunt him throughout the twenties. He had entered the party and the political Left at a time of unusual unanimity. A perpetually fractionalized Left had already undergone serious divisions domestically over the question of American support for the war and had split off from the international Left by becoming the standard-bearers of the Second International's commitment to oppose capitalist wars even as the vast majority of European Socialists turned nationalistic in 1914. When Nearing entered the party, the factional differences over the St. Louis platform had been resolved by significant defections, so that with the war and then the Russian Revolution, the Socialist party gravitated with some harmony leftward, united by antimilitarism, antiimperialism, internationalism, and working-class solidarity. Yet even with reduced hostility among its various wings and tendencies, by 1919, the party faced an insurmountable crisis.

Repercussions from the failure of the Second International and the success of the Russian Revolution began to be felt at home in 1917 as a new left wing of the Socialist party became vocal through the *Class Struggle*, edited by Louis Frania, Ludwig Lore, and Louis Boudin.[72] One important difference between the leadership of the party, those like Hillquit, and the left wing was over the proximity of pacifist groups to the party. The left wing echoed the Bolshevik's hatred for pacifists; pacifism was defined by Lenin as the "means employed to fool the working class."[73] Whereas the Hillquit wing of the party supported political affiliation with pacifist groups, in particular the People's Council, the council became a special target of the left wing because it "did not square with our revolutionary aims." It was a "bourgeois pacifist" organization from which the Socialists should dissociate themselves.[74]

The rhetoric of these battles, although virulent at times, may have appeared, at least initially, more absolutist than it actually was. For instance, when the *Revolutionary Age: A Chronicle and Interpretation of International Events* appeared in November 1918 as a new forum for the left wing, with Frania as its editor, Nearing joined John Reed, N. I. Hourwich, Sen Katayama, G. Weinstein, and Lore as a contributing editor. The magazine had lamented Nearing's congressional loss in 1918 since he was one "who would have laid a good foundation for the more numerous Socialist congressional delegations of the future."[75] Yet this was again an increasingly turbulent time for the Left, and Nearing's pacifism became problematic. In the February 3, 1919, issue of *Revolutionary Age*, the left wing took up the struggle of the Third International, announced from Moscow the month before, which had called for international revolution and the immediate establishment of "a dictatorship of the working class," through "mass action."[76] This program of insurrectionary action precluded cooperation with liberals or reformers and necessitated a split from centrist and right-wing elements in the party, along with unconditional loyalty to the Communist International. Thus, the magazine published a "Manifesto and Program of the Left Wing of the American Socialist Movement" advocating that it "throw off its parliamentary opportunism."[77] By the end of February, Nearing had left the staff of *Revolutionary Age*.

His pacifism and devotion to the Russian Revolution left him in an untenable situation. He wholeheartedly allied himself with the Soviet workers-council idea, and he wanted to move beyond the reformist tendencies of the Socialist party, yet he also wanted revolution without violence. In March he joined a "centrist" group within the party that tried mediating between the ever distancing extremes.[78] A letter appearing in the *Call*, signed by Nearing and other centrists, claimed that the party faced "a national and international crisis" and called for the end of "organized separation and division." The centrists adopted the left-wing position of "abolition of all social reform planks," and they claimed that the party "must teach, propagate, and agitate exclusively for the overthrow of capitalism and the establishment of industrial democracy" by assisting "revolutionary unionism."[79] They had strategically called for "industrial democracy" instead of a dictatorship of the proletariat, advocated propaganda instead of insurrection, and avoided mentioning the Bolsheviks by name as the only revolutionary party. The left wing responded to this position through *Revolutionary Age:* "The center must be smashed as a necessary means of conquering the party for the party, for revolutionary socialism."[80]

By April, this narrow path had led to a painful dilemma. At a lecture at the Rand School on April 19 before an audience of between four and five hundred, Nearing discussed "the programme of the American Socialist Party." He said the present party program was out of date because it was oriented toward "reform" and not "revolution." Revolution, he declared, was "the only way to change the existing order of things."[81] While this sounded as if he were advocating violent insurrection, in keeping with the left-wing line—as it did to the Justice Department agents who covered his lecture—Nearing had in mind a specific kind of "revolution." On April 28, in a debate with Albert Bushnell Hart, Nearing was pushed to define his conception of revolutionary activity. He replied: "When I spoke of revolution, I meant the people should take control of their own means of production. I mean a peaceful revolution. A revolution can be carried on by peaceful means unless the counterrevolutionaries insist on bloodshed as the only method." Knowing that this explanation would likely not satisfy Hart or be acceptable to the left wing, Nearing admitted that he was "one of those despised creatures, a pacifist."[82]

He took the high road by publishing a plea for nonviolence in a pamphlet entitled *Violence or Solidarity; or, Will Guns Settle It?* On its cover appeared a statement by Lenin: "It is with ideas, not with armies, we shall conquer the world." The bulk of Nearing's argument was above the battles of the party; he condemned the violence of the capitalist class in international conflicts and in domestic repression. Violence, he wrote, would not settle questions of war, radical opposition, or labor unrest. Late in the pamphlet he addressed the left wing's tactic of violence in a workers' revolution.

> The workers have used violence—violence against property of their employers, violence against the scabs who were taking their jobs. Has this violence won them their battle? Not at all! . . . The Russians won their point through economic justice at home, propaganda and open diplomacy. Not their army but their philosophy and example spread revolution over Europe. The Russians may fail in their great experiment. . . . If they fail in this the Red Army will help them fail.

"Violence in the labor movement," he argued, "is no substitute for solidarity." He pleaded for "common purpose, common thought, common understanding, courage, solidarity—these things make labor's triumph and not resort to force." He closed by addressing both the capitalists and the leftists.

Guns, he pleaded, "will not suppress ideas nor prevent crime, nor preserve peace, nor win the battle of labor, nor play any part in setting up the institution of the dear love of comrades. Even when they are used for good purposes they lead to bad results."[83]

Again Nearing came under attack from the Left. The *New York Communist*, the organ of the left wing of the party in New York edited by John Reed, lashed out at Nearing's pamphlet early in June. "Comrade Nearing seems to think that the reason for revolution is entirely a moral one. He implies that the reason the working class wishes to take over the power, and *ought* to take over the power, is because such an action is *right*."

> The inference from this argument is that all one has to do in order to persuade the vast majority of the people that Socialism is best, is to employ the weapons of peace argument and propaganda. But the question is not whether Socialism is morally right, the point is that the Socialist Commonwealth is the only possible way to save civilization and reconstruct human society. . . . The capitalist class is not going to be convinced of its moral duty to abolish itself, no matter how great a majority of the workers decide that this is right.

Tactics such as "passive resistance" were "utopian," and there was "no way to meet the violence of the capitalist class except by violence." But the Left also worried about the timing of the pamphlet's appearance. Coming "when the Socialist movement is split into two factions," it had the effect of tarnishing their position. "We resent," said the response, "the implication that we stand for violence because it is violence; and that we are against 'solidarity.'" Slamming Nearing for attempting "to preach 'the Social Revolution by Brotherly Love,'" the Left declared that "pacifism disarms the working class, and exposes it to the most fearful dangers." As for Nearing, the left wing claimed, "there is no place for pacifists in the Social Revolution."[84]

By the time of the August convention of the Socialist Party, Nearing maintained his desire to see the party move leftward yet avoid the excesses of the left wing. There is no evidence that he involved himself in the nuts and bolts of party politics or that he took part in the disastrous convention where the left wing was expelled and the Left itself divided into two rival Communist parties. Nearing told Granville Hicks in 1934 that he remembered urging John Reed not to try to capture the party for the Left at the convention but "to maneuver for six months and then take over the SP apparatus" because "at that stage they could have had the whole thing."[85] With the Left utterly fragmented, Nearing was resigned to staying in the Socialist party. His own position paralleled the party's to a large degree. He could agree that revolutionary conditions did not yet exist in the United States, although he advocated revolutionary educational propaganda to prepare the workers for the revolution ahead. And as long as the Socialists continued to support the Soviet government, its policy was consistent with Nearing's beliefs regarding "the Russian revolution . . . as the epoch making event, the dividing line between capitalism and socialism."[86] Devotion to the ideals of the Revolution did not necessarily mean that the Soviet model could be applied to America, so the Socialists looked to other models, particularly the labor movement in Great Britain. Nearing, too, would follow British labor with great interest, using it as a barometer of sorts to see whether legal parliamentary activity could bring about revolutionary social change. Finally, pacifism was wholly consistent with the party's analysis of its potential and its assessment of the American working class. He stood to the left of the party, but not far enough left to step into divisive oblivion.

As a native intellectual of considerable influence with a reputation for standing up for radical principles, Nearing was considered an important party asset. When *The American Empire* appeared, the party leader James Oneal lavishly praised Nearing as "one of the keenest of contemporary observers of the present transition." Nearing's study served the party's political purposes. Oneal claimed it was "a distinct acquisition to the American Socialist movement." Deriding the Communists' belief in the adaptability of the Russian situation to America, he went on to point out that Nearing's book was "devoted exclusively to American economic conditions." And finally he asked a question aimed only at the Communists: "Will some of our devoted adherents consider it 'treason' to the Russian Revolution to assert that here is a book written in plain and simple English that will do more to enlighten the worker of this country than all the theses that may be written on the 'dictatorship of the proletariate?' "[87] There was no escaping the fact that Nearing could not avoid political squabbles by devoting himself to a course of social science and education that would serve the revolution. Whatever he said, his voice resounded through the dark canyons of the political Left in the twenties.

# Can We
# Live Up to Our Ideals?

## Chapter 14

THE years 1922 and 1923 were a time of intensely agonizing soul-searching for Nearing. He was dissatisfied with the Socialist Left, repelled by the factions and dogma of the Communist Left, wary of the Soviet government, and unsure of himself. At this critical point in his life, he wrote in anguish that "most of us feel an interest in life; we want to go on living even though we must suffer."[1] He began questioning his own social role, and in trying to reassess his task, he engaged in dialogues with himself that he presented as lectures at the Rand School and then published in the *Call*. In January 1922, he looked back over the past year and determined that it had been for the Left nothing but "a year of drifting; people have been rudderless, pilotless, purposeless" and that "the radicals have drifted with the rest." The radical, he wrote, "stands in the position where his fondest hopes have been frustrated, so he says there is nothing to be done and he sits back and waits." There remained but one immediate task of importance, "and that is to stop the drift." "Everyone who does not commit suicide," he said in a desperate tone, "must choose between drifting and not drifting, between passivity and activity, between not doing something and doing something."[2]

One course of action for radicals that would replace drift with mastery was also a direct criticism of the leadership of both the Communist parties and the Socialist party, which, Nearing intimated, remained aloof from the rank and file and were out of touch with the American worker. For "those of us who are disappointed radicals," he advised, they "would do well to get out and rub elbows with those people" who existed "under reduced circumstances" and "live their lives and strike their blows, and thus get a re-established balance." "The tired radical," he contended, "would do well to rub elbows with the people who are doing the world's work" because "whether a state be Communist or capitalist, the ordinary work of the world must be done, and you must choose whether or not you will help do it." He admonished fellow radicals to "take some active part in the organic life of the community, and the man who takes the most active and vigorous part will be one of the most active and vigorous members of the community."[3]

He also raised questions about Soviet Russia, hegemonic control, and revolutionary tactics. He admitted that "for years the workers in every great capitalist country looked toward Russia to find the torch bearers," yet he was critical of the leadership coming from the Soviet government. "Russia was to show the way and the others were to follow," he conceded, "but Russia has not done this."[4] The Soviet government imposed a dogmatism that was as destructive of an enlightened citizenry as the control enforced by capitalists. He worried that "if the social revolution were to come tomorrow, with the same teachers that we have today, there would be little improvement; they would simply teach Bolshevism instead of capitalism—they would put the child through the Bolshevik instead of the capitalist machine."[5] Finally, he saw other similarities between the Communists and the capitalists in adopting deceptively simplistic solutions to society's most difficult problems. Most people "seem to think that you can buy life with money, that if you have enough money you can have anything you want." But "the radical is just as bad: He thinks that he can buy life with revolution, with direct action, with some means except the only one—paying the price."[6]

Reassessment of the Left also led Nearing to determine what meaning the work of Karl Marx had for American radicals. Contrary to the Communists' use of Marx to enunciate hairsplitting decrees to be followed to carry out the party's version of the revolution, Nearing focused little on Marxian theory and claimed that in Marx's works "there is present neither a program of tactics nor a program of economic structure."[7] Marx had "based his theories on the idea that man would act the same way under similar economic circumstances, but historic circumstances differ." Marx, Nearing argued, "never saw an organized industrial society, such as we have today."[8] Thus, there remained the need to formulate "a basis of tactics and a form of social revolution." "The question," he claimed, was "not what Marx meant in a particular paragraph and chapter, but how to overthrow the established order and how to put in a new one."[9] But if one were to try to make Marx's words relevant to the present, Nearing directed attention to his comments in the *Communist Manifesto* that revolution did not have to mean insurrectionary and destructive violence. He quoted: "The class struggle . . . oppressor and oppressed, stood in constant opposition to each other . . . that each time ended either in revolutionary reconstitution of society at large or in the ruin of contending classes."[10]

Marxian theory was open to criticism, according to Nearing, yet regarding "the class struggle, exploitation and surplus value," Marx's ideas were "practically unassailable." His analysis of industrial capitalism was particularly useful in understanding how the type of economic system affected the rest of society. Marx showed how "the forms of production not only shape the forms of society but also shape the morals, the thought, the whole social context." Furthermore, Marx had focused men's thinking on the question of "economic justice—the doctrine that the worker should get the full value of what he creates or receive in proportion to his needs." "Marx's single greatest contribution to humanity" was in his conception of human agency—that man was not a victim of social forces but was master of his life. "Under the old idea," wrote Nearing, "the worker and his kind were doomed for all eternity, but Marx hurled at it the bomb of evolutionary thought" and made it clear that "the only thing to do [was] to go out and assist destiny."[11]

Most important, Marx seemed to serve as a model, as did Tolstoy, for radicals like Nearing. The question of how he lived his personal life was more important than his economic and social analysis. He described Marx as "a bourgeois intellectual" who, "like Kropotkin and Tolstoi," was in a social position "above the middle classes." "He had all the comforts of life and an opportunity to become a leader in the established order," yet "he rejected these opportunities and became active in the revolutionary movement." In that movement "he endured great economic hardships and privations, even hunger." Marx was a role model who instilled confidence in Nearing. When he wrote about Marx, he wrote about himself: "He not only gave up his position in the established order and his scholastic opportunities, but he suffered economically for his faith."[12]

▬▬ Part of Nearing's agonizing doubt arose not from the public and political state of the nation but from the deeply personal circumstances of his family life. Although he never revealed his deepest feelings about the gradual disintegration of his marriage during the twenties, there are some clues to its causes, and its personal consequences must be weighed when explaining this turbulent time in Nearing's life.

Part of the reason lies in his attempt to live a personal creed that would avoid the trappings of a culture that he saw dominated by a pervasive and destructive capitalist hegemony. His own life experiences since about 1915 had driven him to resist vigorously all aspects of the dominant culture that would impinge upon his individuality or co-opt his intellectual independence. Yet those closest to him—his wife, family, and friends—had not fully shared his experiences, nor did they arrive at his analysis of cultural control. When Nearing began to live his creed of resistance in his daily life, it affected the lives of those with whom he lived, and as he explained in a rare moment in his autobiography, "I found myself in hot water at once, domestically and socially. My immediate family and associates did not live in accordance with my golden rule. They usually argued that human happiness varies directly with the total available volume of goods, services, and private property. I replied that on all counts the more the worse."[13]

He admitted that his "immediate family . . . had to put up with many of my idiosyncrasies." Visitors to the Nearing household could not help but notice his unusual behavior, as did Joseph Freeman, who commented that Nearing "wore flannel or denim shirts, coarse trousers, and farmers shoes" and that this professional economist and intellectual "liked physical labor on his Jersey farm, and often prepared his own meals, consisting chiefly of raw fruits and vegetables."[14] Nearing began "protesting at the creeping incursion of lace dollies and cut-glass into our household." To spurn the corrupting effects of these luxuries, he started taking all his meals in a single wooden bowl, using wooden utensils.[15] Unfortunately, his family did not share his fervor for this notion of the simple life, lived with a vengeance.

It appears too that for his wife, Nellie, there were other issues. Although she shared a belief in the social divisiveness of capitalism and sympathized with generally socialist reforms—by the mid 1920s, she served as the executive secretary of the Rand School and on the executive committee of the League for Industrial Democracy—she faced domination and restrictive control as they related to gender. While her husband was often away from home trying to save mankind—as she would write, while the wife remained domestically bound, for "mental, and even emotional stimulus, her husband goes elsewhere"—Nellie assumed the family duties alone and found her intellect stifled.

In a revealing article she published in 1922 under her maiden name, she lashed out at the patriarchal notion that "the ideal of conduct to instill in every young woman was to become as proficient as her talents would permit in the art of conducting a home." In what was undoubtedly an autobiographical mode, she described this stultifying ideal from a woman's perspective.

> To excel as a seamstress, dress-maker, even a tailor when occasion demanded; to function culinarily not as an amateur but as an expert; to become thorough, painstakingly economical and even scientific in general household management; to be a patient, loving and necessary self-sacrificing mother to the next generation; to furnish, nay even become a congenial background for one of the more virile sex, whose task it was to take his place in the front trenches of life, generously protecting her thereby from any of the harder realities of life. . . . The place of the woman was in the home.

As in the past, she claimed, if a woman wanted to "capture" a man, "she had to become the kind of woman a man wanted." The woman's choice "was Hobson's, no choice at all." But, she added, "the world is moving on." "No longer does . . . the woman accept the categorical dictum confining her to the home; she can function without it or provide it for herself if she desires it." Women wanted to be "intellectually emancipated" because "this life of emancipation is obviously more interesting, far more stimulating."

This self-questioning made it an agonizing time for Nellie as well as Scott. She recognized that women's "pursuit of the intellectual life involved departure from the straight and narrow path." Some would be "willing to gloom over the monotonous side of domestic life" while others would "seek to pass beyond these limitations." "If she chooses the home as the field of her activities, her triumph is short-lived. Once let her become settled into the groove of household routine, her fate is fixed. If she is satisfied, efficient therein, it is proof uncontrovertible that her mind never rises above dishes or the wash-tub, and intellectual flights are reckoned beyond her ken." Why, she asked, exhort women "to excel in the virtues of house wifery? Is it not time we squared our theories with the facts?" As with Scott's conception of freedom and social reconstruction, the liberation sought by women like Nellie would entail difficult, even painful struggle. She acknowledged that the kind of emancipation she envisioned could "seldom be accomplished without the overturn of all that once seemed to count most in life. . . . The price is so high, the chance of success is so slight."[16]

Nellie did succeed, but she had to do it without Scott. They quietly drifted apart during the latter 1920s, and although their marriage effectively ended, they never formally divorced. Nellie went on to devote herself to the field of educational reform worldwide, visiting schools in England, Germany, Switzerland, Holland, Belgium, and the Soviet Union. She attended the meetings of the International Educational Conference in Switzerland in 1927 and in Denmark in 1929. From 1927 through 1932, she served as the director of the experimental Manumit School in Pawling, New York. From there she went on to become the Works Progress Administration (WPA) supervisor of adult education for the New York State Department of Education, and during World War II directed the adult education division of the Federal War Labor Board as a specialist in curriculum development and teacher training.[17] For Scott, resisting accommodation to the values and restrictions of capitalist culture meant standing outside its institutions, whether that meant its religious and educational institutions or even the institution of marriage. Nellie's struggle for freedom was focused more fundamentally against social norms in a male-dominated society; unlike her husband, she found emancipation for worthwhile experience within a capitalist culture.[18]

▬ In his public and personal distress, Nearing leaned heavily for moral perseverance, hope, and comfort on his religious faith. After the war, he had not only moved away from the corrupting influence of the Church for his religious belief but had also traveled away from Christianity as his religious anchor. He arrived at an esoteric faith both mystic and spiritual. His mysticism consisted of a unifying vision of a "god" conceived as a transcendent and unifying totality, a cosmic ultimate reality that had immense human importance. His approach to knowing this cosmic reality was through a spiritualism that allowed him to explore willfully the inner resources of his life; to explore deliberately one's inner resources became a kind of moral preparation through which one's inner spiritual composure, physical health, and even economic well-being flowed from unity with the cosmos. Roger Baldwin, a friend close enough to Nearing to know his personal mysteries, thought of Nearing as "essentially a religious man, with a mystic's sense of destiny."

> He lives by faith—faith not only in the future freedom of mankind but in a cosmic order over and above directed human effort. Indeed, his social philosophy flows from his religion. He believes, rather naively it seems to a non-mystic, in a world behind the appearance of reality. The real world is yet unknown. He is eager to explore. He has approached it via spiritualism.[19]

Because men were aggrieved by their situation in the world of the twentieth century, they were, according to Nearing, "looking about for some answer that does not appear in the conduct of their common lives." "We are living today," he wrote in February 1923, "and for a long time have been living, a sick people in a sick world. . . . It is a sick world and people are trying to find some answer."[20] In such a situation, he thought it was a profound error for the radical to overlook this most basic human need. Surely this was in part a response to the Marxians' tendency to dismiss religion as false belief that would placate the masses in their struggle. Yet it was also in all likelihood a response to an increasingly secularized liberal political culture. "Radicals and many who call themselves liberals," Nearing contended, were "in the habit of dismissing the church with a wave of the hand, and religion with a phrase, when as a matter of fact the church and religion are two of the most important factors which have to be reckoned with in any consideration of social problems." These institutions were "an expression of a very definite and potent human need."

The religious belief he referred to was "religious" in a broad sense, extending its meaning to mystical limits. "The subject matter of this body of belief that we call religion," he explained, encompassed "God, or good, the future, and the unknown, or destiny." While the radical and liberal might "say that man has no business to be interested in those things," the fact was that it was "part of his human makeup."[21] "No person," Nearing stated, "can live in the present generation and not realize that there is a tremendous upheaval which betokens an effort to get a grip on the unconscious and to get hold of a new source of power." Reacting against a crass materialism that was coming more and more to define the meaning of freedom in America, Nearing envisioned "society growing to a stage where people think more about what is going on . . . about the mental, rather than the physical."[22]

He was deeply concerned with "man's interest in the good, the eternal and the thing that is called destiny." This interest led him to take seriously ways of knowing this transcendent reality, so he looked to a broad array of spiritual practices such as oriental spiritualism and Christian Science. He also took seriously attempts at mental healing, or "auto-suggestion," as when the

Frenchman Emile Coué, a prophet of solving personal problems of health and success through positive thinking and inner power, made a tour of the United States early in 1923.[23] Nearing was disturbed that liberals and radicals laughingly sneered at Coué, and he was especially upset by "a flippant editorial" about the Frenchman that appeared in the *Nation*. "The Nation and its editorial," said Nearing, "writes as if there were no issue—it makes a joke out of Couéism."[24]

It was no joke to Nearing. Coué was offering something important to a mystic like Nearing. He compared "Couéism" to other spiritualist methods to indicate its merits. He said that Coué's "so-called mental cure" was not "new, but as a matter of fact, it is a very old practice" going back at least to faith healing among the Greeks. He noted "three kinds of mental healing" that were "being utilized now." There was Christian Science, whose practitioners "go to the source, namely spirit, and permit it to dominate his mortal mind. Christian Science goes to God, not as a person, but as a Spirit." There was also a Japanese "form of faith healing" whose "adherents live a simple austere life and refuse to follow the conventional standards." The Japanese approach, he claimed, was "more dynamic and dangerous than Christian Science, the followers of the latter being mostly well-to-do people." But then there was Coué, who, Nearing explained, went "to the individual . . . to first causes" while the Christian Scientist went "to God." His point was that "any sympathetic understanding has got to be built on a knowledge of these big movements."[25]

He was particularly sympathetic to "the mental scientists" like Coué. Their "main ideas" were "first, that we can interfere with nature, and second, that we can interfere with nature by processes of the mind projecting against obstacles of the body." The mental scientists did "not talk about God at all" but instead asked the question "What is my body?" They answered, he explained, that "it is the expression of cosmic energy. The energy has many manifestations, but at bottom there is one primary cause. . . . [The mental scientist] builds his case on the science of the mind as opposed to the science of matter, forces as opposed to manifestations, first causes as opposed to second causes." Coué's use of "auto-suggestion" was based upon the premise "that the imagination is greater than the will, that it is more important." His spiritualism pointed to the proposition that "just beneath the sphere of the conscious mind there is a greater reservoir of experience called the subconscious mind, and if the lid can be taken off this reservoir and . . . be tapped, great recreative forces will flow into the life of the individual."[26]

There is an unmistakable quality to Nearing's conception of spiritual and mystical religiosity that in other terms might be mistaken for Freudian psychological unveiling of the individual unconscious. The psychoanalytic approach to inner harmony and resolution of personal conflict was much more popular among intellectuals and writers of the Left by the 1920s than what Nearing was describing. Yet Nearing consistently shied away from a therapeutic substitute, possibly because it was too intensely individualistic. Even though Nearing's spiritualism appears to be overwhelmingly personal, it was in fact inseparably related to social salvation. He argued that "a community in harmony is a community where people live together with a minimum of friction; an individual in harmony is one whose organs are working together properly and whose mental state is free." "We say that we are trying to win freedom," he explained, but "what is this liberation?" On the one hand it was "freedom from inner conflict . . . for harmony inside." But "liberation takes two forms," so it was also "the freeing of the individual and the freeing of the community."[27]

Nearing rarely wrote about these religious beliefs. His only published writings that discuss mysticism and spiritualism appeared early in 1923 during this period of unrest in his life. Baldwin noted that Nearing's "religious approach to life"—which was "increasingly cosmic, synthetic"—"can hardly be detected in his debates, his speaking, and his writing. It is only the overtone, the large outlines, that reveal the mystical aspect of his nature." Baldwin does not offer an explanation for this, although he alludes to a problem Nearing undoubtedly encountered. His religious views did not square with the revolutionary theories of the Left. In explaining that Nearing was "philosophically an idealist [who] begins with the cosmos, the unseen world, and accepts the material world only as an aspect of the greater," Baldwin contrasted this with the fact that "the orthodox Communist is first a materialist; he accepts the natural world as the only reality."[28] While Nearing searched for harmony through mystical religion, the means he found was paradoxically difficult to harmonize with his political views.[29]

━━━ What was the role of the distraught radical intellectual in this age of spiritual demise and capitalist entrenchment? The answer was that he had no choice but to take the path of idealism and activism, a course of conscience and suffering. In social terms, the radical was "one of the most important assets there is when it comes to making any sort of progressive step," and in the present age "his function" became "very important . . . a vital necessity."[30] He upheld "ideals, beliefs, concepts—those things which play so vital a part in shaping the lives of the people."[31] Furthermore, the radical's social role meant that he sided with the workers in the present struggle. The "intellectual," he stated, "is a dealer in ideas." Like the "producers, whose function is to create or transform," the intellectuals "create the material, mental and moral aspects of our civilization. On the face of it, the intellectual belongs with the producer."[32]

The radical intellectual had a positive role to play in social reconstruction but faced the dilemma of how to turn words into deeds. The radical was "of necessity burdened with too much talking and not enough action, with too much idealism and not enough realism." "We talk and dream of what we will do when a certain situation arises," he noted, "but what are we actually doing in the meantime?"[33] He did not take "the attitude of cynical contempt and throw the job over" but did "his best to build something out of the chaos."[34] "Some folks," he realized, "confuse radicalism with universal negation"—a criticism directed mostly to the Left—and "they forget that they are human beings." He urged his critics on the Left to recall that "three often forgotten virtues are honesty, loyalty and efficiency," virtues "just as important in a Communist society as in a capitalist one."[35] Of course, Nearing understood that whether one's concern focused on the capitalists or the Communists, the final problem of the intellectual's idealism remained the same: "Is idealism practicable?" The answer posed an inescapable paradox. "There are two main lines of action," Nearing argued—"to follow ideals, resist society, and enact a tragedy, or to accept what comes and thus tragically submit."[36]

Nearing would not submit to capitalist cultural hegemony or to any kind of social domination. He would not tolerate those who relinquished their intellectual independence and self-dignity by compromising with or submitting to the dictates of wealth or the dogma of revolution.

> The function of the radical is not an administrative function and not a group function in the sense that he is held responsible for the present order. The Communist radical of today will be the administrator of tomorrow, and the Communist society will need the radical as badly as the capitalist society needs him now. It will then be the business of the radical, as it is now . . . not to perform any particular function as a part of the established order. His is primarily a critical function, representing minority, possibly revolutionary opinion. . . . A radical who wished to continue a radical cannot do so if he is an essential part of the established order, for then he owes a certain fealty to his position.[37]

He upheld this "critical function" by denouncing a revolutionary resistance that subordinated and manipulated the worker instead of raising him to the level of enlightened self-determination. The intellectual, as a "dealer in things of the mind, cannot serve by becoming the secretary of his local union." He could not "serve labor by becoming its accepted leader." "The intellectual should not be a guide in the labor movement but a servant in the movement." Possibly with the Wobblie Ralph Chaplin in mind as a model of the intellectual rebel, Nearing advised that "those of you who have creative ability in the world of art, write a good rebel song, turn out a piece of any kind of artistic creation." This kind of "aesthetic expression in proletarian America" would "be a far greater contribution to labor than if you tried to lead the movement."[38]

Nearing's notion of the intellectual was that of the "propagandist" who functioned as "the prophet and the advocate." In this prophetic role, the intellectual "says that this system is rotten to the core, that this method of life is not conducive to human well-being." The prophet became "a great leader" because "he denounces wrong and cries out in the name of right." "There is nothing more important than the intellectual as a prophet," claimed Nearing, because "young men and women growing up need wise guides, not coercion."[39]

A prophetic role included the possible fate of being crucified for one's ideals. Prophets throughout history—Nearing provided the examples of Socrates, Gandhi, and Debs—had to endure a painful paradox: "Man after man has suffered imprisonment, torture and death for his ideals, and these ideals have had a tremendous influence on the ideals of subsequent generations." "The living of an ideal involves the payment of a certain price. . . . The further the ideal is removed from the common practice of the man the higher the price must be paid for it. . . . If your ideal is to live a mentally active, mentally honest life, to seek the truth, then you may have to sacrifice food, clothing, and shelter to get it." Living according to one's ideals could lead to a kind of Thoreauvian isolation, a complete alienation from society, not as one who was persecuted but who intentionally chose a separate dignified existence. "The hermit who goes off to live all alone," he argued, "need not go as a martyr; he makes a choice between one mode of living and another—he is going along another highway and paying toll there."[40]

There remained the final agonizing paradox surrounding the dilemmas of retreat and influence, the individual and society. On the one hand, "the ideal of the individual" was "one of personal salvation." The further the individual went in living up to his personal ideals, "the more he will get out of life." That such a course of action "may cost him his liberty," was "relatively unimportant." "If the individual is robust mentally and physically," he contended, "he should go just as far as he can in following his ideal." The problem with this kind of prophetic monasticism was that "the individual whose ideal is the elevation of society can only go so far as he is able to keep in touch with society." For the radical to avoid relegating himself to an impotent imperial self, "society must be within sound of his voice." "These two problems," he argued, were "separate and distinct; one is the problem of personal salvation," while "the other is the problem of the elevation of society."[41] Not only was Nearing revealing that the severity of his situation pressed upon him the reality of mutually independent choices—either personal or social salvation—but he was tacitly acknowledging the reality of cultural fragmentation. His organic community ideal that fused public with private, personal with social, had given way to community disintegration, placing each in its "separate and distinct" realm. The problems of freedom for the self and freedom for society presented a terrible paradox that tore at Nearing from within and from without.

# I Didn't Say It
# Because Marx Said It

## Chapter 15

HOPING for some vital signs, Nearing kept his finger on the pulse of the Left, watching with keen interest the activities of the Communist factions. What separated him from the Communists was the issue of tactics; the party line called for violent revolution, a means that alienated a pacifist who foresaw a long struggle of educating the worker toward a revolutionary social consciousness. Suddenly in 1922 things began to change. The Comintern tacitly admitted that its strategy for international revolution had been a failure and had officially adopted a "united front" policy late in 1921 as a policy of seeking alliances with non-Communist organizations. On the surface, this differed little from the Socialist party position, yet the united-front policy defined by the Third International in December 1921 was specifically "for the purpose of *strengthening the Communists* through direct propaganda inside organizations taking part in this movement." In common parlance, it meant "boring from within."[1]

During the following year, the details of this new policy were worked out. The party explained that "the tactics of the United Front imply the leadership of the communist vanguard in the daily struggles of the large masses of the workers for their vital interests."[2] The effect of the united-front policy for American Communists was profound. The shift in tactics made a divided insurrectionary, underground Communist presence in the United States untenable. Along with ordering the American Communists to adopt the united front, the Comintern also ordered a united legal party apparatus. By

December 1922, this new codification unified the American Communists into a single Workers Party of America.

Coincidentally, 1922 was a year of rumblings on the Left in the United States as well as in Moscow. A coalition-building group called the Coalition for Progressive Political Action (CPPA) had called a conference for February in Chicago to form a new political movement, seeking to run a third-party candidate without forming a third party. The united-front policy had not yet transformed the Communist movement in the United States; thus the party was unwilling to compromise with the less-than-revolutionary labor or socialist organizations of the CPPA. In fact, the Communists had not been invited to attend the conference, at which the Socialist party, the Farm–Labor party, and other labor and farmer organizations were represented.[3] By the time of the second CPPA conference in December, the Communists, now the single Workers party, voiced the international united-front party line. This time they sent a delegate to the conference, and even though he was rejected by the CPPA, he had found support from the Farm–Labor delegation at the conference.[4]

The policy of the united front had in part superseded previous critiques of pacifism and had allowed Nearing to enter into Communist debates without being immediately vilified. But the fact that Nearing's conception of the party's task did not square with the party line (Communist or Socialist) became increasingly apparent in 1923. With the December 1922 CPPA convention, the Workers party had found a united-front ally in the Federated Farmer–Labor party of Chicago. Their strategy was to form a united front alliance between the Farmer–Labor party and the third-party movement coalescing behind Robert La Follette. Nearing immediately dissented from this collaboration.

Such an alliance, he said, confused La Follette's liberalism with radicalism. "The liberal in the United States," Nearing claimed, "is one who can promise changes that he cannot effect." La Follette, Nearing asserted, wanted "to restore the conditions of Jeffersonian Democracy, but Standard Oil was born after Jefferson died." While he admired La Follette "as a fighter," La Follette was "fighting not for a Socialist or Communist order, but for a decent, purified capitalist system" and had "no vision of a new world." "Nothing," Nearing said, advising the Left against collaboration, "can be accomplished without a revolutionary program with a revolutionary purpose."[5]

The coming election in 1924 brought instructions from Moscow requiring the united-front policy. The party line adhered to a pessimistic analysis of the viability of capitalism and thus an optimistic assessment of the revolutionary potential of the masses in America. The Communists conceived of turning the united front of 1923 into a third-party alliance in 1924 behind La Follette. The Farmer–Laborite coalition had called for a convention on May 30, 1924, to adopt a platform and nominate its candidate. Early in May, Nearing engaged William Z. Foster, who had assumed the chairmanship of the Workers party in 1923, in a debate in the pages of the Communist *Daily Worker*.

He took issue with Foster's published assertions that the rank and file of American labor would vote for a revolutionary program and that the average worker was far more radical than the union leadership. The rank and file, argued Nearing, acquiesced in the present economic order. Their consent had been exacted from the capitalists

> by lining up the rank and file throughout the most complete system of propaganda, lies, diversions, amusements, excitements and thrills that the world has ever produced. The whole machinery of education is in the hands of the business interests and they do not hesitate to use the newspaper or the movie to put their interpretation on events, to suppress information or to deliberately misrepresent the facts. . . . The rank and file of American workers have come to believe what they are told.

Nearing acknowledged that he was "well aware that this is not the accepted opinion of the left, but I am basing my judgement on a very considerable contact with members" of organized labor. What he was describing, he said, was "not apathy at all but tacit consent . . . to the present economic system." Foster was simply wrong to assume that there was revolutionary sentiment among American workers. The workers, Nearing observed, were "discontented, but they assume 'times will pick up' under the present system." "Whatever revolutionary sentiment there is in the country today," he concluded, "cannot be described as in any sense 'American mass sentiment.'"

Nearing's diagnosis of the American working class led him to assert that "those of us who believe that there must be radical changes in the economic and social life of the United States find ourselves in a position where the radical sentiment must be created." This line of argument assigned priority to the task of educating the worker, which, Nearing admitted, "places us in quite opposite camps when it comes to the tactics that should be pursued." If Nearing's analysis was correct, "the revolutionary movement in America must" realize that it was a minority movement, "highly localized" and "divided by foreign admixtures."

Most critical, the movement had to devote its energies to building its power slowly and thoroughly, fostering "effective and cooperative activities" to "preserve morale and efficiency." "It is not 'radical' to build rapidly," he admonished Foster. "It is radical to build fundamentally, and it is fundamental building that the movement needs in the United States." The revolutionary movement in the United States faced "a vast wall of ignorance and opposition" and therefore "must preserve stern integrity, strict discipline and live revolutionary ideals." "As a matter of tactics," he told Foster, "you . . . are following a policy based on Russian experience, which is quite unfitted to cope with the situation you confront in the United States, and which will drive your party to ruin if you pursue it." Nearing worried that "if the Workers Party enters the May 30th convention, nominates a man like La Follette, and campaigns for him, its position will be misunderstood by its own members; its militance will be dissipated; its members will be discredited with the labor movement; its candidates will be crushingly defeated, and the party will loose itself in the maze of American politics."[6]

Foster replied to Nearing's contentions by declaring that his conclusions were "inexcusably erroneous," "especially coming from one undertaking to use the Marxian form of analysis." He disingenuously argued that the tactics of the party were not based on Russian experience but were "in line with Communist tactics and experience all over the world"—which still missed the point that the American situation might prove to be an exception to the party's historical determinism. Nearing's "program of peaceful education and organization," he asserted, "will not do." It was undeniable, said Foster, that there was "a volume of revolutionary discontent among the masses of American workers and farmers." "This discontent, it is true, is mostly unconscious, blind, stupid, timid, and easily misled," he said, annoyed with this pacifist intellectual: "It is the raw stuff of which revolutions are made. Revolutions are not brought about by the type of clear-sighted revolutionaries that you have in mind, but by stupid masses who are goaded to desperate revolt by the pressure of social conditions, and who are led by straight thinking revolutionaries who are able to direct the storm intelligently against capitalism."[7]

As the third-party movement unfolded over the summer, the Communists, unable to control the alliance or collaborate with La Follette while at the same time criticizing him, turned to Moscow for instructions. But the Soviets themselves were working out new answers amid their own inner-party turmoil following Lenin's death in January 1924. In the end, La Follette denounced those in the Workers party as "the moral enemies of the progressive movement and democratic ideals," and the glamour of the united front faded as the Comintern allowed the American party to run its own candidates, William Z. Foster for president and Benjamin Gitlow as his running mate.[8]

▬ Despite reservations, Nearing broke ranks with the Socialists, dropped out of the party, and looked to the Communists as the most viable revolutionary movement for the Left by early 1923.[9] He reported that on his recent trip through America's heartland he "found the Socialist party almost extinct." "The Workers Party," he argued, "has fallen heir to the present radical position in the United States." Having placed the Communists in a preeminent position on the Left, even though he had not joined the party, he then took up his "critical function" and pointed to the problems with the Workers party.

> Is it built to represent the American worker? So far the radical movement has represented the European worker in the United States. The opportunities for a radical political party are as great as ever, or greater than ever before; the important problem before the Workers Party is to get radical ideas before the workers. Its second and more serious problem is to establish proper relations with Moscow. Moscow is strong; the Workers Party is weak; Moscow can dominate without any trouble.

One way of controlling Moscow's "system of dictation" was by "federating divergent groups and working out the various problems involved." He was suggesting that the principles of federation could take root in the party itself. Instead of serving the interests of Russian nationalism, the Communists could build a true internationalism, and maintain a degree of autonomy for the American Left.[10]

Nearing's defection was a terrible blow to the Socialists. James Oneal responded to Nearing's reevaluation of the Left by pointing out the failure of his analysis while at the same time trying not to alienate him further.[11] The Communists were equally exuberant about their new ally. One party leader praised the "fine culture represented by Scott Nearing" and portrayed him as a Socialist who had seen the light of the united-front policy.[12] James P. Cannon, chairman of the Workers party, declared a coup: "Scott Nearing," he said, "is a significant figure."

> In a movement [the Socialist party] which, as yet, is too much given to loose thinking and careless, exaggerated statement, he stands out conspicuously as a tireless student, a painstaking searcher after facts, a master of simple, homely exposition. But he is much more than that. We have not forgotten the rebel professor who got himself kicked out of the bourgeois universities, the courageous fighter against the imperialist war who ran for Congress in the war years as a revolutionist. This, in my opinion, is the real Scott Nearing. This is the man who fired the imagination of the radical workers and took a firm hold of their affection.

This was united-front policy pure and simple: use this towering figure of the Left to bolster the Communist cause. If he strengthened the party, his pacifism could now be overlooked. Yet some things could not be ignored; a federationist scheme contradicted the Third International's acute centralization.

Nearing, Cannon continued, was "not yet ready, it seems, to go full length." He was "on his way to Communism but has not yet arrived." "Our idea of proper relations" with Moscow, he claimed, "does not coincide with his" because "an International Federation of autonomous National parties, for which he spoke . . . will not suffice in this period of intensified class struggle on a world-wide scale. . . . Federalism was one of the basic weaknesses of the Second International." Cannon, in "flatly reject[ing] the idea of a decentralized international," created a serious dilemma for Nearing. He was devoted to the social ideals of communism, but rejected the Bolshevik form of political organization. Could he throw his support behind the former without adhering to the latter?[13]

▬▬ One issue in particular that had driven Nearing away from the Socialists was the question of upholding the mantle of the Soviet experiment. Although the Socialist party had been friendly toward the Soviets since the Revolution, it had been so frustrated by the constant attacks of the Third International and American Communists and by defections from the Socialist party into the

Communist camp that it drifted slowly away from looking to the Bolsheviks as the strategic model for American radicalism. The Socialists concurrently gravitated toward an anti-Soviet position and toward the model of the British Labour party as more relevant to American conditions.[14] This Socialist stance, as much as anything positive he attributed to the Communists, drove Nearing away from the Socialist party. He had become convinced that British labor proved that collaborationist tactics and parliamentary procedures could not bring about revolutionary change. He was equally convinced that the path toward a revolutionary future lay with the Soviets, whatever their deficiencies.[15]

Because of the failure of collaborationist techniques, the only road to a revolutionary future, according to Nearing, was the one begun with the Russian Revolution and attempted by the Soviets. Yet while he adhered to the goals of the Revolution, he envisioned a revolutionary course of action independent of the Soviet government. This position, which again deviated from the party line, was made clear in a 1924 debate with the British philosopher, pacifist, and supporter of Ramsey MacDonald's Labour government Bertrand Russell on the question "Can the Soviet idea take hold of America, England and France?" Nearing, in the affirmative, addressed what he called "the greatest contributions of the Russian system." Because the economic analysis and political solutions he enunciated had a familiar ring to them, Russell at one point in the debate labeled Nearing a Marxist. Nearing responded that he had "never mentioned Karl Marx," although he had "no objection to having what I said called Marxian." "I didn't say it because Marx said it," he asserted; "I said it because I believe it was true."[16]

He was searching out such an arduous position that Russell could not accept his argument. Nearing wanted his opponent to "distinguish between two very important elements in the Bolshevik situation."

> When I described them, I described them in two categories. I described the aspects of power under the Communist Party, the dictatorship, and I also described the economic forms which the Soviet Government was realizing, namely economic constituencies, the scientific organization of economic life and the demand that everyone should be rewarded in proportion to his service, not in proportion to his property.[17]

"Mr. Russell," he said, "doesn't like bolshevism: neither do I."[18] But, he argued, the whole Soviet experiment should not be judged on the deficiencies of bolshevism, since "the Soviet form of government is a temporary or transition form to bridge over the abyss between capitalism and socialism." The government of Soviet Russia, he argued, was "not a socialist or communist government." He told the audience that he sincerely wished that "there was another way out" and that "Mr. MacDonald's way was the way." "I wish that the people were intelligent enough in America to make economic and social changes by act of Parliament." But reality contradicted such dreams.

The hope for the future lay in "the communist philosophy," not with the present form of government in Soviet Russia. "If the Russians haven't found the right way" to make the Communist ideal take hold, Nearing declared, "it is up to Mr. Russell and me to help Americans find the right way."[19]

▬ The pervasiveness of capitalist hegemony raised the thorny issue of collaboration with political elements that while advocating broad reform stopped short of a radical transformation of the social and economic structure. Because he had been wary of collaboration that would ultimately sidetrack radical measures, Nearing had earlier voiced deep reservations about the relationship between farm–labor parties and the radical parties of the Left. When the labor party movement had made advances and became a national movement by 1919, Nearing had expressed hostility toward proposals to unite the Socialist party with the trade-union movement.[20] He had again expressed caution when the CPPA met, contending that the CPPA's coalition was "neither new nor radical."[21]

By 1922, Nearing seemed to have found an answer to the question he raised once again: "What can the radical do?" It looked as if the united-front policy solved the apparently intractable problem of radical action. Previously he had been left with the choice either to abandon institutional affiliation or to set up rival institutions; now there was another alternative—to "bore from within." "It seems to me," he said, "as we look over the field, that Foster is essentially right—that if the radicals leave the organizations they leave them in the hands of the conservatives. If you stay in, you speak with the authority of the institution: therefore the better part of wisdom is to stay in as long as you can and speak, organize, and do what may be done while you are in the institution." Sensing self-deluding optimism, he maintained deep reservations about any collaborationist strategy, adding that "the time may come when your self-respect and your honesty will no longer permit you to stay in; then, of course, get out irrespective of consequences."[22]

Very quickly, with the failure of the CPPA, collaborationist "boring from within" proved to be a shattered hope. As Nearing repudiated this tactic and took his anticollaborationist interpretation into other areas of analysis, he advocated the creation of cooperatives and the development of union activity outside the conservative AFL, and he found himself tangled in the nuances of the party line. The Communist leader Earl Browder found Nearing's pronouncements sufficiently serious to respond to his position on the issue of collaboration. Browder, writing in the party's periodical the *Workers Monthly*, praised "such an influential figure as Comrade Nearing" because "there are large numbers of workers who listen with respect to what he says." At the same time, Browder criticized Nearing as "a famous liberal who is painfully fighting his way toward the position of communism" but "who has not worked out as yet all the implications of his position." What particularly concerned the party was that the logical conclusion to which Nearing took the problem of collaboration contradicted the policy of the united front. The party's position was that "all talk of abandoning the trade unions, because of their class collaboration policies, in favor of new 'fighting unions,'" went against the united front. In a forceful correction, Browder instructed Nearing on the proper party position: to follow the united front meant "to fight within cooperatives, the trade unions, and every other working class organization equally against dualism and class collaboration."[23]

Yet Nearing found legitimacy for his repudiation of collaboration not only in the American situation but in the experience of the British labor movement. He had at one time claimed that it was "the mother of modern trade unionism"[24] and hoped that the British Labour party could "demonstrate that a producer's society can replace a profiteer's society by due process of law." The British experience symbolized "the final test of the Second International and its theories" of "collaboration" with the bourgeois parties in bringing about the end of capitalism.[25] On the one hand, he conceded that the British Labour party held out the last best hope for transforming the existing order from within it. On the other hand, it became clear to Nearing that the Labour Ministry headed by Ramsey MacDonald, which took office in January 1924, had proven the failure of reform tactics. "Collaboration did not bring in the new social order," argued Nearing; "on the contrary, it merely prolonged the life of the old order." The Second International "had not taken into account the vitality and the coercive power of the capitalist state."[26] "If the state is built upon a social contract in which all have participated," he explained, "and if it represents the interests of the community," then "constitutional action is the only legitimate means for the making of social progress." However, if "the state is an agency of the dominant economic group and if that ruling economic group uses the state primarily for the purpose of advancing its interests," then this theory of constitutionalism "is far removed from reality."[27]

According to Nearing, the failure of collaborationist tactics was proven once and for all by the British General Strike of 1926, which was "an important test in the workers' struggle for power." The General Strike had "called into question the theory of constitutional procedure and substituted the idea of direct united working-class action."[28]

> Two lines of action presented themselves: one constitutional; the other direct. If British labor was to follow constitutional means, it would elect its representatives to local government bodies and to parliament, and would transform British society by a series of constitutional, legislative, and administrative acts from a capitalist empire into a workers' republic. If it was to employ direct action, it would seize the economic and political machinery, smash the structure of the old order and establish a working class government by the direct action of organized workers. The MacDonald administration was a gesture in the direction of constitutional order. The General Strike was the beginning of direct action and revolution.[29]

The events in Britain, especially those connected with the General Strike, Nearing contended, emphasized "the view that the state is an agency of the ruling economic class" and that "those who support the state, therefore inevitably support the ruling class."[30]

▬ By 1925, Nearing was an independent American Communist in search of a party. He had reservations about the Workers party at least equal to those that the party leadership had with him. He admittedly "disagreed with some of their tactics and in part with their principles, [but] they were the only group actively trying to cope with the situation in the United States." Consequently, "from 1922 until 1927," he "wrestled with these questions and suffered emotionally and politically as a consequence." He "hesitated" joining the party, he explained, "for several reasons." First, he was "engaged in some pioneering research and writing on empire building and its larger aspects," and second, the party "was deeply involved in factional disputes." He did not want "to give up my serious work in social science and devote myself to taking sides in factional squabbles." He would eventually apply for membership in the party, even if that meant overlooking significant deficiencies for more glorious possibilities promised in the future.[31]

He traveled to Russia in late 1925 through early 1926 as "an interested and sympathetic outsider,"[32] in part for the purposes of social science. He went to study the Soviet educational system, which he wrote about extensively while there and when he returned. This, of course, was in keeping with his central ideal of the school as the fundamental core of the society and education as the basis for social progress.[33] He saw in the Soviet educational system confirmation of his beliefs. With workers' control and the destruction of a dominating economic ruling class, education had been liberated. "The economic power, based on the ownership of the means of production," he explained, "extends through all social institutions," so that the working class was now in control of "the state, the church, the schools, the press, etc."[34] The Soviet system was succeeding in part because "the center of power in Russia has been shifted . . . to a comparably large group of organized workers."[35] The Soviets were "pioneers" who were struggling toward their ideal society. This meant, he acknowledged, "that mistakes would occur and that numerous changes would be made as experience showed which methods would succeed and which would fail."[36] "The workers and peasants of the Soviet Union have not been able to put all of these principles into practice," he claimed. "There is not a Communist in the Soviet Union who would venture to suggest that a full measure of Socialism has been achieved." More important than its deficiencies, he emphasized that the Soviet Union had been able "to create an economic organization that is without parallel anywhere in the world."[37] In Soviet Russia the "new social order has been tested . . . and with amazing success." It stood out "as the most important single experiment that is being made anywhere on the planet," where "the economic foundations of the new world order are being built."[38]

When he returned "after two months in Moscow, Kharkov, Rostov, Tiflis, Baku, and other cities and villages of Soviet Russia," he admitted that he was "a little dazed." Struck by the "profound" differences between Soviet society and Western civilization, he had trouble getting "used to the fact that I am back in America." "I am home from the first workers' republic," he wrote in the premier issue of the *New Masses*, to America, but "not my America." After being in the Soviet Union, the anthem of the capitalist nation from which he felt alienated sounded very different:

> My country 'tis of thee; sweet land of a leisure class running treasure island balls and throwing bathtub parties; of thee I sing and thy skilled, organized, comfortable labor aristocracy defending the wage slave system with all its might while 6/7 of the workers—unorganized, underpaid, defenseless—are toiling in dirty factories, or pounding the streets looking for work, or striking for the right to exist among the rocks and rills.[39]

No one, he declared, needed to "waste further time talking about American liberty."[40] In the "imperial epoch," the "ruling class of the United States" had become *"the ruling class of the ruling class of the world . . . the leader for the right to exploit the planet, both from the point of view of physical resources and from the point of view of labor."*[41] This meant, in the end, that the two forces shaping the world were Soviet communism and American capitalism. Between the two, he decided, there could be "no compromise; men either believe that the present economic system is satisfactory or they do not; either they believe that the profiteers should run the country or that the workers should run the country." Collaboration with capitalism was out of the question: "On economic rights and wrongs at this stage it is impossible to compromise."[42]

He had arrived at the conviction that "workers as a whole can no longer hope to gain by cooperating with the owning class." This dictum also came to mean that those envisioning a Socialist future could no longer do anything to harm the success of the Soviet experiment. It had become a zero-sum struggle. Criticism of the Soviet Union boosted capitalism, just as criticism of capitalism reinforced the policies of Soviet Russia. This was the position Nearing explained to a packed house—which included Justice Department agents—at the Play House in Washington, D.C., on May 8, 1926. Under the auspices of the League for Industrial Democracy, he spoke on "The Stability of the Soviet Government." During the lecture, he acknowledged some of the glaring problems and inequalities under the Soviet government but then stressed that these conditions also existed outside of Soviet Russia and that, most important, Russia's superiority to capitalism was the overriding factor to be considered. He told the audience that he stood on the side of the Soviet government in Russia and in opposition to all capitalist governments.

Late in the evening, during the question-and-answer period, a woman whom the Justice Department officials identified as the half sister of Emma Goldman, asked Nearing about the dreadful prison conditions under the Communist regime. He acknowledged that such conditions existed but then went on to warn the audience about the dangers in publicizing such conditions, which, he explained, only aided the capitalist press in attacking the Soviets. He claimed that those who exposed the deficiencies of Soviet Russia, as recorded in the federal agents' report, "whether they realized it or not, were enemies of Soviet Russia, because they furnish ammunition to the enemy, although they might think they are friends of the Soviet government."[43] No matter his resentment toward the capitalist system, or the conviction with which he pronounced his hopes for the Soviet experiment, he argued for separating means from ends, convinced it seems that nonhumanitarian means could lead to an enlightened, egalitarian, and just social order in the future.

The issue of support for Soviet Russia, which had in part gradually eased him away from the Socialist party, had driven him solidly into the Communist camp by 1926. Although he was not a party member, even as his sympathies lay clearly with the Communists, he would still participate in what were essentially Socialist-sponsored events. One instance was the annual convention of the League for Industrial Democracy, whose executive director was the Socialist leader Norman Thomas, held at Camp Tamiment in upstate New York in June 1926. Nearing joined a host of leftist intellectuals and leaders to discuss "New Tactics in Social Conflict." When speaking to the Socialist Left, he sounded a much more optimistic note than he did before the Communists. Standing clearly to the left of the other participants, he told those attending the conference that "out of that great, unorganized, incoherent mass of workers in the United States to-day, without expression, without newspapers, without union organizations, without any means of speaking its mind, something or other will come some time or other in the not distant future."[44]

When the symposium was published in book form, Nearing reviewed it and the conference in *New Masses*. The title of the book, *New Tactics in Social Conflict*, he said, would be more appropriately called "*Dodging the Bricks* or, perhaps, better still, *Comfort under Capitalism*." The conference, he explained, consisted of "a group of comfortable men and women" who "met for three days in a pleasant summer camp" and whose "discussion reflected [their] secure economic position." The papers presented "merely described the different ways in which the ruling class of the United States was postponing conflict by buying out the working class and by increasing its wealth and its capacity for exploitation." The conference was not "devoted to the tactics of the workers in their struggle against employers." Neither organized labor nor the Socialist party, he argued, had worked out new tactics of struggle. But, he added, "the Communists have been hammering consistently at the issue. The theory of Third International tactics is essentially different from that of Second International tactics. If any contribution to the tactics of social conflict have been made since the war, the Communists have made it." The way to a new social order would not be paved "by comfortable men and women in pleasant summer camps." It would "arise out of the mass struggle for a new social order."[45] The future lay with the Communists.

▄▄▄ Nearing first tried to join the party in 1925, sometime just before his pilgrimage to the socialist mecca. Here his autobiography is somewhat unreliable since he recalls a decision to join the party, wariness on the part of party officials, a lengthy inquiry into his ideological position, and acceptance in 1927. While this chain of events did occur, it does not accurately account for a much more complex reality. We are not to discount Nearing's recollection that he applied for membership only "after long hesitation and despite many misgivings" or his contention that the party leaders were "wary of me and my turn of mind."[46] But once Nearing had made the decision to enter the party, his acceptance was not a foregone conclusion. Joseph Freeman recounted that Nearing's initial application to the party in 1925 was rejected, which is consistent with Baldwin's claim that his admission was held up for a year. Nearing, it seems, applied to the party at least twice, yet according to Mike Gold, Nearing "applied for admission at least five times before he was admitted."[47] To explain why Nearing gained entry to a party that initially rejected him, we can cite not a change in Nearing's views but a shift in the American party's leadership and policy. Nearing wrote in notes for his autobiography that "as the inner party struggle continued, I found myself more and more inclined to join the Party + help straighten out Party affairs."[48]

When he applied for membership in 1925, the Workers party was in the throes of a leadership struggle that pitted Charles E. Ruthenberg against William Z. Foster. Unable to settle their internal struggle, the factions appealed to Moscow for help. When Ruthenberg and Foster went off to Moscow to win favor with the Comintern, the party was left in the hands of Foster's ally in the struggle, Earl Browder.[49] Joseph Freeman recounted that "after wrestling with his soul, Nearing applied for membership" but that "Earl Browder, then acting secretary," informed Nearing that "the Central Executive Committee, required him to answer a series of questions." The party wanted to know:

> What was his estimate of the present situation in the United States and the immediate tasks of the Party?
> What was his position on the Proletarian dictatorship and on the historic role of the Communist party?
> What were his views on imperialism, war, pacifism and social revolution?
> [What] were Nearing's views on national and international discipline.

The last question was of particular concern since "the matter of discipline in the Party and in the Comintern," Browder instructed, "was of paramount importance."[50] The questions themselves are revealing in that they indicate less a process of inquiry than a predetermined statement of serious differences with Nearing.

Nearing answered Browder in a thirty-two-page reply. On the question of the dictatorship of the proletariat, he described it as "a transition stage from capitalism to communism," a necessary if temporary means, through which the workers would control the economic machinery and take over the state, which was simply a tool of the dominant class. "At this stage of social development," he argued, "there seems to be no other way in which the transition from capitalism to communism can be achieved."[51] He wrote that in comparison with Italian fascism or class collaboration in Britain, the course taken by Soviet Russia was the best possible solution.

While his assessment so far may have passed dogmatic muster in the party, his assessment of the revolutionary situation in the United States deviated seriously from the party line. The United States, he claimed, had emerged from the war years in a position of international dominance with its economic system reinforced. As Freeman recalled, Nearing told Browder that "the American ruling class occupied a very strong position; it had no organized opposition; no other class was prepared to oppose or even seriously question it. Furthermore, the American workers occupied a favored position in the capitalist world."[52] While there were class-conscious elements in labor, Nearing argued, the large majority of American workers were unprepared for any kind of class action. He knew that this was not accepted party policy. Nor was the conclusion he drew from it. The Workers party, he argued, would have to be a propaganda movement and not a mass movement.[53] Its approach would be different when the capitalist system collapsed, but Nearing was not sure whether a severe economic depression would occur in 1926 or 1927. He proposed, according to Freeman, that the work of the party should be devoted "to organizing workers and toward maintaining effective propaganda organization."[54]

Nearing was most interested in "the principles and purposes" of communism.[55] In describing the role of the party, Nearing attempted to refashion Communist political doctrine, transforming party dogma, which he abhorred, into strenuous individual discipline. He suggested that "every effort should be made by the C.P. to cultivate the highest standards of personal integrity—sound health, clean living; trained vigorous and courageous thinking; honest, straightforward dealing." The "new life" upholding a personal ethic of strict moral conduct, social responsibility, vigorous living, and intelligent action, he declared, could be lived "now within the ranks of the revolutionary movement." Thus, the party should "maintain in its internal life a standard of generosity and mutual aid that will make the party, on small scale, the kind of cooperative fellowship we are seeking to establish on a world scale."[56] And in words that would come back to haunt him he agreed to party discipline, defined, to his liking, as personal accountability. Nearing had to know that the nuances of his answer would be seen as an attempt to submit to party conformity as much as to avoid it. "You ask whether I am willing to accept Party control over my writings and educational activities. I understand that to mean that the discipline of the Party extends to the writings and utterances of its members who are held accountable for the expression of opinion on public questions. I believe this is sound policy and would accept it and support it."[57]

It appears to be only a coincidence that Nearing was in the Soviet Union in late 1925 and early 1926 at exactly the same time that Ruthenberg and Foster were pleading their cases to the Comintern. There is no evidence that Nearing tried to influence political events or even that he could have, since he was not a member of the party. By early spring, Soviet officials had given control of the Workers party to Ruthenberg, who returned triumphantly from abroad. It was Ruthenberg who finally replied to Nearing's application for membership; he was rejected.

On the questions of the proletarian dictatorship, explained Ruthenberg, and especially on the situation in the United States and the tasks of the party, his views did not conform with those of the Central Executive Committee. "Your conception of the Communist Party is that of a propaganda society," he told Nearing, and, "the difference between a Communist propaganda society and a Communist Party . . . is the difference between a party such as you outline . . . and a Party which *enters into the immediate struggles of the workers, endeavors to become the leader of the struggle, and in the process, builds its influence and its organization.*" Because Nearing had been incorrect in his assessment of the revolutionary potential of the American worker, he misperceived the party's task. "While all the work which you describe in your statement is necessary for the upbuilding of the Communist Party in the United States," Ruthenberg continued, "it is not sufficient. We would never be able to build a mass movement of the workers against capitalism if we restricted our efforts to the proposals which you outline." In the end, Ruthenberg concluded, "on this point of Communist tactics you seem to be in disagreement with our party and the Communist International."[58]

Nearing again sought membership in spring 1927 at a time of new leadership struggles within the party. Ruthenberg had died suddenly on March 2, 1927, and by May was succeeded by Jay Lovestone, his right-hand man, by direction of the Comintern. Lovestone brought with him one unique ideological characteristic, a belief that American capitalism was "on the upgrade," that the United States was not adhering to the formula of economic decline and disintegration. This peculiar notion of American economic and political "exceptionalism" was unique not only to the United States but to Lovestonites; it was also an assessment consistent with Nearing's view of Coolidge prosperity.[59]

It is likely that Nearing reapplied during the time between Ruthenberg's death and Lovestone's ascendancy. He recalled that weeks went by before he heard from the party. When a reply came, it was from Jay Lovestone, as party secretary, who requested answers to a list of questions from this wayward leftist.[60] While we don't know what he wrote to Lovestone, there is no evidence to indicate that the answers Nearing provided expressed any views significantly different from the answers he supplied in 1925. We might speculate that the same answers were accepted by the party this time. Lovestone may have seen in Nearing an ally in his belief that the United States was an exception to the rule of capitalist decay. While he may have been less willing to adopt what Nearing saw as the logical tasks of the party, it is possible that the political advantage weighed more heavily than Nearing's deviations from party policy. There are indications, too, that Lovestone could count on Nearing in the internal party battles, particularly in opposition to Foster's faction. On one occasion, Nearing had moved perceptibly against Foster, changing his vote on a resolution to unseat Foster from the board of the Garland Fund.[61]

The fact remains that after another delay, Nearing was accepted into the party and assigned to a party local in New York City.[62] The party Nearing joined had fewer than ten thousand members, the vast majority of whom were recent European immigrants. Even in New York City, which claimed one-third of the total membership, the party could pull only about ten thousand votes in 1927.[63] Nearing did not participate in internal Party affairs but began "speaking at public meetings, teaching in the Workers' School, writing for Party publications."[64] Nothing in his thinking should have made him any more suited to enter the party in 1927 than in 1925; it was not Nearing who changed, but the party. The problem was, if the party changed again, what would become of Nearing?

▬▬ When Nearing attended the next annual conference of the League for Industrial Democracy in June 1927, he was still far to the left of the rest of the predominantly Socialist participants, and because of his recent party affiliation, he found his intellectual independence questioned. He defended his views by stating that he did "not represent the Communist party, although I am a member of the Party."[65] To the Socialists, his rigid noncollaborationist position made him sound like a spokesman for Communist revolutionary dogma. His advocacy of "direct action" was, in fact, nothing new.

> Nothing short of fundamental remedies will meet the situation in which the farmers and the unskilled workers of the United States quite generally find themselves. . . . Politics consists of a series of compromises between groups that are not too far apart to compromise, or that have to compromise. . . . The economic and social needs, cannot be met by any system of politics, and can only be met by direct action . . . unconstitutionally, illegally, by direct action.[66]

Direct action on the part of the workers was justified, he contended, because "when the basic interests of the business class in the United States are threatened . . . the dominant economic group resorts to direct action."

He chided the Socialists for questioning his characterization of the U.S. government as "the establishment of a domestic dictatorship" that exercised repressive violence: "Of course, you will say our traditions aren't like that, but if you will read the record of the last fifteen years you can see where we are going and how fast."[67] He noted that this position differed "fundamentally from [that of] Morris Hillquit," although that fact was readily apparent to the rest of the participants. His discussion of direct action left some, like the

Socialist labor lawyer Louis Waldman, dumbfounded. Waldman was astonished at this call for what he saw as "force and violence" and "the dictatorship of the proletariat." Hillquit agreed that Nearing seemed to be advocating violence.[68]

Of interest here is that Nearing did not refute their accusations. He followed up his argument by stating that "the second point in my program of political action is to utilize those measures and those agencies we can command" in order "to tell people what kind of a system we are living under in the United States"—in other words, the united front for purposes of propaganda. The capitalists, he declared, "have the newspapers, and the movies, and the machinery of public opinion, and they have told you a certain story of prosperity. . . . It is a great big lie. . . . We have got to tell the other side of the prosperity story." "Don't let's waste time telling the working people in the United States that they have anything in particular to hope for in the way of permanent prosperity under the present system. Let's tell them they have got to change the system. That is straight class-conscious propaganda. . . . It is not political compromise."[69]

The role for the radical that prepared the workers for direct action sounded remarkably like the party notion of a Communist "cadre," Lenin's idea of the revolutionary who worked full-time for the party.[70] Nearing proposed to the other participants at Camp Tamiment the organization of "a professional revolutionary class" whose task was to organize "a revolution in the United States, preparing to seize power." Here, he said, was "an opportunity for adventure and constructive effort in an organized revolutionary movement." He was proposing the moral equivalent of immediate revolutionary violence. The careful preparation by the professional revolutionary, he noted, "may take us a generation or two." "What we need in every society is a group that will continue to be idealists, revolutionists, anything you like in spite of the rewards that respectable society offers," he asserted, "to fight the battles of a new social order."[71]

We can detect here a subtle but important shift in Nearing's thought on the question of pacifism. He seems to have reached the position of believing that what he earlier referred to in *Violence or Solidarity* as "counter-revolutionary" violence, violence by the capitalists against the political and labor radicals, necessitated violence by the workers. The pacifist regretfully accepted violent revolutionary action as the inevitable means to seize power from the capitalists. This argument—that he would condone violence, only after a long period of educational propaganda by trained revolutionaries, as a purposeful violence of last resort but ultimately necessary—was a position similar to if not quite as extreme as that reached by the Protestant theologian Reinhold Niebuhr in his *Moral Man and Immoral Society* in 1932. Like Niebuhr, Nearing had to struggle with the morality of pacifism in relation to the immorality of the economic and political system under capitalism. Niebuhr ultimately condoned violence as a decisive step toward revolution, as did Nearing. Of course, Nearing's prescription allowed that one not wrestle too much with his or her conscience, since the day of reckoning, he suggested, was in the distant future. The important point, however, was that Nearing conceived of, and apparently condoned, the possibility of future revolutionary violence.[72]

⸻ As a citizen of the world and a member of the movement for a revolutionary future, as Nearing saw it, one of the most difficult obstacles to the creation of a noncapitalist united world was imperialism. In fact, as the Soviet Union began to exercise its influence in the world, the question arose whether Soviet international adventures were not like the subjugation, exploitation, and domination of capitalist imperialism. The test case for evaluating the character of Soviet foreign policy was the Far East—in particular, China. By 1926, Nearing was interested not only in China's revolution but also in its foreign relations with the Soviet Union. China had undergone social and political upheaval since the fall of the Ch'ing Dynasty in 1911. Ancient warlord control and rampant imperialism had turned Chinese nationalism into a potent political cause. Under Sun Yat-sen, this new nationalism found new power. After unsuccessfully appealing to the Japanese, Great Britain, and the United States for aid and support for his political party, the Kuomintang, Sun received aid from Soviet Russia in the form of military advisors and material and political guidance. The Kuomintang was reorganized in the shape of Bolshevik centralization. The Soviets provided military training and instruction in party ideology, strongly emphasizing anti-imperialism and nationalism. They also fostered the creation of an anti-imperialist, united-front alliance between the Kuomintang and a small Chinese Communist party, despite opposition from the right wing of the Kuomintang in January 1924. By the time of Sun's death in March 1925, his party controlled Canton and exercised even wider influence.

The domestic and international issues embodied in China's revolutionary situation caught Nearing's attention as a test case for anti-imperialism and Soviet foreign policy. In early 1927, he compiled data and assembled the study *Whither China?: An Economic Interpretation of Recent Events in the Far East.* Nearing saw something unique in Chinese development. Industrialization, although initiated by imperialists, was now being advanced by the Chinese and formed the basis for the "new China." "The direction of this movement," he claimed, "depends upon an understanding of its true character, and an appreciation of the fact that China is not moving from a village economy toward capitalist imperialism, but from a village economy, past capitalist imperialism, toward a new form of social organization." For this reason, he argued, China was "closer to the Soviet Union than to any of the great empires."[73]

When he studied China, he was also studying Soviet Russia. The Russian Revolution, he said, brought with it "the idea of local cultural self-determination." "The shift in the form of economy" in Russia following the Revolution "removed the economic pressure in the direction of foreign exploitation."[74] The Soviets had "presented a simple formula to the Asiatic people: Co-operate and be free." The only possible choice for subjugated peoples, Nearing asserted, "lay between this formula and the continued exploitation and oppression of western imperialism." "The U.S.S.R.," he declared, "speaks for an order of society which was born with the worldizing influences of modern economic life."[75] China became the focus for assessing its success because "the new Soviet plan for handling relations with the racial minorities and with the exploited peoples had its first real test in Asia."[76]

For this reason among others, Nearing claimed that "the Chinese Revolution is one of the most important social revolutions in modern times."[77] "The Chinese movement" was "without parallel" as "a movement toward a new social order in a portion of the world hitherto largely untouched by modern economic and social developments."

> If China can shake off the grip of Western imperialism, avoid the worst abuses of private capitalism, and establish the foundations of a new social order, freed from economic competition and war, this whole Asiatic area may be able to follow suit. Since the Asiatic area includes two-thirds of the world's population, such a development would carry in its train unprecedented advantages for the human race.

The hope for China was that "a new social form is emerging"; and just as significantly, it was "under the spiritual leadership of the U.S.S.R."[78]

Dissatisfied with the available information in the United States, he explained, he "decided to go to China and see the situation at first hand."[79] Unknown to him until he arrived in Shanghai, the Revolution had suffered a terrible blow in the spring of 1927. In the leadership struggle following Sun's death, the military leader of the Kuomintang, Chiang Kai-shek, allied himself with rightwing forces within the party and conservative elements without, and seized control of the party, ordering a purge of Communist elements. The "White Terror" brutally eliminated Chinese Communists and instigated a break with the Kuomintang's left wing and the Soviets. Nearing arrived in China to observe its Revolution at the same time the Revolution was being crushed by Chiang's White Terror. Instead of the Revolution, he would witness counterrevolutionary violence in action.

Before sailing for the Orient, Nearing spent a month crossing Canada to lecture on the American empire, imperialism, and war. By an odd coincidence, it was in Canada that his blind idealism about the Soviet Union was challenged by another visitor on a Canadian lecture tour, Emma Goldman, by then a disillusioned critic of the Bolshevik regime. Nearing had arrived at the extreme position that there could be no compromise with the capitalists and that criticism of the Soviet government qualified as collaboration with capitalism. According to Goldman, while she and Nearing were in Canada, it was proposed that they debate on the question "Life under the Dictatorship" in Soviet Russia. Goldman agreed, although she "preferred some Communist who had lived in Russia longer and knew the situation better." As she recalled the incident, Nearing refused to meet her on the platform: "His reply was that if E.G. were dying and he could save her life, he would not go around the corner to do so."[80]

Nearing sailed from Vancouver, stopping over in the Philippines before going on to China. When he arrived on the mainland, he found himself in an awkward, even dangerous situation. His contacts in China were with the political Left, yet he found in Shanghai that "leftists were being liquidated on sight." He even witnessed "some heads mounted on poles" as a warning to revolutionaries. When he traveled to Peking, he found that the White Terror "was in full swing." Clearly this was not the society he had anticipated. He was contacted by a student rebel to give a talk at Yenching University on American imperialism. On the evening of his lecture, Nearing was picked up and taken to the university where he was led into an unlit room and told that his audience was waiting in the dark. They would hear Nearing's ideas but could not jeopardize themselves by revealing their identities. In total darkness, Nearing delivered his talk, hearing only his voice and breathing in the crowd. When he finished, he was led out of the building and taken back to his room.[81]

After three months in China, he left for Moscow as a U.S. representative of the Friends of the Soviet Union for a conference that coincided with the November 7 celebration of the tenth anniversary of the Russian Revolution.[82] He was particularly impressed with Joseph Stalin, whom he revered as the ideal type of revolutionary, one "who worked unusually hard and lived with unusual frugality and had no thought but socialism."[83] When Nearing looked at Stalin, he saw only a reflection of himself. From Moscow, he stopped in Berlin where recently "the aggressive, expansionist National Socialist Party of Germany (Nazis) gained its first electoral victory."[84] While there, he met with his friend, the American Socialist Agnes Smedley, who had arranged for him to lecture at the Charlottenburg town hall on the topic of the U.S. imperialism in the Philippines.[85] Then it was home to the United States. He had traveled around the world not to escape America but to gather intellectual ammunition for the revolutionary struggle at home. He had left for China shortly after his long-awaited acceptance into the party. Now, back in the States, he would learn about life in the party.

# The Farce
# of Political Democracy

## Chapter 16

UPON his return to the States, Nearing took up his activities in the party. By August, he had been chosen to run as the Communist candidate in the election for governor of New Jersey.[1] This was an odd choice and a seemingly incongruous move for Nearing. As he had explained to the participants at the League for Industrial Democracy conference the previous summer, he felt that the workers should not "waste their time going to the polls to vote. . . . Have them pull a boycott or a strike or some other kind of direct action demonstration." "The basis for any political program," he had said then, was "to use economic direct action." He advocated using "all the agencies of propaganda, including a political labor party, but without in our minds believing that a political labor party is an answer to the question. . . . A political labor party is a propaganda agency, but not a means of electing people to office."[2]

This ambivalence regarding the role of political activity was reflected in his campaign. While he did some campaigning in the state, he spent nearly all of September and part of October touring southern states—Florida, Alabama, Georgia, Tennessee, Kentucky, West Virginia—on behalf of the party. Additionally, he spent a week during mid-October touring the Midwest for the Communist cause.[3] His "campaign" reflected a tactic of propaganda to educate the masses, not a strategy for getting elected. He clearly was not out to win the election, nor would it have advanced the revolutionary goals of the party, so he believed, if he had been successful. The dismal result of his own run and that of the party candidates in general only confirmed his analysis of the task of a revolutionary party.

That Nearing's assessment of party tactics created serious if not yet debilitating problems within the Party was indicated by an article explaining his evaluation of the 1928 elections that was printed in the party journal, the *Communist*. It appeared with the editor's warning: "The article . . . is widely at variance with the viewpoint of the Party on a whole series of questions." In the election, Nearing noted, the Workers party candidates had met with "stiffened bourgeois resistance." The lessons of the campaign were that

> the American masses are not ideologically prepared for the program of the Workers (Communist) Party; the ruling class in the United States is too well organized, too class conscious, too well equipped with police, sedition laws, etc., to permit effective campaigning by the Communists; there is no reason to suppose that the American masses can be reached [by] Party political propaganda in the immediate future. The Party can not hope to function between 1928 and 1932 as a political force.

His view of tactics was tied to an analysis of American exceptionalism. There was no widespread revolutionary movement in the United States, and even the "dissatisfied farmers, oppressed Negroes, exploited wage earners, and dispossessed petit-bourgeois elements" were "not yet prepared, ideologically, to accept the implications of class struggle." This not only meant that "open participation by a revolutionary party is, for the moment, politically impossible," but it also led Nearing to question the united-front policy. The party, he said, "must send its members into the new organizations, without any hope of 'controlling' or 'capturing' but for the purpose of directing left-wing policy and tactics." He warned the party against indulging "in utopian dreams." American circumstances, he claimed, determined that "the most the . . . Party can hope for . . . is a steady increase in membership and a broadening of sympathetic support in that small minority of the American farmer-worker masses who are already conscious of the class nature of American society."[4]

While the 1928 election only reinforced Nearing's earlier dissent from the party line, it did have the effect of reawakening him to the problem of racial discrimination in the United States. His southern campaign swing for the party reflected in part a change in Comintern policy, officially formulated at the Sixth World Congress in Moscow in 1928. The Communist party had long struggled with "the Negro question" but now announced a policy of the "Right of Self-Determination for Negroes."[5] This new policy had its roots in Lenin's analysis of imperialism and the colonial question. As the most exploited person in the United States, the Negro, according to the party, was a natural recruit who would not only empower the proletarian movement in America but would awaken and lead the oppressed races of the rest of the world to overthrow capitalism. Included was the notion of Negro self-determination in the Deep South, with an eventual separatist movement among Southern Negroes followed by an inevitable revolutionary crisis. Finally, just as previous radical movements in the United States had done, the party subordinated the issue of race to an economic class analysis, propounding the view that the Negro's oppression was to be solved through class struggle.[6] The Comintern's 1928 policy declared that only the Negro's "close union with the white proletariat and joint struggle with them against the American bourgeois can lead to their liberation from barbarous exploitation, and that only the victorious proletarian revolution will completely and permanently solve the agrarian and national question in the Southern United States in the interests of the overwhelming majority of the Negro population of the country."[7]

No doubt, Nearing's interest in racism followed the party line, merging as it did his study of imperialism and the party's interest in the question of colonialism as an approach to the question of race. But this was not simply a matter of marching in step to dictates from Moscow. More correctly, the party's policy in 1928 coincided to a large degree with Nearing's long-standing interest in "the race question" and his reassessment of it. In his 1908 textbook *Economics*, Nearing had addressed the educational needs of blacks in the South, applauding the approach taken by Booker T. Washington and carried out by his Tuskegee Institute. At that time, Nearing saw that this approach shared merit with Manual Schools in providing purposeful education. Tuskegee, wrote Nearing, "has made an attempt, and a successful one, to make the education fit the needs of the population."[8] In 1913, he went into the Deep South for the first time.[9] He would later abandon his earlier view and adopt a position that reflected the influence of W. E. B. Du Bois's critique of Washington's position as a policy of submission and accommodation as well as a socialist analysis emphasizing class instead of race oppression.

This new position emerged by 1917 and was indicated by Nearing's contributions to and sympathy for the black radicalism of A. Philip Randolph's and Chandler Owen's *Messenger*. The *Messenger*, which proclaimed itself to be "the only radical Negro magazine in America," emerged in the fall of 1917, protesting American intervention in the war and applauding the Bolshevik Revolution. It advocated racial solidarity in labor organization, the labor tactics of the IWW, and the politics of the Socialist party.[10] Nearing contributed to its first and its subsequent issues.[11] In a letter to Randolph and Owen in the September 1919 issue of the magazine, Nearing applauded them, stating, "The work you are doing is vital. Your people constitute more than a tenth of the total population of the United States. We are all native born Americans. If there is to be progress made, particularly in the great Southland, by the Socialist movement, it must be made by and through colored people." The admiration was mutual. The editors awarded him "unstinted praise" as "one of the finest figures in America. . . . Race, creed, color and sex produce no prejudice in Nearing."[12] The back cover of the June 1922 issue was devoted to a salute to Nearing: "His latest book, *The American Empire*, gives more truth about the Negro, the treatment of Haiti and American Negro slavery, than you would find during years in most Negro publications."[13] With his journey into the Deep South in 1928, the Negro situation in the

United States suddenly became a touchstone for testing his values and the meaning of freedom in American culture.

▬▬ Nearing took up the problem of racism in the United States in a systematic fashion for the first time with his historical-sociological study *Black America*. The "Negro question" forced him to confront most fundamentally the problem of freedom as well as the issues of Northern racism, pacifism, and class struggle. When he looked into the "abstract principles of freedom and self determination" for blacks, he determined that even the gains made through the Civil War were but "paper liberation." The war was heralded as " 'the freeing of the slaves,' " but, he asked, "freeing from what? For what?" "Theoretically and legally the Negro was freed from slavery," he explained, but "practically, and economically, the Negroes were still under the necessity of making a living on land owned by white Southern men."[14]

As Nearing interpreted black history, World War I became a pivotal event for black freedom. Migration out of the South and the industrial opportunities of war production pushed the issue of race forcefully out of the South and brought the Negro into confrontation with the capitalist system, so that "to be Black, in the United States," wrote Nearing, "is to be proletarian." "The war was fought ostensibly for democracy, freedom and self-determination," but it left in its wake disturbing questions about democratic freedom at home and capitalist imperialism abroad. From this perspective, he explored the situation of black Americans, claiming that "among the great modern empires only one contains a subject race within its homeland."[15]

But was the oppression of blacks a matter of race or of class? The answer would suggest vastly different strategies for achieving freedom. At one point in his study, Nearing claimed that "the authority of any ruling class rests upon its economic power. . . . The whites therefore spare no means to keep the centers of economic power under their exclusive control." Yet to state that "economic power in the United States remains a function of the white race"[16] meant that there were problems in this analysis for explaining the exploitation of working-class whites. A more refined view noted that while blacks "carry the normal burden of workers under capitalism," they also had to "shoulder the special burden of economic discrimination which the exploiting whites of the United States have laid upon the shoulders of Negro workers in industry."[17] Thus, "the subjugation and exploitation of black men by white men is, at bottom, an economic phenomenon," and "the solution to the problem must be found in the field of economic reorganization." The white ruling class in the United States, argued Nearing, "own economically and dominate politically." Blacks, he concluded, were "the victims of economic discrimination . . . practiced today when Negroes are 'free.' " It was part of the technique used by "the white ruling class" to "keep exploited blacks in a position where they can neither resist nor escape exploitation."[18]

Yet the years surrounding the Great War, Nearing observed, were "an era of enlarged Negro race consciousness," which "forced the Negro into a position where they (sic) were compelled to organize for self defense and self advancement."[19] Their "bitter experience," however, had created a situation where "intelligent American Negroes no longer expect emancipation through the franchise." No longer was politics "the avenue along which freedom must be won." Lamenting "the farce of political democracy," Nearing noted that "participation in political activity is ordinarily a function of the ruling class," for the Negro, merely "a delusion." Political action and the franchise, he claimed, "are not means of emancipation for an exploited class but are tools employed by the ruling class in the exercise of class power."[20]

This position reiterated the strategy of direct action, even violence, as a response to violent oppression, as a means of social transformation. Nearing took particular interest in retaliatory violence on the part of Northern blacks following the war, especially the circumstances of race riots in Northern cities. In *Black America,* he described the "race war" that took place in Chicago during the summer of 1919. Culling his facts from a 1922 study by the Chicago Commission on Race Relations, *The Negro in Chicago,* he reported the incident in detail, from its beginnings in the stoning of a black who strayed onto the white section of a segregated beach to black demands for justice, "mass white attacks," and violent defiance by blacks.[21] In the postwar years, the white strategy for black emancipation, he wrote critically, was to be "in accordance with a 'pacific' formula."[22] For blacks to achieve freedom, he strongly intimated, nonviolent political means were not enough.

What was needed, above all, was racial cooperation for the class struggle. This, he said, clearly echoing the party line, would benefit both white and black workers. "There is no more vital task before the American workers today," he explained, "than that of establishing working class solidarity along race lines." Whites "have not yet waked up to the situation," and they still believe "the ruling class propaganda about 'racial inferiority.' "[23] As for blacks, he wrote, "the sooner they discover their logical allies and work out a scientific plan of campaign, the sooner they will win the emancipation they seek." "There can be no victory for the working-class while workers are divided along race lines. Black and white workers must stand together for working class emancipation." Black freedom (and white freedom) could "only come when the Negro working masses have joined the white working masses in smashing the economic and social structure built upon individual and race exploitation, and by replacing it with a cooperative economic system under working-class control."[24]

A unique feature of *Black America* was that it included photographic evidence. He recalled that he took hundreds of photographs for the book, and 159 of them appeared in the text. They revealed the life and work of blacks in the South and the North, in rural and urban settings, in agriculture and industry. They also documented racial discrimination through segregation, whether in Washington, D.C., schools, playgrounds, and apartments or a

Florida hotel or streetcars in North Carolina, Baltimore homes, a Richmond lunchroom, a Birmingham restaurant. The most disturbing and searing photographs recorded white violence against blacks. He witnessed and photographed a gruesome hanging in Tennessee, the hanging and burning of a black man by a frantically enthusiastic white crowd in Waco, Texas, a hanging in Houston, another in Florida, multiple hangings and burnings at the stake in Tennessee and Mississippi. His photographs unveiled the harsh, brutal reality of racial discrimination, but they also reveal the formative personal experience of the photographer.

Nearing never indicated what led him to choose the medium of photography to convey his social analysis. While the camera would become in the 1930s as James Agee noted, "the central instrument of our time,"[25] for Nearing in 1928, it was an important tool for reporting social facts. While there was an inherent anti-intellectual quality to the photograph's appeal since it relied upon evoking an emotional rather than a rational response, Nearing's presentation emphasized an intelligent political consciousness via the combination of documentary photography and social analysis. There were other tensions as well. Photography could serve as an art form or it could, as it did for Nearing, have a social focus as a propaganda tool employed to help change society.

Perhaps it was for Nearing most crucially an instrument of propaganda that could evade the dominant cultural values. Undistorted by capitalist cultural hegemony, the photograph allowed the viewer to witness the evidence directly. The photographer could communicate an unaltered authenticity of experience that could not be achieved in type. Just as social analysis could be turned toward educational propaganda, so could the camera be diverted from its aesthetic function and aimed with a social purpose. Nearing's use of photography suggested that it had counterhegemonic potential, that the camera was a revolutionary weapon in the class struggle.[26]

━━━ Nearing's view of the social function of the photograph was consistent with his increasing concern over the social purposes of art, expressed earlier in the art-show critique that he communicated to Joseph Freeman and in his enthusiasm for Ralph Chaplin's poetry. By 1929, he focused his attention on literature as yet another art form with revolutionary potential. He took up the question of social fiction with Joseph Freeman, who felt that a novel of the working class could not be written while the United States was still in the process of moving from capitalism to socialism. "Could not a part of that process of interpretation," he asked Freeman, "be placed in the realm of fiction? . . . You were saying that one could not write a novel yet about U.S.A. Why not? Is not transition a part of life?" He encouraged Freeman to try his hand "at a real proletarian American novel."[27] Soon after publishing *Black America*, Nearing wrote his only novel, *Free Born*, about a Southern black man, Jim Rogers, who migrates from the South to the industrial North, discovering that the discrimination of wage slavery lives at the root of his oppression and the oppression of his race. According to one student of American literature it was "the first revolutionary novel of Negro life," and in the words of another, it was "at least as noteworthy for containing probably the most ghastly lynch scene in American literature."[28]

While the notion of proletarian art had a self-contradictory ring to it, as suggested by Max Eastman when he decried the concept of "artists in uniform," it gained vital currency among Communist intellectuals in the 1920s who were committed to a theory of literature that ennobled the tough, virile working class as an alternative to a theory of art for art's sake. Marxian theory regarded art as an example of the highly complex and indirect relationship between the mode of production and cultural expression, between the productive base and the cultural superstructure. The notion of proletarian art emerged out of this fertile theoretical contention that art signified an instance of autonomy in the Marxian base–superstructure relationship and could therefore serve to challenge the predominant ideological beliefs.[29] After the Revolution, the Bolsheviks gave official sanction to this analysis in efforts to develop a working-class culture called Prolet-Kult.[30] The first party declaration on literature came from Moscow in 1925—the same year Trotsky took up the issue in his *Literature and Revolution*[31]—pronouncing art as a class weapon in establishing a working-class culture and collectivist values as it rejected bourgeois culture. In 1928, the party's Central Committee issued a decree that literature must serve the interests of the party.[32]

American intellectuals became familiar with Soviet theories of art and literature during the twenties primarily through three publications, the *Liberator*, the *New Masses*, and the *Modern Quarterly*—all magazines with which Nearing was closely associated. Michael Gold, a leading translator of Soviet proletarian literary criticism for American intellectuals, issued one of the first calls for proletarian art in the pages of the *Liberator* in February 1921.[33] The fusion of literature and revolution was later promoted when the magazine was turned over to the Workers party in 1922. In September 1923, Nearing became a contributing editor for the *Liberator*, and his name appeared in the masthead until its last issue in October 1924. Joseph Freeman and Mike Gold further advanced the theory of proletarian art in the pages of the *New Masses*, a magazine initially financed by the Garland Fund and unofficially an organ of the party, which appeared in May 1926 with Nearing as a contributing editor.[34] In 1927, the magazine sponsored a symposium on the question "May society properly demand of the artist, not merely good craftsmanship and good reporting, but the transvaluation of values—and the creation of new social values?"[35] When Gold assumed the editorship in 1928, Nearing wrote in a letter to the magazine that under Gold's "new management," the *New Masses* should become "a real paper—determined, hard-hitting, satirical—full of understanding and sympathy for the class struggle."[36]

Finally, another key disseminator of Marxian analysis applied to literature and art was V. F. Calverton's independently radical *Modern Quarterly*, for which Nearing wrote regularly. First issued in March 1923, it explored a sociological view of art and revolutionary theories coming from the Soviet Union.[37] In its pages in 1927, Freeman deplored "the Wilsonian era in American literature" because, he claimed, "the capitalist nature of this civilization is ignored." Due to this "thoroughgoing evasion of American reality," he argued, "the literature dealing with the decisive impact of the classes, with life in the mill, factory, or mine, is as yet meager." It was time, he proclaimed, for American writers "to deal with American literature with reference to American social conditions."[38] By the late 1920s, Marxian views of art and literature were widely discussed in America and achieved a certain popularity among intellectuals wanting to exchange expatriation for commitment.[39]

Revolutionary literature offered Nearing an experimental means of expressing his social message. Proletarian literature was not merely another form of propaganda but also offered a new role for the intellectual. In *Free Born*, the merging of propaganda and art allowed Nearing to speak for the lower class, for the worker as the hero of the social struggle. In the end, the novel was devoted to one class and the destruction of capitalism. To explore the intricacies of American freedom, Nearing chose to write of the oppression of blacks, to elevate the significance of their struggle in the nation's history. To capture the "real" life of blacks, he wrote about the details of their lives, and in a break with literary convention—a typical strategy of proletarian literature—he even tried to capture their speech. While his attempt at conveying black dialect is unconvincing—particularly because it is unchanged through the novel, even after the protagonist goes to law school in the North and reads Marx, Lenin, and Upton Sinclair—it was used as a technique that emphasized racial separation. The dialect in the novel is a dialect of race; North or South, the whites have no dialect. The dialogue stresses the split between races.

Typical too of proletarian fiction, the novel is thinly veiled autobiography, not in the sense that Nearing's experience could be equated with that of a Southern black, but as personally introspective in the realm of ideas. Nearing's disillusionment was inseparable from what he had to say about American society. It is a novel of education and growth toward consciousness that begins in the teens and in which the war becomes a critical, pivotal event. In its autobiographical vein it becomes, metaphorically, an expatriate memoir: the protagonist is exiled from his homeland and experiences a life of flight, escape, and searching until he reaches a crisis by the mid-twenties, when suddenly his exile from his native land ends with commitment to the cause of the working class and the Communist movement.

While the novel offers economic and social commentary and class analysis, it is deeply personal in its discussion of radical commitment, pacifism, and conjugal relations. At a critical turning point in the novel, Jim is saved by Jane Wilson, a laundry worker who is also an activist. More important, she is a Communist. She wants to prevent Jim from committing suicide because, she says, "Yo' is a brother human, an' 'cause you' is needed." In a confessional scene, Jim pours his heart out to this savior, telling her everything about his past. Jim rushes to her, and all she symbolizes, "to save himself from a black abyss." Jane takes him to her apartment, and in a short time he has undergone a conversion to a working-class consciousness. Jane, it is learned, is a member of a union, and while she works all day, she spends many evenings in union activities. Her communism, she explains to Jim when telling him about a union meeting, is much like Nearing's.

> "It's a fight fo' power. De right wing in de union is conservative—dey all voted fo' Coolidge las' year. But de lef' wing is . . . communist."
> "Communist," he questioned. "Is that the same as Bolshevik?"
> "No," she said briefly. "Dey is different."[40]

When Jim tells her that he is studying to become a lawyer, she confronts him with a question: " 'Ain't it de lawyers what fastens de masters' fetters on de hands an' minds of de workin' class?' " She teaches him of collaboration and capitalist hegemony.

> "But de people need leaders," Jim protested.
> "Leaders—not deserters!" [replied Jane.]
> "But Ah wouldn't be that kind of lawyer."
> "Yo' think yo' wouldn't. But lemme ask yo'—can yo' with your own hands smash dis hyar system of poverty an' wage slavery?"
> "Mebbe not alone," Jim admitted.
> "Den yo'se part of it—an yo'se part of the master class, or yo'se part of the slave class. Ninety-nine lawyers an' more, in every hundred, is part of de master class. . . . But yo' forget de res' of us. Yo' think we're satisfied jes caise we is livin' in de mud an' de stink. An whut do yo' do? Yo' begin to climb out of de mud; yo' want to move away from de stink. How 'bout de res' of us? . . . Will we be any happier? Will we be any better?"[41]

Almost immediately, Jim's consciousness has been changed. He admits to Jane that " 'Ah always thought Ah could get somewhere by climbing out of the mess we're livin' in. Now Ah see Ah've got to get to work an' clean up the mess!' " "He could not say what had happened to him," explained Nearing; "something curious certainly,—but he saw things differently."[42]

Jane shows Jim a different side to education, an education outside the control of the dominant classes. While he is with Jane being revitalized for the fight, he has access to her books—Jack London, Lenin, Marx, Sinclair, Dostoevsky, Tolstoy. He reads Marx's *Value, Price and Profit* as well as Sinclair's *The Jungle*. Jane recommends Sinclair's *The Goose Step* as 'a good one . . . Its 'bout education—goose-steppin' de mind.' " Reading Lenin's *State and Revolution* produces in Jim a conversion of sorts, a complete reorientation of thinking.

> "Lenin is a-tryin' to say: rights an' liberty an' justice fo' de rulin' class o'course—an' fo' de slaves, to all slaves—hard work an' de policeman's club! . . . Ah've learned more from dat book than from all de law classes Ah ever took!"

These were, wrote Nearing, "ideas he had never encountered," yet "the ideas dovetailed, point by point, with his own experience." "'Yo ain't never don much studyin','" Jim tells Jane, "'but Ah'se learned mo' from yo' shelf o' books in five days dan Ah has from de library in two years.'"[43]

The personal implications of Jane's radicalism touch more significantly on the institutions of marriage and the family. Nearing's discussion of these issues is the only indication of how he resolved them in the twenties. *Free Born* is unusual in proletarian fiction in that it links revolutionary goals with sexual freedom, upholding "free love" as a repudiation of the institution of marriage.[44] Jane explains to Jim that most women "'is a-lookin' fo' a meal ticket in a man!'"

> "Ain't yo' lookin' fo' a man?" Jim asked furtively.
> "Fo' somebody to love me? Of course Ah is! Who don' want to be loved? Fo' a piece o' property, lak mah hat an' mah shoes? Of course Ah is not! Who wants slaves aroun' de house? De slave days is Ovah!"

"'Mah body,'" she tells him, "'is mah own . . . an Ah only gives it to the man Ah loves, an only fo' so long as Ah loves him.'" Jim wonders if "'dat what de call 'free love?'"" to which Jane answers, "'Dey ain't no other kind.'" Jim argues that without marriage and "a good home" that she could never have any children, but she counters that parents trying to provide for their children under capitalism become "'caught like rats in a trap.'" The situation, she explains, is even worse for "revolutionary workers," since not only the children suffer but so does the revolution. Marriage and a family, she contends, "'makes yo' tame—tame slaves for de system. . . . It cripples yo' to much for de fight.'"[45]

In the final section of the novel, Jim is convinced that he must take up the fight of the working class, even if that means leaving Jane—the revolution comes first. Until the individual takes a stand, Jane tells him, "'until he does fight he ain't never really satisfied.'" For Jim, expatriation is scrapped for partisan commitment. As he tells her, "'Ah ain't never mo' unhappy dan when Ah runs away.'"[46] Jim ships out of Chicago with his first opportunity for work. He soon finds himself in the place of Nearing's roots, the coal mines of Pennsylvania, brought in with other blacks as strikebreakers. Under dangerous working conditions, a black worker next to Jim gets killed in the mine. Workers' anger turns toward a white supervisor, and Jim won't submit to his orders. He discovers that "in the crisis, he had become their spokesman, articulating what they all felt." When his fellow workers look to him for leadership, he "felt a sense of power that comes to a man when others stand before him, waiting for orders." When a black Communist newspaper is smuggled in to the workers, Jim reads it and offers to write a story about scab recruiting, which appears in the next issue. In the meantime, discontent among the blacks erupts, and a guard is struck by a brick and killed. When a search of the workers' quarters turns up a copy of the radical newspaper as well as the Communist party's campaign handbook in Jim's bunk, the owners jail him for the murder of the guard.

Jim goes on trial, not for the alleged crime but for his beliefs. The prosecution reads from the Workers party handbook and accuses Jim of calling "the workers to rise against the duly constituted authority and to overthrow the democratic institutions founded by the revered fore-fathers of this great Republic." Without any deliberation, the jury finds him guilty. But before sentencing, Jim makes a final defiant statement to the court.

> "Judge, you said this is a free country. Per'aps it looks that way to you. You are a white man an' a judge. . . . Suppose instead of bein' a white judge you were a black worker. Would de country look as free to you as it does now? . . . Ah was free born. . . . Ah found out dat de country was free for de rich and powerful, an' for de workers, it was just a fight to live. . . . What's all this talk about a free country anyway? . . . In Chicago when Ah couldn't get a good job, Ah thought it was because Ah was black. Then Ah learned that de very identical things was a'happenin' to plenty of white workers. Skins have different colors, judge, but a worker is a worker, no matter what his color. . . . De won't never have freedom till they learns to stand together—white an' black—man an' women an' children—an' take de things their labor produces, an de machines necessary to produce de food an' clothes they need. . . . This is a class fight."[47]

The novel ends as the judge angrily sentences him for his "dastardly attempt to undermine American institutions."[48] With his trial, he confronts American law corrupted by the values of capitalism, and, reminiscent of Nearing's 1919 trial, he preaches to the court the ideals of freedom and justice, and the betrayal of those ideals in America.

The pessimistic message of the ending, implying the weakness of the counterhegemonic impulse, was further confirmed as Nearing tried to get the novel published. He attempted to secure a publisher in vain until the summer of 1930 when he sent it to Freeman. He asked him to "take a look at it and give me your frank opinion regarding its worthwhileness." Freeman suggested the possibility of making some of the material suitable for magazine publication as a way of getting it out. "It looks to me now," Nearing told Freeman, "as though no commercial publishing house would be willing to handle the book. . . . If, however, through its publication we can get some of these facts and this point of view before an enlarged reading public I will do what I can to bring it out in some form."[49] Confronting what he saw as the ubiquitous control of the dominant class, he faced what he called in notes for his auto-biography as "the dramatist's ideal nightmare." "Something to say (as I conceive it) of life and death interest to the human race which I should communicate, without any way to reach and warn those who should hear in order that they may understand what is going on and act before it is too late. The situation . . . reads like a tragedy for me. For mankind it is the tolling bell of destiny."[50]

*Free Born* was finally published in 1932 by a small New York City publishing house with the subtitle *An Unpublishable Novel,* and with a publisher's note explaining that the manuscript had been rejected in the States and abroad, the last time with a favorable critique but with the caveat that it was "obviously impossible for it to be handled by any ordinary publisher."[51] Nearing explained years later that *Free Born* was an "experiment in a researched field that failed."[52] The experiment itself, along with the frustrated efforts to disseminate its message, fueled a desperate situation. Was public enlightenment impossible when one encountered the pervasive influence of capitalist hegemony? Was the connection between the personal and social struggle for freedom completely severed? What did it matter if one was only freeborn?

# Twilight

## Chapter 17

AS WAS indicated earlier regarding Nearing's assessment of the Communist strength in the 1928 elections, which the party reluctantly published, his views did not blindly follow the party line. The party's own ambiguous response to Nearing's heterodoxy reflected deep party turmoil rooted in political struggles and intrigue in Moscow and in the new period of Communist struggle. The "Third Period"—following the revolutionary period immediately after the 1917 Revolution and the second period of capitalist stabilization—was announced at the World Congress of the Communist International, which met from July through September 1928. With it, Stalin officially imposed a "left turn" on the international Communist movement, proclaiming that "the era of capitalism's downfall had come" and that the movement had entered into an ultrarevolutionary phase of class struggle.[1] This sharp shift in policy was fueled not by objective economic conditions but by internal power struggles over Soviet economic policy among Stalin, his political critic on the left, Trotsky, and his opponent on the right, Bukharin.[2] The political fighting in Moscow had serious repercussions in the American party. It caused bitter factionalism, further weakened the party,[3] and ended Lovestone's leadership.

Yet it was not specifically his misalliances with Stalin's enemies that explained why Lovestone suddenly found himself ideologically out of step. His problem was his identification with the theory of American "exceptionalism."[4] How could a swing to the left, necessitating struggle against reformist elements and premised on the imminent decline of capitalism, hold true everywhere except in America? How could the American economy be in "an epoch of affluence and magnificence, of peace and prosperity," as Lovestone claimed late in 1928, while the Comintern said that world capitalism was declining? If the American party could interpret economic conditions independently of the Comintern, was not that a return to the failed independent parties of the Second International? Political expediency in the American party meant imitating the struggles in Moscow. For the opposition, consisting of Cannon, Foster, Browder, and others, the "Right danger" in the United States—their Bukharin—was Lovestone. The primary charge against him was his overestimation of American capitalism and hence his diminished view of radical potential. What is important here is that Nearing was caught in the same tangled political web as Lovestone—and would suffer a similar fate. He was not purged with the Trotskyites and would write V. F. Calverton that he liked "Trotsky personally, but politically he is a menace, + I am anxious to avoid giving aid and comfort to him or to any group that backs him."[5] Neither was he driven out with the Lovestonites; he was not closely associated with the political leadership in the party. But in the new ultrarevolutionary period, all his unorthodox views came under renewed scrutiny, and the party would no longer tolerate his independent communism.

Nearing crossed the Rubicon of deviance in the interpretation of imperialism presented in his new study, *The Twilight of Empire: An Economic Interpretation of Imperialist Cycles*. With this book, Nearing embroiled himself in politically charged and highly controversial issues. When he had completed the manuscript, he turned it over to Alexander Trachtenberg of International Publishers, the official party publishing house. For months, Nearing tried to persuade him to publish it; in the meantime, Trachtenberg sent the manuscript to the party leadership in Moscow for approval.[6] Nearing knew of this and wrote Freeman that he had "sent a copy across and is waiting for an answer." Nearing added that Trachtenberg was "friendly enough, but careful as usual." He also shared with Freeman his view that "the C.P. situation here is not encouraging. I guess it is less rooted in USA life."[7]

The interpretation of imperialism offered in the *Twilight of Empire* was not only influenced by Hobson; Nearing also acknowledged the inspiration of Lenin's *Imperialism: The Highest Stage of Capitalism*. "Hobson stressed the economic aspect of imperialism," wrote Nearing, while "Lenin added the developmental aspect—placing imperialism in its historical setting."[8] Nearing's analysis followed the party line, straight and narrow. Even when he appeared to deviate slightly as he did with his definition of imperialism, he veered back sharply to a Leninist position. Lenin had described imperialism, Nearing acknowledged, as "a particular phase of capitalist development." Nearing, however, universalized the phenomenon, defining it as "the stage of economic and political development during which a ruling class conquers and exploits beyond the boundaries of the civil state."[9] In what was a seriously non-Marxian historical view, he detected "cycles of imperialism" following a pattern that occurred throughout the rise and fall of the ancient Egyptian, Persian, Greek, and Roman empires. While he argued that imperialism "has been characteristic of the whole era of civilization," his interpretive scheme recovered a Leninist orientation by arguing that "in the closing decades of the eighteenth century the sequence of the modern imperial cycle was broken by the industrial revolution." Thus, "the imperial cycle, instead of following its normal course, was disrupted by the industrial revolution."[10]

Nearing was mindful of non-Marxian interpretations dealing with the rise and fall of civilizations, particularly that of Oswald Spengler, whose "patterns" of decay the party denounced as the work of a "bourgeois" historian. Nearing's work reflected the influence of Spengler's *Decline of the West* (1928), particularly in its universalizing of the concept of imperialism and in discovering a pattern, or "cycles," in the rise and fall of great civilizations. Spengler goes virtually unacknowledged in the *Twilight of Empire*, but Nearing had written in 1927 that Spengler, and others like him, were wrong with their dire predictions. "They see capitalism toppling; they feel the foundations of civilization crumbling under their feet, and they have neither the knowledge nor the understanding to realize that the labor movement is already building a new social structure upon the ruins of civilization." "Comfortable philosophers may be satisfied with daily resorts to pessimism," he contended, but "the workers are not so free." What Spengler "does not understand," he argued, is "that the passing of civilization means, not destruction, but emancipation."[11]

In an interpretation that continued along essentially orthodox ideological lines, even while it perhaps stressed federalism more than centralization, Nearing explained that the industrial revolution resulted in two important developments. First, it meant greater international economic activity, which in turn led to a world economic system. The new era, "with its wider area of business activity, called into being a new kind of state—the confederation or federal organization of sovereign states" that left a "balance between localism and federalism that would leave the local areas culturally free and at the same time centralize their chief economic interests under one sovereign jurisdiction."[12] Second, there was the evolution toward "financial capitalism" by the late nineteenth century when world economic expansion had reached all areas of the globe, resulting in economic rivalry. Thus, the end of the century was marked by the struggle of industrial empires. The Great War was "the military phase of the struggle between great imperial powers." But the postwar world, with the realignment of imperial rivalries, ushered in seemingly contradictory developments; on the one hand, capitalist development had brought international interdependence, while on the other it had led to "the most intense foreign conquest and exploitation."[13]

In the face of these economic forces, Nearing declared, "only from the Soviet Union comes a ringing voice of protest, and a call for the workers and the farmers of the world to throw off the shackles of imperialism, wipe out the capitalist system, abolish poverty and war, and lay the foundations of a world co-operative society."[14] The proletarian revolution in the Soviet Union held out hope for "the transition from the imperial state to the world federation of producer groups."[15] From the workers there had emerged "a class consciousness and a sense of class solidarity, then a labor movement, and finally the Proletarian revolution, which broke the spiral of imperialism."[16]

While this part of Nearing's interpretation adhered closely to party dogma and could have been only mildly offensive, he courted trouble with his conviction of the exceptional revolutionary circumstances in America, commenting that "even to-day the American workers are so little class conscious that more than 95 percent of them vote the same ticket as the men who own their jobs, without any realization of what they are doing."[17] If he was convinced of the correctness of his assessment of American radicalism, he was still struggling with the question of pacifism, and while he did not confront the issue directly, he reasserted a covert yet unmistakable critique of violence at the root of his interpretation. He did not address the fundamental question of how the transition away from capitalist imperialism would come about, but he made it clear that it would be gradual, evolutionary, and implicitly nonviolent.[18] When Nearing concluded that "within its own structure, imperialism carries the seeds of its own destruction" and leads to "a higher economic level than conflict and exploitation . . . beyond imperialism,"[19] he was clearly no longer following Lenin—a particularly acute problem during the new military revolutionary Third Period. It would be hard to miss the implications of Nearing's overall argument, which essentially repudiated the Third Period. Not only did he not accede to the notion of a sudden new phase of revolutionary ferment, but he failed to acknowledge the party as the fundamental force behind revolutionary change. In fact, in response to the implications of the Third Period, Nearing seemed to have retreated from his concessions to violence and reverted to his earlier absolute pacifism.

At bottom, it was the issue of pacifism that led Nearing to break with the party's interpretation of imperialism. The dominant issue for Lenin, and the point of departure for Nearing, was his perception of the basic contradiction of capitalism, "the contradiction between monopoly and free competition that exists side by side with it."[20] Lenin wrote that "monopoly, which has grown out of free competition, does not abolish the latter, but exists over and along side of it; and thereby gives rise to a number of very acute, intense antagonisms, frictions and conflict."[21] It was, said Lenin in his *Imperialism*, notions of "pacifism and 'democracy' in general, which have no claim to Marxism whatever," that led to the argument (much like Nearing's) that "monopolies in economics are compatible with non-monopolistic, non-violent, non-annexationist methods in politics."[22] It was meaningless, Lenin claimed, to allude to the possibility that capitalism would transform itself beyond its "highest stage" to an international nonexploitive order. Imperialism, he wrote, was "leading to annexation, to increased national oppression, and, consequently, also to increasing resistance . . . towards violence and reaction."[23] The contradiction inherent in capitalism led only to domination and inevitable violence. "How else," wrote Lenin, "can the solution of the contradictions be found, except by resorting to *violence?*"[24] Nearing, in the *Twilight of Empire*, would not grant that the destruction of capitalism would have to come through violence, and he even invoked Marx as the authoritative voice leaving open the possibility for nonviolent revolutionary change. "Marx notes," Nearing pointed out (as he had done earlier), "that open class struggle ends 'either in a revolutionary reconstruction of society at large, or in the common ruin of contending classes.' "[25]

Finally, word came from the party: permission to publish was denied. Trachtenberg explained to Nearing that the defect of the study was that contrary to Lenin's position, its imperialism was a phase in the history of modern capitalism and not a universal social pattern. "We would like to publish the book here," conceded Trachtenberg, but "over there they are more interested in party politics than they are in social theory."[26] Nearing knew that publication outside party channels "would be a violation of party discipline" and was left to weigh "the issue carefully, with its conflicting loyalties and the stark political consequences."[27] He decided to quit the party and publish. He sent in his letter of resignation, explaining that the rejection of the *Twilight of Empire* had left him with three alternatives.

1. To abandon the idea of publishing the manuscript. This I do not care to do, as I believe it presents an important historical synthesis heretofore unstated.
2. To publish the manuscript outside Party channels. This action might lead to additional inner Party controversy. Already we have too much of that.
3. To resign from the Party and publish the study.

He had decided, he wrote the Central Committee of the party, to take the "third course" and resign his membership while "continuing, as in the past, to uphold the principles of the Party and to support the Party work."[28]

The Party, however, preferred expelling members rather than accepting resignations, and in their announcement dropping Nearing it became clearer that his recalcitrance was more serious than a matter of the history of imperialism. Nearing's decision to contest the decision of "the authoritative Marxian body in Moscow" simply indicated "how little fit intellectuals of the type of Nearing are to stand the pressure which the duties of the revolution put upon a revolutionist." "Scott Nearing was never a Marxian," the committee stated, "but his subordination under Party direction and discipline could have made him of service to the proletarian revolution." Instead, because of his "non-Marxian conceptions," the party decided to dump him "on the scrap heap of the revolution."[29]

The party's vaguely critical explanation and denunciation of Nearing's "non-Marxian" ideas was more than simply a case of the party's impatience with the troublesome independent thinking of a party intellectual. The party's initial response may be explained by its own turmoil. Its leadership was still suffering repercussions from Stalin's war against his political enemies and the expulsion of Lovestone and his supporters. Moscow had appointed Max Bedacht as interim secretary of the American party by the time Nearing resigned. But as the dust from the Third Period left turn began to settle, a new leader of the American party emerged, a strong supporter of the new Comintern line and a hard-line critic of the Lovestonites. Earl Browder was the Comintern's chosen man and would climb to the leadership of the party by the end of the year.[30] His rising preeminence in the party explains why in June 1930 he wrote an eleven-page critique of Nearing's manuscript in the party journal for those "who are impressed with the prestige of Nearing's long record as scholar and teacher."[31]

According to Browder, Nearing went astray because he was not sufficiently revolutionary. The problem was partly his relentless idealism, his religious "faith," which wreaked havoc with his scientific Marxism, and partly his view that the hard reality of American conditions was an exception to the belief in worldwide capitalist decay and increased revolutionary fervor. In the *Twilight of Empire*, Browder argued, "Nearing finally demonstrates his inability to understand Marxism, demonstrates his fundamentally mystic or religious philosophy, which prevents him from understanding or contributing to that revolutionary movement to which he gives emotional allegiance." His method was "neither dialectical nor material; it is eclectic and idealist."

Because Nearing looked to history instead of the party to determine the course of the future, he was lumped with Spengler in finding a "pattern" as "our basis of prediction." "Then we cannot predict the coming of socialism, we can predict nothing but the eternal recurrence of the pattern." "If anyone," he continued, "can believe this 'pattern' as a basis for the perspectives of the future, then he can be a revolutionist only as an act of faith (religious), and not as a matter of scientific conviction, the conviction that the revolutionary Party is itself carrying through the historical process." Nearing, Browder concluded, "uses the words and phrases of science, but his thought is determined by the same religious preconceptions as that of Spengler, the bourgeois idealist philosopher."[32] Nearing was not, according to Browder, awarding proper legitimacy to the party or its new revolutionary line and thus sounded "like Lovestone describing the 'Hooverian Age' of the American Empire, a period of peace and prosperity, of riches, magnificence and stability, with nary a hint of revolt."[33] Nearing could not stay in the party because he could not make the leap into the party's Third Period.

"Scott Nearing," Michael Gold wrote later in the *Daily Worker*, "had remained in the Party for several years, and always seemed to be in hot water." His problem was that he "had lapsed into a moment of mystic individualism." "In Scott Nearing one always felt this conflict going on," Gold claimed, that "the man of science never could shake off the barnacles of his churchly past."

He was more than anything else "an individualist, he followed his own mystic impulses and logic."[34] Roger Baldwin noted that Nearing's "exit from a party to which he was never temperamentally adapted was a foregone conclusion." As a "revolutionary economist," he was "no spokesman for a movement" but was a figure who stood "above parties and movements."[35]

Nearing contended that "politically and personally the consequences of the decision to publish *Twilight of Empire* were cataclysmic." The effect was "overwhelming," he said. "The Communist Party was my last institutional connection."[36] With that connection broken, Nearing relinquished his place in all radical organizations, resigning his "directorships and committee positions" in the Workers School, the Garland Fund, the Civil Liberties Union, "and all other organizations in which I held responsible positions."[37] He had reached the twilight of a long fight, and at the age of forty-six, he faced critical life choices. The struggle took its toll on the man. "It would be hard to call Nearing a happy man," wrote Baldwin shortly after Nearing's expulsion; "among the strong lines of a face weather-beaten and tanned by much outdoor living are the lines of conflict, even suffering. He is not the happy warrior."[38] Nearing recalled that "the break from the Left was as final as the expulsion from academia which marked a break with the Center and the Right. Again I was out in a cold, cold world."[39] Yet despite the isolation and alienation of his crisis, those close to him, like Baldwin, knew that he could not "help continuing his essential drive." "For thousands in the radical movement," Baldwin prophesied, "he will continue to be an inspiration as a teacher, not through his propaganda so much as through rare qualities of rigid honesty, a loveable selflessness, and the essential integrity of the contradictory virtues that go to make up his character."[40]

# Living the Good Life

**Part Five**

# To a Cyclone
# Cellar in New England

## Chapter 18

*The custodians of culture hope, at bottom, merely to survive its collapse. The will to build a better society, however, survives, along with traditions of localism, self-help, and community action that only need the vision of a new society, a decent society, to give them new vigor. The moral discipline formerly associated with the work ethic still retains a value independent of the role it once played in the defense of property rights. That discipline—indispensable to the task of building a new order—endures most of all in those who knew the old order only as a broken promise, yet who took the promise more seriously than those who merely took it for granted.*

Christopher Lasch,
The Culture of Narcissism (*1979*)

AS the Depression decade opened, Nearing, like the nation, faced an acute crisis. His was a personal and a political predicament. In his struggle against the overpowering dominance of capitalist hegemony, he had given his all to what he saw as the last best hope on the left for social transformation, the Communists. Yet the party could not fulfill his social vision. Furthermore, cultural fragmentation had become so severe that personal and social salvation seemed to occupy vastly different realms. That Nearing sensed the disconnected nature of American culture is apparent in his autobiography, which he subtitled *A Political Autobiography*. For the part of his life through World War I, the "political" linked the personal and the public. After that point, the structure of his recollections changed dramatically. He alternately provided analyses of public affairs and private endeavors, but they occupied distinctively separate spheres. The self and society had become disengaged.[1]

But an essential pursuit continued—a struggle for greater freedom. That quest would remain a central preoccupation for the next half-century, as an intellectual concern and in his day-to-day life. In his most important writings in the years from 1930 to 1983—*Democracy Is Not Enough* (1945), *Living the Good Life* (1954), and *Freedom: Promise and Menace* (1961)—he examined the prospects for true freedom in America.

With his break from the Left in 1930, he had cut himself loose from public associations to find personal freedom. In fact, the only hope for individual liberation was to maintain a separation from capitalist society and culture. As he had throughout his life, he turned to religious faith in time of crisis. He found spiritual comfort when he met Helen Knothe, twenty years his junior, in Ridgewood, New Jersey. Helen was a vegetarian and deeply involved in Theosophy, a movement that embraced all religions. She would serve as the model for the female characters in *Free Born* whose feminine nurture brought salvation to Jim Rogers.[2] Her intense spirituality was in part Scott's redemption. She was like the female character who claimed, "'Ah ain' nebber feun' nobody befor' whut done enjoy hisself in de Holy Lan' de way yo' all has. . . . We'se chums, Jim! We both understan'.'" And Nearing was like Jim, who "had fallen, for the first time, over a precipice, into the life of another human being with whom he had no previous contact. He had gazed into her eyes; had seen the depth. . . . At last, after all these years, he had found someone who understood."[3] And there were other parallels. Like Jim and Jane in the novel, Scott and Helen lived together unmarried and had no children.[4] Helen was in some ways his Jane Wilson, the one who pulled him out of a "black abyss."

Helen came from a privileged background similar to Scott's. Her mother, a native of Holland, was trained as an artist, and her father was a successful New York businessman. Brought up in an intellectually rich environment, she showed promise as a musician. After graduating from high school, Helen went to Europe to continue her music studies. While in Amsterdam, she came into contact for the first time with key figures in the Theosophical Society, particularly the young spiritual leader Krishnamurti to whom she was greatly attracted. As she explained years later, Krishnamurti led her "from a paramount interest in music to the study of Eastern Religions and Theosophy." Helen's spiritual training took her to India in the early 1920s, and then to Australia as she journeyed along "the Path of Discipleship." Her "supernal relations with Krishnamurti" became strained in 1926, and she returned to the United States. When she and Scott met, it appeared on the surface that they had little in common. She had, she admitted, her "head in the clouds and . . . no knowledge of what had been going on in the world. . . . I was a complete political ignoramus."[5]

Scott offered Helen a political education, and she provided him with spirituality. While they lived in an unheated cold-water apartment in lower Manhattan, he persuaded her to take on a factory job to get "in touch with reality." She took jobs at minimum wage, and when she asked for better pay, she was fired. Thus started her "real-life education."[6] Scott, for his part, absorbed the teachings of Theosophy. This was particularly disturbing to some on the left like Michael Gold who remained attentive to Nearing's activities. Nearing had become, wrote Gold critically, "an ardently naive disciple of theosophy." "You may say," claimed Gold, "that anyone has a right to any private religious belief, if in his public life he is loyal to the working class." The problem was that "more and more, in his public life, the economist . . . has yielded to the theosophist." How could anyone, Gold lamented, "reconcile Madame Blavatsky [a founder of the Theosophical movement] and Lenin?"[7]

▬ Nearing knew there were limits to his idealism, that "fidelity to truth," as he put it, "butters no parsnips. If the business interests could freeze me out of my profession and starve me besides, the game would be up."[8] The solution to his dilemma came in 1932 during the depth of the Great Depression when he and Helen used all their available resources to purchase a run-down farmhouse in the Green Mountains of Vermont. In an expansive version of his earlier Arden experience,[9] they intended "to set up a semi-self-contained household unit, based largely on a use economy and, as far as possible, independent of the price-profit economy." They began only as "summer folk," and "at the outset" they "thought of the venture as a personal search for a simple, satisfying life on the land." It quickly became a year-round enterprise, and "with the passage of time and the accumulation of experience," they came to regard their effort as "a laboratory in which we were testing out certain principles and procedures."[10] Their objective was partly economic—to live "as independently as possible from the commodity and labor markets"—and it was partly "social and ethical," "to liberate and disassociate ourselves . . . from the cruder forms of exploitation."[11] The productive unit of the "subsistence farmstead"[12] allowed for the expression of values associated with earned income, strenuous living, practical ethics, and a widened field of free will. "Freedom," Nearing explained,

> is opportunity to make choices and decisions and to formulate them into action,—unrestricted, uncoerced, independent, sovereign. Freedom requires self-determination, whether the involved entity be an individual or a social group. Freedom exists when the individual or social group has an unrestricted opportunity for self expression,—physically, emotionally, mentally, spiritually.[13]

"Vermont life" was thus " 'free' in the sense that it placed before the individual and the household a wide range of choices."[14] "For the individual or family that wishes independence of plutocratic control," Nearing advised, "the subsistence farm offers important possibilities."[15]

There was, of course, one critical problem. Even though their retreat to a "cyclone cellar in New England,"[16] as Scott metaphorically referred to it, was not an attempt to "escape"—"we were not shirking obligations, but looking for an opportunity to take on more worthwhile experiences"—it remained "an individual experience."[17] The Nearings "looked upon association with the community as a necessary aspect of life" and "were cooperators in theory," yet theirs was never to become a community endeavor.[18] The crusty Vermonters were attuned neither to the Nearings' social vision nor their lifestyle. As Paul Goodman explained it, the Nearings brought a postindustrial mind-set into a preindustrial community.[19] Their neighbors, they decided, were under the pervasive influence of dominant values of the capitalist culture and therefore exhibited "no deep concern to cooperate." Conversely, the Nearings were "not willing to conform to their patterns of living." They despaired that any attempt "to cooperate effectively" would result in "failure because the social set-up doomed such an experiment before it was born." The local Vermonters were "conditioned from birth by the professions and practices of a private enterprise, individualistic life pattern."[20] While the Nearing's rural experiment was personally unifying, "linking vocation and avocation,"[21] it failed to harmonize the self and society, and there remained "the absence of effective neighborhood cooperation."[22]

With some regret, the Nearings acknowledged "the social inadequacy of our Vermont project" and that their "solution to the problem" was "a personal one." In the long run, their effort was "a personal stop-gap, an emergency expedient." "But in the short view," they explained, it was "a way of preserving self-respect and of demonstrating to the few who are willing to observe, listen and participate, that life in a dying acquisitive culture can be individually and socially purposeful, creative, constructive and deeply rewarding."[23] Nearing granted that "it is quite possible to argue that homesteading is not an ideal way of life because it lays too much emphasis on the individual family and overlooks the larger social groups,"[24] yet he hoped that "the one who has broken away from the established group pattern has distinguished himself and thus set himself up as an example for others."[25] The Nearings recognized that their contribution to social "advance" was "only a tiny one," expressed best by those they influenced "through precept or example."[26]

When he assessed the significance of their homesteading experiment, Nearing argued that

> Any consideration of freedom in actions should include some reference to the numerous casual experiments designed to enlarge the areas in which individuals or groups of human beings make choices and implement them. All such experiments call into question the theoretical bases of the established order, violate property laws, attempt by extra-legal means to correct injustices and challenge . . . the existing folkways, which are predominantly restrictive and coercive.[27]

Demands for freedom, he declared, "come frequently from idealists outraged by the needless suffering, injustice and inefficiency and the slowness of social change, who are eager to move rapidly into a social pattern that will bring men closer to realizing their loftiest aspirations."[28]

▬ At the same time that Nearing reassessed his life and chose a less-beaten path to the Vermont woods, his sons were coming of age and in search for a direction of their own. Even as he and Nellie drifted farther apart and he was absent from the day-to-day lives of his boys, he was always the concerned, loving father, ever ready to offer advice, search out their thinking, and point out correctives to faulty ideas or activities. The shadow he cast often made it difficult for his sons to find their own way as they matured, and John would complain to his father of being unable to break free of the family and a "feeling of subordination."[29]

The boys experienced a privileged education, at the Friends Seminary in New York City in the late teens and then at the public schools in Ridgewood. In 1925, the whole family went to Europe, and while Scott and Nellie pursued their own interests, Bob and John attended an exclusive school in Switzerland where John excelled in the study of languages. When the family returned, Bob continued his schooling at the Manumit School, soon to be under Nellie's direction, and John went on to graduate from the George School in Philadelphia. Bob would attend an agricultural school and eventually turn his talents to farming. In 1929 John enrolled in the University of Wisconsin's Experimental College, a creation of Alexander Meiklejohn, where the radical educational program offered a curriculum founded on the classics of ancient Greece and the study of the moral and political values of Western civilization.

Out from under the immediate domination of his family, John aspired to be a writer, but quickly his social conscience wreaked havoc with his art. During his first semester of study, he composed an autobiographical essay in which he wrestled with his choice of vocation. "The important thing," he wrote, "is the class struggle." But, he asked, could he "serve the class struggle better if he stayed in school in his little white room and looked at the whole thing objectively and then went out as a leader?" The answer was no, "the place where there is work to be done now is among the workers themselves." While he would "stay in his white room a while longer," it was "Marx and not Plato that he will concentrate on," realizing "that his place is with the workers helping to set up a new world."[30] Before his first year at Wisconsin was over, John wrote to Scott that his plans for the future might include returning to the university to study math or engineering, or perhaps to go to Russia to work. "I am getting very stale here," he confided to his father; "school is getting very meaningless."[31]

While at Wisconsin in 1931, John wrote to Scott that he had "come to the conclusion that American civilization for the last 300 years has produced no culture at all." Scott's reply, in part, consisted of the following:

1. The structure of American society was built by exploiting interests whose objective was the possession of the largest possible quantity of economic goods. USA society is necessarily colored throughout by these forces of profiteering.
2. In such a society the emphasis would necessarily be on outward appearances and exteriors, since wealth itself is entirely exterior to human life, although it necessarily has some influence on it. . . .
3. These motivating forces applied in an undeveloped natural environment led to the fabrication of materials,—wood, iron, etc. The very abundance of natural resources such as petroleum, yielding their enormous profits, drove the whole nation headlong towards mass production.

4. Under such circumstances, there could be few of the graces of life,—little decoration on the buildings; little art; little literature. The pursuit of profits is so narrow a phase of human activity that it does not permit of much elaboration. Then, the thinness of life left very little to express even where decoration was attempted. Dreiser's *American Tragedy* tells the story. So the books of Sherwood Anderson. The whole scheme of life falls flat when it is subjected to the least critical examination. It explodes like a gas balloon the moment it is pricked.

5. Even the American philosophers seldom get below the surface, but confine themselves like James, to a rather superficial phase of relativity (pragmatism) or worse still, as with most of the modern philosophers, they build their work on experimental psychology. . . .

6. In order to have a way of life such as that for example of the Greeks, which can impress contemporaries with its dignity, and which can make an historic impress, it is necessary to go further than either pragmatism or behaviorism. . . .

7. The cosmos is a larger unit of which man is a very small part. In order to build a dignified or an enduring culture, some concept of the relation between man and the cosmos is indispensable. Emerson knew something of this relation. Also of course, Whitman. William James was aware of it. . . .

. . . I think however that the USA is going to create a culture. . . . Before it can achieve such a result however, it must eliminate its profit economy and take what it can from the wisdom of the world. This means of course that men and women must settle down as they did in earlier societies and spend their time and energy in "searching for the truth. . . ."

Always keep in mind the above analysis. It is not your turn now. Get your engineering training; make a go of your profession; bring up a family; perform your duties as a "householder." But when you are 45 years old or so, leave the "Hall of Knowledge" in which you have been living and working, and set out on the path that leads to the "Hall of Wisdom."[32]

John's ambivalence regarding his choice of study may have been a reflection of the difficulty he experienced trying to create an identity free of the father whose influence he both revered and resisted. While he turned to Scott for counsel, he also struck off in directions simultaneously deferential and rebellious. In explaining his new course of study, he wrote to Scott of the need for "the Chemistry of dye industry; the Math of Bridge construction; and the Physics of machine designing or of electrical engineering. All the advanced theory can come later. It is in Economics and in applied science that the big job is to be done now."[33] At the same time, John found his voice as a youthful revolutionary, criticizing the timidity of the Communist party in fighting for revolutionary change. This in turn was received with stern advice from Scott, who warned John that he was "laboring under the delusion that fighting will bring Communism." "You are entirely too impatient," he admonished. "The movement in the USA is now full of young men and women with no trades or professions or training. They hinder more than they help."[34] Scott's shadow, it seems, reached all the way to Wisconsin, and while John was there, in an act symbolic of both liberation and the deepening paradox that surrounded his relationship with his father, he dropped his last name, changing his name to John Scott. Late in his life he would explain that "everyone I met either would compliment me on being my father's son, or reproach me with his opinions," so he "decided I'd like to be someone myself."[35]

John's desire to go to Russia intensified in 1931, fueled by his father's encouragement. While Nearing was in Leningrad in the summer of that year, he wrote to John of workers "going to the Urals" and of his own experience working in a brickyard. He hoped to return "possibly to the Urals or Siberia + work on building construction or else in a factory." He added that "life is hard. Living quarters rough + rather monotonous. But it is *enormously interesting.*"[36] With his sights set on Russia, John left college in 1931 and on Scott's advice prepared himself for a useful trade. "No matter what the field," Scott explained to John, "a worker must have some technical training if he is to be of use."[37] At the General Electric Plant in Schenectady, New York, John completed a training course and earned a welders certificate. In August 1932, Scott and John traveled to Amsterdam as part of the American delegation of the World Congress against War. While John attended the conference as an organizer for the Electrical Workers Union, his destination was Moscow. With his welders certificate in hand, he went from there to the industrial city of Magnitagorsk on the eastern slopes of the Ural Mountains.[38]

As John described his expatriation, he had left "an America sadly dislocated, an America offering few opportunities for young energy and enthusiasm." He had gradually come "to the conclusion that the Bolsheviks had found the answers to at least some of the questions Americans were asking each other." He wanted to "lend a hand in the construction of a society which seemed to be at least one step ahead of the American." In Magnitagorsk John hoped to get "away from the fetishization of material possessions," which, he explained, "my good parents had taught me, was one of the basic ills of American society."[39]

John lived hard in Magnitagorsk, yet he thrived on the intensity of the life he found. He learned Russian, enrolled in a party university, and worked his way from a welder to foreman and chemist in a coke and chemicals by-products plant. By 1934, John's letters revealed a new self-confidence and maturity. He didn't hesitate taking his father to task on points of disagreement, as when he questioned "What are you driving at when you talk about the over estimation by the communists of the role of reasoning power in human affairs in general. You didn't finish your thought in the letter, and, I don't see what you are getting at."[40] When Scott criticized John's life and "the raggedness of [his] letters, clothes, beard, and life; and of life in general," John's reply was self-assured.

You tell me to learn all I can. I am learning every day so much that if I manage to assimilate half of it I will be a Socrates by next free day. . . . I am not wasting my time here. If you lived here a week and saw how much sleep I get, and what I do with my day, you would agree with me. . . . My life is on a much higher [level] than it has ever been before (many times higher), and is ever approaching the high level attained by yourself since 1883 and especially since 1920.[41]

John married a Russian woman in 1934, and Scott traveled to Magni-tagorsk that summer; he would return to see John for the next three years. When John visited the United States briefly in 1937, he returned to Russia accompanied by Bob, who was "at loose ends" in America and anxious to find meaningful work.[42] But the Russia the brothers encountered was not the one that John had left only months before. Stalin's purges were reaching to the heart of Soviet society. Foreigners were now suspect and were unable to find work, and Bob returned to the States after a matter of months. John eventually went to Moscow to write as a correspondent for a French news agency. He was stymied in his efforts to get his family out of the country and haunted by what he saw as the split reality of Soviet Russia—social progress undermined by senseless repression. Personally and culturally, the horrors of Stalinism destroyed the promise of a fulfilling way of life.

John was expelled from the Soviet Union in 1941 for slandering Soviet foreign policy but he secured safe passage for his wife and two daughters, so that the entire family came to the United States. The anticommunism that he brought back with him drove an ever deepening wedge between him and Scott, as did other aspects of his life. He settled in Ridgefield, Connecticut, and began work on a large house that required him to borrow heavily. He went to work for Henry Luce's *Time* magazine, variously as a specialist on the Soviet Union, a correspondent, an editor, and a roving lecturer as well as assistant to the publisher.

This prompted Scott to chide John for the "group of scandalous associates" with whom he had allied himself. It was only a short step for his disagreements with John's cold-war views to lead to a greater objection over his son's lifestyle, which, from the father's perspective, betrayed all of his earlier promise and youthful potential. Scott wrote John that he was "dismayed when a person of your background + capacity" could write that "Soviet power is on the offensive throughout the world." There was no point, he insisted, in "denouncing the USSR as the enemy of mankind and the source of all our ills." "Once upon a time you did know better," wrote Scott, but "either you have forgotten what you knew a few years ago or else the economic pressure of your family + of your ill-starred venture in Ridgefield have led you to choose self + power rather than integrity." "This is a crucial and terrible issue in your life. . . . Above all you must determine what part economic factors are to play in your life. Whether you are to be dominated + driven by them, or whether you are to give truth, order, harmony + beauty the priority in making your decisions."[43]

━━━ While homesteading, Nearing remained an American communist and defended the Soviet Union as the only real alternative to U.S. capitalism, even as he became disillusioned with the Soviet regime. It was a rare occasion that he criticized the Soviet Union publicly, since, as he had made clear in the twenties, he feared such criticism would only aid the capitalists. Yet privately he expressed misgivings, perhaps because of the knowledge gained from John, first with Stalin's purges. He wrote to V. F. Calverton in 1938 that he felt "helpless re the Soviet trials." He feared that "maybe this is Socialism—the servile state."

> Ideally, the content of socialism is quite different, but actually what will it be? Perhaps the USSR is the answer.
>
> Certainly no social order can be built upon fear, hate, suspicion + coercion. They will tear the fabric of society to pieces—as they are now tearing that of the USSR.
>
> Ever since National Socialism got power in Germany I have been asking myself the question: What is Socialism, after all? . . . If we win socialism + lose all our freedoms—are we paying an excessive price? . . . I am convinced that there is something fundamentally at fault about the C.P. approach and organiza- tion. . . . It needs a lot of rethinking. The history of the past 20 years has made mince-meat out of more than the outstanding theories of K. Marx.

The Nazi–Soviet Pact of August 1939 only furthered his disenchantment. It made the "USSR one of the aggressors," he wrote Calverton. "As for its effect on the C.P.," he added, "that can be mitigated only if the C.P. is willing to cut itself off entirely from U.S.S.R. + make its own path in the woods."[44]

Still, the liberating "social pattern" that provided an alternative to capitalist society, in a general sense, was socialism. For Nearing, socialism retained the expansive meaning it had in the early years of the century. Unconfined by any rigid dogma, it was characterized by a pragmaticlike, vital openness. "Socialism," Nearing wrote in his autobiography, "is unfinished business rather than an accomplished fact . . . a growing, changing, develop- ing, evolving cluster of social institutions."[45] Thus, although he admired Marx, when he referred to socialism, he did not mean its Marxian rendering. After his battles in the Communist party, he decided that "you probably cannot combine the principle of free will with the principle of dialectical materialism." This was one reason, he said, that explained why he was "not an orthodox Marxist. I believe in the principle of free will."[46] Another reason was that he was "a pacifist and [I] do not believe in the efficacy or righteousness of the use of violence."[47] Finally, he was "never really a 100% Marxian socialist" since he was not an "orthodox materialist."[48]

Marxism's "emphasis on economic development" led Nearing to view it as "a doctrine" that "bypasses the individual and the cosmos. . . . We ignore at our peril any aspect of human nature and any phase of human experience." "One of the things that has bothered me about socialism as it is developing in the socialist countries," he noted, was "the tendency to confine socialism to the plane of daily necessities: food, clothing, housing." "More goods and services may provide physical comforts and social amenities; they cannot meet the demands for constructive, creative living." He proposed a "reformed socialism" that would answer needs "beyond physical gratification" and address "the entire range of man's urge to know, to aspire, to participate, to create. It is in these realms only that the greatest satisfactions and the real fulfillments are to be found." If socialism was to make "a distinctive contribution to human culture," it would be by reaching "beyond the welfare state" and into "a new field of initiative, inquiry, and creativity."[49] He conceived of socialism in the same terms he used to explain the purpose of the homesteading experiment: "The ultimate end of the economy is the stimulation of human will and genius to efforts which will improve the social environment, keep it fluid and thus enlarge opportunities for the building of individual character."[50]

▬ When *Living the Good Life* appeared in 1954, it was compared immediately with Thoreau's *Walden*.[51] Here was a twentieth-century *Walden*, an account signifying an act of deliberate liberation through an alternative way of life. There was a distinct echo from Thoreau resonating through the Nearings' writing. Not only did the publication of their book coincide with the centenary of *Walden*, but they drew on Thoreau directly.[52] Like *Walden*, *Living the Good Life* revealed the Nearings' quest as an act of "liberation," a way of life by which they "had freed ourselves from dependence upon a market economy."[53] They would shun capitalist cultural hegemony and "assume a large measure of self-sufficiency and thus make it more difficult for civilization to impose its restrictive and coercive economic pressures."[54] This was on one level an act of civil disobedience, "a psychological and political resistance" as well as an example of "a self-respecting, decent, simple life" through the "principles and practices of an alternative social system."[55]

*Living the Good Life* was the culmination of an attempt by the Nearings to formulate the practical and theoretical basis for their homesteading experiment. This process of self-reflection began in the late 1940s when they had achieved a large degree of success with their alternative way of life. In 1949, Scott explained that "we can picture clearly to ourselves what we mean by 'the good life.' . . . We can refuse to take part in any effort to preserve the institutions of life of the old social order."[56] "The self-containment" of homesteading, he wrote, "is based on the production of goods which we consume ourselves, without the intervention of the market. . . . We have freed ourselves largely from direct dependence upon price-profit economy."[57]

Initial attempts to give an account of the ultimate meaning of their lives fell short. Helen became the voice of the practical aspects of the "good life," while Scott shunned the practical for the philosophical and, as it turned out, autobiographical. When *The Maple Sugar Book* appeared in 1950, it was primarily Helen's handiwork, and while it made reference to the purposeful attempt to "control our own source of livelihood," it also carried the disclaimer that the book "by-passed the theories almost entirely and concentrated . . . on practical economic and social detail."[58] Scott groped toward a more philosophical account in *Man's Search for the Good Life.*

In 1951, Scott and Helen tried again at a coherent "report on the entire Vermont enterprise . . . dealing with the project as a whole."[59] When they outlined their new project, Scott was assigned the abstract sections, Helen the concrete.[60] That year they also decided to reinvigorate their experiment by leaving Vermont to begin again in Maine. When John Scott expressed dismay over his father's plan, Scott replied:

> Your outlook on life differs from mine. You want rootedness in a *place*. I do not ask or expect rootedness. I want to be able to do the job at hand, + when it is finished, to go on to the next one.
>
> We have been here for two decades . . . + built up the place + made a success of the business. We could stay here indefinitely + live comfortably on the syrup-sugar business. But that is status—ergo retrogression.

Abandonment of the Vermont experiment also coincided with the disheartening realization that the hope of creating a community would not be realized. That Scott and Helen were "living in a community"—the title of a final chapter in *Living the Good Life*—was simply an illusion. The transition to Maine symbolized a tacit acknowledgement of the failure of the community ideal and the beginning of a new, purely individualist effort. Scott explained to John that he and Helen would spend a year living frugally "+ do some reading + writing."[61] During that year, their own *Walden* began to take shape.

The genius of *Living the Good Life,* much like that of *Walden,* lay in its ability to elevate a practical way of life to a level of social and moral criticism. The fundamental issue was human freedom. How could one achieve human liberation—economic, political, and spiritual—in a fragmented culture controlled by the values of the dominant class? Freedom became a matter of finding a way of life that dignified self-determination and individual activity. It required that one's conduct and principled beliefs harmoniously converge. If they "diverged . . . it splits theory away from practice and divides the personality against itself." Thus, "the most harmonious life is one in which theory and practice are unified."[62] More than "a life pattern rich in simple values and productive of personal and social good," the Nearings unveiled "an alternative cultural pattern" that challenged the economic and ethical foundations of capitalist culture.[63] At bottom was the view that unearned income was immoral and socially destructive, echoing back to Nearing's earliest economic writings. "We were against the accumulation of profit and unearned income by non-producers," the Nearings explained. They advocated the principle of rendering "a service in exchange for income, thus eliminating the social divisions which develop when a part of the community lives on unearned income."[64]

Helen and Scott Nearing in the Soviet Union, 1938. Courtesy of Helen Nearing

Helen and Scott Nearing in Vermont in the 1950s. Courtesy of Helen Nearing

Nearing, always the teacher, Forest Farm, Harborside, Maine, in late 1950s. Courtesy of Helen Nearing

Nearing at Forest Farm, Maine, 1976. Emmett Mears photo, courtesy of Helen
Nearing

Nearing at work, Forest Farm, late 1970s. Lou Penfield photo, courtesy of Helen Nearing

The most important message they imparted was that individual freedom was severely restricted by a daunting capitalist cultural hegemony. "The closer we have come to this social order, the more completely we are a part of it. Since we reject it in theory, we should, as far as possible, reject it also in practice." "Keep out of the system's clutches," they warned, "and you have a chance of subsistence, even if the oligarchs disapprove of what you think and say and do. Accept the system . . . and you become a helpless cog in an impersonal, implacable, merciless machine."[65] He and Helen "wanted to find a way in which we could put more into life and get more out of it."

> We were seeking an affirmation . . . that would provide at least a minimum of those values which we considered essential to the good life. . . . Making a living under conditions that would preserve and enlarge joy in workmanship, would give a sense of achievement, thereby promoting integrity and self-respect.[66]

▬ Homesteading marked a further break with American culture, an estrangement made complete when the United States dropped the atomic bomb on August 6, 1945, Nearing's sixty-second birthday. He rushed off a letter of protest to President Truman:

> Your government is no longer mine. From this day onward our paths diverge: you to continue your suicide course, blasting and cursing the world. I turn my hand to the task of helping to build a human society based on cooperation, social justice and human welfare.[67]

The remorseless intransigence of his later years could become emotionally inhibiting and eventually destroyed his relationship with his son John. Scott's disdain for his son's way of life spilled out in a letter he sent John in 1952.

> Dear John,
> When you returned to U.S.A. ten years ago I suggested that you live very modestly in some town . . . where there was a good library + spend a year or two studying + reading,—thus getting theoretically oriented for the change which was sure to come + actually on the way.
> You chose, instead to go and work for one of the U.S.A. top ranking predators—Henry Luce, to build a baronial mansion, with neither economic foundation nor social reason for existence + to ally yourself with progressively reactionary groups. . . . It would be even less reactionary + anti-social if you went into piracy or highway robbery on your own account, because your chances of getting anywhere would be inconsequential. But in selling your talents to the Luce . . . interests you are allying yourself to a major anti-social force which today is the chief threat to the peace + happiness of mankind.
> As you look back over this ten year record
> 1. I should think that you would seriously question the validity of your decision of ten years ago.
> 2. Realize that you are serving the interests most opposed to human welfare.
> 3. And make a right about face.
> Such an experience would be painful.

But a continuance of your present line will be increasingly painful as you come to realize more fully how completely you have fallen into the hands of the world's most reactionary elements, and to understand how thoroughly you have surrendered your affirmations of 20 years ago for a disagreeable = unhealthful acceptance of "whatever is."

This is strong medicine. But a desperate situation warrants desperate + drastic treatment.

Much love,
Scott[68]

In 1963, after a testimonial dinner given in New York City to celebrate Nearing's eightieth birthday, Roger Baldwin, once a close friend, wrote apologetically to John Scott to express his complete opposition to his father's "whole outlook on the world."[69] John agreed that "Scott's attitudes have frozen long since." "The only countervailing comments I can make," he continued, "are to the effect that when one talks to Scott . . . he is much more preoccupied with philosophical—even cosmic—concepts than with the parochial issues of our immediate environment." John added that this was "most painful for me, particularly since I respect much that Scott has done, and perhaps even more what he is."[70] For years, Scott and John maintained a strained relationship. When John retired from *Time* in 1973, he went on to become vice president of Radio Free Europe—Radio Liberty. In the end, Scott cut his ties with his son. Only two months before John died of a heart attack in 1976 while in Chicago on a speaking tour, the tragedy of John's struggle with filial devotion ended when Scott gave Bob an unopened letter to return to his brother.[71]

This same intransigence contributed to a general unsettling ambivalence toward Nearing, sustained by the impression that Nearing's dreams of a better world were seemingly contradicted by a certain hard-heartedness, a cold rationality, a disregard for the possibility of human frailty. A reviewer of *Living the Good Life* could not ignore in the prescription for well-being "a certain aloofness, a dogmatism which will not take into account the weaknesses and foibles of mankind, an unreality which expects cool reason to determine men's actions, a lack of warmth or of human[ity]."[72] Similarly, one of Nearing's neighbors in Vermont saw that "the real tragedy of our valley in this: The people possessing the hard-won technical ability to adjust to the strenuous environment had somehow failed to acquire the deep-running human warmth necessary to draw people to them on any sort of permanent basis."[73] This ambivalence was not unlike the misgivings Jane Addams had expressed about Tolstoy, raising the question whether he was "more logical than life warrants? Could the wrongs of life be reduced to the terms of unrequited labor and all made right if each person performed the amount necessary to satisfy his own wants?"[74]

By the middle of the century, Nearing's notoriety and tumultuous past had largely been forgotten. He was reintroduced to new generations largely through *Living the Good Life* when the book was rediscovered in the early 1970s as a bible of the "back-to-the-land" movement, selling over two hundred thousand copies.[75] With its reissue, one reviewer noted the "acknowledgement that what was once a personal and eccentric solution to the ills of American society has become a movement, relevant and growing."[76] Nearing's resurrection appeared to be less a matter of his politics, which many of his admirers knew little if anything about, than the allure of the man.

He seemed to serve as a personal model for disaffected middle-class youth who had burned out on the activism of the sixties and had turned inward as they lost hope in political solutions for social change. He became, in a sense, a countercultural hero, attracting thousands of "disaffected bourgeois youth" to "Forest Farm" every year. The Nearings described their visitors as

> wanderers and seekers, feeling their way toward an escape from orthodoxy and superficiality, with the nervous dissatisfaction that characterizes people who do not have a home base in any real sense. Perhaps they can be described as unsettled. Never before in our lives have we seen so many unattached, uncommitted, insecure, uncertain human beings.[77]

It was precisely the youths' lack of commitment to any program or purposeful social values that led the Nearings to "observe them with mixed feelings"[78] and generated a clash between the older radical values and the intensely personal quality of the new liberation. The strenuous, disciplined, constructive lifestyle of the Nearings left no place for the sexual and sensory hedonism of the counterculture. The counterculture was, the Nearings perceived, more nearly anticultural, abandoning all social structures and conventions without offering an alternative vision, program, or purpose.[79]

> Almost universally they favor "freedom"; that is, the pursuit of their personal goals and fancies. They are not joiners and not members of any group more specific than is implied by the adoption of a specific diet or the practice of some yoga exercises.[80]

They were the disillusioned remnants of capitalist society whose inability to break through their self-absorption imperiled the significance of homesteading. There was the possibility that the therapeutic goal of psychic self-preservation could subvert the aim of personal and social improvement and lead homesteading down the path of accommodation. In 1974, Nearing would express the apprehension that "what begins as a search for the good life can gradually be rechanneled into acquisition, competition, combat, and an all absorbing search for wealth and power. At any point along the difficult path the good life may be submerged and smothered by its opposites."[81]

In his last years, Nearing was looked upon as a popular curiosity, a subject suitable for *People* magazine, a story fit for ABC's "20/20" program. He was a dinosaur of sorts, a living remnant of a forgotten past, and in the 1982 film *Reds*, he was a "witness" to the American radicalism of the early part of the century. Yet as he worked on his last book—unfinished and tentatively titled *Social Forces*—he realized that his ideas were no longer being taken seriously. He admitted at the age of ninety-five that "my friends tell me what I have to say is less interesting than it used to be. I regret this deeply."[82] In his ninety-ninth year, only months before he died on August 24, 1983, he said that he had "been trying for a whole century to do something to move the mass and I would say with phenomenally little success."[83] But he knew, too, as he had written in *Living the Good Life*, that "the value of doing something does not lie in the ease or difficulty, the probability or improbability of its achievement, but in the vision, the plan, the determination and perseverance, the effort and the struggle which go into the project. Life is enriched by aspiration and effort, rather than by acquisition and accumulation."[84]

*He held his purpose—*
*Through the glad spring hours*
*Along the panting reach of sultry days*
*Into the autumn glory.*

*Then, like a leaf*
*That has thrown back the afterglow,*
*And beckoned to the morning star;*
*That has kept rain and sun and wind*
*From grateful travelers,*
*He slipped the world's harsh bondage*
*And is free.*

*He held his purpose through the years.*
*He holds it still.*
*His place on life's great evergreen*
*Must now be filled by others*
*Who, with equal courage,*
*Greet the sun;*
*Bide the storm;*
*Glory in the star-shine,*
*And at last*
*Loosen their hold on life, and move*
*Into the great beyond.*

*Those best can go who best have served.*
*He lived and labored ardently.*
*Our debt to him is paid*
*As we take up his tasks.*

*Scott Nearing,*
*"October," 1920*

Notes
Manuscript Sources
Bibliography: The Works of Scott Nearing
Index

# Notes

## Introduction

1. Nearing's only biographer chose to "forego thorough analysis of Nearing's ideas" under the assumption that "his thought cannot bear the weight of intensive scrutiny" and thereby presupposed little lasting influence in his thought. Alan Lawson has noted that this approach missed "an important measure of Nearing's significance." Stephen J. Whitfield, *Scott Nearing: Apostle of American Radicalism* (New York: Columbia University Press, 1974), p. vii; R. Alan Lawson, "The New Left and New Values: A Review Essay," *America Quarterly* 28 (Spring 1976):121.

2. Sidney Hook, *Out of Step: An Unquiet Life in the 20th Century* (New York: Harper & Row, 1987), p. 357.

3. Joseph Freeman, *An American Testament* (London: Gollancz, 1938), p. 300.

4. Nearing, "The Teacher, the School, and Democracy," lecture given at the Garrick Theater, Chicago, March 12, 1916. Stenographer's Transcript, Military Intelligence Division, Record Group 165, National Archives, Washington, D.C., p. 3.

## Chapter 1

1. Nearing, *The Making of a Radical: A Political Autobiography,* 1972, p. 36. (Complete citations to Nearing's works can be found in the bibliography of Nearing's works that follows the notes.)

2. Ibid., p. 134.

3. See ibid., p. 15; Eva Grover, *Historical Highlights of Morris Run, Pennsylvania* (1932) (Wellsboro, Pa.: Tioga County Historical Society, 1984), p. 8.

4. Nearing, *Making of a Radical,* p. 15; Grover, *Historical Highlights,* p. 8.

5. Grover, *Historical Highlights,* p. 9; *History of Tioga County, Pennsylvania* (New York: R. C. Brown and Co., 1897), pp. 625–26.

6. John L. Sexton, Jr., *History of Tioga County, Pennsylvania* (New York: W. W. Munseu and Co., 1883), p. 22.

7. Ibid., pp. 179, 181. The Welsh Baptist Church was organized in 1864, and by 1874 the Welsh were listed as the most numerous immigrant group in an ethnically diverse local population. Of W.S.N.'s religious views, Scott Nearing would recall in his autobiography that his grandfather was both skeptical and tolerant. When a Methodist

minister came for dinner and offered a prayer, W.S.N. was reported to have replied, "Why not? It won't do any harm."

8. Nearing, *Making of a Radical*, p. 76.

9. This characterization of Louis Nearing is derived largely with the aid of information provided by Robert Nearing of Troy, Pa., Scott Nearing's younger son; interview with author, Troy, Pa., November 8–9, 1986.

10. George Olin Zabriskie, *The Zabriskie Family: A Three-Hundred-and-One-Year History of the Descendants of Albrecht Zaborowski*, Salt Lake City, 1963, p. 1002; Nearing, *Making of a Radical*, pp. 5–11.

11. Nearing, *Making of a Radical*, pp. 9–11, 13, 16; draft of *Making of a Radical*, November 2, 1966, May 23, 1967, bk. 4, p. 3, DG 124, Scott Nearing Papers, Swarthmore College Peace Collection, Swarthmore, Pa. (hereafter, SCPC); on the Victorian sensibility generally, see Daniel Walker Howe, ed., *Victorian America* (Philadelphia, University of Pennsylvania Press, 1976).

12. Nearing, *Making of a Radical*, pp. 11–13.

13. Ibid., p. 17.

14. Nearing, "Education for What?" 1925, p. 578.

15. Thorstein Veblen, *The Theory of the Leisure Class* (1899) (New York: Penguin, 1986), pp. 15, 33, 94, 259.

16. Nearing, *Making of a Radical*, p. 16. In a later study that Nearing wrote on the anthracite industry, he in all likelihood drew upon his youthful experiences when he explained that "perhaps the most effective weapon in the hands of the operators, for controlling the men through their jobs, is surplus labor. . . . The alien groups have been pressed hard upon one another." Nearing, *Anthracite: An Instance of a Natural Resources Monopoly*, 1915, p. 204.

17. "The Aged Autocrat of Morris Run," *New York Herald*, magazine sec., May 7, 1905, p. 5; see also *Making of a Radical*, pp. 15–16.

18. Scott Nearing Papers, draft of *Making of a Radical*, November 19, 1968, bk. 6, p. 91, DG 124, SCPC.

19. Nearing, *Making of a Radical*, p. 5.

20. Ibid., pp. 46, 60.

21. On the educational reform associated with the rise of manual training schools, see Lawrence Cremin, *The Transformation of the Schools; Progressivism in American Education, 1876–1957* (New York: Vintage, 1964), pp. 25–35.

22. Scott Nearing Papers, draft of *Making of a Radical*, November 19, 1968, bk. 6, p. 92, DG 124, SCPC.

23. Nearing and Henry Reed Burch, *Elements of Economics*, 1912, p. 4.

24. Nearing, *Making of a Radical*, pp. 30–31; Edward Bellamy, *Looking Backward* (1887) (New York: Penguin, 1985).

25. Walter Rauschenbusch, "Why I am a Baptist," 1905, repr. in Sydnor L. Stealey, ed., *A Baptist Treasury* (New York: Ayer Co., 1980), pp. 163–83.

26. Henry F. May, *Protestant Churches and Industrial America* (New York: Harper, 1949), pp. 199–200.

27. Nearing, *Making of a Radical*, p. 32.

28. Russell H. Conwell, *Acres of Diamonds* (New York: Harper, 1915), p. 30.

29. Ibid., p. 18.

30. Nearing, *Making of a Radical*, pp. 32–34.

31. See James Dombrowski, *The Early Days of Christian Socialism in America* (1936) (New York: Columbia University Press, 1966), p. 24.

32. Nearing, *Making of a Radical*, p. 24; "The Dawn of Optimism," *The Public*, February 9, 1912, pp. 135–36. Contrary to one scholar's claim that Nearing had "analyzed and eventually dismissed the merits of religion along with the possibilities of becoming a minister," he dismissed the Church while maintaining a deeply religious sensibility. See Gerald Stuart Coles, "Political Economy and Education in Progressivism and Socialism, 1905–1932: Scott Nearing," Ph.D. diss., State University of New York at Buffalo, 1974, p. 109.

33. Nearing, *Making of a Radical*, p. 34.

34. Ibid., pp. 19–21.

35. On the influence of the German-university ideal upon American scholars and its role in the development of the American university, see Richard Hofstadter and Walter P. Metzger, *The Development of Academic Freedom in the United States* (New York: Columbia University Press, 1955), pp. 367–83; Laurence R. Veysey, *The Emergence of the American University* (Chicago: University of Chicago Press, 1965), pp. 125–33; Carol S. Gruber, *Mars and Minerva: World War I and the Uses of the Higher Learning in America* (Baton Rouge: Louisiana State University Press, 1975), pp. 17–23; Barton J. Bledstein, *The Culture of Professionalism* (New York: Norton, 1978), pp. 309–31. For the more specific contributions to the development of the Wharton School, see Steven A. Sass, *The Pragmatic Imagination: A History of the Wharton School, 1881–1981* (Philadelphia: University of Pennsylvania Press, 1982), pp. 55–129.

36. Quoted in Sass, *Pragmatic Imagination*, pp. 22–23.

37. Ibid., pp. 72–83.

38. Joseph Dorfman, *The Economic Mind in American Civilization, Volume 3, 1865–1918* (New York: Viking, 1949), p. 186.

39. Nearing, *Educational Frontiers: Simon Nelson Patten and Other Teachers*, 1925, p. 81.

40. Simon Nelson Patten, "The Reconstruction of Economic Theory" (1912), repr. Rexford G. Tugwell, ed., *Essays in Economic Theory* (New York: Knopf, 1924), p. 279.

41. From Patten's 1908 presidential address to the American Economics Association, quoted in Nearing, *Social Adjustment*, 1910, p. 312.

42. Scott Nearing Papers, working outline, *Making of a Radical*, December 23, 1965, p. 3, DG 124, SCPC.

43. Rexford Tugwell's observation of his teacher, quoted in Joseph Dorfman, *Economic Mind, Vol. 5, 1918–1933*, p. 503.

44. See generally Joseph Dorfman, "The Background of Institutional Economics," in Dorfman et al., *Institutional Economics* (Berkeley: University of California Press, 1963), pp. 1–44; Dorfman, *Economic Mind, Vol. 3, 1865–1918*, pp. 161–62, 183, 276–78, 343; Sidney Fine, *Laissez Faire and the General Welfare State* (Ann Arbor: University of Michigan Press, 1956), pp. 198–221; Daniel M. Fox, *The Discovery of Abundance, Simon Nelson Patten and the Transformation of Social Theory* (Ithaca: Cornell University Press, 1967).

45. John R. Everett, *Religion in Economics* (New York: King's Crown Press, 1946), p. 33.

46. Patten, "The Reconstruction of Economic Theory," repr. *Essays in Economic Theory*, p. 276.

47. Patten, "Theory of Dynamic Economics" (1892), repr. *Essays in Economic Theory*, pp. 53–54.

48. Patten, "The Conflict Theory of Distribution" (1908), repr. *Essays in Economic Theory*, p. 219.

49. Dorfman, *Economic Mind*, Vol. 3, p. 183.

50. Patten, "Pragmatism and Social Science" (1911), repr. *Essays in Economic Theory*, p. 260.

51. Dorfman, *Institutional Economics*, pp. v., 5, 9, 42; Dorfman, *Economic Mind*, Vol. 3, p. 343; see also David Hollinger, "The Problem of Pragmatism in American History," *Journal of American History* 67 (1980):88–107.

52. Dorfman, *Economic Mind*, Vol. 4, p. 125.

53. Patten, *The Social Basis of Religion* (New York: Macmillan, 1914), p. vi.

54. Patten, "The Reconstruction of Economic Theory" (1912), repr. *Essays in Economic Theory*, p. 274.

55. Patten, "Pragmatism and Social Science" (1911), repr. *Essays in Economic Theory*, p. 264.

56. Patten's social criticism never strayed far from the question of how to find restraints amid economic abundance, both for the individual and for the nation. Daniel Horowitz's writings on the culture of consumption provide important insights into Patten's thought but are limited regarding Nearing; see his *The Morality of Spending: Attitudes towards the Consumer Society in America, 1875–1940* (Baltimore: Johns Hopkins University Press, 1985), and "Consumption and Its Discontents: Simon N. Patten, Thorstein Veblen, and George Gunton," *Journal of American History* 67 (1980):302–7.

57. Patten, "Is Christianity Ethics or Religion?" *The Independent*, March 30, 1911, p. 656.

58. Ibid., p. 657.

59. Patten, *Social Basis of Religion*, p. 210.

60. Ibid., p. v.

61. Mary Furner, *Advocacy and Objectivity, A Crisis in the Professionalism of American Social Science, 1865–1905* (Lexington: University Press of Kentucky, 1975), p. 51; see also Charles Hopkins, *The Rise of the Social Gospel in American Protestantism, 1865–1915* (New Haven: Yale University Press, 1914), pp. 273–74; particularly helpful is Everett, *Religion in Economics*, pp. 124–36.

62. Patten, "The Reconstruction of Economic Theory" (1912), repr. *Essays in Economic Theory*, p. 279.

63. Quoted in Everett, *Religion in Economics*, p. 119.

64. Patten, "The Economic Causes of Moral Progress" (1893), repr. *Essays in Economic Theory*, p. 164.

65. On the tension between professionalism and social advocacy, see generally Furner, *Advocacy and Objectivity;* Thomas L. Haskell, *The Emergence of Professional Social Science* (Urbana: University of Illinois Press, 1976); Dorothy Ross, "The Development of the Social Sciences," in Alexandra Oleson and John Voss, *The Organization of Knowledge in Modern America, 1860–1920* (Baltimore: Johns Hopkins University Press, 1979), pp. 107–38, and "Socialism and American Liberalism: Academic Social Thought in the 1880s," *Perspectives in American History* 11 (1977–78):5–79.

66. Patten, "The Reconstruction," p. 293.

67. Simon Nelson Patten, *The New Basis of Civilization* (1907) (Cambridge, Mass.: Belknap Press, 1968), p. 40.

68. Ibid., p. 158.

69. Simon Nelson Patten, *Product and Climax* (New York: B. W. Huebsch, 1909), pp. 41, 44, 57–60, 65–66.

70. Patten, "The Reconstruction," p. 293.

71. Ibid., p. 292.

72. Ibid., pp. 292–93.

73. Patten, *New Basis of Civilization*, pp. 70–71.

74. Patten, "The Conflict Theory of Distribution" (1908), repr. *Essays in Economic Theory*, p. 219.

75. Patten, "The Reconstruction," p. 289.

76. See Everett, *Religion in Economics*, pp. 123, 133–34, and see generally, Dorfman, *Institutional Economics*.

77. Patten, "The Reconstruction," pp. 277–78, 291.

78. On the German ideal and the question of academic freedom as it was transformed in the United States, see Hofstadter and Metzger, *Development of Academic Freedom*, pp. 383–412, and Veysey, *Emergence of the American University*, pp. 381–418; Gruber, *Mars and Minerva*, pp. 17–23; Bledstein, *Culture of Professionalism*, pp. 309–31.

79. Patten, "Making of Economic Literature" (1908 presidential address), rept. *Essays in Economic Theory*, p. 240.

80. Ibid., pp. 240–41.

81. Ibid., pp. 242–47.

82. Nearing, *Making of a Radical*, p. 54.

83. Ibid.

84. Ibid., p. 56.

85. Nearing's vitae in 1914 listed contributions to these publications, general Wharton School File, 1914, University of Pennsylvania Archives, Philadelphia.

86. Nearing, *Making of a Radical*, p. 45.

87. Ibid., p. 33.

88. Ibid., p. 38.

89. Nearing, *Educational Frontiers*, pp. 16–17.

90. Nearing, *Making of a Radical*, pp. 56–57.

91. Nearing, *Educational Frontiers*, p. 17.

92. Nearing, *Making of a Radical*, p. 82.

93. Nearing, *Educational Frontiers*, p. 4; *Making of a Radical*, p. 21.

94. Nearing, *Making of a Radical*, p. 21.

95. Ibid., p. 37.

96. Nearing, *Educational Frontiers*, pp. ix, x.

97. Scott Nearing Papers, draft of *Making of a Radical*, May 31, 1967, bk. 4, p. 69, DG 124, SCPC.

98. Nearing, *Making of a Radical*, p. 36.

## Chapter 2

1. Nearing and Frank Watson, *Economics*, 1908, p. 28.

2. Ibid., pp. 350–51.

3. Scott Nearing Papers, draft of *Making of a Radical*, October 9, 1967, bk. 6, p. 175, DG 124, Swarthmore College Peace Collection (SCPC).

4. Nearing and Henry Reed Burch, *Elements of Economics*, 1912, p. 135.

5. Nearing, *Social Adjustment*, 1910, p. ix.

6. Nearing and Nellie Seeds Nearing, "New Year Greetings," 1913, p. 38.

7. Nearing and Watson, *Economics*, p. 1.

8. Nearing, *Social Adjustment*, p. 11.

9. See Nearing, "Welfare and the New Economics," 1913, p. 505. In the textbook he coauthored with Frank Watson, Nearing wrote that "the fathers of our science were imbued with the belief in unalterable economic laws. . . . Of such were their statements of the 'Iron Law of Wages,' The Wage Fund Theory, Ricardo's Theory of Rent, The Law of Diminishing Returns, and the Law of Population as stated by Malthus. To them it was preposterous to think of trying to overcome the operation of deep fundamental economic laws." *Economics*, pp. 443–44.

10. Nearing, *Social Sanity*, 1913, pp. 70–71.

11. Ibid., p. 341.

12. Nearing, *Reducing the Cost of Living*, 1914, p. 119.

13. Nearing, *Social Adjustment*, p. 9. It should be noted too that the strong antideterministic reaction against natural-law philosophy had the consequence that Nearing apparently never seriously explored the advances in psychology at the turn of the century. While many radicals discovered Freudian psychology as a panacea for personal liberation, Nearing seems to have shied away from the individualistic and deterministic implications of the subconscious. In 1952, Nearing referred to Freud as one who "did more than any other . . . to perpetuate the myth of individualism." See his *World Events* newsletter, summer 1952, p. 23, Scott and Helen Nearing Papers, Boston University Special Collections, Boston, Mass., box 9, folder 7. Nearing's only other comment on Freud, appearing on an undated notecard, read, "Sex is associated with one of the urgent hungers magnified by Freud and others out of all proportion to its balanced relation."

14. Nearing, *Reducing the Cost of Living*, p. 119.

15. Nearing, "Welfare and the New Economics," p. 506.

16. Ibid., p. 504.

17. Ibid., p. 507.

18. Ibid., p. 506.

19. Ibid., p. 509.

20. Ibid., p. 507.

21. Nearing often cited Ruskin in his work. Typical was his tendency to turn to Ruskin to emphasize that economics had to be judged by moral standards, that "reason tells us that we must judge wealth by its effects upon human life and human well being." Thus, he relied heavily on "Ruskin['s] . . . famous statement: 'There is no life but wealth.' . . . These were his standards of economics." Nearing, *The Human Element in Economics*, pamphlet, 1919.

22. Nearing and Burch, *Elements of Economics*, p. xiv.

23. Ibid., p. 504.

24. Nearing and Watson, *Economics*, p. 445.

25. Nearing, *Income*, 1915, p. 198.

26. See generally Daniel M. Fox, *The Discovery of Abundance: Simon Nelson Patten and the Transformation of Social Theory* (Ithaca: Cornell University Press, 1967), and Patten's classic, *The New Basis of Civilization* (1907) (repr. Cambridge, Mass.: Belknap Press, 1968). His teacher, claimed Nearing, had focused on "consumption as the logical goal of economic endeavor," which "theoretically . . . seems to be justified" but "practically it is impossible, at least at the present stage of human knowledge. . . . It is in no sense a point of departure for income facts." Nearing, *Income*, pp. xvi–xvii.

27. Nearing, *Making of a Radical*, p. 37.

28. Fox, *Discovery of Abundance*, p. 125.

29. Nearing, *Social Adjustment*, pp. 4–5.

30. Nearing, *Social Religion*, pamphlet, 1910, p. 23.

31. Rexford G. Tugwell, *To the Lesser Heights of Morningside: A Memoir* (Philadelphia: University of Pennsylvania Press, 1982), pp. 28–29.

32. Nearing and Watson, *Economics*, p. 341.

33. Ibid., p. 18.

34. Nearing, *Making of a Radical*, p. 56.

35. Scott Nearing Papers, draft of autobiography, bk. 4, April 18, 1968, p. 28a, DG 124 SCPC.

36. Nearing, *Income*, p. 18.

37. Ibid., p. 61.

38. Ibid., p. 17.

39. Thorstein Veblen, *The Theory of the Leisure Class* (1899) (New York: Penguin, 1986), pp. 39, 209.

40. Tugwell, *Lesser Heights of Morningside*, pp. 48, 67.

41. Alvin S. Johnson, "Our National Income," *The Nation*, August 28, 1915, pp. 107–8.

42. "Professor Nearing's Attitude on Economics and His Dismissal from The University of Pennsylvania: A Plea for Freedom in University Teaching of Economics," n.p., 1915, pp. 10–11.

43. Nearing, "The Why of Income," 1915, pp. 745–62.

44. Nearing, "The Service-Property Conflict," 1915, p. 385.

45. Nearing, "Service Income and Property Income," 1914, pp. 236–37.

46. Nearing, *Income*, p. 155. See also Nearing, "Wages and Salaries in Organized Industry," 1915, p. 478.

47. Nearing and Watson, *Economics*, pp. 24–26.

48. Nearing, *Income*, p. 184.

49. Ibid., p. viii.

50. Nearing, *Reducing the Cost of Living*, p. 65. Veblen, in his *Theory of the Leisure Class*, pp. 204–5, 209, 246, made similar observations that the idle rich had become social parasites debasing the workers and inhibiting reform. "The institution of the leisure class," he explained, "acts to make the lower classes conservative by withdrawing from them as much as it may of the means of sustenance, and so reducing their consumption and consequently their available energy, to such a point as to make them incapable of the effort required for the learning and adoption of new habits of thought." It was "this direct inhibitory effect of the unequal distribution of wealth . . . [that] hinders cultural development."

51. Nearing, *Making of a Radical*, p. 46.

52. Nearing, *Poverty and Riches: A Study of the Industrial Regime*, 1916, p. 206.

53. Ibid., pp. 200–201.

54. Nearing, *The Human Element in Economics*, 1919.

55. Ibid.

56. Nearing, *Social Sanity*, pp. 161, 169.

57. Nearing, *Poverty and Riches*, p. 220.

58. Nearing, *Human Element in Economics*.

59. *Chautauquan Daily*, July 16, 1915, p. 2.

60. Nearing, *Social Sanity*, p. 161.

61. Ibid., pp. 228–32.

62. Nearing, *Income*, pp. 20–21.

## Chapter 3

1. Nearing, *Reducing the Cost of Living*, 1914, p. 77.

2. Scott and Helen Nearing Papers, card file, "Writing Plans," January 11, 1944, Boston University Special Collections, Boston. In full, the card reads, "Philosophy—way of life. Wealth is meaningless and sterile. There may be some gleaming of wisdom in this legacy."

3. Nearing, "Social Decadence," 1913, p. 629.

4. The literature on republicanism is extensive. My own work has benefited most from the following studies: Joyce Appleby, *Capitalism and the New Social Order: The Republican Vision of the 1790s* (New York: New York University Press, 1984); "Liberalism and the American Revolution," *New England Quarterly* (March 1976):3–26; "The Social Origins of the American Revolutionary Ideology," *Journal of American History* 64 (1978):935–58; Bernard Bailyn, *The Ideological Origins of the American Revolution* (Cambridge, Mass.: Belknap Press, 1967); John P. Diggins, *The Lost Soul of American Politics* (New York: Basic Books, 1984); and Gordon S. Wood, *The Creation of the American Republic, 1776–1787* (Chapel Hill: University of North Carolina Press), 1969). For a discussion of republican ideology in the thought of American Progressives, see John P. Diggins, "Republicanism and Progressivism," *American Quarterly* 37 (Fall 1985):572–98.

5. Nearing, *The Super Race: An American Problem*, 1912, p. 57.

6. Nearing and Nellie Seeds Nearing, *Women and Social Progress*, 1912, p. 141.

7. Nearing, *Human Element in Economics*.

8. Quoted in Lawrence A. Cremin, *The Transformation of the School: Progressivism in American Education, 1876–1957* (New York: Vintage, 1964), p. 100.

9. Nearing, *The New Education: A Review of the Progressive Educational Movements of the Day*, 1915, p. 3.

10. See generally Cremin, *Transformation of the School*.

11. Nearing, *New Education*, pp. 22, 42.

12. Nearing, *Social Adjustment*, 1910, pp. 17, 21; for a discussion of the positions of Spencer and Ward in the educational debates of the Progressive Era, see Cremin, *Transformation of the School*, pp. 90–100.

13. Nearing, *Social Adjustment*, p. 313.

14. Ibid., pp. 50–51; on the transfer of the responsibility of apprenticeship from industry to the schools, see Cremin, *Transformation of the School*, pp. 34–41.

15. Nearing and Jessie Field, *Community Civics*, 1916, p. 129.

16. Dewey wrote approvingly of Gary schools in *Schools of Tomorrow* (New York: Dutton, 1915), as did Bourne, *The Gary Schools* (Boston: Houghton Mifflin, 1916).

17. Nearing, *New Education*, p. 82.

18. Nearing and Field, *Community Civics*, p. 141.

19. Ibid., p. v.

20. Nearing, *Social Adjustment*, p. 318.

21. Nearing, *New Education*, p. 222.

22. Nearing, *Social Adjustment*, pp. 317, 320.

23. Ibid., p. 314.

24. Ibid., p. 288.

25. Ibid., pp. 285–86.

26. Ibid., p. 323.

27. Ibid., p. 374.

28. Ibid., p. 322.

29. Ibid., p. 372.

30. Ibid., p. 32.

31. Ibid., p. 234.

32. Ibid., p. 140.

33. Nearing and Nellie Nearing, *Women and Social Progress*, pp. 54–55.

34. Ibid., p. 128.

35. Ibid., pp. 128–37.

36. Ibid., pp. 138–39.

37. Ibid., pp. 141–42.

38. Ibid., p. 141.

39. Ibid., p. 146.

40. Ibid., pp. 145–46.

41. Nearing, *Social Religion*, 1913, p. 208.

42. Nearing, *Super Race*, pp. 81–83.

43. See Nearing and Nellie Nearing, *Women and Social Progress*, p. 199.

44. Nearing and Nellie Seeds Nearing, "Four Great Things a Woman Does at Home," 1912, p. 12.

45. Nearing and Nellie Nearing, *Women and Social Progress*, p. xi.

46. Nearing, *Poverty and Riches*, 1916, p. 234.

47. Nearing, *Social Adjustment*, p. 137.

48. Ibid., p. 145.

49. Nellie Seeds Nearing kept a travel journal, "Our First Trip to Europe, Sailed from Philadelphia, June 10, 1911," detailing their purposeful vacation, mixing evenings at the theater with days of research and writing. Her journal is in the possession of Robert Nearing, Troy, Pa.

50. Rexford G. Tugwell, *To the Lesser Heights of Morningside: A Memoir* (Philadelphia: University of Pennsylvania Press, 1982), p. 39.

51. Nellie Seeds Nearing, *Education and Fecundity*, repr. Publications of the American Statistical Association, June 1914, abstract of thesis, Chautauqua Print Shop, 1917, p. 19.

52. Charles Hopkins, *The Rise of the Social Gospel in American Protestantism, 1865–1915* (New Haven: Yale University Press, 1940), p. 141.

53. Nearing, *Social Religion*, p. xi; it is interesting to note that Walter Rauschenbusch, in his *Christianizing the Social Order* (New York: Macmillan, 1912), p. 248, cited Nearing's *Wages in the United States*, writing: "Mere living is not yet life. The economic organization of our nation does not meet even that minimum requirement. In spite of the wealth of our national resources and the comparative spaciousness of our population, several millions of workers have not enough income to keep themselves at normal physical efficiency."

54. Nearing, *Social Religion*, p. xiii.

55. Nearing, debate with John Haynes Holmes, *Can the Church Be Radical?* 1922, p. 36.

56. For the relationship between the social gospel and social science, see generally Hopkins, *Rise of the Social Gospel*, John R. Everett, *Religion and Economics* (New York: King's Crown Press, 1946), and James Dombrowski, *The Early Days of Christian Socialism* (1936) (New York: Columbia University Press, 1966).

57. Nearing, *Poverty and Riches*, p. 220.

58. Nearing, *Social Sanity*, 1913, p. 59.

59. Tugwell, *Lesser Heights of Morningside*, p. 59.

60. Nearing, *Social Religion*, p. 2.

61. Ibid., p. 11.

62. Ibid., p. 197.

63. Ibid., p. 170.

64. Nearing, debate with Percy Ward, *Would the Practice of Christ's Teachings Make for Social Progress?* 1920, p. 14.

65. Nearing, *Social Religion*, p. xiii.

66. Nearing, *Social Adjustment*, p. 289.

67. Nearing–Ward, *Practice of Christ's Teachings*, p. 43.

68. Nearing, *Social Adjustment*, p. 290.

69. Nearing, "Can the Church be Pacifist?" 1922, p. 665; *Social Religion*, pp. xv, x.

70. Nearing, *Social Religion*, pp. 193–94.

71. Ibid., pp. xii–xiii.

72. Nearing, *Social Religion*, pamphlet, p. 8.

73. Nearing, *Social Religion*, p. xiv.

74. Ibid., p. 200.

75. Nearing, *Social Adjustment*, p. 5.

76. Ibid., p. 5.

77. Nearing, *Social Religion*, pp. 170, 197–98.

78. Ibid., p. 201.

79. Nearing, *Social Sanity*, p. 7.

80. Ibid., p. 245.

81. Ibid., p. 100.

82. Nearing, *Social Religion*, p. 215.

83. Ibid., p. 5.

84. Ibid., pp. 5–7.

85. *Chautauquan Daily*, July 17, 1915, p. 2.

86. Nearing, *Social Religion*, p. 168.

87. Ibid., p. xvi.

88. Ibid., p. xvi.

89. Morton White, *Social Thought in America: The Revolt against Formalism* (New York: Oxford University Press, 1976), p. 107.

90. Simon Nelson Patten, *The Social Basis of Religion* (New York: Macmillan, 1910), pp. xii–xiii.

91. Nearing, *Making of a Radical*, p. 30; *The Next Step*, 1922, p. 145; *Making of a Radical*, pp. 36–37.

92. Scott and Helen Nearing Papers, card file 2, Nearing quoted from William Caldwell, *Pragmatism and Idealism*, London, 1913, Boston University Special Collections, Boston.

93. Nearing, *New Education*, p. 251.

94. Nearing, "Education and the Open Mind," 1925, p. 284; *Man's Search for the Good Life*, 1974, p. 21.

95. Scott and Helen Nearing Papers, card file 1, n.d., Boston University Special Collections, Boston.

## Chapter 4

1. Nearing, *Poverty and Riches: A Study of the Industrial Regime*, 1916, pp. 92, 109.

2. Nearing, *Conscience of a Radical*, 1965, pp. 10–11.

3. Jackson Lears has observed of turn-of-the-century American culture that critics of the "overcivilized" bourgeoisie "culture of material comfort and spiritual blandness" hoped to rekindle "intense experience to give some distinct outline and substance" to artificial lives. For the late Victorian bourgeoisie, intense experience— whether physical or emotional—seemed a lost possibility. There was no longer the opportunity for bodily testing provided by rural life, no longer the swift alternation of despair and exhilaration characterized by the old-style Protestant conversion. . . . Bourgeoisie existence seemed a narrow path. . . . No wonder, then, that late Victorians began to feel that they had been cut off from 'reality,' and that they had experienced life in all its dimensions second hand, in books rather than action." See his *No Place of Grace: Antimodernism and the Transformation of American Life, 1880–1920* (New York: Pantheon, 1981), pp. 32, 48.

4. Nearing, *Making of a Radical*, 1972, p. 225; on McFadden, see also James C. Whorton, *Crusaders for Fitness: A History of American Health Reformers* (Princeton: Princeton University Press, 1982), pp. 296–303.

5. Joseph Freeman, *An American Testament* (London: Gollancz, 1938), p. 271.

6. Thorstein Veblen, *The Theory of the Leisure Class* (1899) (New York: Penguin, 1986), pp. 247, 250, 255, 261, 271.

7. William James, *The Varieties of Religious Experience* (1902) (New York: Modern Library, 1929), p. 357.

8. William James, "The Moral Equivalent of War," in John J. McDermott, ed., *The Writings of William James* (Chicago: University of Chicago Press, 1977), pp. 663, 666, 669.

9. Theodore Roosevelt, "The Strenuous Life" (1899), in *The Works of Theodore Roosevelt*, Vol. 13 (New York: National Edition, 1926), pp. 320, 322, 323, 331; see also George M. Fredrickson, *The Inner Civil War: Northern Intellectuals and the Crisis of Union* (New York: Harper, 1965), pp. 217–38.

10. Nearing, *The American Empire*, 1921, p. 112.

11. Nearing, *Social Sanity*, 1913, pp. 117, 122, 123.

12. Nearing, *Reducing the Cost of Living*, 1914, p. 210.

13. Ibid., p. 209.

14. Ibid., p. 215.

15. Nearing, *Poverty and Riches*, p. 79.

16. James, "Moral Equivalent of War," p. 669.

17. James, *Varieties of Religious Experience*, pp. 359–60.

18. Ibid., p. 360.

19. Scott Nearing Papers, "The Spirit of Revolt," undated, DG 124; quote is from *Christianizing the Social Order*, 1912, p. 102, scpc.

20. "Thoreau," *Atlantic Monthly,* August 1862.

21. Nearing, *Making of a Radical,* p. 2.

22. See generally Morton and Lucia White, *The Intellectual versus the City* (1964) (New York: Oxford University Press, 1977); see also Whorton, *Crusaders for Fitness,* pp. 164–67.

23. Nearing, *Reducing the Cost of Living,* p. 218.

24. Nearing and Jessie Field, *Community Civics,* 1916, pp. 146, 178–81; *Social Adjustment,* 1910, p. 65.

25. Nearing and Field, *Community Civics,* pp. 37, 39, 42.

26. Nearing, *Reducing the Cost of Living,* pp. 20, 217–19, 227, 228; for an excellent discussion of the simple life as an ideal in American history with a disappointingly brief and superficial treatment of Nearing, see David Shi, *The Simple Life: Plain Living and High Thinking in American Culture* (New York: Oxford University Press, 1985).

27. Nearing, *Man's Search for the Good Life,* 1974, p. 10.

28. Quoted in Shi, *Simple Life,* pp. 176, 179; see also Whorton, *Crusaders for Fitness,* pp. 164–67.

29. Frank Stephens, "The Arden Enclave," in Charles White Huntington, *Enclaves of Single Tax,* Vol. 4 (Harvard, Mass.: F. Warren, 1924), p. 72.

30. Huntington, *Enclaves of Single Tax,* Vol. 5, 1925, p. 50. Stephens explained that he and Price had "learned that nothing could be done for Art till we have bridged the terrible gulf between the rich and the poor. We were so disgusted with civilization that we determined . . . to go out into the open and make a better one in which the land theory of Henry George should make the social basis for the industrial theory of Kropotkin and the art theory of William Morris." See Stephens, "Arden Enclave," p. 72.

31. Stephens, "Arden Enclave," p. 73.

32. In 1909, Nearing was the head of the economics "gild"; in 1913, he is listed as the "gildmaster" of the "Folk Gild." See the Amy Potter Cook Collection, Arden, Delaware, "Club Talk," December 1909, and "Gild News," December 1912–January 1913. I am indebted to Vivien Dreves for bringing this material to my attention.

33. Huntington, *Enclaves of Single Tax,* Vol. 1, pp. 37–38.

34. Nearing, *Man's Search for the Good Life,* pp. 1–10; *Making of a Radical,* p. 40; see also Stephen Whitfield, *Scott Nearing: Apostle of American Radicalism* (New York: Columbia University Press, 1974), pp. 15–17.

35. Upton Sinclair, *American Outpost: A Book of Reminiscences* (Pasadena, Calif.: the author, 1932), p. 230.

36. Scott Nearing Eightieth Birthday Album, letter from Donald Stephens to Scott Nearing, October 28, 1963; in the possession of Helen Nearing.

37. Nearing, *Social Adjustment,* pp. 299, 360; Nearing explained in *Economics,* 1908, p. 474, the essential difference between the socialists and the single taxers: The Socialist "feels that the single taxer stops short in his reforms in confining common ownership to only two means of life, farming and mining."

38. Ella Reeve Bloor, *We Are Many* (New York: International Publishers, 1940), p. 71.

39. Sinclair, *American Outpost,* p. 232.

40. Scott Nearing Papers, draft of autobiography, bk. 4, October 5, 1967, p. 167, DG 124, SCPC.

41. An indispensable source for understanding health reform is Whorton, *Crusaders for Fitness.*

42. Nearing and Field, *Community Civics*, p. 178.

43. Sinclair, *American Outpost*, p. 231.

44. Nearing, *Making of a Radical*, p. 210.

45. Nearing to Frances Perkins, May 27, 1912, Frances Perkins Papers, Columbia University Archives, New York. Nearing wrote to inform her that he would be in the city "to deliver a lecture on the relation between vacations and efficiency."

46. Nearing, "The New Education," 1917, p. 147.

47. Nearing, *Social Adjustment*, p. 26.

48. See Robert and Helen Lynd, *Middletown* (New York: Harcourt, Brace, 1929).

49. Nearing, "New Education," p. 147.

50. Nearing, *Making of a Radical*, p. 210.

51. Nearing Papers, October 5, 1967, bk. 6, p. 167, DG 124, SCPC; according to Shi's *Simple Life*, such attempts to define leisure activity as a remedy to economic problems worked to sanction the prevailing capitalist system. He writes that "simple living during the Progressive Era was being used by some as a placebo to calm frayed nerves before plunging back into the maelstrom of metropolitan life," thereby creating the "creeping embourgeoisment of simplicity." This paradox has interpretive appeal because it helps to explain the demise of alternative cultures—they held within them the seeds of their own destruction. Yet if the contradictory qualities of these subgroups helps to explain their demise—which I think it does—it does not help to explain their existence. T. J. Jackson Lears has argued that in the period 1877–1919 there are numerous examples of groups that did not consent to the hegemony of industrial capitalism and that cultural openness allowed for counterhegemonic alternatives to flourish. Only when the culture becomes closed to divergent sets of values does the paradox of simplicity have interpretive merit. While openness remains, counterhegemonic tendencies form an inseparable part of the totality of attitudes and practices; only when it breaks down do there emerge self-destructive contradictions, and counterhegemonic meanings serve not to transform a dominant set of values but merely to reinforce them. See Lears, "The Concept of Cultural Hegemony; Problems and Possibilities," *American Historical Review* (June 1985):567–93; on the concept of free cultural spaces, see Sara M. Evans and Harry C. Boyte, *Free Spaces: The Sources of Democratic Change in America* (New York: Harper & Row, 1986), and Boyte, "Populism and the Left," *democracy*, April 1981, pp. 53–66.

52. Nearing, *Making of a Radical*, p. 59; on Chautauqua, see Theodore Morrison, *Chautauqua: A Center for Education, Religion, and the Arts in America* (Chicago: University of Chicago Press, 1974); Henry May, *Protestant Churches in Industrial America* (New York: Knopf, 1949), p. 206; Charles H. Hopkins, *The Rise of the Social Gospel in American Protestantism* (New Haven: Yale University Press, 1940), p. 163; Arthur E. Bestor, *Chautauqua Publications: An Historical and Bibliographical Guide* (Chautauqua, N.Y.: Chautauqua, 1934); Eldon E. Snyder, "The Chautauqua Movement in Popular Culture: A Sociological Analysis," *Journal of American Culture* 8 (Fall 1985):79–90; and David Mead, "1914: Chautauqua and American Innocence," *Journal of Popular Culture* 1, no. 4 (Spring 1968):339–56.

53. William James, "What Makes Life Significant," in John J. McDermott, ed., *The Writings of William James* (Chicago: University of Chicago Press, 1981), pp. 646–47.

54. *Chautauquan Daily*, July 19, 1912, p. 2; July 14, 1914, p. 1.

55. *Chautauquan Daily*, July 24, 1917.

56. *Chautauquan Daily*, July 14, 1915, p. 6.

57. *Chautauquan Daily*, July 15, 1914, p. 3.

58. *Chautauquan Daily*, July 17, 1915, p. 2.

59. *Chautauquan Daily*, July 16, 1914, p. 2.

60. For James's comments on Chautauqua, see "What Makes Life Significant" and *The Letters of William James*, ed. Henry James, Vol. 2 (repr. New York: Kraus, 1969), pp. 243–44.

61. *Chautauquan Daily*, July 14, 1914, p. 1.

62. See Beverly Seaton, "Helen Reimensnyder Martin's 'Caricatures' of the Pennsylvania Germans," *Pennsylvania Magazine of History and Biography* 104 (January 1980):86–95.

63. I am indebted to Robert Nearing for pointing out the association of Martin and his father and the striking resemblance of his father to the characters in her novels. Nearing's copy of *Fanatic or Christian?* is in the possession of Robert Nearing. The full inscription is "Given to Scott Nearing 'the hero,' by Helen R. Martin, inscribed by N. M. S., since Scott was too modest and Mrs. Martin forgot." Biographical details of Martin's life and her enthusiasm about Nearing's views were provided by her son Frederick T. Martin, letter to author, February 7, 1987.

64. Helen R. Martin, *Fanatic or Christian?* (Garden City, N.Y.: Doubleday, 1918), pp. 88, 91.

65. Ibid., pp. 92–93.

66. Ibid., pp. 148, 256.

67. Ibid., p. 96.

68. Helen R. Martin, *The Church on the Avenue* (New York: Dodd, Mead, 1923), pp. 236–37, 284.

## Chapter 5

1. Nearing, *Reducing the Cost of Living*, 1914, p. 13.

2. Nearing and Nellie Nearing, *Women and Social Progress*, 1912, p. 213.

3. Nearing, *The Super Race: An American Problem*, 1912, p. 51.

4. Nearing, *The Solution of the Child Labor Problem*, 1911, p. 134; *Reducing the Cost of Living*, pp. 206, 207, 257; *Chautauquan Daily*, July 18, 1914, p. 3.

5. Nearing, *Super Race*, p. 86.

6. See Simon Nelson Patten, *Heredity and Social Progress* (New York: Macmillan, 1903); "An Analysis of Mental Defects," *The Monist* 30 (January 1920):107–12; "The Reconstruction of Economic Theory" (1912), repr. in Rexford G. Tugwell, ed., *Essays in Economic Theory* (New York: Knopf, 1924), p. 330.

7. Nellie Seeds Nearing's travel journal, "Our First Trip To Europe, Sailed from Philadelphia, June 10, 1911," in the possession of Robert Nearing, Troy, Pa.

8. Rexford G. Tugwell, *To the Lesser Heights of Morningside: A Memoir* (Philadelphia: University of Pennsylvania Press, 1982), pp. 27–28n.

9. Nearing, "Social Decadence," 1913, p. 634.

10. Nearing and Nellie Nearing, *Women and Social Progress*, p. 152.

11. Nearing, *Super Race*, pp. 53, 16, 75, 56, 78; on the movement of eugenics generally, see Daniel J. Kevles, *In the Name of Eugenics: Genetics and the Uses of Human Heredity* (New York: Knopf, 1985); Donald K. Pickens, *Eugenics and the Progressives* (Nashville, Tenn.: Vanderbilt University Press, 1968); and Michael Freeden, "Eu-

genics and Progressive Thought: A Study in Ideological Affinity," *Historical Journal* 22, no. 3 (1979):645–71.

12. The word *race* was used by eugenicists not in a strict biological sense but rather in a loosely construed notion of a cultural community, often with both prejudiced and nationalistic overtones.

13. Nearing, *Super Race*, pp. 34, 41–42, 35, 40, 33, 71–72, 40–41, 155, 41.

14. Nearing, "Social Decadence," pp. 634, 639.

15. Nearing, "Race Suicide v. Overpopulation," 1911, p. 81.

16. Ibid., p. 83.

17. *Toledo Blade*, February 1, 1916. Nearing wrote on eugenics in this way: "conclusively that this method is not the most effective one . . . [he was] for education rather than eugenics."

18. Llewellyn Jones, Review of *The Super Race*, *The Public*, November 8, 1912, p. 1073.

19. Nearing, *Super Race*, pp. 72, 42.

20. Ibid., p. 49.

21. Ibid., p. 52.

22. Ibid., p. 73.

23. *Toledo Blade*, February 1, 1916.

24. Nearing and Frank Watson, *Economics*, 1908, p. 144.

25. Nearing, "The Child Labor Problem," 1910, p. 357.

26. Nearing and Watson, *Economics*, p. 488.

27. Ibid.

28. Nearing, "Child Labor and the Child," 1910, p. 496.

29. Nearing, *The Solution of the Child Labor Problem*, 1911, pp. 39–40.

30. Nearing, "Child Labor and the Child," p. 495; *Solution of the Child Labor Problem*, p. 41.

31. Nearing, *Solution of the Child Labor Problem*, p. 41.

32. Nearing, *Social Adjustment*, 1910, p. 253.

33. Nearing, "Child Labor and the Child," p. 441.

34. Nearing, *Solution of the Child Labor Problem*, p. 29.

35. Nearing, "Child Labor and the Child," pp. 413–14.

36. Nearing, *Solution of the Child Labor Problem*, pp. 50, 51, 58–59.

37. Ibid., p. 23.

38. Ibid., p. vi.

39. Ibid., p. 125.

40. Ibid., pp. 129, 133, 134, 9.

41. Dorothy Ross, "The Development of the Social Sciences," in Alexandra Oleson and John Voss, *The Organization of Knowledge in Modern America, 1869–1920* (Baltimore: Johns Hopkins University Press, 1979), p. 128.

42. Nearing, *Reducing the Cost of Living*, p. 297.

43. Nearing, *Social Adjustment*, p. 351.

44. Ibid., pp. 317, 357.

45. Ibid., p. 307.

46. Nearing and Henry Reed Burch, *Elements of Economics*, 1912, p. 342.

47. Nearing, *Social Sanity*, 1913, p. 225.

48. Ibid., p. 226.

49. Ibid., pp. 225–26.

50. Nearing, *Social Adjustment,* p. 363.

51. Nearing, *Social Sanity,* p. 53.

52. Nearing, *Social Adjustment,* p. 366.

53. Nearing, *Anthracite,* 1915, p. 229.

54. Nearing and Burch, *Elements of Economics,* p. 346.

55. Nearing and Watson, *Economics,* pp. 339, 470, 474–75.

56. [Roger Baldwin], "A Puritan Revolutionist: Scott Nearing," in Devere Allen, ed., *Adventurous Americans* (New York: Farrar and Rinehart, 1932), p. 267. The unsigned article, according to Nearing, was written by Baldwin. Interview with author, Harborside, Me., March 20, 1983.

57. Nearing and Watson, *Economics,* pp. 475–76, 483, 492, 476–78.

58. Nearing, *Social Sanity,* p. 255.

59. On the community ideal generally in the late nineteenth and early twentieth century, see Jean B. Quandt, *From the Small Town to the Great Community* (New Brunswick, N.J.: Rutgers University Press, 1970), and R. Jackson Wilson, *In Quest of Community: Social Philosophy in the United States, 1860–1920* (New York: John Wiley, 1968).

60. Nearing, *Educational Frontiers,* 1925, p. 144.

61. Ibid., pp. 162, 192.

62. Ibid., p. 212; Scott Nearing Papers, lecture notes, March 3, 1916, lecture 24, "The Teacher, the School, and the Democracy," Swarthmore College Peace Collection (SCPC).

63. Nearing, *Educational Frontiers,* p. 155.

64. Lecture 24, "Teacher, School, and Democracy," SCPC.

65. Nearing, *Educational Frontiers,* pp. 186, 159.

66. "The Darrow–Nearing Debate," *Modern School,* March, April 1917, p. 207.

67. Nearing, *Income,* 1915, p. 195.

68. "Darrow–Nearing Debate," pp. 203–4, 231–32.

69. Ibid., pp. 211, 213, 214, 225, 228–29.

70. Randolph Bourne, Review of *Poverty and Riches, Intercollegiate Socialist* 5, no. 2 (December–January 1916–17):17.

71. James Kloppenberg, *Uncertain Victory: Social Democracy and Progressivism in European and American Thought, 1870–1920* (New York: Oxford University Press, 1986), p. 62.

## Chapter 6

1. Nearing, *Social Sanity,* 1913, p. 20; *Poverty and Riches,* 1916, p. 126.

2. Nearing, *Income,* 1915, p. 193.

3. Nearing, "The Impending Conflict," 1915, p. 606.

4. Ibid., p. 191.

5. Nearing, "The Parasitic Power of Property," 1915, p. 537.

6. Nearing, "Impending Conflict," pp. 606–7.

7. Rexford G. Tugwell, *To the Lesser Heights of Morningside: A Memoir* (Philadelphia: University of Pennsylvania Press, 1982), pp. 30, 39, 45, 46.

8. Nearing, *The Making of a Radical,* 1972, p. 45.

9. Stephen A. Sass, *The Pragmatic Imagination: A History of the Wharton School, 1881–1981* (Philadelphia: University of Pennsylvania Press, 1982), pp. 117–18.

10. Edward Potts Cheyney, *The History of the University of Pennsylvania, 1740–1940* (Philadelphia: University of Pennsylvania Press, 1940), p. 376.

11. The Wharton School faculty's role in the gas wars is recounted in Sass, *Pragmatic Imagination,* pp. 111–13.

12. Quoted in Sass, *Pragmatic Imagination,* p. 112.

13. Lincoln Steffens, "Philadelphia: Corrupt and Contented," *McClure's Magazine* 21 (1903):249; on the history of reform attempts in Philadelphia during this period, see Donald Disbrow, "The Progressive Movement in Philadelphia," Ph.D. diss., University of Rochester, 1956, and Lloyd Abernathy, "Insurgency in Philadelphia, 1905," *Pennsylvania Magazine of History and Biography* 87 (January 1963):3–20.

14. Tugwell, *Lesser Heights of Morningside,* p. 39n.

15. Cheyney, *History of the University of Pennsylvania,* p. 362.

16. Editorial, *Alumni Register,* March 1911, p. 23.

17. Quoted in Sass, *Pragmatic Imagination,* p. 119; see also Cheyney, *History of the University of Pennsylvania,* pp. 371ff.; Lightner Witmer, *The Nearing Case: The Limitation of Academic Freedom at the University of Pennsylvania by Act of the Board of Trustees, June 14, 1915* (New York: B. W. Huebsch, 1915), pp. 63, 103–6; Nearing, *Educational Frontiers,* 1925, pp. 48, 78–79; Upton Sinclair, *The Goose Step: A Study of American Higher Education* (Pasadena, Calif.: the author, 1923), pp. 98, 97–101.

18. See Nearing, *Educational Frontiers,* pp. 77–79; editorial, "The New Board of Trustees," *Alumni Register,* March 1911, p. 12.

19. "The New Board of Trustees," p. 12.

20. Witmer, *Nearing Case,* p. 96.

21. Editorial, "State Appropriations," *Alumni Register,* March 1911, p. 23.

22. Nearing, "Postscript," interviews conducted in 1981, 1982, in Craig Kaplan and Ellen Schrecker, *Regulating the Intellectuals: Perspectives on Academic Freedom in the 1980s* (New York: Praeger, 1983), p. 242.

23. Ibid., p. 243.

24. Witmer, *Nearing Case,* p. 116.

25. See ibid., p. 116, and Sass, *Pragmatic Imagination,* p. 119.

26. Nearing, *Making of a Radical,* p. 58.

27. Witmer, *Nearing Case,* p. 116.

28. See Cheyney, *History of the University of Pennsylvania,* pp. 364–67, and Sass, *Pragmatic Imagination,* pp. 119–20.

29. Quoted in Sass, *Pragmatic Imagination,* p. 120.

30. Tugwell, *Lesser Heights of Morningside,* pp. 39, 26.

31. "The Case of Scott Nearing—University of Pennsylvania 1915," Nearing Case File, American Association of University Professors, Washington, D.C., pp. 1–2.

32. Witmer, *Nearing Case,* pp. 79, 87–90. "The trustees' actions were closely related to the growing discontent among leaders of the general alumni society. Ten of the twenty-four trustees were nominees of the society." Clyde Barrow, *Universities and the Capitalist State: Corporate Liberalism and the Reconstruction of American Higher Education, 1894–1928* (Madison: University of Wisconsin Press, 1990), p. 215.

33. "Report of the Committee of Inquiry on the Case of Professor Scott Nearing of the University of Pennsylvania," *Bulletin of the American Association of University Professors* 2 (1916):20 (hereafter cited as "AAUP Report on Nearing").

34. Witmer, *Nearing Case,* p. 81.

35. Editorial, "Academic Freedom," *Alumni Register,* March 1912, p. 140.

36. Editorial, "Changes in the College," *Alumni Register*, September 1912, p. 43.

37. See editorial, "A Partnership," *Alumni Register*, June 1913; Witmer, *Nearing Case*, pp. 116–17.

38. *Proceedings of the American Political Science Association, 1913*, p. 42.

39. On the formation of the AAUP, see Barrow, *Universities and the Capitalist State*, pp. 170, 208.

40. Nearing Dismissal Scrapbook, p. 3, Wharton School 1915, Archives, General Manuscript Collection, University of Pennsylvania Archives, Philadelphia.

41. Philadelphia *Ledger*, January 4, 1914, Nearing Dismissal Scrapbook, p. 1, University of Pennsylvania Archives, Philadelphia.

42. Editorial, "The Professors' Union," *Alumni Register*, February 1914.

43. Editorial, *New Republic*, July 3, 1915, p. 214.

44. Nearing, *Making of a Radical*, pp. 57–58.

45. Ibid., p. 38.

46. Witmer, *Nearing Case*, pp. 117–18.

47. Ibid., p. 118.

48. Ibid., pp. 118–19.

49. Ibid., p. 120.

50. Ibid., p. 120.

51. "AAUP Report on Nearing," p. 17.

52. Scott Nearing to Joel Springarn, February 9, 1914, Joel Springarn Papers, box 9, folder 2, Rare Books and Manuscripts Division, Astor, Lenox and Tilden Foundations, New York Public Library, New York.

53. Trustee Minutes, May 11, 1914, University of Pennsylvania Archives, Philadelphia.

54. Professor Ordinarius, "Academic Freedom—A Confession," *New Republic*, January 2, 1915, p. 18.

55. Resigning was possibly viewed as the most satisfactory course of action, with the ready example of President Andrews of Brown University, who had resigned in a 1897 case instead of submitting to trustees' restrictions.

56. "AAUP Report on Nearing," p. 9.

57. Editorial, "Free Speech Again," *Alumni Register*, November 1914, pp. 69–70.

58. See Howard Crosby Warner, "Academic Freedom," *Atlantic Monthly*, November 1914, pp. 689–99. In a listing of the key academic freedom cases in America, Warner reviewed the Ely, Bemis, and Ross cases, and brought his compilation up to date by noting the situation of Nearing and others at the Wharton School who "had been denied promotions on account of some statistical inquiries relating to local and state enterprises."

59. Nearing, response to "Freedom of Teaching in the United States," by Ulysses G. Weatherly, and "Reasonable Restrictions upon the Scholar's Freedom," by Henry Pritchet, 1914, p. 165.

60. Ibid., response by Ross, p. 166; on the conference, see also Herman Schwendinger and Julia R. Schwendinger, *The Sociologists of the Chair: A Radical Analysis of the Formative Years of North American Sociology, 1883–1922* (New York: Basic Books, 1974), pp. 531–38.

61. On the founding of the AAUP, see Ellen Schrecker, *No Ivory Tower: McCarthyism and the Universities* (New York: Oxford University Press, 1986), p. 17; the

association published *List of Charter Members of the American Association of University Professors* in May 1915.

62. Disbrow, "Progressive Movement in Philadelphia," pp. 199–210; *The Pennsylvanian*, January 9, 1915, p. 1, February 13, 1915, p. 1, March 13, 1915, p. 1; Sass, *Pragmatic Imagination*, p. 120.

63. Witmer, *Nearing Case*, p. 52.

64. Quoted in William G. McLoughlin, Jr., *Billy Sunday Was His Real Name* (Chicago: University of Chicago Press, 1955), p. 238.

65. *The Pennsylvanian*, March 15, 1915, p. 1.

66. Witmer, *Nearing Case*, p. 49.

67. Nearing, *Making of a Radical*, p. 79.

68. Witmer, *Nearing Case*, pp. 54–55; Nearing, *Making of a Radical*, pp. 77–79.

69. On the Gompers incident, see Witmer, *Nearing Case*, p. 51; Samuel Gompers, *Seventy Years of Life and Labor: An Autobiography*, Vol. 1 (New York: E. P. Dutton, 1925), p. 141; editorial, *New Republic*, March 15, 1915, p. 1; Kenneth Fones-Wolf, "Trade Union Gospel: Protestantism and the Labor Movement in Philadelphia, 1865–1915," Ph.D. diss., Temple University, 1985, p. 415.

70. On the Stotesbury incident, see Tugwell, *Lesser Heights of Morningside*, pp. 67–68, "AAUP Report on Nearing," p. 18, Sass, *Pragmatic Imagination*, p. 121; on Stotesbury, see Witmer, *Nearing Case*, p. 105.

71. From the constitution of the ISS; see Max Horn, *The Intercollegiate Socialist Society, 1905–1921: Origins of the Modern American Student Movement* (Boulder, Colo.: Westview Press, 1979), app. A.

72. Quoted in Horn, *Intercollegiate Socialist Society*, p. 30.

73. Intercollegiate Socialist Society Papers, "Report of Organizer of ISS," reel 27: R2656, Tamiment Institute, New York University, New York.

74. Horn, *Intercollegiate Socialist Society*, p. 28.

75. Henry Flury, "College Men and Socialism," *International Socialist Review* August 1908, 131–34.

76. *Intercollegiate Socialist*, February–March 1915, 19.

77. Paul Howard Douglas, editorial, "Professors and Free Speech," *Intercollegiate Socialist*, February–March 1915, 3–4.

78. Nearing, *Income*, 1915.

79. N. I. Stone, Review of *Income*, *Intercollegiate Socialist*, February–March 1916, 31.

80. Nearing, "The Parasitic Power of Property," 1915, pp. 536–37; Nearing, "The Impending Conflict," 1915, pp. 606–7.

81. Nearing, *Making of a Radical*, p. 84.

82. Nearing defined academic freedom in sweeping terms. By 1916, he claimed that the university "has the right to dismiss the members of its faculty for intellectual dishonesty, scientific incompetency, and moral cowardice, but for no other cause! . . . The university is an institution which is founded to seek, to proclaim and to apply the truth. . . . There is no limit to freedom of discussion in the school—there is no limit to freedom of discussion in the college—either speech is free, or it is not free!" See his "The Teacher, the School, and the Democracy," lecture given at the Garrick Theater, Chicago, March 12, 1916. Stenographer's transcript, Military Intelligence Division, Record Group 165, National Archives, Washington, D.C.

83. Nearing, *Making of a Radical*, p. 104.
84. Editorial, "The Professor's Calling," *Alumni Register*, January 1915, p. 246.
85. Editorial, "Public Utterances," *Alumni Register*, February 1915, p. 319.
86. Editorial, *Alumni Register*, p. 322.
87. "AAUP Report on Nearing," p. 15.
88. Ibid., pp. 17–18.
89. Ibid., p. 17.
90. Editorial, *New Republic*, May 1, 1915, p. 314.
91. Quoted in Witmer, *Nearing Case*, p. 84.
92. Editorial, "Our Universities," *New Republic*, May 22, 1915, pp. 57–58.
93. Editorial, *New Republic*, April 17, 1915, p. 271.
94. Nearing, *Making of a Radical*, p. 83; Witmer, *Nearing Case*, p. 15.

## Chapter 7

1. Lightner Witmer, *The Nearing Case: The Limitation of Academic Freedom at the University of Pennsylvania by Act of the Board of Trustees, June 14, 1915* (New York: B. W. Huebsch, 1915), p. 83; Louis C. Madeira to Edgar F. Smith, September 29, 1915, Wharton School 1915, Archives, General Manuscript Collection, University of Pennsylvania Archives, Philadelphia.
2. Witmer, *Nearing Case*, p. 19.
3. Ibid., p. 35.
4. Ibid., p. 31.
5. "Report of the Committee of Inquiry on the Case of Professor Scott Nearing of the University of Pennsylvania," *Bulletin of the American Association of University Professors* 2 (1916):33 (hereafter cited as "AAUP Report on Nearing").
6. Clyde Barrow, *Universities and the Capitalist State: Corporate Liberalism and the Reconstruction of American Higher Education, 1894–1928* (Madison: University of Wisconsin Press, 1990), p. 216.
7. Nearing, *The Making of a Radical*, 1972, pp. 85, 93–94; Steven A. Sass, *The Pragmatic Imagination: A History of the Wharton School, 1881–1981* (Philadelphia: University of Pennsylvania Press, 1982), p. 122.
8. Nearing, *Making of a Radical*, p. 84.
9. Nearing folder, newspaper clipping no. 1205, University of Pennsylvania Archives, Philadelphia.
10. Nearing, *Making of a Radical*, pp. 84–85.
11. Rose Pastor Stokes Papers, box 2, folder 56, June 22, 1915, Tamiment Institute, New York University, New York.
12. Nearing, *Making of a Radical*, p. 85.
13. Editorials, *New Republic*, June 26, 1915, front page; July 3, 1915, p. 214; October 9, 1915, pp. 245–46.
14. McCrea to Smith, June 22, 1915, Wharton School 1915, Archives, General Manuscript Collection, University of Pennsylvania Archives, Philadelphia.
15. J. Russell Smith, "Dismissing the Professor," *Survey*, November 6, 1915, pp. 131–34.
16. Witmer, *Nearing Case*, pp. 16–17.
17. Edward Potts Cheyney, *The History of the University of Pennsylvania, 1740–1940* (Philadelphia: University of Pennsylvania Press, 1940), p. 370.

18. Witmer, *Nearing Case*, pp. ix, 120.

19. Rexford G. Tugwell, *To the Lesser Heights of Morningside: A Memoir* (Philadelphia: University of Pennsylvania Press, 1982), p. 68.

20. Witmer, *Nearing Case*, pp. 20, 42–44, 59–60.

21. Tugwell, *Lesser Heights of Morningside*, p. 68.

22. "AAUP Report on Nearing," p. 33.

23. Witmer, *Nearing Case*, p. 122.

24. Edward Cheyney, "Trustees and Faculties," *School and Society*, December 4, 1915, p. 794.

25. Witmer, *Nearing Case*, p. 51.

26. Scott Nearing Papers, draft of autobiography, bk. 6, April 30, 1968, p. 85b, DG 124 (SCPC).

27. Review of Nearing's *Wages in the United States*, *International Socialist Review* (December 1911): 355.

28. Debate, *Should Socialism Prevail?* 1915, pp. 12–13, 30–32.

29. John Dewey, "Is the College Professor a Hired Man?" *Literary Digest*, July 10, 1915, p. 65.

30. On the National Civic Federation generally, see James Weinstein, *The Corporate Ideal in the Liberal State, 1900–1918* (Boston: Beacon Press, 1968), pp. 3–39.

31. Quoted, ibid., p. 22.

32. Quoted, ibid., p. 128; on the NCF and its crusade against socialism generally, see pp. 117–38.

33. Ibid., p. 28.

34. Easley to Bell, July 2, 1915, box 15, general correspondence, 1915, National Civic Federation Papers, Rare Books and Manuscripts Division, New York Public Library, Astor, Lenox and Tilden Foundations, New York; Schwendinger and Schwendinger, in their *Sociologists of the Chair* (New York: Basic Books, 1974), p. 543, argue forcefully that NCF interest in the Nearing case reveals coercive and repressive capitalist cultural hegemony. Yet their thesis is often unrefined, and in this instance it is due to lack of care in handling the evidence. By placing the date of the Easley letter sometime in 1914, they have concluded that the NCF was instrumental in forcing Nearing out. Since the letter was written after Nearing's dismissal, this of course was not the case.

35. Bell to Easley, July 3, 1915, and November 9, 1915, box 15, general correspondence, 1915, National Civic Federation Records, Rare Books and Manuscripts Division, New York Public Library, Astor, Lenox and Tilden Foundations, New York.

36. Dewey, "Is the College Professor a Hired Man?" p. 65; on the "employee idea," see Barrow, *Universities and the Capitalist State*, pp. 166–67.

37. Randolph Bourne, "Who Owns the Universities?" *New Republic*, July 17, 1915, repr. Olaf Hansen, ed., *The Radical Will: Randolph Bourne, Selected Writings 1911–1918* (New York: Urizen, 1977), pp. 216–22.

38. "AAUP Report on Nearing," pp. 13, 29, 34; Douglas, "Professors and Free Speech," pp. 3–4; B. Boyesen, "What the Universities Need," *The Masses*, November 1915, p. 16; John Dewey, "The Case of the Professor and the Public Interest," *The Dial*, November 8, 1917, pp. 435, 437.

39. "AAUP Report on Nearing," p. 25; Nearing, *Making of a Radical*, p. 89; Sass, *Pragmatic Imagination*, p. 124.

40. McCrea to Smith, June 22, 1915, Wharton School 1915 Archives, General Manuscript Collection, University of Pennsylvania Archives, Philadelphia.

41. Cheyney, "Trustees and Faculties," pp. 794, 808.

42. Nearing, *Making of a Radical*, p. 94.

43. Tugwell, *Lesser Heights of Morningside*, p. 69.

44. Cheyney, *History of the University of Pennsylvania*, pp. 370–71; Oswald Garrison Villard, "Academic Freedom," *The Nation*, December 23, 1915, pp. 245–46; "What the Nearing Case Won," *Literary Digest*, January 8, 1916.

45. Tugwell, *Lesser Heights of Morningside*, p. 70; Sass, *Pragmatic Imagination*, pp. 124–25.

46. When Dean McCrea resigned, reportedly on account of the dismissal of Nearing, his replacement, W. L. McClellan, was announced without consultation with the faculty of the Wharton School. Shortly after his appointment, he issued guidelines prohibiting the faculty from engaging in activity of a "public nature," which was widely interpreted to mean that certain Wharton faculty members would be restricted in their civic activities. Protests over McClellan's actions were lodged with the AAUP, which conducted a preliminary investigation. See Chairman, Committee on Academic Freedom and Academic Tenure, AAUP to Dean W. L. McClellan, November 27, 1916, and A. A. Young to the Members of the Committee on Academic Freedom and Academic Tenure, March 9, 1917, Nearing Case File, American Association of University Professors, Washington, D.C.

47. Nearing, *Educational Frontiers*, 1925, pp. 62, 76.

48. Daniel M. Fox, *The Discovery of Abundance: Simon Nelson Patten and the Transformation of Social Theory* (Ithaca: Cornell University Press, 1967), p. 126.

49. H. L. Mencken, *Prejudices, Third Series* (London: Jonathan Cape, 1923), pp. 280–84, 287–88.

50. The turmoil had boiled over in the mid-1890s when the popular economist Richard T. Ely had come under attack by the University of Wisconsin Board of Regents. In 1895, one of Ely's students, Edward T. Beemis, after entering into political controversy over the role of the government in economic reform, had his academic career ended with his dismissal from the University of Chicago. The circumstances were similar in the case of another of Ely's students, Edward A. Ross, who as an academic professional and public intellectual became embroiled in economic and political controversy and was forced to resign from Stanford in 1900. See Ellen W. Schrecker, *No Ivory Tower; McCarthyism and the Universities* (New York: Oxford University Press, 1986), pp. 12–19; John Brubacher and Willis Rudy, *Higher Education in Transition* (New York: Harper & Row, 1968), p. 312; Laurence R. Veysey, *The Emergence of the American University* (Chicago: University of Chicago Press, 1965), pp. 381–88; Carol S. Gruber, *Mars and Minerva: World War I and the Uses of the Higher Learning in America* (Baton Rouge: Louisiana State University Press, 1975), pp. 162–212; Clyde Barrow, *Universities and the Capitalist State: Corporate Liberalism and the Reconstruction of American Higher Education, 1894–1928* (Madison: University of Wisconsin Press, 1990), pp. 186–220.

51. "AAUP Report on Nearing," p. 4.

52. The new circumstances reflected in the Nearing case are perhaps one reason his case has been revived in recent literature on academic freedom. See Russell Jacoby, *The Last Intellectuals: American Culture in the Age of Academe* (New York: Basic Books, 1987), pp. 125–26, 209; Schrecker, *No Ivory Tower*, pp. 19–21, 26–27; Schrecker, "Academic Freedom: The Historical View," in Craig Kaplan and Schrecker, eds.,

*Regulating the Intellectuals: Perspectives on Academic Freedom in the 1980s* (New York: Praeger, 1983), pp. 29–30; see also "Postscript: Scott Nearing," in Kaplan and Schrecker, *Regulating the Intellectuals*, pp. 241–47.

53. Bertell Ollman, "Academic Freedom in America Today: A Marxist View," in Kaplan and Schrecker, *Regulating the Intellectuals*, p. 45. Ely recanted his reformist beliefs and maintained his academic position, and while Beemis was fired, he had tried to convince the president of the University of Chicago of his conservative intentions. Thus, regarding Beemis, Ollman writes that he finds "it difficult to view him as the first radical to lose his job because of his political beliefs. That honor belongs to Scott Nearing." Clyde Barrow claims that "no other single case brought the class conflict between intellectuals and the business trustees into such relief by intertwining" issues of tenure "with the problems of ideology and academic freedom"; *Universities and the Capitalist State*, p. 214.

54. Harry W. Laidler, "Academic Freedom," in *The American Labor Yearbook*, Vol. 1, New York, 1916, p. 319.

55. See Bruce Kuklick, *Churchmen and Philosophers: From Jonathan Edwards to John Dewey* (New Haven, Conn.: Yale University Press, 1985), pp. 196–97.

56. *Report of Committee on Academic Freedom and Academic Tenure*, American Association of University Professors, December 1915.

57. Randolph Bourne, "The Idea of a University," *The Dial*, November 22, 1917, pp. 509–10.

58. Thorstein Veblen, *The Higher Learning in America: A Memorandum on the Conduct of Universities by Businessmen* (1918) (New York: Hill and Wang, 1957), p. 134.

59. John Dewey, "Academic Freedom," *Educational Review*, January 1902, pp. 10–13.

60. Jacob H. Hollander to E. R. A. Seligman, June 29, 1915; E. R. A. Seligman to J. H. Hollander, July 2, 1915; B. M. Anderson, Jr. to Seligman, August 5, 1915; U. G. Weatherly to Seligman, June 26, 1915; "Reference Scott Nearing," p. 1, Nearing Case file, American Association of University Professors, Washington, D.C.

61. For important discussions of the emergence of the modern university and the rise of professionalism and their effects on academic freedom, see Gruber, *Mars and Minerva*, pp. 34–35; Burton J. Bledstein, *The Culture of Professionalism: The Middle Class and the Development of Higher Education in America* (New York: Norton, 1976), pp. 92–93, 287–331.

62. Arthur Livingston, "Academic Freedom," *New Republic*, November 17, 1917, p. 70.

63. *Chautauquan Daily*, July 6, 1915, pp. 1, 2.

64. Nearing File, from the New York *Sun*, October 19, 1915, University of Pennsylvania Archives, Philadelphia.

65. "Scott Nearing in College Opening Week," *The Survey*, October 9, 1915, p. 35; *The Survey*, January 22, 1916, p. 449.

66. Morris Hillquit, *Loose Leaves from a Busy Life* (New York: Macmillan, 1934), p. 60.

67. See generally, Frederick Cornell, "History of the Rand School," Ed.D. diss., Columbia University Teachers College, 1976; *American Labor Yearbook*, Vol. 1, New York, 1916, pp. 151–53, Vol. 3, 1919–1920, pp. 206–7; Papers of the Rand School of Social Science, reel 54, R2683, Tamiment Institute, New York University, New York.

68. *American Labor Yearbook*, Vol. 3, 1919–1920, New York, p. 207.

69. Nearing, "Teacher, School, and Democracy," p. 19.

70. Nearing, *Making of a Radical*, p. 96; Trustee Minutes, July 26, 1915, Toledo University Archives, Toledo, Ohio.

71. Monroe Stowe, "The Work of a Municipal College of Arts and Science," *School and Society*, November 27, 1915, p. 786.

72. Nearing, *Making of a Radical*, p. 98.

73. Editorial, *Toledo Blade*, October 15, 1915, and Nearing, "Grave Faults of the Wage System," *Toledo Blade*, October 21, 1915, Toledo University Archives, Toledo, Ohio.

74. Nearing, *Making of a Radical*, pp. 97, 99.

75. Ibid., p. 87.

76. Nearing, *Anthracite*, 1915, p. 9.

## Chapter 8

1. John Dewey, Introduction to Jane Addams, *Peace and Bread in Time of War* (1922) (New York: Garland Press, 1971), p. ix.

2. Nearing, *The Making of a Radical*, 1972, pp. 177, 127–28.

3. See A. M. Stowe, "Work of a Municipal College of Arts and Sciences," *School and Society*, November 29, 1915, pp. 786–88.

4. Quoted in Elliot J. Anderson, "The Scott Nearing Controversy in Toledo, 1916–1917," *Northwest Ohio Quarterly* 29 (1957):72–88, 161–73, 206–33.

5. Morris Hillquit, ed., *The Trial of Scott Nearing and the American Socialist Society* (New York: Rand School, 1919), p. 31.

6. Quoted, ibid., p. 208.

7. Nearing, *Making of a Radical*, p. 99.

8. Quoted in Anderson, "Scott Nearing Controversy," p. 79.

9. Ibid.

10. Ibid., p. 84.

11. Scrapbook, *Toledo Blade*, January 14, 1916, Toledo University Archives, Ward M. Canaday Center, University of Toledo, Toledo, Ohio.

12. Ibid., January 31, 1916.

13. See David M. Kennedy, *Over Here: The First World War and American Society* (New York: Oxford University Press, 1980), pp. 41, 47; Arthur S. Link, *Woodrow Wilson and the Progressive Era, 1910–1917* (New York: Harper, 1954), pp. 180–82; see also C. Roland Marchand, *The American Peace Movement and Social Reform, 1898–1918* (Princeton, N.J.: Princeton University Press, 1972), pp. 244–48.

14. Anderson, "Scott Nearing Controversy," p. 162.

15. The notes for the lecture can be found in the Scott Nearing Papers, lecture 24, March 3, 1916, Swarthmore College Peace Collection (SCPC); a transcript of the lecture, as delivered at the Garrick Theater, Chicago, on March 12, 1916, can be found in the Military Intelligence Division, Record Group 165, National Archives, Washington, D.C.

16. *Intercollegiate Socialist* (April–May 1916):35.

17. Editorial, *Toledo Blade*, February 14, 1916, Toledo University Archives, Ward M. Canaday Center, University of Toledo.

18. Anderson, "Scott Nearing Controversy," p. 85.

19. Quoted, ibid., pp. 85–86.

20. Ibid., pp. 210, 163.

21. *Toledo Blade*, May 9, 1916, Toledo University Archives, Ward M. Canaday Center, University of Toledo; Anderson, "Scott Nearing Controversy," pp. 162–64.

22. *Toledo Blade*, May 12, 1916, Toledo University Archives, Ward M. Canaday Center, University of Toledo; Anderson, "Scott Nearing Controversy," pp. 80–81.

23. "Report of the Committee of Inquiry on the Case of Scott Nearing of the University of Pennsylvania," *Bulletin of the American Association of University Professors* 2 (March 1916):38.

24. Anderson, "Scott Nearing Controversy," pp. 207–8.

25. See Link, *Woodrow Wilson and the Progressive Era*, pp. 223–51.

26. *Chautauquan Daily*, July 25, 1916, p. 1.

27. Hillquit, *Trial of Scott Nearing*, p. 32.

28. *Chautauquan Daily*, July 25, 1916, p. 1.

29. Nearing, "What is America?" 1916, p. 360.

30. Nearing, *The Germs of War*, pamphlet, 1916, pp. 18, 11, 30.

31. Ibid., pp. 28–29.

32. Anderson, "Scott Nearing Controversy," p. 80.

33. Scrapbook, newspaper clipping, December 13, 1916, Toledo University Archives, Ward M. Canaday Center, University of Toledo.

34. *Toledo Blade*, January 8, 1917, Toledo University Archives, Ward M. Canaday Center, University of Toledo.

35. Anderson, "Scott Nearing Controversy," p. 165; scrapbook, newspaper clipping, February 14, 1917, Toledo University Archives, Ward M. Canaday Center, University of Toledo.

36. See Merle Curti, *Peace or War: The American Struggle, 1636–1936* (New York: Norton, 1936), pp. 251–59; Charles DeBenedetti, *The Peace Reform Movement in American History* (Bloomington: University of Indiana Press, 1980), pp. 96–99; Charles Chatfield, *For Peace and Justice: Pacifism in America, 1914–1941* (Knoxville: University of Tennessee Press, 1971), pp. 21–27; Blanche Wiesen Cook, "Democracy in Wartime: Antimilitarism in England and the United States, 1914–1918," in Charles Chatfield, ed., *Peace Movements in America* (New York: Schocken Books, 1973), pp. 40–43; and Marchand, *American Peace Movement*, pp. 179, 241–45.

37. See Anderson, "Scott Nearing Controversy," pp. 166–67, 211–12.

38. *Toledo Blade*, March 10, 1917, Toledo University Archives, Ward M. Canaday Center, University of Toledo.

39. Nearing, "A Letter of Explanation," 1917.

40. Anderson, "Scott Nearing Controversy," p. 213.

41. *Toledo Blade*, March 10, 1917, Toledo University Archives, Ward M. Canaday Center, University of Toledo; quoted in Anderson, "Scott Nearing Controversy," p. 215.

42. Anderson, "Scott Nearing Controversy," p. 216.

43. Toledo *Union Leader*, March 16, 1917, Toledo University Archives, Ward M. Canaday Center, University of Toledo.

44. Quoted in Anderson, "Scott Nearing Controversy," pp. 216–17.

45. Ibid., p. 214.

46. *Intercollegiate Socialist* (April–May 1917).

47. Marchand, *American Peace Movement*, pp. 252–53.

48. See Cook, "Democracy in Wartime," pp. 40–43; DeBenedetti, *Peace Reform in American History*, p. 96; Marchand, *American Peace Movement*, pp. 241–45.

49. Quoted in Marchand, *American Peace Movement*, pp. 244–45. Nearing had

been a spokesman for the movement as early as April 1916 and was a member of the executive committee by May 1917. See Lillian D. Wald to Wilson, April 21, 1916, Arthur S. Link, ed., *The Papers of Woodrow Wilson*, Vol. 36 (Princeton, N.J.: Princeton University Press, 1981); see also American Union Against Militarism Papers, microfilm reel 1, "A Challenge Accepted," [April] 1916, "Wartime Program of the AUAM," May 1917, SCPC.

50. Quoted in Stephen Whitfield, *Scott Nearing: Apostle of American Radicalism* (New York: Columbia University Press, 1974), p. 60; on the formation of the AUAM, see Donald Johnson, *The Challenge to American Freedoms: World War One and the Rise of the ACLU* (Lexington: University Press of Kentucky, 1963), pp. 1–23.

51. University of Toledo Board of Trustees, Minutes, March 11, 1917, Toledo University Archives, Ward M. Canaday Center, University of Toledo; Anderson, "Scott Nearing Controversy," pp. 217–18.

52. Quoted in Anderson, "Scott Nearing Controversy," p. 218.

53. University of Toledo Board of Trustees, Minutes, March 11, 1917, Toledo University Archives, Ward M. Canaday Center, University of Toledo.

54. Quoted in Anderson, "Scott Nearing Controversy," p. 169.

55. Nearing, *Making of a Radical*, p. 100.

56. University of Toledo Board of Trustees, Minutes, April 18, 1917, and newspaper clippings, April 18, 1917, Toledo University Archives, Ward M. Canaday Center, University of Toledo; Anderson, "Scott Nearing Controversy," p. 219.

57. Scrapbook, newspaper clipping, May 4, 1917, Toledo University Archives, Ward M. Canaday Center, University of Toledo.

58. Newspaper clipping, April 21, 1917, Toledo University Archives, Ward M. Canaday Center, University of Toledo; Anderson, "Scott Nearing Controversy," p. 169.

59. Nearing, *The Menace of Militarism*, 1917, pp. 29–30.

60. *Toledo Blade*, April 2, 1917, Toledo University Archives, Ward M. Canaday Center, University of Toledo; Anderson, "Scott Nearing Controversy," pp. 169–72.

61. Nearing, *Making of a Radical*, p. 100; Nearing, "The Right and Duty of Free Speech," 1917.

62. Carol Gruber, *Mars and Minerva: World War I and the Uses of the Higher Learning in America* (Baton Rouge: Louisiana State University Press, 1975), p. 82; on intellectuals' support of the war generally, see Roland Stromberg, *Redemption by War: The Intellectuals and 1914* (Lawrence: Regents Press of Kansas, 1982).

63. Ibid., pp. 82, 174.

64. American Association of University Professors, "Report of Committee on Academic Freedom in Wartime," *Bulletin of the American Association of University Professors* 4 (February 1918):29.

65. Quoted in Gruber, *Mars and Minerva*, p. 170.

66. See AAUP, "Report of Committee on Academic Freedom in Wartime," pp. 29–47.

67. Nearing to Henry Raymond Mussey, December 4, 1917, Henry Raymond Mussey Papers, Houghton Library, Harvard University, by permission of the Houghton Library, Cambridge, Mass. This was a view shared by antiwar critics. Randolph Bourne had written in "War and the Intellectuals" in June 1917 that it was "a war made deliberately by the intellectuals!"

68. Scott Nearing Papers, handwritten notes for autobiography, n.d., SCPC.

69. Nearing, *Making of a Radical,* p. 193.

70. Scott Nearing Papers, draft of autobiography, bk. 6, June 27, 1967, p. 78, SCPC.

71. Nearing, *Making of a Radical,* p. 126.

72. Ibid., pp. 103, 104, 126–27.


**Chapter 9**

1. Randolph Bourne, "A War Diary," in Carl Resek, ed., *War and the Intellectuals: Essays by Randolph Bourne, 1915–1919* (New York: Harper & Row, 1964), p. 45.

2. Nearing, *The Making of a Radical,* 1972, pp. 121, 127–28.

3. Nearing, *The Menace of Militarism,* pamphlet, 1917, pp. 17, 22.

4. Morris Hillquit, ed., *The Trial of Scott Nearing and the American Socialist Society* (New York: Rand School, 1919), p. 121.

5. Ibid., p. 193.

6. Nearing, *The Germs of War, A Study in Preparedness,* pamphlet, 1916, p. 18.

7. Nearing, *The Next Step: A Plan for Economic World Federation,* 1922, p. 34.

8. Nearing, *Germs of War,* p. 27.

9. Nearing, *Making of a Radical,* p. 121; Hillquit, *Trial of Scott Nearing,* p. 123.

10. Hillquit, *Trial of Scott Nearing,* p. 123.

11. Nearing, *Open Letters to Profiteers,* pamphlet, 1916, p. 10.

12. Hillquit, *Trial of Scott Nearing,* pp. 60–61.

13. Ibid., pp. 62, 63, 66.

14. Nearing, *Irrepressible America,* pamphlet, 1922, p. 16.

15. Nearing, *A Nation Divided; or, Plutocracy versus Democracy,* pamphlet, 1920, p. 16.

16. Nearing, *Open Letters to Profiteers,* p. 10; in *Nation Divided,* p. 15, Nearing wrote: "No one can question the control which the plutocracy exercises over the jobs, the industrial product, and the economic surplus of the community. These facts are admitted on all hands. The corollaries which flow naturally from these axioms of present day economic life are not so readily accepted."

17. Cultural hegemony as an analytical concept originated with the Italian Marxist Antonio Gramsci; see his *Prison Notebooks* (New York: International Publishers, 1971), and Joseph V. Femia, *Gramsci's Political Thought* (New York, Oxford University Press, 1981). It has recently gained renewed attention as a means of understanding the complexities of control and acquiescence, domination and subordination, consent and coercion in industrial America. See T. J. Jackson Lears, "The Concept of Cultural Hegemony: Problems and Possibilities," *American Historical Review* (June 1985):567–93, and "Power Culture, and Memory," *Journal of American History* (June 1988):137–40; Thomas L. Haskell, "Capitalism and the Origins of Humanitarian Sensibility," *American Historical Review* (April 1985):339–61, (June 1985):547–66; "Convention and Hegemonic Interest in the Debate over Antislavery," *American Historical Review* (October 1987):829–78; John Patrick Diggins, "Comrades and Citizens: New Mythologies in American Historiography," *American Historical Review* (June 1985):614–38; and "The Misuses of Gramsci," *Journal of American History* (June 1988):141–45; David Byron Davis, "Reflections on Abolition and Ideological Hegemony," *American Historical Review* (October 1987):797–812; John Ashworth, "The Relation between Capitalism and Humanitarianism," *American Historical*

*Review* (October 1987):813–28; Leon Fink, "The New Labor History and the Powers of Historical Pessimism: Consensus, Hegemony, and the Case of the Knights of Labor," *Journal of American History* (June 1988): 115–36; George Lipsitz, "The Struggle for Hegemony," *Journal of American History* (June 1988):146–50.

18. Nearing, *Next Step*, p. 117.

19. Ibid., p. 38.

20. Bourne, "The State," in Resek, *War and the Intellectuals*, p. 71; see also Charles Chatfield, "World War I and the Liberal Pacifist in the United States," *American Historical Review* (December 1970):1934–35; Charles Chatfield, *For Peace and Justice: Pacifism in America, 1914–41* (Knoxville: University of Tennessee Press, 1971), pp. 61–62.

21. Nearing, *Menace of Militarism*, pp. 4, 29.

22. Hillquit, *Trial of Scott Nearing*, p. 37.

23. Nearing, *Next Step*, p. 15.

24. Nearing, *Nation Divided*, p. 31.

25. Nearing, debate with Percy Ward, *Rationalism v. Socialism: Is the Economic Factor or the Mental Factor More Important in Social Evolution?* 1921, p. 3.

26. Hillquit, *Trial of Scott Nearing*, p. 127; Nearing, *Next Step*, pp. 153, 163; *Nation Divided*, p. 19; *Menace of Militarism*, p. 41.

27. Nearing, *Next Step*, p. 163.

28. Nearing–Ward, *Rationalism v. Socialism*, p. 3.

29. Nearing, *Menace of Militarism*, p. 49.

30. Nearing, "The Master Blunder," *Bulletin of the People's Council of America*, November 28, 1917; *U.S. Military Intelligence Reports, Surveillance of Radicals in the United States, 1917–1941*, ed. Randolph Boehm (Frederick, Md.: University Publications of America, 1984), microfilm, reel 5, 0001-10110-219.

31. Jane Addams, *Peace and Bread in Time of War* (1922) (New York: Garland, 1971), p. 143; see also Chatfield, "World War I and the Liberal Pacifist in the United States," pp. 1926, 1929–31; Chatfield, *Peace and Justice*, p. 35; Carol Gruber, *Mars and Minerva: World War I and the Uses of the Higher Learning in America* (Baton Rouge: Louisiana State University Press, 1975), pp. 89–93.

32. Joseph Freeman, *An American Testament* (London: Gollancz, 1935), p. 101.

33. Bourne, "Twilight of Idols," in Resek, *War and the Intellectuals*, p. 53.

34. Addams, *Peace and Bread*, pp. 133, 150.

35. Dewey, "Conscience and Compulsion," in Joseph Ratner, ed., *Characters and Events*, Vol. 2 (1929) (New York: H. Holt, 1970), p. 577.

36. Dewey, "Conscription of Thought," p. 566, "In Explanation of our Lapse," pp. 571–75, in Ratner, *Characters and Events*.

37. Dewey, "The Future of Pacifism," in Ratner, *Characters and Events*, pp. 583–84.

38. See Bourne, "A War Diary," in Resek, *War and the Intellectuals*, pp. 39, 40, 42.

39. Randolph Bourne, "Conscience and Intelligence in War," *The Dial*, September 13, 1917, p. 193.

40. Ibid.

41. Ibid., pp. 193–95.

42. Bourne, "A War Diary," in Resek, *War and the Intellectuals*, p. 39.

43. Ibid., p. 42.

44. Bourne, "Conscience and Intelligence in War," p. 194.

45. Bourne, "War and the Intellectuals," in Resek, *War and the Intellectuals*, p. 13.

46. Randolph Bourne, "Radicals in Wartime," *A Voice in the Wilderness*, December 1917, p. 17.

47. Bourne, "Twilight of Idols," in Resek, *War and the Intellectuals*, pp. 55, 59.

48. Nearing, *Irrepressible America*, p. 23.

49. Nearing, *Germs of War*, p. 3.

50. Ibid., p. 4; Nearing, *Menace of Militarism*, p. 4.

51. Nearing, *Nation Divided*, p. 28.

52. Ibid., p. 28.

53. Nearing, *Menace of Militarism*, p. 4.

54. Dewey, "Conscience and Compulsion," in Ratner, *Characters and Events*, p. 577; on the issue of conscription, see Chatfield, "World War I and the Liberal Pacifist," pp. 1927–28; H. C. Peterson and Gilbert Fite, *Opponents of War, 1917–1918* (Madison: University of Wisconsin Press, 1957), pp. 21–42.

55. Nearing, *Menace of Militarism*, pp. 5, 7.

56. Ibid., p. 6.

57. Nearing, *Next Step*, p. 137.

58. Nearing, debate with Percy Ward, *Will the Practice of Christ's Teachings Make for Social Progress?* 1920, pp. 5–6. Nearing took the affirmative in the debate.

59. Nearing, "Education and the Open Mind," 1925, pp. 282, 284.

60. Nearing, *Educational Frontiers*, 1925, pp. 155–56.

61. Nearing, "Education and the Open Mind," p. 282.

62. [Roger Baldwin], "A Puritan Revolutionist: Scott Nearing," in Devere Allen, ed., *Adventurous Americans* (New York: Farrar and Rinehart, 1932), p. 266; Rexford G. Tugwell, *To the Lesser Heights of Morningside: A Memoir* (Philadelphia: University of Pennsylvania Press, 1982), p. 60.

63. Nearing–Ward, *Practice of Christ's Teachings*, p. 47. In an important exchange in a 1921 debate on "Rationalism vs. Socialism," Nearing told the audience at one point: "[My opponent] might have defined mind as 'God,' and said that there was a great force in the universe that manifested itself in planets and mountains and rivers and apes and people. And then he would have had me backed off the platform. He might have said with the Buddhists, that each soul comes old and full grown into the world, trailing its Karma with it, and carrying into the world all the power of that accumulated mental force." Nearing–Ward, *Rationalism vs. Socialism*, pp. 10–11.

64. Nearing–Ward, *Practice of Christ's Teachings*, p. 42.

65. Nearing, *World Events*, Summer 1952, letter 75. *World Events* was a newsletter Nearing published privately. A nearly complete collection of this newsletter can be found in the Scott and Helen Nearing Papers, Boston University Special Collections, Boston.

66. Scott Nearing Papers, draft of autobiography, bk. 6, temp. box 6, February 10, 1969, p. 444, DG 124 (SCPC).

67. Nearing, *The One Big Union of Business*, 1920, p. 31.

68. Nearing, "The Teacher, the School, and the Democracy," lecture given at the Garrick Theater, Chicago, March 12, 1916, Stenographer's transcript, Military Intelligence Division, Record Group 165, National Archives, Washington, D.C., p. 2.

69. Chatfield, *For Peace and Justice*, p. 60.

70. Nearing, *Irrepressible America*, pp. 26–27.

71. Nearing, *Next Step*, p. 149.

72. Hillquit, *Trial of Scott Nearing*, pp. 102, 175.

73. Nearing, *Next Step*, p. 86. In the aftermath of being dropped by Macmillan, Nearing concentrated his writing almost exclusively on pamphlet literature, most of which was published and distributed by the Rand School.

74. Hillquit, *Trial of Scott Nearing*, p. 99. Discussing the labor movement in his *Where is Civilization Going?* 1927, p. 60, Nearing wrote: "Propaganda institutions of the labor movement are numerous and effective. Labor papers and magazines, labor tracts, pamphlets and books, labor schools and forums, labor temples and centers of social activity all play their part. All of these efforts have been begun under the capitalist system. At the same time they are all aimed, more or less consciously, at the protection of the workers against the present economic and social system and their ultimate emancipation from it."

75. Nearing and Alexis Fermi, debate, *Has Propaganda Any Value in Education?* 1925, pp. 7, 10, 20, 22–24.

76. See James Weinstein, *The Decline of Socialism in America, 1912–1925* (1967) (New Brunswick: N.J.: Rutgers University Press, 1984), pp. 125–29, and David A. Shannon, *The Socialist Party of America* (Chicago: Quadrangle, 1955), pp. 93–98.

77. "Socialists and the Problem of War: A Symposium," *Intercollegiate Socialist*, April–May, 1917, p. 20.

78. Nearing, *Making of a Radical*, p. 145.

79. Hillquit, *Trial of Scott Nearing*, p. 110.

80. Ibid., pp. 124–25.

81. Ibid., pp. 120, 195, 197.

82. *Survey*, May 19, 1917, p. 180. Simon Patten was also among the signers. See also People's Council of America for Democracy and Peace Papers, reel 3.1, SCPC.

83. Quoted in Morris Hillquit, *Loose Leaves from a Busy Life* (New York: Macmillan, 1934), p. 171.

84. Freeman, *American Testament*, p. 106.

85. *The American Labor Year Book, 1919–1920*, New York, 1920, p. 80.

86. On the People's Council, see also, Roland Marchand, *The American Peace Movement and Social Reform, 1898–1918* (Princeton, N.J.: Princeton University Press, 1972), pp. 294–322, and Peterson and Fite, *Opponents of War*, pp. 74–80.

87. Hillquit, *Trial of Scott Nearing*, p. 105.

88. Frank C. Grubbs, Jr., *The Struggle for Labor Loyalty: Gompers, the A.F. of L. and the Pacifists, 1917–1920* (Durham, N.C.: Duke University Press, 1968), pp. 26–28.

89. Hillquit, *Trial of Scott Nearing*, p. 108.

90. Ibid., p. 108.

91. *U.S. Military Intelligence Reports, 1917–1941*, December 8, 1917.

92. Hillquit, *Trial of Scott Nearing*, p. 174.

93. Grubbs, *Struggle for Labor Loyalty*, p. 49.

94. Quoted in Chatfield, "World War I and the Liberal Pacifist," p. 1934.

95. People's Council Statement, "Why We Went to War" [Fall 1917], *U.S. Military Intelligence Reports, 1917–1941*, pp. 34–35.

96. The Reminiscences of Roger Baldwin, Part 1 (1954), pp. 55–56, in the Oral History Collection of Columbia University, New York.

97. Quoted in Peggy Lamson, *Roger Baldwin* (Boston: Houghton Mifflin, 1976), p. 73.

98. See Christopher Lasch, *The American Liberals and the Russian Revolution* (New York: McGraw-Hill, 1962), pp. 23, 27, 30; Adam Ulam, *The Bolsheviks* (New York: Macmillan, 1965), pp. 314–31; Peter Filene, *America and the Soviet Experiment, 1917–1933* (Cambridge, Mass.: Harvard University Press, 1967), pp. 9, 13.

99. Freeman, *American Testament*, p. 106.

100. Bourne, "Twilight of Idols," in Resek, *War and the Intellectuals*, p. 57.

101. While the name "council" has been explained as an attempt at a direct translation of the Russian *soviet*—see Marchand, *American Peace Movement*, p. 306. Nearing had used the term "people's council" in 1915 in his description of the social function of the classroom. See *Chautauquan Daily*, July 6, 1915, pp. 1–2.

102. People's Council Papers, microfilm, reel 3.1, SCPC.

103. Nearing, *Open Letters to Profiteers*, p. 11.

104. On the People's Council's emulation of Soviet Russia, see Frank C. Grubbs, "Council and Alliance Propaganda, 1917–1919," *Labor History* (Spring 1966):157; Merle Curti, *Peace or War: The American Struggle, 1636–1936* (New York: Norton, 1936), p. 259; Marchand, *American Peace Movement*, p. 311. There was no direct connection between the Soviets and the People's Council. Asked at his trial if the council had any "relation to any policy or program or anything in line with the Soviets," Nearing answered: "Well, except that they advocated a certain line of publicity with regard to it: no annexations and no indemnities, and free development of all peoples. That is one of the planks of the Council, I believe, and that was one of the planks of the Soviet Government platform." Hillquit, *Trial of Scott Nearing*, p. 174.

105. Quoted in Chatfield, "World War I and the Liberal Pacifist," p. 1929.

106. Grubbs, *Struggle for Labor Loyalty*, p. 22.

107. Donald Johnson, *The Challenge to American Freedoms: World War I and the Rise of the ACLU* (Lexington: University Press of Kentucky, 1963), pp. 18–19.

108. Ibid., pp. 19–20.

109. Chatfield, *For Peace and Justice*, pp. 28–29.

110. Johnson, *Challenge to American Freedoms*, pp. 22–23; American Union Against Militarism Papers, Lillian Wald to Crystal Eastman, August 29, 1917, microfilm, reel 1, SCPC.

111. Quoted in Marchand, *American Peace Movement*, p. 259.

112. Peterson and Fite, in *Opponents of War*, concluded that "by the Fall of 1917 [the People's Council] was the most important organization fighting for a quick peace" (p. 74). With the September convention, Nearing became the chairman of the executive committee of the council.

113. Nearing, *Making of a Radical*, p. 11; the executive committee of the AUAM voted to accept Nearing's resignation on October 9, 1917, AUAM Papers, Minutes of October 9 Meeting, microfilm, reel 1, SCPC.

114. See Charles DeBenedetti, *The Peace Reform in American History* (Bloomington: University of Indiana Press, 1980), pp. 103–4.

115. The proclamation and letter of protest are reprinted in Arthur S. Link, ed., *The Papers of Woodrow Wilson*, Vol. 44 (Princeton, N.J.: Princeton University Press, 1983), Louis Lochner to Woodrow Wilson, August 28, 1917, pp. 78–79.

116. *U.S. Military Intelligence Reports, 1917–1941*, September 4, 1917.

117. The best account of the convention appears in Grubbs, *Struggle for Labor Loyalty*, pp. 58–64.

118. Link, *Papers of Woodrow Wilson,* Vol. 43, Wilson to Albert Burleson, August 7, 1917, pp. 382–83.

119. Ibid., Memorandum for the Postmaster General, August 8, 1917, pp. 394–96.

120. Ibid., Burleson to Wilson, August 8, 1917, pp. 396–97.

121. Ibid., Memorandum for the Postmaster General, August 15, 1917, pp. 480–82.

122. Ibid., Wilson to Heath Dabney, August 13, 1917, p. 437.

123. *Papers of Woodrow Wilson,* Vol. 44, Diary of Joseph Daniels, August 31, 1917.

124. The most thorough and revealing account of this propaganda war is Grubbs, "Council and Alliance Propaganda: 1917–1919," pp. 156–72; see also Grubbs, *Struggle for Labor Loyalty,* pp. 40–43, and Weinstein, *Decline of Socialism in America,* p. 131.

125. Quoted in Peterson and Fite, *Opponents to War,* p. 76.

126. Quoted in James Weinstein, *The Corporate Ideal in the Liberal State, 1900–1918* (Boston: Beacon Press, 1968), p. 244; see also Stephen J. Whitfield, *Scott Nearing: Apostle of American Radicalism* (New York: Columbia University Press, 1974), pp. 82–85; and Lasch, *American Liberals and the Russian Revolution,* p. 39.

## Chapter 10

1. See Frank C. Grubbs, *The Struggle for Labor Loyalty: Gompers, the A.F. of L. and the Pacifists, 1917–1920* (Durham, N.C.: Duke University Press, 1968), p. 87; Adam Ulam, *The Bolsheviks* (New York: Macmillan, 1965), p. 331.

2. "Our Ninth Convention," *The Intercollegiate Socialist* (February–March 1918):20.

3. New York *Call,* October 7, 1918; September 29, 1918; October 18, 1918. The year 1918 was the first in which women had the right to vote in New York State.

4. See Charles Leinenweber, "Socialist in the Streets: The New York City Socialist Party in Working Class Neighborhoods, 1908–1918," *Science and Society* 41 (1977):157.

5. See Lowell M. Limpus and Burr W. Leyson, *This Man LaGuardia* (New York: Dutton, 1938), pp. 76–78.

6. Morris Hillquit, ed., *The Trial of Scott Nearing and the American Socialist Society* (New York: Rand School, 1919), p. 93.

7. Elizabeth Gurley Flynn, *The Rebel Girl: An Autobiography, My First Life, 1906–1926* (New York: International Publishers, 1955), p. 239.

8. As to wartime prosecutions, "the total number of all prosecutions during the war (from April 6, 1917, to November 11, 1918) involving freedom of speech, press, and assemblage, is estimated roughly at 4,500 to 5,000. Of these, 998 were under the Espionage Act (to July 1, 1918). This is exclusive of the draft act cases of men liable for military service. Of this total, some 1,500 are estimated to have been convicted and sent to prison." Regarding prosecution under state and city ordinances, "the total number of these cases can only be estimated as the laws invoked to control discussion and meeting were varied. . . . In New York City alone, scores of cases were brought before municipal judges." Alexander Trachtenberg, ed., *The American Labor Yearbook, 1919–1920* (New York: Rand School, 1920), pp. 91, 93–94. See also Paul L. Murphy, *The Meaning of Free Speech* (Westport, Conn.: Greenwood, 1972), p. 4.

9. James Weinstein, *The Decline of Socialism in America, 1900–1925* (1967) (New Brunswick, N.J.: Rutgers University Press, 1984), p. 145.
10. New York *Call*, August 30, 1918.
11. *New York Times*, September 12, 1918.
12. Editorial, New York *Call*, August 18, 1918.
13. Collection 6, microfilm, reels 9, 10, Socialist Party Minutes, Regular Meeting of the Executive Committee of local New York, December 12, 1917, Socialist Collection, Tamiment Library, New York University, New York; see also Fiorello LaGuardia, *The Making of an Insurgent: An Autobiography 1882–1919* (Philadelphia: Lippincott, 1948), p. 197.
14. Quoted in Limpus and Leyson, *This Man LaGuardia*, p. 72.
15. Editorial, *New York Times*, July 2, 1918.
16. Collection 6, microfilm, reels 9, 10, July 13, 1918, Socialist Collection, Tamiment Library, New York University, New York.
17. *New York Times*, July 15, 1918; LaGuardia, *Making of an Insurgent*, p. 198.
18. New York *Call*, August 30, 1918.
19. Weinstein, *Decline of Socialism*, pp. 90, 99.
20. New York *Call*, September 4, 1918.
21. Zechariah Chafee, Jr., *Freedom of Speech* (New York: Harcourt, Brace, 1920), pp. 120, 159.
22. New York *Call*, September 1, 1918.
23. Ibid.
24. *New York Times*, September 5, 1918.
25. Ibid.
26. New York *Call*, September 7, 1918.
27. Quoted in Limpus and Leyson, *This Man LaGuardia*, p. 64.
28. Nearing, *The Debs Decision*, pamphlet, 1919, p. 17.
29. Editorial, New York *Call*, September 14, 1918.
30. New York *Call*, September 23, 1918.
31. *American Labor Yearbook, 1919–1920*, pp. 91–92.
32. New York *Call*, October 24, 1918.
33. New York *Call*, October 27, 1918.
34. Ibid., September 12, 1918; *New York Times*, September 12, 1918.
35. *New York Times*, September 12, 1918; New York *Call*, September 22, 1918.
36. New York *Call*, September 11, 1918; September 22, 1918.
37. Nearing, *Letter of Acceptance*, no. 1, Wednesday, September 11, 1918, in Scott Nearing Papers, temp. box 15, Swarthmore College Peace Collection (SCPC).
38. New York *Call*, October 3, 1918.
39. Ibid., October 16, 1918.
40. Moses Rischin, *The Promised City: New York Jews, 1870–1914* (Cambridge, Mass.: Harvard University Press, 1962), pp. 133–35.
41. New York *Call*, October 11, 1918.
42. Ibid., October 17, 1918, October 19, 1918.
43. Ibid., September 12, 20, 22, 29, 1918; October 13, 23, 1918.
44. Louis Waldman, *Labor Lawyer* (New York: Dutton, 1944), pp. 82–83.
45. Nearing, *Profiteering*, pamphlet, 1918, pp. 1, 3.
46. Nearing, *The Cost of Living*, pamphlet, 1918, pp. 1, 2.
47. Nearing, *Who Owns the United States*, pamphlet, 1918, pp. 1, 2.

48. Nearing, *Profiteering*, p. 3; *Cost of Living*, p. 3; *Who Owns the United States*, p. 3.

49. New York *Call*, October 7, 1918; Nearing also published an article entitled "Patriotism" in the New York *Call*, October 20, 1918.

50. Ibid.

51. Ibid., October 14, 1918.

52. Ibid., October 21, 1918.

53. Ibid., October 20, 21, 1918.

54. Ibid., October 19, 28, 1918; see also Art Young, *Art Young's Political Primer: Scott Nearing for Congress*, 1918, in Scott Nearing Papers, temp. box 15, SCPC.

55. New York *Call*, October 30, 1918.

56. Telephone interview with Morris Novik, September 18, 1989. Novik was a Nearing supporter who in later years went on to work for LaGuardia during his long political career in New York City.

57. *New York Times*, October 29, 1918; Limpus and Leyson, *This Man LaGuardia*, p. 75.

58. LaGuardia, *Making of an Insurgent*, p. 199.

59. Quoted in Howard Zinn, *LaGuardia in Congress* (New York: Norton, 1959), p. 31.

60. Bella Rodman, *Fiorello LaGuardia* (New York: Hill and Wang, 1962), pp. 70–71.

61. New York *Call*, November 1, 1918.

62. Ibid.

63. Quoted in LaGuardia, *Making of an Insurgent*, p. 101.

64. Limpus and Leyson, *This Man LaGuardia*, p. 32.

65. Zinn, *LaGuardia in Congress*, p. 32; Limpus and Leyson, *This Man LaGuardia*, p. 77.

66. New York *Call*, November 2, 1918.

67. *New York Times*, November 2, 1918.

68. New York *Call*, November 2, 1918.

69. Editorial, ibid., November 7, 1918.

70. Board of City Record, *The City Record*, supplement; Official Canvas of the Votes, December 1918.

71. *The Liberator*, December 1918.

72. [Roger Baldwin], "A Puritan Revolutionist: Scott Nearing," in Devere Allen, ed., *Adventurous Americans* (New York: Farrar and Rinehart, 1932), p. 270.

73. New York *Call*, November 6, quoted in Stephen J. Whitfield, *Scott Nearing: Apostle of American Radicalism* (New York: Columbia University Press), p. 110.


Chapter 11

1. While federal records are becoming increasingly available and can prove a treasure trove of evidence, piecing together the scattered information can be difficult. During the war there was no clear operative center for surveillance activities. Hence, agents from various branches of the Justice Department undertook similar activities. Most important of these was Military Intelligence, often listed as MIBED (Military Intelligence Branch, Espionage Division) or simply MID (Military Intelligence Division). MID records are available through the National Archives, Washington, D.C.,

Record Group 165. An edited record of MID files is available on microfilm under the title *U.S. Military Intelligence Reports: Surveillance of Radicals, 1917–1941*, ed. Randolph Boehm (Frederick, Md.: University Publications of America, 1984). In Nearing's case, these two MID sources were unusually rich in material pertaining to his lectures. A common procedure of the agents would be to hire a stenographer to attend meetings and speeches; hence verbatim lectures, unavailable elsewhere, were reproduced. Less useful but still important were investigative case files of the Bureau of Investigation, 1908–1922, also available at the National Archives. The Bureau of Investigation was the precursor of the FBI and had responsibility more specifically for domestic activities. While this agency reported minimally on Nearing during the war, it became the chief agency conducting surveillance against him in the 1920s. Regarding Nearing's indictment and trial, Justice Department file no. 9-19-1758, also available through the National Archives, is an important source. All the above material has been declassified and is readily available. Under the Freedom of Information Act, previously classified material has been released, including a 327-page correlation summary of the Nearing case file totaling more than 1,550 pages, as well as other documents. These are for the most part heavily "sanitized," with excision purportedly made for reasons of "national security." The FBI files on Nearing show that material was collected pertaining to his activities as late as 1969. All the papers gathered under the FOIA have been deposited in the Scott and Helen Nearing Collection, Special Collections, Boston University, Boston.

2. Name index to Correspondence of the Military Intelligence Division of the War Department General Staff, 1917–1941, reel 162, 9140-1160, July 10, 1917.

3. See Zechariah Chafee, Jr., *Freedom of Speech* (New York: Harcourt, Brace, 1920), pp. 42–43.

4. U.S. Military Intelligence Reports, Surveillance of Radicals in the United States, 1917–1941, microfilm, reel 7–8, 0001-10110-559, report dated July 30, 1917 (hereafter cited as Military Intelligence Reports).

5. Ibid., reel 5, 0001-10110-219, report dated September 4, 1917.

6. Ibid., reel 7–8, 10110-559, report September 20, 1917; see also Justice Department File, Memorandum for Mr. Bettmann, April 11, 1918, no. 9-19-1758, National Archives, Washington, D.C.

7. Quoted in Elliot J. Anderson, "The Scott Nearing Controversy in Toledo, 1916–1917," *Northwest Ohio Quarterly* 29 (1957):172.

8. Military Intelligence Reports, reel 5, 0001-10110-219, October 8, 1917, October 23, 1917, November 12, 1917, November 16, 1917.

9. Ibid., reel 8, 0001-10110-559, October 23, 1917; reel 5, 0001-10110-219, October 23, 1917.

10. Ibid., reel 5, 0001-10110-219, November 28, 1917.

11. Ibid.

12. Ibid., reel 8, 0001-10110-559, December 8, 1917.

13. Ibid., stenographer's report, January 28, 1918, pp. 19–22.

14. Ibid., reel 5, 0001-10110-219, February 20, 1918.

15. Ibid., reel 8, 0001-10110-559, March 15, 1918.

16. Ibid., March 13, 1918.

17. Ibid., reel 5, 0001-10110-219, February 25, 1918.

18. Alexander Trachtenberg, ed., *The American Labor Yearbook, 1919–1920* (New York: Rand School, 1920), p. 108.

19. Justice Department File, Alfred Bettmann to John O'Brian, February 18, 1918, file no. 9-19-1758, National Archives, Washington, D.C.

20. Ibid., Bettmann to O'Brian, February 21, 1918.

21. Ibid., O'Brian to Francis Caffey, February 28, 1918.

22. Ibid., Bettmann to O'Brian, February 18, 1918.

23. Reel 54, R2683, The Papers of the Rand School of Social Science, Tamiment Library, New York University, New York.

24. On June 6, 1917, the publications committee of the Rand School authorized the publication of three pamphlets: (1) on the position of the party with reference to the war, (2) on the Russian Revolution, and (3) on militarism. Two of the pamphlets eventually published were written by Nearing, *The Great Madness*, and *The Menace of Militarism*. See *United States v. American Socialist Society*, 260 F. 885, at 889.

25. Frederick Cornell, "A History of the Rand School of Social Science," Ph.D. diss., Columbia University Teachers College, 1976, pp. 64, 68, 105.

26. Military Intelligence Reports, reel 8, 0001-10110-559, March 29, 1918.

27. Morris Hillquit, ed., *The Trial of Scott Nearing and the American Socialist Society* (New York: Rand School, 1919), p. 121.

28. Nearing, *The Great Madness*, pamphlet, p. 5.

29. Ibid., p. 36.

30. Ibid., pp. 12–13. Nearing referred to the article by Bourne only by the date and the magazine it appeared in, the *Seven Arts*. And while he cites the July 1917 issue of the magazine, in which appeared Bourne's article "Below the Battle," he quotes from "War and the Intellectuals," which appeared in the June issue.

31. Ibid., p. 12.

32. *United States v. Nearing*, 252 F. 223 (S.D.N.Y., 1918).

33. Ibid., pp. 225–26.

34. Ibid., pp. 226, 228.

35. Ibid., pp. 226, 228.

36. Military Intelligence Reports, reel 5, 0001-10110-219, April 12, 1918.

37. Ibid., reel 8, 0001-10110-559, April 11, 1918.

38. Ibid., August 5, 1918.

39. Ibid., reel 5, 0001-10110-219, May 26, 1918.

40. Ibid., June 8, 1918.

41. Ibid., July 15, 1918.

42. Ibid., September 11, 1918.

43. Joseph Freeman, *An American Testament* (London: Gollancz, 1938), p. 156.

44. Arturo Giovannitti, "Scott Nearing Reprieves Democracy," *The Liberator*, April 1919, p. 5.

45. Hillquit, *Trial of Scott Nearing*, pp. 117, 157.

46. Nearing, *Address to the Jury*, pamphlet, 1918, pp. 5, 11, 12, 19–20, 24–25, 28.

47. Ibid., pp. 7, 9, 10–11, 13.

48. Hillquit, *Trial of Scott Nearing*, p. 249; *United States v. American Socialist Society*, 260 F. 885 (S.D.N.Y., 1919).

49. Nearing, *The Making of a Radical*, 1972, p. 117.

50. *United States v. American Socialist Society*, 260 F. 885, 886, 888, 891.

51. *American Socialist Society v. United States*, 266 F. 212 (2d Cir., 1920).

52. Cornell, "History of the Rand School," p. 87.

53. Ibid., pp. 88, 89, 90.

54. Charles Recht, "The Prosecution of the Rand School of Social Science," in *American Labor Yearbook, 1919–1920*, p. 109.

55. This resolution pledging support to the Rand School was adopted by both the national and state conventions, and was printed in the New York *Call*, July 6, 1920. It also became evidence in the Lusk Committee investigation and was reprinted in their report, *Revolutionary Radicalism, Report of the Joint Legislative Committee Investigating Seditious Activities, The Senate of the State of New York, Part 1, Vol. 2*, Albany, N.Y., 1920, p. 1786.

56. Hillquit, *Trial of Scott Nearing*, p. 3.

57. *Case of the Rand School*, pamphlet, 1919, p. 1.

58. Cornell, "History of the Rand School," pp. 95–98.

59. Ibid., p. 121.

60. Nearing, *Address to the Jury*, 1918, pp. 28, 29–30.

## Chapter 12

1. Nearing, ed., *War, Patriotism, Peace* by Leo Tolstoi (New York: Vanguard, 1926), p. v.

2. Ibid., pp. iii, iv.

3. Ibid., p. 50.

4. Ibid., p. 88.

5. Ibid., p. 51.

6. Ibid., p. 42.

7. See Clair R. Goldfarb, "William Dean Howells: An American Reaction to Tolstoy," *Comparative Literature Studies* (December 1971):317–35; Kenneth S. Lynn, *William Dean Howells: An American Life* (New York: Harcourt Brace Jovanovich, 1971), pp. 282–304; Peter Brock, *Pacifism in the United States from the Colonial Era to the First World War* (Princeton, N.J.: Princeton University Press, 1968), p. 934; Henry F. May, *Protestant Churches and Industrial America* (New York: Harper, 1949), p. 153.

8. Nearing, *The Making of a Radical*, 1972, p. 29.

9. Nearing, *Where is Civilization Going?* 1927, pp. 49–51.

10. Nearing, "Why American Teachers Do Not Think," 1925, pp. 225, 226, 229.

11. Nearing, *Where is Civilization Going?* p. 46.

12. Nearing, *The Next Step: A Plan for Economic World Federation*, 1922, p. 159.

13. Nearing, *Work and Pay*, pamphlet, 1917, pp. 3–4.

14. Nearing, "The Man and the Machine," 1917, p. 47.

15. Nearing, *Work and Pay*, p. 4.

16. Nearing, *Next Step*, pp. 158, 162.

17. Nearing, *A Nation Divided; or Plutocracy versus Democracy*, pamphlet, 1920, p. 25.

18. Nearing, *Next Step*, p. 162.

19. Ibid., p. 160.

20. Nearing, *Where is Civilization Going?* p. 100.

21. Nearing, *Next Step*, pp. 153, 163.

22. Ibid., p. 161.

23. Nearing, *Making of a Radical*, pp. 26–29.

24. Joseph Freeman, *An American Testament* (London: Gollancz, 1938), p. 299.

25. See Nearing, *Making of a Radical*, pp. 79–82; "Report of Committee of Inquiry concerning Clark University," *Bulletin of the American Association of University Professors* 10 (October 1924):40–107; Upton Sinclair, *The Goose Step: A Study in American Education* (Pasadena, Calif.: the author, 1923), pp. 287–302; J. E. Kirkpatrick, *The American College and its Rulers* (New York: New Republic, 1926), pp. 133–34, 147.

26. "Report concerning Clark University," pp. 67–68; Nearing, "The Control of Public Opinion in the United States," 1922, pp. 421–23.

27. Sinclair, *Goose Step*, p. 293.

28. "Report concerning Clark University," pp. 63–69.

29. Ibid., pp. 68–69; Nearing, *Making of a Radical*, p. 80.

30. Haven D. Brackett, letter to the editor, *The Nation*, April 5, 1922, p. 397.

31. Nearing, *Making of a Radical*, p. 80.

32. "Report concerning Clark University," pp. 40–41.

33. Arthur Warner, " 'Fiat Lux'—But No Red Rays," *The Nation*, March 29, 1922, p. 364.

34. Bruce Bliven, "Free Speech, But—?" *New Republic*, April 5, 1922, p. 161.

35. Nearing, *Educational Frontiers: Simon Nelson Patten and Other Teachers*, 1925, p. 182.

36. Nearing, *Making of a Radical*, pp. 74–75, 158, 172.

37. Nearing, "Control of Public Opinion," p. 422.

38. Scott Nearing Papers, draft of autobiography, bk. 6, June 24, 1967, p. 74, DG 124 (SCPC).

39. Nearing, *The Menace of Militarism*, pamphlet, 1917, p. 42.

40. Nearing, debate with John Haynes Holmes, *Can the Church Be Radical?* 1922, pp. 17–18.

41. Ibid., pp. 21–22, 33–34.

42. Ibid., pp. 21, 23, 38.

## Chapter 13

1. Nearing, *War: Organized Destruction and Mass Murder By Civilized Nations*, 1931, p. 97.

2. Scott Nearing Papers, draft of autobiography, chapter 8, July 7, 1968, Swarthmore College Peace Collection (SCPC).

3. Nearing, *The Making of a Radical*, 1972, p. 136.

4. Nearing, *The Next Step*, 1922, p. 13.

5. Scott and Helen Nearing Papers, November 25, 1919, "Lecture with Darrow," box 9, F 1, Boston University Special Collections, Boston.

6. Nearing, *Making of a Radical*, p. 138; the quote comes from a slightly different version in a written draft of his autobiography in Scott Nearing Papers, DG 124, n.d., n.p., SCPC.

7. Nearing, *Making of a Radical*, p. 137.

8. Ibid., pp. 198, 199.

9. Scott Nearing Papers, written draft of autobiography, Scott Nearing Papers, DG 124, n.d., n.p., SCPC.

10. Nearing refers to this reorientation of his thought in *Making of a Radical*, p. 137, yet he deals with it more extensively in various versions of the draft of his autobiography, from which the previous quotes were taken; Scott Nearing Papers, bk. 6, June 23, 1967, p. 73, DG 124; bk. 6, June 24, 1967, pp. 74–75, SCPC.

11. Nearing, *Next Step*, p. 34.

12. Nearing, *Oil and the Germs of War*, pamphlet, 1923, p. 26.

13. Nearing, *The American Empire*, 1921, p. 24.

14. Ibid., pp. 23, 24, 15.

15. Ibid., pp. 24, 14, 169, 21.

16. J. A. Hobson, *Imperialism: A Study* (1902) (Ann Arbor: University of Michigan Press, 1962), p. 90.

17. Scott and Helen Nearing Papers, "The Role of Revolution," lecture, 1938, p. 3, Boston University Special Collections, Boston.

18. Nearing, *American Empire*, pp. 261, 255.

19. Ibid., p. 241.

20. Nearing, *British Labor Bids for Power: The Historic Scarboro Conference of the Trade Union Congress*, 1926, p. 29; *American Empire*, pp. 243, 250.

21. Nearing, "The Human Element in Economics," 1919?

22. Nearing, *American Empire*, p. 244.

23. Ibid., p. 254.

24. Ibid., pp. 244, 265, 254–55.

25. Scott Nearing to George Goetz [V. F. Calverton], December 23, 1924, box 11, V. F. Calverton Papers, New York Public Library, Astor, Lenox and Tilden Foundations, Rare Books and Manuscripts Division, New York.

26. Nearing, *Next Step*, p. 143.

27. Nearing, "What Can the Radical Do?" 1923, p. 5.

28. Nearing, "Taking Stock of American Labor," 1922, pp. 11–13; New York *Call*, November 19, 1922, p. 9.

29. Nearing, "Old Mexico," 1921, p. 4.

30. Letter from Nearing to Robert Nearing, October 4, 1924, in the possession of Robert Nearing, Troy, Pa.

31. Guest book, Ridgewood, N.J., in the possession of Robert Nearing, Troy, Pa. All the visitors mentioned were at Ridgewood between 1918 and 1927.

32. Joseph Freeman, *An American Testament* (London: Gollancz, 1938), p. 301.

33. Joseph Freeman, "A Blue Print of Utopia," *The Liberator*, May 1923, p. 43; Rexford G. Tugwell, *To the Lesser Heights of Morningside: A Memoir* (Philadelphia: University of Pennsylvania Press, 1982), p. 591; Nearing, *Next Step*, p. 35.

34. Nearing, *Next Step*, pp. 7, 74.

35. Ibid., p. 117.

36. Sondra R. Herman, *Eleven against War: Studies in American International Thought, 1898–1921* (Stanford, Calif.: Hoover Institution Press, 1969), pp. ix, 7–8, 137–38, 220; Herman, in Charles Chatfield, ed., *Peace Movements in America* (New York: Schocken, 1973), p. 172.

37. Nearing, *Next Step*, pp. 23–24; on the postwar proposals to build a league on an economic basis, see also Warren F. Kuehl, *Seeking World Order: The United States and International Organization to 1921* (Nashville, Tenn.: Vanderbilt University Press, 1969), pp. 252–53.

38. Nearing, "On Joining the World Court," 1923, p. 25.

39. Nearing, *Labor and the League of Nations*, pamphlet, 1919, p. 10.

40. Ibid., pp. 17, 20.

41. "Notes on the Tenth Annual Convention, I.S.S.," *Intercollegiate Socialist*, February–March 1919, p. 27.

42. Nearing, *Labor and the League of Nations*, p. 25.

43. Nearing, *Next Step*, pp. 167, 59.

44. Ibid., p. 113.

45. Ibid., p. 100.

46. Ibid., pp. 104, 107; on the prevalence of the idea of adopting U.S. federalism as a model for world federation, see Kuehl, *Seeking World Order*, pp. viii, 37, 54, 86.

47. Nearing, *Next Step*, pp. 148, 149.

48. Nearing, "What Can the Radical Do?" p. 5.

49. Justice Department, MID files, 10110-741, National Archives, Washington, D.C.

50. Nearing, "The Control of Labor Education," 1923, pp. 35, 36, 37.

51. This symposium was published as Scott Nearing, leader, *The Laws of Social Revolution: A Cooperative Study by the Labor Research Study Group*, 1926; see also Nearing, *Making of a Radical*, p. 174.

52. Whittaker Chambers, *Witness* (New York: Random House, 1952), pp. 201, 211, 212; Chambers's veracity as a "witness" must always be scrutinized. For instance, while he claims that Nearing had attended the Pan-Asiatic Congress in Baku "shortly after the Russian Revolution" in the summer of 1920, Nearing did not attend, nor did he travel to the Soviet Union until 1925. Curiously, the only other reference alluding to Nearing's alleged trip to the Soviet Union in 1920 appears in a report to J. Edgar Hoover on July 15, 1925, to the effect that "in 1920 he [Nearing] was rumored to have left the United States without a passport to attend the Third Internationale at Moscow." A. B. Lane to J. Edgar Hoover, U.S. Department of State, Doc. 61-1273, Case Control no. 8801789.

53. Freeman, *American Testament*, p. 302.

54. Nearing and Freeman, *Dollar Diplomacy: A Study in American Imperialism*, 1925, pp. v, xii; Freeman, *American Testament*, p. 303; *Dollar Diplomacy* was one of the first comprehensive studies of its kind to emerge from radical scholars and to be widely regarded by radicals in the twenties and thirties as an important work on the subject. Its lasting influence as an important survey of the first decades of American imperialist expansion is attested to by its reissue in 1966.

55. Nearing, *Making of a Radical*, pp. 171, 158–70.

56. On the American Fund for Public Service, see Gloria Garrett Samson, "Toward a New Social Order—the American Fund for Public Service: Clearinghouse for Radicalism in the 1920s," diss., University of Rochester, 1987; Peggy Lamson, *Roger Baldwin* (New York: Houghton Mifflin, 1976), pp. 148–49; The Reminiscences of Roger Baldwin, Part 1 (1954), Oral History Collection of Columbia University, New York, pp. 225–33; Nearing, *Making of a Radical*, p. 48. At the same time that Nearing became a trustee of the Garland Fund, he was also an officer of the American Civil Liberties Union and belonged to the League for Industrial Democracy and the Fellowship of Reconciliation, among other left-wing organizations.

57. Quoted in Samson, "Toward a New Social Order," p. 41.

58. "Memorandum Regarding Fund Policy for Consideration at May 14th

*Use this card as a bookmark, then tell us what you think...*

Chelsea Green publishes books on a variety of subjects related to sustainable living. Return this card for a complete catalog of our books. Please indicate the subject(s) that interest you most:

___ Renewable Energy ___ Shelter ___ Food ___ Gardening ___ Nature ___ Environment

Other topics that interest you: _____

In which book was this inserted? _____ Where purchased? _____

How would you describe your satisfaction with this book?

___ Exceeded expectations ___ Met expectations ___ Could be improved ___ Disappointed

Comments for the author or publisher: _____

_____

_____

_____

Name: _____

Address: _____

*Thank you very much!*

*People who dare to build a utopia use the same materials available to anyone, but they find surprising ways to combine them.* ∼ Gustavo Yepes, in Alan Weisman's *Gaviotas*

*Books for Sustainable Living*

CHELSEA GREEN PUBLISHING
POST OFFICE BOX 428
WHITE RIVER JUNCTION, VT

05001

*Visit us at our website*
www.chelseagreen.com

PLACE
POSTAGE
HERE

Meeting, from Scott Nearing," n.d.; "Consistent Educational Work Looking to the Establishment of a New World Order," April 3, 1924, Am 1888.3 (160) (159) Lewis Gannett Papers, by permission of Houghton Library, Harvard University, Cambridge, Mass.

59. Ibid., "American Fund for Public Service, Press Release," April 12, 1923; Reminiscences of Roger Baldwin, Part 1 (1954), p. 328; Lamson, *Roger Baldwin*, p. 149.

60. "American Fund for Public Service, Press Release," April 12, 1923; Lewis Gannett Papers, by permission of Houghton Library, Harvard University; Nearing, *Making of a Radical*, p. 173; *Revolutionary Radicalism: Its History, Purpose and Tactics: Report of the Joint Legislative Committee Investigating Seditious Activities, Filed April 24, 1920, in the Senate of the State of New York*, Vol. 2, Albany, N.Y., 1920, p. 1991; *Federated Press Bulletin*, Vol. 1, no. 1, April 9, 1921; p. 2; Vol. 1, no. 12, June 25, 1921, p. 2.

61. Arthur Warner, "Enter the Labor Press," *The Nation*, June 1, 1921, quoted in *Federated Press Bulletin*, June 11, 1921, p. 2; *Revolutionary Radicalism*, Vol. 2, pp. 1996–97.

62. Freeman, *American Testament*, p. 303.

63. Nearing, *Irrepressible America*, pamphlet, 1922, pp. 26, 27.

64. Nearing, *Making of a Radical*, p. 114; Ralph Chaplin, *Wobblie: The Rough and Tumble Story of an American Radical* (Chicago: University of Chicago Press, 1948), pp. 281–82; Nearing, "Industrial Heretics," 1922, p. 6.

65. Nearing, *Making of a Radical*, p. 114.

66. Nearing, Introduction to *Bars and Shadows: The Prison Poems of Ralph Chaplin* (New York: Leonard Press, 1922), p. 5.

67. Nearing, "Industrial Heretics," p. 6.

68. Nearing, Introduction to *Bars and Shadows*, pp. 7, 10, 11.

69. Donald Winters, Jr., *The Soul of the Wobblies: The IWW, Religion, and American Culture in the Progressive Era, 1905–1917* (Westport, Conn.: Greenwood, 1985), p. 15.

70. Nearing, Introduction to *Bars and Shadows*, p. 5.

71. Nearing, "Industrial Heretics," p. 6.

72. Milton Cantor, *The Divided Left: American Radicalism, 1900–1975* (New York: Hill and Wang, 1978), p. 67; Theodore Draper, *The Roots of American Communism* (New York: Viking, 1957), p. 87.

73. Quoted in Draper, *Roots of American Communism*, p. 111.

74. Ibid., pp. 111–12; Lewis Coser and Irving Howe, *The American Communist Party: A Critical History, 1919–1957* (New York: Praeger, 1962), p. 21; James Weinstein, *The Decline of Socialism in America, 1912–1925* (1967) (New Brunswick, N.J.: Rutgers University Press, 1984), pp. 188–89; Cantor, *Divided Left*, p. 55.

75. Quoted in Weinstein, *Decline of Socialism*, p. 189.

76. Ibid., p. 192.

77. "Manifesto and Program of the Left Wing of the American Socialist Movement," *Revolutionary Age*, February 3, 1919.

78. On the "centrist" position, see Draper, *Roots of American Communism*, pp. 143–44; Cantor, *Divided Left*, p. 69; Bertrand D. Wolfe, *A Life in Two Centuries: An Autobiography* (New York: Stein and Day, 1981), pp. 209–10. Wolfe was unable to overlook the contradiction that Nearing "had a stubborn streak of pacifism in him

along with his gently bloodthirsty injunctions to wipe out all the elites in the countries to which the revolution spread."

79. New York *Call*, March 23, 1919, p. 7.

80. Draper, *Roots of American Communism*, p. 154.

81. MID files, April 21, 1919, "Sub: Scott Nearing (lecture at Rand School)," National Archives, Washington, D.C.

82. New York *Call*, April 28, 1919, p. 2.

83. Nearing, *Violence or Solidarity; or, Will Guns Settle It?* 1919, pp. 10, 11.

84. "Violence or Solidarity?" *New York Communist*, June 14, 1919, p. 7.

85. Nearing to Granville Hicks, September 9, 1934, Granville Hicks Papers, George Arendts Research Library for Special Collections at Syracuse University, Syracuse, New York.

86. Nearing, debate with Edwin R. Seligman, *Resolved: That Capitalism Has More to Offer the Workers of the United States than Has Socialism*, 1921, p. 38.

87. James Oneal, "The American Empire," *Call Magazine*, March 6, 1921, p. 5.

## Chapter 14

1. Nearing, "What Shall I Do in the Next War?" 1923, p. 1.

2. Nearing, "The New Year," 1922, p. 8.

3. Ibid.

4. Ibid.

5. Nearing, "Thought Factories," 1922, p. 5.

6. Nearing, "New Year," p. 8.

7. Nearing, "Karl Marx and Economic Emancipation," 1923, p. 9.

8. Nearing, "The Industrial Worker," 1922, p. 8.

9. Nearing, "Karl Marx and Economic Emancipation," p. 9.

10. Ibid., p. 8.

11. Ibid., pp. 8, 9.

12. Ibid., p. 8.

13. Nearing, *The Making of a Radical*, 1972, p. 44.

14. Joseph Freeman, *An American Testament* (London: Gollancz, 1938), p. 298.

15. Nearing, *Making of a Radical*, p. 45.

16. Nellie Marguerite Seeds, "Why Martha," *Call Magazine*, May 7, 1922, p. 2; I am indebted to Robert Nearing for sharing with me some of the more intimate details of his family's life in the twenties and the circumstances of his parents' estrangement.

17. Nellie M. Seeds, "Essentials of Teacher Education," *Our Weekly News*, June 9–11, 1941, sec. 2, p. 1, in possession of Robert Nearing, Troy, Pa.

18. See *League for Industrial Democracy News Bulletin*, March–April 1924, p. 6; November 1926, p. 5; Nellie M. Seeds, "William M. Fincke, The Founder of Brookwood and Manumit," *Labor Age*, August 1927, p. 10; *New York Times*, December 5, 1946, p. 31.

19. [Roger Baldwin], "A Puritan Revolutionist: Scott Nearing," in Devere Allen, *Adventurous Americans* (New York: Farrar and Rinehart, 1932), p. 273.

20. Nearing, "Couéism," 1923, p. 6.

21. Nearing, "The Social Significance of Dr. Grant," 1923, p. 7.

22. Nearing, "Couéism," p. 7.

23. Nearing, "Couéism," p. 7; see also Sydney E. Ahlstrom, *A Religious History of the American People*, Vol. 2 (New York: Image, 1975), p. 391, and Frederick Lewis Allen, *Only Yesterday, An Informal History of the 1920s* (1931) (New York: Harper & Row, 1959), p. 69.

24. Nearing, "Couéism," p. 6.

25. Ibid., pp. 6, 7.

26. Ibid., p. 7.

27. Ibid.

28. [Baldwin], "Puritan Revolutionist," p. 273.

29. On mystical thought in twentieth-century America, see generally Hal Bridges, *American Mysticism, from William James to Zen* (New York: Harper & Row, 1970). I am also indebted to Robert Nearing for helping to explain and clarify his father's religious beliefs in the twenties and in his later life.

30. Nearing, "What Can the Radical Do?" 1923, p. 5.

31. Nearing, "What Can the Intellectual Do?" 1922, p. 4.

32. Ibid.

33. Nearing, "Can We Live Up to Our Ideals?" 1923, p. 1.

34. Nearing, "What Can the Intellectual Do?" p. 4.

35. Nearing, "What Can the Radical Do?" p. 5.

36. Nearing, "Can We Live Up to Our Ideals?" p. 1.

37. Nearing, "What Can the Radical Do?" p. 5.

38. Nearing, "What Can the Intellectual Do?" p. 4.

39. Ibid.

40. Nearing, "Can We Live Up to Our Ideals?" p. 2.

41. Ibid.

## Chapter 15

1. On the united-front policy, see James Weinstein, *The Decline of Socialism in America, 1900–1925* (1967) (New Brunswick, N.J.: Rutgers University Press, 1984), pp. 269–71; Milton Cantor, *The Divided Left: American Radicalism, 1900–1975* (New York: Hill and Wang, 1978), p. 76; Theodore Draper, *The Roots of American Communism* (New York: Viking, 1957), pp. 327–29, 343.

2. Quoted in Theodore Draper, *American Communism and Soviet Russia* (1960) (New York: Vintage, 1986), p. 34.

3. On the CPPA and the Communists, see Draper, *American Communism*, pp. 30–31.

4. Ibid., pp. 36–37.

5. Nearing, "What Can La Follette Do?" 1923, p. 3.

6. Nearing, "Scott Nearing and Party Policy," 1924, pp. 4–5.

7. William Z. Foster, "Foster's Reply to Nearing," *Daily Worker*, magazine supplement, May 17, 1924, pp. 4, 5.

8. Quoted in Draper, *American Communism*, p. 114; on the 1924 Third Party fiasco generally, see pp. 96–123.

9. Nearing, *The Making of a Radical*, 1972, p. 146.

10. Nearing, "What Can the Radical Do?" 1923, p. 5.

11. James Oneal, "The Future of the Socialist Party," *Call Magazine*, February 11, 1923, pp. 3, 9.

12. John Pepper, "The S. P.—Two Wings without a Body," *The Liberator*, May 1923, p. 33.

13. James P. Cannon, "Scott Nearing and the Workers' Party," *The Worker*, February 24, 1923, pp. 1–2.

14. See Weinstein, *Decline of Socialism in America*, p. 331, also pp. 243–44, 246; Cantor, *Divided Left*, p. 89.

15. [Roger Baldwin], "A Puritan Revolutionist: Scott Nearing," in Devere Allen, ed., *Adventurous Americans* (New York: Farrar and Rinehart, 1932), p. 270.

16. Nearing, debate with Bertrand Russell, *Resolved: That the Soviet Form of Government Is Applicable to Western Civilization* (Nearing in the Affirmative), pamphlet, 1924, pp. 24, 51.

17. Ibid., p. 51.

18. Ibid., p. 53.

19. Ibid., pp. 23, 54, 55.

20. "American Labor and Socialist Party Symposium," *Intercollegiate Socialist*, April–May 1919, pp. 11–12.

21. Nearing, "The Chicago Conference," 1922, p. 4.

22. Nearing, "The Social Significance of Dr. Grant," 1923, p. 9.

23. Earl R. Browder, "What is Collaboration of Classes?" *Workers Monthly*, June 1925, pp. 366–68.

24. Nearing, *The British General Strike*, 1926, p. 100.

25. Nearing, *Can Britain Escape Revolution?* pamphlet, 192[4], pp. 3, 4.

26. Ibid., pp. 2, 3.

27. Nearing, *British General Strike*, p. 18.

28. Ibid., pp. vi, 2.

29. Ibid., p. 13.

30. Ibid., p. 18.

31. Nearing, *Making of a Radical*, p. 146.

32. Nearing, *Glimpses of the Soviet Republic*, pamphlet, 1926, p. 3.

33. Nearing, *Making of a Radical*, p. 140. The writings from this trip included articles he wrote for the *Federated Press Bulletin* as well as *Glimpses of the Soviet Republic*, 1926; *Education in Soviet Russia*, 1926; "The Organizing of Educational Workers in Soviet Russia," 1926; "Higher Education in Russia," 1926; and "Russianizing American Education," 1926.

34. Nearing, *Education in Soviet Russia*, p. 151.

35. Harry Laidler and Norman Thomas, eds., *Prosperity? A Symposium* (New York: Vanguard, 1927), p. 59.

36. Nearing and Jack Hardy, *The Economic Organization of the Soviet Union* 1927, p. 39.

37. Ibid., pp. xvii–xviii, 221.

38. Nearing, *World Labor Unity*, 1926, p. 4; "The Soviet Union Forges Ahead," 1929, p. 12.

39. Nearing, "Return of the Native," 1926, p. 18.

40. Nearing, "Answering Uncle Sam," 1923, p. 19.

41. Nearing, symposium with Sam A. Lewisohn, M. C. Rorty, and Morris Hillquit, *The Future of Capitalism and Socialism in America*, pamphlet, 1927, p. 20.

42. Nearing, "Answering Uncle Sam," p. 21.

43. Military Intelligence Division, Record Group 165, "Stability of Russian

Soviet Government—Scott Nearing Meeting Held under the Auspices of the League for Industrial Democracy—Play House, Washington, D.C.—Saturday, May 8, 1926," pp. 1–3. National Archives, Washington, D.C.

44. Harry W. Laidler and Norman Thomas, eds., *New Tactics in Social Conflict* (New York: Vanguard, 1926), p. 27.

45. Nearing, "Conflict and Avoidance," 1927, p. 26.

46. Nearing, *Making of a Radical*, p. 147.

47. Baldwin's account is in "A Puritan Revolutionist: Scott Nearing," p. 270; Joseph Freeman, *An American Testament* (London: Gollancz, 1938), p. 309; Michael Gold, "Change the World," *Daily Worker*, January 31, 1935, in the Scott and Helen Nearing Papers, Boston University Special Collections, Boston.

48. Scott Nearing Papers, handwritten notes, April 29, 1969, bk. 4, p. 85E, DG 124, Swarthmore College Peace Collection (SCPC).

49. See Draper, *American Communism*, p. 219.

50. Freeman, *American Testament*, p. 309.

51. Quoted, ibid., p. 311.

52. Ibid., p. 311.

53. Quoted, ibid., p. 311.

54. Ibid., pp. 311–12.

55. Quoted, ibid., p. 312.

56. Quoted, ibid., p. 313.

57. Quoted, ibid., p. 310.

58. Quoted, ibid., pp. 313–14.

59. Draper, *American Communism*, pp. 243, 249, 272, 298; Cantor, *Divided Left*, p. 93.

60. Nearing, *Making of a Radical*, p. 147.

61. See Gloria Garrett Samson, "Toward a New Social Order—the American Fund for Public Service: Clearinghouse for Radicalism in the 1920s," diss., University of Rochester, 1987, p. 298. Samson claims that the shift in Nearing's vote from September 1926 to January 1927 was "unexplained and unexplainable." The evidence indicates that party politics offers a partial explanation.

62. Ibid., p. 147.

63. Draper, *American Communism*, p. 268.

64. [Baldwin], "Puritan Revolutionist," p. 271; Nearing, *Making of a Radical*, p. 147.

65. Harry Laidler and Norman Thomas, eds., *Prosperity? A Symposium* (New York: Vanguard, 1927), p. 228.

66. Ibid., p. 205.

67. Ibid., pp. 207, 209.

68. Ibid., pp. 214–16.

69. Ibid., pp. 212–13.

70. Draper, *American Communism*, p. 197; Harvey Klehr, *The Heyday of American Communism: The Depression Decade* (New York: Basic Books, 1984), p. 7.

71. Ibid., pp. 213, 214, 230.

72. [Baldwin], "Puritan Revolutionist," p. 264.

73. Nearing, *Whither China?: An Economic Interpretation of Recent Events in the Far East*, 1927, p. 12.

74. Ibid., pp. 63, 64.

75. Nearing, *Russia Turns East: The Triumph of Soviet Diplomacy in Asia*, pamphlet, 1926, pp. 29, 30.

76. Nearing, *Whither China?* p. 65.

77. Nearing, "Revolution in China," 1930, p. 16.

78. Ibid., pp. 183, 184, 206.

79. Nearing, *Whither China?* p. 11. Over the course of his life, the reasons Nearing gave for traveling to China varied. In 1927, he claimed to want to see the Revolution firsthand, which would not have been unlike his motive for wanting to observe the social circumstances firsthand elsewhere, whether in the United States, Mexico, Europe, or the Soviet Union. There is no indication that his trip had any connection to his membership in the party or that he traveled in an official capacity for the party. In his autobiography, he recounts that he had been invited by a former student at the Wharton School, now an important figure in China, to join the Railway Administration as an advisor. This, he explains, was the reason for his interest in China, the writing of the book, and his trip. He added that he left "expecting to stay for years."

Since Nearing went to China via a lecture tour across Canada, stayed for only three months before going on to the Soviet Union for November 7 celebrations, then on to Berlin, and then back to the United States, his trip was in keeping with his pattern of firsthand study and travel throughout the decade. Given the larger body of evidence, including his recent, long-awaited acceptance into the party, it would appear odd for him to have left the United States for another country for an extended length of time.

80. Emma Goldman, *Living My Life* (1931) (Salt Lake City, Utah: Gibbs H. Smith, 1982), p. 987.

81. Nearing, *Making of a Radical*, pp. 140, 142–43.

82. Ibid., p. 144.

83. Joseph Freeman, *American Testament*, p. 531.

84. Ibid., p. 183.

85. Janice R. MacKinnon and Stephen R. MacKinnon, *Agnes Smedley: The Life and Times of an American Radical* (Berkeley: University of California Press, 1988), p. 364.

## Chapter 16

1. *Daily Worker*, August 9, 1928, p. 1.

2. Harry Laidler and Norman Thomas, eds., *Prosperity? A Symposium* (New York: Vanguard, 1927), pp. 211, 228.

3. *Daily Worker*, August 30, 1928; September 18, 1928.

4. Nearing, "The Political Outlook for the Workers (Communist) Party—a Discussion Article," 1928, pp. 756–59.

5. Theodore Draper, *American Communism and Soviet Russia* (1960) (New York: Vintage, 1986), pp. 349, 354.

6. Wilson Record, *The Negro and the Communist Party* (Chapel Hill, N.C.: University of North Carolina Press, 1951), pp. 14–15; Draper, *American Communism*, pp. 349, 354.

7. Quoted in Draper, *American Communism*, p. 349.

8. Nearing and Frank Watson, *Economics*, 1908, pp. 134–35.

9. Scott Nearing Papers, draft of autobiography, bk. 6, June 29, 1969, p. 84, DG 124, Swarthmore College Peace Collection (scpc).

10. Jervis Anderson, *A. Philip Randolph: A Biographical Portrait* (Berkeley: University of California Press, 1986), pp. 85–93.

11. Nearing, "Business and War," 1917, pp. 11–12; "War Shouters and War Contracts," 1918, pp. 11–12; "The Big Ten," 1919, pp. 27–28.

12. "Scott Nearing," *The Messenger*, March 1919, p. 23.

13. *The Messenger*, June 1922.

14. Nearing, *Black America*, 1929, pp. 5, 221–22.

15. Ibid., pp. 5, 132, 249.

16. Ibid., p. 70.

17. Ibid., p. 106.

18. Ibid., pp. 7, 142.

19. Ibid., p. 256.

20. Ibid., pp. 223, 227, 228.

21. Ibid., pp. 153, 209–12.

22. Ibid., p. 257.

23. Ibid., pp. 262, 261.

24. Ibid., p. 262.

25. Quoted in William Stott, *Documentary Expression in Thirties America* (New York: Oxford University Press, 1973), p. 76.

26. On the cultural implications of photography, see Stott, *Documentary Expression*, and Susan Sontag, *On Photography* (New York: Farrar, Straus and Giroux, 1980).

27. Nearing to Joseph Freeman, April 7, 1929, Joseph Freeman Collection, Hoover Institution Archives, Stanford, Calif.

28. Walter B. Rideout, *The Radical Novel in the United States, 1900–1954* (New York: Hill and Wang, 1956), p. 194; Sterling Brown, *The Negro in American Fiction* (1937) (Port Washington, N.Y.: Kennikat Press, 1968), p. 181.

29. See generally Raymond Williams, *Marxism and Literature* (Oxford: Oxford University Press, 1977), and Terry Eagleton, *Marxism and Literary Criticism* (Berkeley: University of California Press, 1976).

30. Daniel Aaron, *Writers on the Left* (1961) (New York: Oxford University Press, 1977), p. 94.

31. It should be noted that Trotsky's discussion of proletarian art argued that the proletariat was a transitory class and should not attempt to perpetuate itself as a class through proletarian art. Its goal was to wipe out all classes and produce classless art. Trotsky's writing on art and revolution appeared in an English translation in 1926.

32. James B. Gilbert, *Writers and Partisans, A History of Literary Radicalism in America* (New York: John Wiley, 1968), pp. 80–81; Eagleton, *Marxism and Literary Criticism*, pp. 37–39.

33. Gilbert, *Writers and Partisans*, pp. 79–84.

34. Aaron, *Writers on the Left*, pp. 101–2; Freeman discusses the founding of the *New Masses* in *An American Testament* (London: Gollancz, 1938), pp. 336–48. According to Freeman, Nearing also ran the business department of the magazine.

35. Gilbert, *Writers and Partisans*, p. 84.

36. Aaron, *Writers on the Left*, p. 209.

37. Gilbert, *Writers and Partisans*, pp. 74–75, 82–84.

38. Freeman, "The Wilsonian Era in American Literature," *Modern Quarterly*, June–September, 1927, pp. 132, 133, 135.

39. See Richard H. Pells, *Radical Visions and American Dreams* (New York: Harper & Row, 1973), p. 151.

40. Nearing, *Free Born: An Unpublishable Novel*, 1932, p. 172.

41. Ibid., p. 166.

42. Ibid., p. 171.

43. Ibid., pp. 169, 177, 181, 183.

44. Rideout, *Radical Novel in the United States*, pp. 219, 317; only one other novel of the genre, Agnes Smedley's *Daughter of Earth* (1929), has a major radical character who advocates free love.

45. Nearing, *Free Born*, pp. 175, 188, 189, 190.

46. Ibid., p. 203.

47. Ibid., pp. 235–36.

48. Ibid., p. 237.

49. Nearing to Joseph Freeman, June 21, 1930, Joseph Freeman Collection, Hoover Institution Archives, Stanford, Calif.

50. Scott Nearing Papers, notes for autobiography, bk. 6, November 2, 1967, p. 196, DG 124, SCPC.

51. Nearing, *Free Born*, "Publishers Note."

52. Helen K. Nearing, Harborside, Me., to author [September 1981].

## Chapter 17

1. On the Third Period, see Theodore Draper, *American Communism and Soviet Russia* (1960) (New York: Vintage, 1986), pp. 300–306; Milton Cantor, *The Divided Left: American Radicalism, 1900–1975* (New York: Hill and Wang, 1978), p. 92.

2. Draper, *American Communism*, pp. 305–6.

3. There were 9,300 party members in 1929. In 1930, the number fell to 7,545. See Harvey Klehr, *The Heyday of American Communism: The Depression Decade* (New York: Basic Books, 1984), p. 9.

4. Ibid., pp. 272, 298, 307, 414–15; Cantor, *Divided Left*, p. 93.

5. Nearing to George Goetz [V. F. Calverton], March 2, 1933, V. F. Calverton Papers, Rare Books and Manuscripts Division, New York Public Library, Astor, Lenox and Tilden Foundations, New York.

6. Nearing, *The Making of a Radical*, 1972, p. 149; Scott Nearing Papers, draft of autobiography, April 29, 1968, bk. 6, p. 85H, DG 124, Swarthmore College Peace Collection (SCPC).

7. Nearing to Freeman, April 7, 1929, Joseph Freeman Collection, Hoover Institution Archives, Stanford, Calif.

8. Nearing, *The Twilight of Empire: An Economic Interpretation of Imperialist Cycles*, 1930, p. 15.

9. Ibid., pp. 15, 16.

10. Ibid., pp. 21, 127, 130.

11. Nearing, *Where is Civilization Going?* 1927, pp. 77, 78, 90.

12. Nearing, *Twilight of Empire*, pp. 136, 137.

13. Ibid., p. 167.

14. Ibid., p. 162.

15. Ibid., p. 169.

16. Ibid., p. 140.

17. Ibid., p. 171.

18. Ibid., pp. 167–68.

19. Ibid., pp. 168, 169.

20. V. I. Lenin, *Imperialism: The Highest Stage of Capitalism* (1916) (New York: International Publishers, 1939), p. 117.

21. Ibid., p. 88.

22. Ibid., pp. 12, 93.

23. Ibid., pp. 121, 91.

24. Ibid., pp. 96–97.

25. Nearing, *Twilight of Empire*, p. 92.

26. Nearing, *Making of a Radical*, p. 149.

27. Ibid.; the quote is actually taken from a slightly different version, which appears in the draft of the autobiography, Scott Nearing Papers, DG 124, April 29, 1969, bk. 6, p. 85J, SCPC.

28. *Daily Worker*, editorial page, January 8, 1930; Nearing, *Making of a Radical*, pp. 151–52.

29. Nearing, *Making of a Radical*. Nearing's departure from the party as well as his continued alliance to it created some confusion about his actual association. When the House Committee on Un-American Activities probed the question of Nearing's membership on September 5, 1939, Earl Browder, secretary of the party, stated: "Oh, I know that Scott Nearing was in and out of the party a number of times. . . . I think once he was expelled and once he dropped out." Browder was wrong about Nearing entering and reentering the party, but he was correct that Nearing was expelled and that he dropped out. Investigation of Un-American Propaganda Activities in the U.S. Special Committee of Un-American Activities, House of Representatives, 76th Cong., H. Res. 282, Vol. 7, p. 4459.

30. Klehr, *Heyday of American Communism*, pp. 17–27.

31. Earl Browder, "A 'Fellow Traveler' Looks at Imperialism," *The Communist*, June 1930, p. 568.

32. Ibid., pp. 564, 565.

33. Ibid., p. 562.

34. Michael Gold, "Change the World," *Daily Worker*, January 21, 1935; February 22, 1935, box 9, file 12, Scott and Helen Nearing Papers, Boston University, Special Collections, Boston.

35. [Roger Baldwin], "A Puritan Revolutionist: Scott Nearing," in Devere Allen, ed., *Adventurous Americans* (New York: Farrar and Rinehart, 1932).

36. Scott Nearing Papers, draft of autobiography, DG 124, April 29, 1968, bk. 6, p. 85L; June 30, 1967, bk. 6, p. 92, SCPC.

37. Nearing, *Making of a Radical*, p. 153.

38. [Baldwin], "Puritan Revolutionist," p. 275.

39. This quote is a composite of the passage that appears in the published autobiography and the earlier unpublished version. Nearing, *Making of a Radical*, p. 153; Scott Nearing Papers, draft of autobiography, April 29, 1968, bk. 6, p. 85L, SCPC.

40. [Roger Baldwin], "A Puritan Revolutionist: Scott Nearing," *World Tomorrow*, July 1930, p. 308.

## Chapter 18

1. This disjointed character of the autobiography was also apparent to Helen Nearing. In acknowledgments in an early draft of the autobiography, Nearing wrote:

"I am particularly grateful because she [Helen] has not agreed with many parts of the book. Her disagreement was particularly resolute when she typed part III. . . . 'This is not autobiography,' she insisted. 'It is just another book—history, economic charts + tables, world events and the rest. Why not write a regular autobiography.'" Scott Nearing Papers, draft of autobiography, bk. 6, July 17, 1968, p. 269D, DG 124, Swarthmore College Peace Collection (SCPC).

2. I am indebted to Helen Nearing for pointing out the parallels Nearing intended between her and the characters in the novel.

3. Nearing, *Free Born: An Unpublishable Novel*, 1932, pp. 86, 87.

4. Scott and Helen married in 1948, upon the death of Nellie Seeds Nearing.

5. Helen Nearing, *The Good Life Album of Helen and Scott Nearing* (New York: Dutton, 1974), pp. 8–9; on Helen's relations with the Theosophical Society and Krishnamurti, see generally Mary Lutyens, *Krishnamurti: The Years of Awakening* (1975) (New York: Avon, 1983).

6. Helen Nearing, *Good Life Album*, pp. 8, 9.

7. Michael Gold, "Change the World," *Daily Worker*, January 21, 1935, p. 7, February 22, 1935.

8. Nearing, "Teaching Is My Job," leaflet, 1944.

9. See Nearing, *Man's Search for the Good Life*, 1974, pp. 1–10.

10. Nearing and Helen Nearing, *Living the Good Life: How to Live Sanely and Simply in a Troubled World* (1954) (New York: Schocken, 1977), pp. vii, 10.

11. Ibid., p. ix.

12. Nearing, *Democracy Is Not Enough*, 1945, p. 98.

13. Nearing, *Freedom: Promise and Menace*, 1961, pp. 6–7.

14. Nearing and Helen Nearing, *Living the Good Life*, p. 194.

15. Nearing, *Democracy Is Not Enough*, p. 98.

16. Nearing, *Making of a Radical*, 1972, p. 207.

17. Nearing and Helen Nearing, *Living the Good Life*, pp. 5, vii.

18. Ibid., pp. 158, 161; see generally chapter 7, "Living in a Community."

19. Paul Goodman, introduction to Nearing and Helen Nearing, *Living the Good Life*, p. xxi.

20. Nearing and Helen Nearing, *Living the Good Life*, pp. 159, 166, 173.

21. Nearing, *Making of a Radical*, p. 211.

22. Nearing and Helen Nearing, *Living the Good Life*, p. 192.

23. Ibid., pp. 126, 185, 192.

24. Nearing, *Making of a Radical*, p. 229.

25. Nearing, *Freedom: Promise and Menace*, p. 11.

26. Nearing and Helen Nearing, *Living the Good Life*, p. 126.

27. Nearing, *Freedom: Promise and Menace*, pp. 82–83.

28. Ibid., p. 62.

29. Scott Nearing to John Scott, January 29, 1931, in the possession of Elka Schumann, Glover, Vt. Elka Schumann, John Scott's daughter, provided extensive correspondence between John Scott and Scott Nearing from the late 1920s to the early 1940s. Also, I am indebted to Robert Nearing for helping me to sort out details of his family's life.

30. Quoted in Stephen Kotkin, introduction to reissue of John Scott's *Behind the Urals* (1942) (Bloomington: University of Indiana Press, 1989), pp. xi–xii.

31. John Scott to Scott Nearing, no date [1930], in the possession of Elka Schumann, Glover, Vt.

32. Scott Nearing to John Scott, August 1931, in the possession of Elka Schumann, Glover, Vt.

33. Ibid.

34. Scott Nearing to John Scott, October 29 [1930], in the possession of Elka Schumann, Glover, Vt.

35. Quoted in Stephen J. Whitfield, *Scott Nearing: Apostle of American Radicalism* (New York: Columbia University Press, 1974), p. 142.

36. Scott Nearing to John Scott, August 1931; Scott Nearing to John Scott, postmarked August 25, 1931; Scott Nearing to John Scott, August 20, 1931, in the possession of Elka Schumann, Glover, Vt.

37. Scott Nearing to John Scott, January 29, 1931, in the possession of Elka Schumann, Glover, Vt.

38. See Kotkin, introduction, pp. xiii–xiv; Whitfield, *Scott Nearing*, p. 181.

39. John Scott, *Behind the Urals*, pp. 3–4.

40. John Scott to Scott Nearing, February 2, 1934, in the possession of Elka Schumann, Glover, Vt.

41. John Scott to Scott Nearing, June 28, 1934, in the possession of Elka Schumann, Glover, Vt.

42. Telephone interview with Robert Nearing, October 10, 1989.

43. Scott Nearing to John Scott, April 30, 1951, in the possession of Masha Scott, Ridgefield, Conn.

44. Nearing to George Goetz [V. F. Calverton], March 13, 1938, September 26, 1939, box 11, V. F. Calverton Papers, Rare Books and Manuscripts Division, New York Public Library, Astor, Lenox and Tilden Foundations, New York.

45. Nearing, *Making of a Radical*, pp. 267–68.

46. Nearing, "Fuhrer Nationalism," lecture, 1938, Scott and Helen Nearing Papers, Boston University Special Collections, Boston.

47. Nearing, *Making of a Radical*, p. 272.

48. Interview with author, Harborside, Me., March 20, 1983.

49. Nearing, *Making of a Radical*, pp. 257, 265, 272.

50. Scott and Helen Nearing to "Friends," September 3, 1949, in the possession of Helen Nearing, Harborside, Me.

51. See reviews of *Living the Good Life* in *Catholic Worker*, March 1955, and *Journal of Natural Hygiene*, April–May 1955, pp. 49–54.

52. Nearing and Helen Nearing, *Living the Good Life*, pp. 4, 162; see also their *The Maple Sugar Book* (1950), 1972, p. xii.

53. Nearing and Helen Nearing, *Living the Good Life*, p. 147.

54. Ibid., p. 6.

55. Ibid., p. viii.

56. Scott Nearing, *World Events* 6, no. 3 (Summer 1949), letter 63, p. 23, box 9, file 5, in Scott and Helen Nearing Papers, Boston University Special Collections, Boston.

57. Nearing to "Friends," September 3, 1949, in the possession of Helen Nearing, Harborside, Me.

58. Nearing and Helen Nearing, *Maple Sugar Book*, pp. 236, 244.

59. Nearing and Helen Nearing, *Living the Good Life*, p. xi.

60. Outline for "Vermont Life," February 4, 1951, box 1, file 1, in Scott and Helen Nearing Papers, Boston University Special Collections, Boston.

61. Scott Nearing to John Scott, October 2, 1951, in the possession of Masha Scott, Ridgefield, Conn.

62. Nearing and Helen Nearing, *Living the Good Life*, p. 183.

63. Ibid., pp. 4, 181.

64. Ibid., pp. ix, 144.

65. Ibid., pp. 184, 187.

66. Ibid., pp. 5, 6.

67. Nearing, *Making of a Radical*, p. 203.

68. Scott Nearing to John Scott, August 4, 1952, in the possession of Masha Scott, Ridgefield, Conn.

69. Roger Baldwin to John Scott, November 10, 1963, box 26, Roger Baldwin Papers, Princeton University Library, Princeton, N.J., published with permission of Princeton University Library.

70. John Scott to Roger Baldwin, November 25, 1963, box 26, Princeton University Library, Princeton, N.J., published with permission of Princeton University Library.

71. Telephone interview with Robert Nearing, October 10, 1989.

72. *Catholic Worker*, March 1955, box 1, file 2, Scott and Helen Nearing Papers, Boston University Special Collections, Boston.

73. Norman Williams to Scott and Helen Nearing, December 5, 1954, Scott and Helen Nearing Papers, Boston University Special Collections, Boston.

74. Jane Addams, *Twenty Years at Hull House* (1910) (New York: Macmillan, 1936), p. 274.

75. When the book originally appeared in 1954, it sold approximately 10,000 copies.

76. Martin Jezer, "Don't Admire the Turnips," *New Republic*, September 12, 1970, pp. 26–28. See also John Thompson, "Away from It All," *Harper's Magazine*, November 1970, pp. 120–22; Sonya Rudikoff, "O Pioneers," *Commentary*, July 1972, pp. 62–74; *The Nation*, June 17, 1972, p. 765; *New Republic*, February 5, 1972, p. 25.

77. Nearing and Helen Nearing, *Continuing the Good Life*, 1979, pp. 150–51.

78. Ibid., p. 156.

79. On this notion of anticulture as distinct from counterculture, see Frances Fitzgerald, *Cities on a Hill* (New York: Simon and Schuster, 1987), p. 408.

80. Ibid., p. 150.

81. Nearing, *Man's Search for the Good Life*, 1974, p. 50.

82. Unfinished manuscript of "Social Forces," draft dated December 6, 1978, p. 4. The full title was "Social Forces and the Human Future: Beyond Sociology and into Cosmology." Scott and Helen Nearing Papers, Boston University Special Collections, Boston.

83. Interview with author, Harborside, Me., March 20, 1983.

84. Nearing and Helen Nearing, *Living the Good Life*, p. 197.

# Manuscript Sources

American Union against Militarism Papers, Swarthmore College Peace Collection, Swarthmore, Pa.

Roger Baldwin, Oral History Collection of Columbia University, New York, N.Y.

Roger Baldwin Papers, Princeton University Library, Princeton, N.J.

Frederick Blossom Papers, State Historical Society of Wisconsin, Madison, Wis.

Randolph Bourne Papers, Columbia University, New York, N.Y.

Earl Browder Papers, George Arendts Research Library, Syracuse University, Syracuse, N.Y.

V. F. Calverton Papers, Rare Books and Manuscripts Division, New York Public Library, Astor, Lenox and Tilden Foundations, New York, N.Y.

Max Eastman Papers, Lilly Library, Indiana University, Bloomington, Ind.

Joseph Freeman Papers, Hoover Institution, Stanford, Calif.

Lewis Gannett Papers, Houghton Library, Harvard University, Cambridge, Mass.

Powers Hapgood Papers, Lilly Library, Indiana University, Bloomington, Ind.

Granville Hicks Papers, Syracuse University, Syracuse, N.Y.

Jacob H. Hollander Papers, Johns Hopkins University, Baltimore, Md.

Charles Humbolt Papers, Yale University, New Haven, Conn.

Intercollegiate Socialist Society, Tamiment Library, New York University, New York, N.Y.

Henry Raymond Mussey Papers, Houghton Library, Harvard University, Cambridge, Mass.

National Civic Federation Collection, New York Public Library, New York, N.Y.

Nearing Case File, The American Association of University Professors Archives, Washington, D.C.

Scott Nearing Papers, Swarthmore College Peace Collection, Swarthmore College, Swarthmore, Pa.

Scott and Helen Nearing Papers, Boston University Special Collections, Boston, Mass.

People's Council for Democracy and Peace Papers, Swarthmore College Peace Collection, Swarthmore College, Swarthmore, Pa.

Frances Perkins Papers, Columbia University, New York, N.Y.

Rand School of Social Science Papers, Tamiment Library, New York University, New York, N.Y.

John Reed Papers, Houghton Library, Harvard University, Cambridge, Mass.
John Scott Papers, State Historical Society of Wisconsin, Madison, Wis.
Upton Sinclair Papers, Lilly Library, Indiana University, Bloomington, Ind.
Socialist Party Collection, Tamiment Library, New York University, New York, N.Y.
Joel Springarn Papers, New York Public Library, New York, N.Y.
Rose Pastor Stokes Papers, Tamiment Library, New York University, New York, N.Y.
Rose Pastor Stokes Papers, Yale University, New Haven, Conn.
Toledo University Trustees Papers, Toledo University, Toledo, Ohio.
Rexford Tugwell Papers, National Archives and Records Administration, Franklin D. Roosevelt Library, Hyde Park, N.Y.
Harvey Weinberger Papers, Yale University, New Haven, Conn.
Wharton School Papers, University of Pennsylvania Archives, University of Pennsylvania, Philadelphia, Pa.
Charles Erskine Scott Wood Papers, Huntington Library, San Marino, Calif.

# Bibliography: The Works of Scott Nearing

## Books

With Frank Watson. *Economics*. New York: Macmillan, 1908.

*Social Adjustment*. Ph.D. diss. New York: Macmillan, 1910.

*The Solution of the Child Labor Problem*. New York: Moffat, Yard, 1911.

With Henry Reed Burch. *Elements of Economics*. New York: Macmillan, 1912.

*The Super Race: An American Problem*. New York: B.W. Huebsch, 1912.

With Nellie Seeds Nearing. *Women and Social Progress: A Discussion of the Biologic, Domestic, Industrial, and Social Possibilities of American Women*. New York: Macmillan, 1912.

*Financing the Wage Earner's Family: A Survey of the Facts Bearing on Income and Expenditures in the Families of American Wage Earners*. New York: B.W. Huebsch, 1913.

*Social Religion: An Interpretation of Christianity in Terms of Modern Life*. New York: Macmillan, 1913.

*Social Sanity*. New York: Moffat, Yard, 1913.

*Reducing the Cost of Living*. Philadelphia: G.W. Jacobs, 1914.

*Wages in the United States, 1908–1910: A Study of State and Federal Wage Statistics*. New York: Macmillan, 1914.

*Anthracite: An Instance of a Natural Resource Monopoly*. Philadelphia: John C. Winston, 1915.

*Income: An Examination of the Returns for Services Rendered and from Property Owned in the United States*. New York: Macmillan, 1915.

*The New Education: A Review of the Progressive Educational Movements of the Day*. Chicago: Row, Peterson, 1915.

With Jessie Field. *Community Civics*. New York: Macmillan, 1916.

*Poverty and Riches: A Study of the Industrial Regime*. Philadelphia: John C. Winston, 1916.

*The American Empire*. New York: Rand School, 1921.

*The Next Step: A Plan for Economic World Federation*. Ridgewood, N.J.: N. S. Nearing, 1922.

With Joseph Freeman. *Dollar Diplomacy: A Study in American Imperialism*. New York: B.W. Huebsch, Viking, 1925.

*Educational Frontiers: Simon Nelson Patten and Other Teachers*. New York: T. Seltzer, 1925.

*The British General Strike*. New York: Vanguard, 1926.

With associates. *The Law of Social Revolution: A Cooperative Study by the Labor Research Study Group*. New York: Social Science, 1926.

Ed. Leo Tolstoi. *War, Patriotism, Peace*. New York: Vanguard, 1926.

With Jack Hardy. *The Economic Organization of the Soviet Union*. New York: Vanguard, 1927.

*Where is Civilization Going?* New York: Vanguard, 1927.

*Whither China? An Economic Interpretation of Recent Events in the Far East*. New York: International Publishers, 1927.

*Black America*. New York: Vanguard, 1929.

*The Twilight of Empire: An Economic Interpretation of Imperialist Cycles*. New York: Vanguard, 1930.

*War: Organized Destruction and Mass Murder by Civilized Nations*. New York: Vanguard, 1931.

*Free Born: An Unpublishable Novel*. New York: Urquart, 1932.

*Democracy Is Not Enough*. New York: Island Workshop, 1945.

*The Tragedy of Empire*. New York: Island, 1945.

*United World: The Road to International Peace*. New York: Island, 1945.

*The Soviet Union as a World Power*. New York: Island, 1946.

*War or Peace?* New York: Island, 1946.

*The Revolution of Our Time*. New York: Island, 1947.

With Helen Nearing. *The Maple Sugar Book*. New York: J. Day, 1950.

*Economics for the Power Age*. New York: J. Day, 1952. Citations in text from 1972 edition. New York: Schocken Books.

With Helen Nearing. *Living the Good Life: How to Live Sanely and Simply in a Troubled World*. Harborside, Me.: Social Science Institute, 1954. Citations in text from 1977 edition New York: Schocken Books.

*Man's Search for the Good Life*. Harborside, Me.: Social Science Institute, 1954.

With Helen Nearing. *USA Today*. Harborside, Me.: Social Science Institute, 1955.

With Helen Nearing. *Brave New World*. Harborside, Me.: Social Science Institute, 1958.

With Helen Nearing. *Socialists around the World*. New York: Monthly Review, 1958.

*Freedom: Promise and Menace, A Critique of the Cult of Freedom*. Harborside, Me.: Social Science Institute, 1961.

*Socialism in Practice: The Transformation of East Europe*. New York: New Century, 1962.

*The Conscience of a Radical*. Harborside, Me.: Social Science Institute, 1965.

*The Making of a Radical: A Political Autobiography*. New York: Harper and Row, 1972.

*Man's Search for the Good Life*. rev. ed. Harborside, Me.: Social Science Institute, 1974.

*Civilization and Beyond: Learning from History*. Harborside, Me.: Social Science Institute, 1975.

With Helen Nearing. *Continuing the Good Life: Half a Century of Homesteading*. New York: Schocken, 1979.

## Pamphlets and Debates

*Social Religion: A Discussion of the Place of Social Welfare in a Religious Program*. Philadelphia: Friends' General Conference, 1910.

Debate with Morris Hillquit, Rev. John L. Bedford, and Prof. Fredrick M. Davenport. *Should Socialism Prevail?* New York: Rand School, 1915.

*Women in American Industry.* Philadelphia: American Baptist Publishing Society, 1915.

*The Germs of War: A Study in Preparedness.* St. Louis: National Ripsaw, 1916.

*Open Letter to Profiteers.* New York: People's Council of America, 1916.

*The Great Madness: A Victory for American Plutocracy.* New York: Rand School, 1917.

*A Letter of Explanation.* Toledo, 1917.

*The Menace of Militarism.* New York: Rand School, 1917.

*The Right and Duty of Free Speech: An Answer to Rev. A. A. Stockdale.* Toledo, April 1917.

Debate with Clarence Darrow. *Will Democracy Cure the Ills of the World?* Chicago: Worker's University Society, 1917.

*Work and Pay.* New York: Rand School, 1917.

*Address to the Jury.* New York: Rand School, 1918.

*The Coal Question.* New York: Rand School, 1918.

*The Cost of Living: Weekly Letter to the Citizens of the Fourteenth Congressional District.* New York, September 1918.

*Profiteering: Weekly Letter No. 2 to the Citizens of the Fourteenth Congressional District.* New York, September 1918.

*Who Owns the United States?: Weekly Letter No. 4 to the Citizens of the Fourteenth Congressional District.* New York, September 1918.

*Before the Court.* New York: People's Print, 1919.

*The Debs Decision.* New York: Rand School, 1919.

*The Human Element in Economics.* Twelve Lessons, Correspondence Dept., Rand School of Social Science. New York: Rand School [1919].

*Labor and the League of Nations.* New York: Rand School, 1919.

*Violence or Solidarity; or, Will Guns Settle It?* New York: Rand School, 1919.

*Europe and the Next World War.* New York: Rand School, 1920.

*Europe in Revolution.* New York: Rand School, 1920.

*Labor and the League of Nations.* New York: Rand School, 1920.

*A Nation Divided; or, Plutocracy versus Democracy.* Chicago: Socialist Party of the United States, 1920.

*The New Slavery; or, the World Made Safe for Plutocracy.* Chicago: Socialist Party of the United States, 1920.

*The One Big Union of Business.* New York: Rand School, 1920.

*Profiteering.* N.p., 1920.

Debate with Percy Ward. *Would the Practice of Christ's Teachings Make for Social Progress?* Girard, Kans.: Appeal to Reason, 1920.

Debate with Percy Ward. *Rationalism vs. Socialism.* Chicago, 1921.

Debate with Edwin R. Seligman. *Resolved: That Capitalism Has More to Offer the Workers of the United States than Has Socialism.* New York: Convention Reporting, 1921.

Debate with John Haynes Holmes. *Can the Church Be Radical?* New York: Hanford, 1922.

*Irrepressible America.* New York: League for Industrial Democracy, 1922.

*Oil and the Germs of War.* Ridgewood, N.J.: N.S. Nearing, 1923.

*The A. F. of L. at the Crossroads.* New York: Rand School, 1924.

Debate with Bertrand Russell. *Bolshevism and the West: A Debate on the Resolution "That the Soviet Form of Government Is Applicable to Western Civilization."* London: G. Allen, Unwin, 1924.

*Can Britain Escape the Revolution?* New York: Rand School, 192[4].

Debate with Alexis Fermi. *Has Propaganda Any Value in Education?* New York: Modern School Press, 1925.

*British Labor Bids for Power: The Historic Scarboro Conference of the Trade Union Congress.* New York: Social Science, 1926.

*Education in Soviet Russia.* New York: International, 1926.

*Glimpses of the Soviet Republic.* New York: Social Science, 1926.

*Russia Turns East: The Triumph of Soviet Diplomacy in Asia.* New York: Social Science, 1926.

*Stopping a War: The Fight of the French Workers against the Moroccan Campaign of 1925.* New York: Social Science, 1926.

*World Labor Unity.* New York: Social Science, 1926.

Debate with Sam A. Lewisohn, M. C. Rorty, and Morris Hillquit. *The Future of Capitalism and Socialism in America.* New York: League for Industrial Democracy, 1927.

*Fascism.* Ridgewood, N.J.: N. S. Nearing, 1930.

*A Humanist Approach to Economics.* Salt Lake City, Utah: The Humanist [1930].

Debate with A. F. Seligman. *Resolved: That Capitalism Offers More to the Workers of the World than Socialism or Communism.* New York: Rand School, 1930.

*A Warless World.* New York, 1931.

*The Decisive Year, 1931: Capitalism, Imperialism, Sovietism before the Bar of History.* New York: Urquart, 1932.

*Must We Starve?* New York: Vanguard, 1932.

*The One Way Out.* New York: Urquart, 1932.

Debate with Norman Thomas and Don D. Lescohier. *Which Offers More for the Future: Communism, Socialism, or Capitalism?* Chicago: Popular Interest, 1932.

*Why Hard Times?: A Study of the Economic and Social Forces That Are Sweeping Away Capitalist Imperialism.* New York: Urquart, 1932.

*An ABC of Communism.* N.p., 1934.

*Europe: West and East.* Ridgewood, N.J.: N. S. Nearing, 1934.

*The European Civil War: The First Twenty Years, 1917–1936.* Baltimore: Christian Social Science Fund, 1936.

Symposium with Dorothy Thompson and Lawrence Dennis. *Public Opinion and the Town Meeting Idea.* New York: American Book, 1936.

*World Perspective: A Survey, Analysis, and Synthesis.* Ridgewood, N.J.: N. S. Nearing, 1937.

*The Rise and Decline of Christian Civilization.* Ridgewood, N.J.: N. S. Nearing, 1940.

*The Second World War: An Evaluation.* Ridgewood, N.J.: N. S. Nearing, 1940.

Debate with Harry Watson. *Should the United States and Great Britain Police the World?* New York: Spinoza Institute, 1943.

*From Capitalism to Communism.* N.p., 1945.

*The New Age—Will It Be Dark or Golden?* Washington, D.C.: World Events, 1946.

*The New World Order and Some of Its Immediate Problems.* Washington, D.C.: World Events, 1946.

*Victory without Peace.* Washington, D.C.: World Events, 1946.

*Sound the Alarm.* New York: Monthly Review, 1949.

*Soviet Education: What Does It Offer to America?* Harborside, Me.: Social Science Institute, 1949.

*To Promote the General Welfare: An Essay on the Powers and Duties of Government and the*

*Rights, Obligations and Responsibilities of Citizens.* Harborside, Me.: Social Science Institute, 1956.

With Helen Nearing. *Our Right to Travel.* Harborside, Me.: Social Science Institute, 1959.

*Economic Crisis in the United States.* Harborside, Me.: Social Science Institute, 1961.

*Cuba and Latin America: An Eyewitness Report on the Continental Congress for Solidarity with Cuba.* Harborside, Me.: Social Science Institute, 1963.

## Articles

With Lawrence W. Trowbridge. "How Pennsylvania Primary Legislation and Party Rules Work in Philadelphia." *National Conference for Good City Government, Proceedings* (1905): 302–8.

With Lawrence W. Trowbridge. "Political Organization and Primary Legislation in Pennsylvania, 1881–1904." *National Conference for Good City Government, Proceedings* (1905): 293–302.

"Can the State Afford to Pay the Cost of Overworking Its Children?" *Charities and the Commons,* February 3, 1906, 602–6.

"The History of a Christmas Box." *Charities and the Commons,* December 29, 1906, 555–58.

"Newsboy at Night in Philadelphia." *Charities and the Commons,* February 2, 1907, 778–84.

"Stanny Mattevitez." *The Independent,* September 26, 1907, 746–47.

"On the Trail of the Pittsburgh Stogie." *The Independent,* July 2, 1908, 22–24.

"The Automobile Point of View." *The Independent,* May 20, 1909, 1081.

"Evolution of the Small Board of Education." *Educational Review* 29 (June 1909): 663–68.

"The Workings of a Large Board of Education." *Educational Review* 38 (June 1909): 43–51.

"The Extent of Unemployment in the United States." *Quarterly Publications of The American Statistical Association* 2 (September 1909): 525–42.

"The Selection of the Board of Education." *Educational Foundations,* December 21, 1909, 246–52.

"The Child Labor Problem." *Educational Foundations,* February 22, 1910, 344–58.

"Child Labor and the Child." *Education* 30 (March–April 1910): 407–515.

"Elementary Economics for the College Freshman." *Journal of Politics and Economics* 18 (June 1910): 444–47.

"Prosperity." *The Public,* November 25, 1910, 1109.

"Race Suicide v. Overpopulation." *Popular Science Monthly* 78 (January 1911): 91–93.

"The Goal of Education As Seen by an Economist." *Journal of Education* 73 (March 1911): 340–41.

"Social Life Insurance." *The Public,* March 3, 1911, 209.

"The Premium on Abnormality." *Survey,* March 4, 1911, 940–42.

"Race Suicide—an Appreciation." *Educational Foundations,* March 22, 1911.

"Most or Best: A Quality Test for Population." *Educational Foundations,* April 22, 1911, 468–71.

"The Increase in Unskilled Labor in American Universities." *Educational Foundations,* June 22, 1911, 603–6.

"Concerning Prejudice." *Everybody's,* September 1911, 289.

"The Barterer." *Everybody's,* January 1912, 1.

"Two O'Clock Sunday Morning." *The Independent,* February 1912, 288–89.

"The Dawn of Optimism." *The Public,* February 9, 1912, 135–36.

"One District Messenger." *The Independent,* February 22, 1912, 412–13.

"Efficiency Wage Standards." *Popular Science Monthly* 80 (March 1912): 257–62.

With Nellie Seeds Nearing. "When a Girl Is Asked to Marry." *Ladies Home Journal,* March 1912, 7.

With Nellie Seeds Nearing. "Four Great Things a Woman Does at Home." *Ladies Home Journal,* May 1912, 12.

"Wages in Massachusetts and New Jersey." *Quarterly Publication of the American Statistical Association* (June 1912): 157–73.

"What Public Schools Have Done." *Journal of Education,* December 12, 1912, 630–31.

With Nellie Seeds Nearing. "New Years Greetings and Suggestions." *The Public,* January 10, 1913, 38.

"The Power behind Our Silk Mills." *The Independent,* February 1, 1913, 255–56.

"An Inquiring Manufacturer." *The Public,* February 14, 1913, 159–61.

With Nellie Seeds Nearing. "Fitting the Public Schools to the Children." *Ladies Home Journal,* March 1913, 20.

"Masters and Slaves. " *Everybody's,* March 1913, 425.

"Elementary Schools That Are Linked to Real Life." *Ladies Home Journal,* April 1913, 19–20.

"Experimental Democracy." *The Public,* April 18, 1913, 377–78.

"High Schools That Are in Step with Life." *Ladies Home Journal,* May 1913, 10.

"Social Decadence." *North American Review* 197 (May 1913): 629–39.

"Welfare and the New Economics." *Popular Science Monthly,* May 1913, 504–9.

"A Challenge to Education." *Journal of Education,* May 15, 1913, 542.

"The New Basis for Education." *Journal of Education,* May 22, 1913, 563–64.

"The Cost of Living: A Fragment." *The Public,* May 23, 1913, 498–99.

"The Child: Social Asset or Liability?" *Kindergarten Primary Magazine,* May 25, 1913, 246–48.

"Bit of Evidence." *Survey,* May 31, 1913, 306.

"Where the Rural School Has Made Good." *Ladies Home Journal,* June 1913, 22.

"Higher Education in Lowville." *Journal of Education,* June 12, 1913, 649–51.

"English as an Education Pass-key." *Educational Foundations,* June 24, 1913, 593–99.

"Wages in the United States." *Annals of the American Academy of Political and Social Science* 48 (July 1913): 41–44.

"Pay Envelope and Market Basket." *Survey,* July 26, 1913, 544–45.

"Watered Farm-Land Values." *The Public,* August 1, 1913, 725–27.

"Prize Apron." *Survey,* August 2, 1913, 562–653.

"The Increase of American Land Values." *Popular Science Monthly,* November 1913.

Response to "Freedom of Teaching in the United States," by Ulysses G. Weatherly and "Reasonable Restrictions upon the Scholar's Freedom," by Henry Pritchet. *Publications of the American Sociological Society* 9 (1914): 165–66.

"The Public School Teacher and the Standard of Living." *National Educational Association, Addresses and Proceedings* 52 (July 1914): 78–94.

"Geographical Distribution of American Genius." *Popular Science Monthly,* August 1914, 189–99.

"Service Income and Property Income." *Quarterly Publication of the American Statistical Association* 14 (September 1914): 236–59.

"A Religious Lesson for Billy Sunday." *The Public,* February 12, 1915, 155.

"The Parasitic Power of Property." *International Socialist Review,* March 1915.

"The Recent Increase in Land Values." *Annals of the American Academy of Political and Social Science* 58 (March 1915): 149–57.

"If Wage Earners Kept Accounts Like Business Concerns." *Survey,* March 13, 1915, 655.

"The Impending Conflict." *International Socialist Review,* April 1915.

"The Service-Property Conflict." *The Public,* April 16, 1915, 385–86.

"The Adequacy of American Wages." *Annals of the American Academy of Political and Social Science* 59 (May 1915): 111–24.

"Wages and Salaries in Organized Industry." *Popular Science Monthly,* May 1915, 478–503.

"The Why of Income." *American Journal of Sociology* 20 (May 1915): 745–63.

"Increasing Land Values and the Cost of Living." *The Public,* June 4, 1915, 550–52.

"Property Philosophy." *The Public,* August 20, 1915, 806–7.

"Migrations of Distinguished Americans." *Science* n.s. 42 (September 1915): 413–15.

"The Sex of Distinguished Americans." *The Public,* October 22, 1915, 1031–33.

"Land Value Increase in American Cities." *The Public,* November 26, 1915, 1149–52.

With Pat H. Tooney et al. "The Fight of the Young Coal Miners." *Coal Miner* [1916].

"The Younger Generation of American Genius." *Science Monthly,* January 1916, 46–61.

"Persistent Prosperity." *International Socialist Review,* March 1916.

"One Hot Meal per Day." *The Public,* March 24, 1916, 272.

"Child Poverty and Child Delinquency." *The Public,* April 14, 1916, 351.

"A Challenge to Education." *Journal of Education,* May 11, 1916, 514.

"British Labor Misled," *The Public,* June 16, 1916, 568–69.

"What Chance Has Worker to Become a Capitalist?" *Appeal to Reason,* August 12, 1916.

"Brigandage." *The Public,* October 13, 1916, 972.

"We Want to Know." *The Public,* November 24, 1916, 1127.

"Beating Germany to It." *The Independent,* December 18, 1916, 487–88.

"The Public Library as an Index of Culture." *School and Society,* December 30, 1916, 980–84.

"The New Education." *Modern School,* January 1917.

"Who's Who on Our Boards of Education." *School and Society,* January 20, 1917, 89–90.

"Germany." *Journal of Education,* March 8, 1917, 260–61.

"Who Is Doing It to Us?" *The Public,* March 9, 1917, 235.

"The High Cost of Living." *American Socialist,* March 24, 1917, 1.

Debate with Clarence Darrow. "Can Democracy Cure the Ills of the World?" *Modern School,* March–April 1917, 201–32.

"Symposium: Socialists and the Problems of War." *Intercollegiate Socialist,* April–May 1917.

"Direct Action." *The Public,* May 18, 1917, 487.

"The Menace of Higher Wages." *The Public,* May 25, 1917, 510–11.

"Farewell to Meat." *The Public,* June 8, 1917, 559–60.

"Farm Youngsters in a Summer Camp." *The Independent,* July 1917, 164–65.

"Who's Who Among College Trustees?" *School and Society,* September 8, 1917, 297–99.

"Ownership and Democracy." *The Public,* September 21, 1917, 920–21.

"Business and War." *The Messenger,* November 1917, 11–12.

"War Shouters and War Contracts." *The Messenger,* January 1918, 11–12.
"Patriotism." New York *Call,* October 20, 1918, editorial page.
"Necessity." *The Commonwealth,* March 1919, 3.
"Twenty Years." *The Commonwealth,* March 1919, 15.
"Symposium: The American Labor and Socialist Parties—Competition or Coopera-tion?" *Intercollegiate Socialist,* April–May 1919.
"The Big Ten." *The Messenger,* August 1919, 27–28.
Introduction to Senator Richard Franklin Pettigrew, *The Course of Empire.* New York: Boni and Liveright, 1920.
"October: A Poem." *Survey,* January 10, 1920, 390.
"Profiteering." *Socialist World,* July 1920, 7–8.
"American Imperialism." *Labour Monthly,* November 1921.
"When Will Work Begin Again." *The Nation,* November 2, 1921.
"The Conference at Washington." *Call Magazine,* December 4, 1921, 8.
"Irrepressible America." *Call Magazine,* December 11, 1921, 7.
"Old Mexico." *Call Magazine,* December 18, 1921, 4.
"Individual Incomes in the United States." In *American Labor Yearbook,* Vol. 4, 114–18. New York: Rand School, 1921–1922.
Introduction to *Bars and Shadows: The Prison Poems of Ralph Chaplin.* New York: Leonard Press, 1922.
"The Irish Free State." *Call Magazine,* January 1, 1922, 9.
"Peace and Good Will," *Call Magazine,* January 15, 1922, 5, 8.
"The New Year." *Call Magazine,* January 22, 1922, 8.
Debate with William D. Guthrie. "Are the Present Day Schools a Menace to Democ-racy?" (Nearing in the affirmative). *Call Magazine,* January 29, 1922, 1–6.
"Taking Stock of American Labor." *Labor Age,* February 1922, 11–13.
"Penroism." *Call Magazine,* February 5, 1922, 7.
"What Does France Want?" *Call Magazine,* February 12, 1922, 7.
"Income in the United States." *Call Magazine,* February 26, 1922, 4, 9.
"The Arms Conference Harvest." *Call Magazine,* March 5, 1922, 8, 9.
"The Industrial Worker." *Call Magazine,* March 12, 1922, 5, 8.
"The Chicago Conference." *Call Magazine,* March 19, 1922, 4.
"What Can the Intellectual Do?" *Call Magazine,* March 26, 1922, 4.
"The Mine Workers Crisis." *Call Magazine,* April 9, 1922, 7.
"The Control of Public Opinion in the United States." *School and Society,* April 15, 1922, 421–23.
"Social Revolution." *Call Magazine,* April 16, 1922, 7, 11.
"Industrial Heretics." *Call Magazine,* April 23, 1922, 6.
"Genoa—Is It Too Late?" *Call Magazine,* April 30, 1922, 6, 7.
"The Workers Toll of the New Society." *Call Magazine,* May 7, 1922, 6.
"Thought Factories." *Call Magazine,* May 14, 1922, 5, 11.
"Pennsylvania: A Study in Godliness and Economic Determinism." *Call Magazine,* December 3, 1922, 3, 10.
"Can the Church Be Pacifist?" *The Nation,* December 13, 1922, 665–66.
"The Election Returns in Terms of Fact." *Call Magazine,* December 17, 1922, 4.
"Oil and the Near East." *Call Magazine,* December 31, 1922, 3, 14.
"What Can La Follette Do?" *Call Magazine,* January 7, 1923, 3.
"This Present Era." *Call Magazine,* January 21, 1923, 7, 9.

"What Can the Radical Do?" *Call Magazine*, February 4, 1923, 5.
"Karl Marx and Economic Emancipation." *Call Magazine*, February 11, 1923, 8.
"Couéism." *Call Magazine*, February 18, 1923.
"The Control of Labor Education." *Modern Quarterly*, March 1923, 35–37.
"The Social Significance of Dr. Grant." *Call Magazine*, March 11, 1923, 2, 9.
"I Recommend." *New Student*, March 24, 1923, 8.
"What Shall I Do in the Next War?" *Call Magazine*, April 1, 1923, 1, 9.
"Labor in Silk Stockings." *Call Magazine*, April 8, 1923, 4, 5.
"Can We Live Up to Our Ideals?" *Call Magazine*, April 29, 1923, 1, 2.
"Answering Uncle Sam." *The Liberator*, May 1923, 19–21.
"The Lap of Luxury." *The Liberator*, June 1923, 23–25.
"On Joining the World Court." *The Liberator*, August 1923, 24–25.
"France and Soviet Russia Join Hands." *The Nation*, January 9, 1924, 33–34.
"France Is Next." *The Liberator*, February 1924, 11.
"Imperial Hari-Kiri." *The Liberator*, March 1924, 9.
"Black Lands." *Labour Monthly*, April 1924, 236–37.
"The Economic Conquest of Canada." *The Nation*, April 16, 1924, 432–33.
"The Crumbling British Empire." *The Nation*, April 30, 1924, 514–15.
"Dear Government." *The Liberator*, May 1924, 12.
"The Imperial Struggle for Canada." *Labour Monthly*, May 1924, 286–92.
"Scott Nearing and Party Policy." *Daily Worker*, magazine suppl., May 10, 1924, 4–5.
"The Dawes Plan." *The Liberator*, June 1924, 7.
"Cooperative Democracy: Will It Work?" *Cooperation*, August 10, 1924, 129–30.
"Why American Teachers Do Not Think." *Modern Quarterly*, April 1925, 222–29.
"Education for What?" *The Nation*, May 1925, 577–79.
"The Labour Situation in Western Canada." *Labour Monthly*, May 7, 1925, 288–93.
"Another Lost Year." *Advance*, May 8, 1925.
"Education and the Open Mind." *Modern Quarterly*, June 1925, 280–89.
"British Labor Turns to the Left." *The Nation*, October 14, 1925, 405–6.
"The Organization of Educational Workers in Soviet Russia." *School and Society*,
    March 13, 1926, 324–27.
"Higher Education in Russia." *New Student*, March 31, 1926, 4.
"Return of the Native." *New Masses*, May 1, 1926, 18–30.
"Russianizing American Education." *Modern Quarterly*, May–June 1926, 189–91.
"British Labour in Transition." *The Nation*, October 6, 1926, 321–22.
"Is This 'Education'?" *New Masses*, November 1926, 20.
"Conflict and Avoidance." *New Masses*, February 1927, 26.
"Crow's Nest Path." *Labour Monthly*, February 1927, 120–23.
"Is Oil Thicker than Blood?" *New Masses*, February 1927, 5.
"See America First." *New Masses*, February 1927, 21.
"Uncle Sam—Buccaneer." *New Masses*, February 1927, 5.
"American Imperialism in the Caribbean." *Labour Monthly*, March 1927.
"Prosperous Profiteers." *New Masses*, March 1927, 24.
"Jay Walking." *New Masses*, May 1927, 12.
"England Runs Amuck." *New Masses*, July 1927, 15.
"What's Ahead in the Caribbean?" *Labour Monthly*, August 1927, 496–505.
"The Movement of World Wealth." *The Nation*, September 7, 1927, 234–35.
"White Terror in China." *The Nation*, December 28, 1927, 734–35.

"On a Chinese River Boat." *New Masses*, January 1928, 20–21.
"Introducing Mr. Hsu." *New Masses*, February 1928, 24.
"Imperial Hong Kong." *The Nation*, February 8, 1928, 150.
"Another Month." *New Masses*, September 1928, 8.
"Free and Fair Elections." *The Nation*, October 31, 1928, 449.
"Democracy." *Labour Monthly*, November 1928, 681–85.
"Sinclair's One Hangover." *New Masses*, November 1928, 7.
"Slave of the Machine." *New Masses*, November 1928, 18–19.
"Soviet Russia and Peace." *New Masses*, November 1928.
"Symposium on Soviet Russia." *Labor Defender*, November 1928.
"The Political Outlook for the Workers (Communist) Party—a Discussion Article."
    *The Communist*, December 1928, 756–59.
"The Coming War with England." *New Masses*, February 1929, 11.
"Academic Mortuaries." *New Masses*, April 1929, 71.
"Hoover and MacDonald." *Labour Monthly*, November 1929, 753–56.
"The Soviet Union Forges Ahead." *New Masses*, November 1929, 17–19.
"The Color Line in Art." *New Masses*, December 1929, 11–12.
"Open Letter." American Fund for Public Service, December 12, 1929.
"The Child in Soviet Russia." In V. F. Calverton and Samuel Schmalhausen, eds., *The
    New Generation*, 23–28. New York: Macaulay Co., 1930.
"Revolution in China." *New Masses*, May 1930, 16.
"The Five Year Plan." *New Masses*, August 1930, 16–17.
"Reparations." *New Masses*, May 1931, 8.
"The Communist Way Out." *Christian Century*, October 12, 1932, 1234–36.
"Drift toward Insurrection." *World Tomorrow*, March 22, 1933, 273–75.
"Marx's Contribution to Social Advance." *World Tomorrow*, March 22, 1933.
"Class against Class." *New Masses*, April 1933, 27–28.
"Symposium: Against Fascist Terror in Germany." *New Masses*, April 1933, 12.
"Dr. Beard Cooperates." *New Masses*, January 2, 1934, 25.
"A Primer for Lambs." *New Masses*, September 11, 1934, 27–28.
"What I Will Do When America Goes to War: A Symposium." *Modern Monthly*,
    September 1935.
"Will Germany Go Left?" *Modern Quarterly* 11 (1939): 62–69.
"Can Democracy Survive?: A Symposium." *Modern Quarterly*, Summer 1939.
"The Second World War: An Evaluation." *Modern Quarterly*, Summer 1940.
"The Shifting Center of World Power." *Modern Quarterly*, Fall 1940.
"Britain's Rivalry." In Latin American Economic Institute, *The Economic Defense of
    the Western Hemisphere: A Study in Conflicts*. Washington, D.C.: American Coun-
    cil on Public Affairs, 1941.
"World Events." Newsletter 1944–1953, Scott and Helen Nearing Papers, Boston
    University Special Collections, Boston.
"What the U.S. Could Do for the World." World Events Committee, Washington,
    D.C., 1948.
"Why I Believe in Socialism." *Monthly Review* 1 (1949): 44–50.
"Statement Presented to the Senate Foreign Relations Committee, Feb. 17, 1950."
    *Simplified Economics*, April 1950.
"Views in Favor of World Government." *Congressional Digest* 31 (August 1952): 214.
"World Events." Monthly column in *Monthly Review*, 1953–1970.

# Index

169, 182, 183, 189, 198, 216, 229–31, 237; and *Dollar Diplomacy*, 186; on *Free Born*, 234
Freud, Sigmund, 272n
Freudian psychology, 201–2
Friends of the Soviet Union, 223

Galton, Francis, 67
Gandhi, Mohandas, 204
Gannett, Lewis, 182; and American Fund for Public Service, 187
Garland, Charles, 182; and American Fund for Public Service, 187
Garland Fund, 187–88, 219, 242. *See also* American Fund for Public Service
Gary, Ind., schools, 39–40
George, Henry, 29, 33, 55, 56
German university ideal, 16, 23
Giddings, Franklin H., 109
Gold, Michael, 216, 230, 241–42, 246–47; and proletarian literature, 230
Goldman, Emma, 222–23
Gompers, Samuel, 145; and American Federation of Labor, 91
Goodman, Paul, 247
Grace Baptist Temple, Phila., 11, 16
Grundy, Joseph, 86–87, 97

Hall, G. Stanley, 169; *Adolescence*, 70
Hand, Judge Learned, 159
Hanna, Paul, 189
Hart, Albert Bushnell, 192
Hassler, Carl, 182
Haywood, Bill, 149, 184
Hicks, Granville, 193
Hillman, Sidney, 187
Hillquit, Morris, 100, 109, 159, 163, 191, 219, 220
Historical school of economics, 18–19
Hobson, J. A., 179–80, 237; *Imperialism: A Study*, 179–80
Hollander, Jacob H., 107
Holmes, John Haynes, 172
Holmes, Justice Oliver Wendell, Jr., 162
Homesteading, 54–57, 247–48, 254–55, 261, 262–63. *See also* Back-to-the-land movement; Country life; Simple life
Hourwich, N. I., 191
Howe, Frederick C., 189
Howells, William Dean, 166

Imperialism, 178–81, 183, 184, 186, 188, 226, 237–42; and Soviet Union, 221–22
Industrial democracy, 116, 122, 150, 151, 152–53, 160–61
Intellectuals, 202–4
*Intercollegiate Socialist*, 77, 93, 138
Intercollegiate Socialist Society, 92–93, 109, 114, 146
International Publishers, 186, 237
*International Socialist Review*, 93, 100
International Workers of the World, 140, 149, 156, 182, 190, 226
Internationalism, 183–85, 190

James, Edmund J., 16
James, William, 19, 136, 250; on Chautauqua, 58, 62; on strenuousness, 51
Johnson, Tom L., 35
Jones, James Weldon, 187
Jordan, David Starr, 103

Katayama, Sen, 191
Kirchwey, Freda, 187
Krishnamurti, 246
Kropotkin, Prince, 197
Kuomintang, 221–22; and "White Terror," 222–23

*Labor Age*, 187
*Labour Monthly*, 187
La Follette, Robert, 206–8
LaGuardia, Fiorello, 147–50, 153–54
League for Industrial Democracy, 198, 214, 219, 224
League of Nations, 184
Lee, Algeron, 182
Leisure, 57–58, 167–68
Lenin, V. I., 191, 192, 208, 220, 239, 247; in *Free Born*, 231, 232; *Imperialism*, 237–40
Levine, Helen, 153
Liberalism, 37
*Liberator*, 154, 187; and proletarian literature, 230
Liggett, Walter, 182
Lochner, Louis, 182; and *Federated Press Bulletin*, 188
London, Jack, in *Free Born*, 232
London, Meyer, 150
Lovestone, Jay, 218–19, 236–37, 241
Luce, Henry, 252, 261

Lusk, Sen. Clayton R., 162; and Lusk Committee, 162–63, 170
Lynd, Robert and Helen, 57, 167

Macmillan, publisher, 125, 186
Magnitagorsk (U.S.S.R.), 251–52
Manual schools, 10, 226
Manual-training education, 10
Manumit School, 249
Martin, Helen R., 62, 63–64; *Church on the Avenue*, 63; *Fanatic or Christian?*, 63; *Maggie of Virginsburg*, 63
Marx, Karl, 19, 22, 25, 29, 33, 72, 74, 78, 131, 181, 196–97, 210, 231–32, 253; and *Communist Manifesto*, 196
Marxism, 177, 181, 196–97, 208, 210, 241, 253; and imperialism, 237–38; and literature, 230–31; and pacifism, 239–40; and religion, 200
*Masses*, 150
McCrea, Roswell Cheney, 85–87, 89, 98, 103, 107
McDonald, Ramsey, 210, 212
McFadden, Bernarr, 50
Mead, Margaret, 182
Meiklejohn, Alexander, 249
Mencken, H. L., 104–5
*Messenger*, 226
Mexico, 182
Mill, John Stuart, 19, 25
Mine Workers Union, 9
Minor, Robert, 182
Mitchell, John, 9
*Modern Quarterly*, 187; and proletarian literature, 230
Mooney, Thomas J., 149, 184
Morris, William, 55, 78
Morris Run, Pa., 7–8
Mysticism, 199–202

*Nation, The*, 124, 171, 187, 201
National Association for the Advancement of Colored People, 115
National Civic Federation, 101
National Security League, 148
National Socialism (Germany), 223, 253
Nazi party, 223
Nazi–Soviet Pact, 253
Nearing, Guy, 92–93
Nearing, Helen (Knothe), 246, 254–55, 261; and Theosophy, 246

Nearing, John Scott. *See* Scott, John
Nearing, Louis, 8
Nearing, Minnie (Zabriskie), 8
Nearing, Nellie Marguerite (Seeds), 43, 97, 123, 163, 182, 197–99, 248–49; at Chautauqua, 58; and education, 43; and Federated Press, 189; with Scott Nearing, *Women and Social Progress*, 43
Nearing, Robert, 43, 182, 249, 252, 262; to Magnitagorsk (U.S.S.R.), 252; at Manumit School, 249
Nearing, Scott, works of; *The American Empire*, 178–80, 186, 194, 226; *Anthracite*, 28; *Black America*, 227–29; "Can the Church be Radical?," 172; "The Control of Public Opinion in the United States," 169; *Democracy Is not Enough*, 245; with Joseph Freeman, *Dollar Diplomacy*, 186, 306n; with Frank Watson, *Economics*, 27, 226; with Henry Burch, *Elements of Economics*, 27; *Financing the Wage Earner's Family*, 27–28; *Free Born*, 229, 231–35, 246; *Freedom: Promise or Menace*, 245; *The Germs of War*, 117; "Grave Faults of the Wage System," 109; *The Great Madness*, 155, 157–61; "The Impending Conflict," 93; *Income*, 28, 34, 93; "The Industrial Regime," 108; with Helen Nearing, *Living the Good Life*, 245, 254–55, 262–63, 264; *The Making of a Radical*, 245; "The Man and the Message," 115; *Man's Search for the Good Life*, 255; with Helen Nearing, *The Maple Sugar Book*, 254–55; "The New Economics and Socialism," 114; *The New Education*, 39; *The Next Step*, 183, 186; "The Parasitic Power of Property," 93; "Pennsylvania: A Study in Godliness and Economic Determinism," 187; *Poverty and Riches*, 77; "Public Opinion and Academic Freedom," 108; *Reducing the Cost of Living*, 52; "The Right and Duty of Free Speech," 123; *Scott Nearing's American Letter*, 185; *Scott Nearing's Article Service*, 185; *Social Forces*, 264; *Social Religion*, 46–47; *Social Sanity*, 28, 35; *The Super Race*, 67, 69; "The Teacher, the Schools, and the Democracy," 114; *Twilight of Empire*, 237–38, 240–42; *Violence or Solidarity?*, 192–93, 220; *Wages in the United States*, 28, 100; "Welfare and the New Economics," 29; *Whither China?*, 221; "The 'Why' of Income," 33; with Nellie Nearing, *Women and Social Progress*, 43

# CHELSEA GREEN

Sustainable living has many facets. Chelsea Green's celebration of the sustainable arts has led us to publish trend-setting books about organic gardening, solar electricity and renewable energy, innovative building techniques, regenerative forestry, local and bioregional democracy, and whole foods. The company's published works, while intensely practical, are also entertaining and inspirational, demonstrating that an ecological approach to life is consistent with producing beautiful, eloquent, and useful books, videos, and audio cassettes.

For more information about Chelsea Green, or to request a free catalog, call toll-free (800) 639–4099, or write to us at P.O. Box 428, White River Junction, Vermont 05001. Visit our website at www.chelseagreen.com.

Chelsea Green's titles include:

  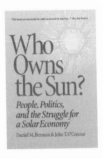